D0430736

LABOR AND EMPL~. ....

RELATIONS ASSOCIATION SERIES

The Gloves-off Economy: Workplace Standards at the Bottom of America's Labor Market

EDITED BY

Annette Bernhardt, Heather Boushey,

Laura Dresser, and Chris Tilly

First Edition

ISBN 978-0-913447-97-0

Price: $24.95

LABOR AND EMPLOYMENT RELATIONS ASSOCIATION SERIES
Proceedings of the Annual Meeting (published electronically beginning in 2009)
Annual Research Volume
LERA 2006 Membership Directory (published every four years)
LERA Newsletter (published quarterly)
Perspectives on Work (published annually)
Perspectives on Work Online Companion (published electronically semiannually)

Information regarding membership, subscriptions, meetings, publications, and general affairs of the LERA can be found at the Association website at www.lera.uiuc.edu. Members can make changes to their member records, including contact information, affiliations and preferences, by accessing the online directory at the website or by contacting the LERA national office.

LABOR AND EMPLOYMENT RELATIONS ASSOCIATION
University of Illinois at Urbana-Champaign
121 Labor and Industrial Relations Building
504 East Armory Ave.
Champaign, IL 61820
Telephone: 217/333-0072   Fax: 217/265-5130
Internet: www.lera.uiuc.edu   E-mail: leraoffice@uiuc.edu

CONTENTS

CHAPTER 1

An Introduction to the "Gloves-off" Economy

ANNETTE BERNHARDT
National Employment Law Project

HEATHER BOUSHEY
Center for Economic and Policy Research

LAURA DRESSER
University of Wisconsin, Madison

CHRIS TILLY
University of California, Los Angeles

At 6:00 a.m. in New York City, a domestic worker wakes up her employer's children and starts to cook breakfast for them, in a work week in which she will earn a flat $400 for as many hours as her employer needs. In Chicago, men are picked up at a homeless shelter at 8:00 a.m. and bussed by a temp agency to a wholesale distribution center to spend the next 10 hours packing toys into boxes, for the minimum wage without overtime. In Atlanta, workers at a poultry processing plant break for lunch, hands raw from handling chemicals without protective gear. At 3:00 p.m. in Dallas, a new shift of nursing home workers start their day, severely understaffed and underpaid. During the evening rush hour in Minneapolis, gas station workers fill up tanks, working only for tips. In New Orleans, a dishwasher stays late into the night finishing the evening's cleaning, off the clock and unpaid. And at midnight, a janitor in Los Angeles begins buffing the floor of a major retailer, working for a contract cleaning company that pays $8 an hour with no benefits.

These workers—and millions more—share more than the fact that they are paid low wages. The central thesis of this volume is that they are part of the "gloves-off" economy, in which some employers are increasingly breaking, bending, or evading long-established laws and standards

1

designed to protect workers. Such practices are sending fault lines into every corner of the low-wage labor market, stunting wages and working conditions for an expanding set of jobs. In the process, employers who play by the rules are under growing pressure to follow suit, intensifying the search for low-cost business strategies across a wide range of industries and eventually ratcheting up into higher wage parts of the labor market.

When we talk about the "gloves-off economy," we are identifying *a set of employer strategies and practices that either evade or outright violate the core laws and standards that govern job quality in the U.S.* While such strategies have long been present in certain sectors, such as sweatshops and marginal small businesses, we argue that they are spreading. This trend, driven by competitive pressures, has been shaped by an environment where other major economic actors—government, unions, and civil society—have either promoted deregulation or have been unable to contain gloves-off business strategies. The result, at the start of the 21st century, is the reality that a major segment of the U.S. labor market increasingly diverges from the legal and normative bounds put into place decades ago.

The workplace laws in question are a familiar list of regulations at the federal, state, and local level. They include laws that regulate wages and hours worked, setting minimum standards for the wage floor, for overtime pay, and, in some states, for rest and meal breaks. They also comprise laws governing health and safety conditions in the workplace, setting detailed requirements for particular industries and occupations. Others on the list include antidiscrimination laws, right-to-organize laws, and laws mandating employers' contribution to social welfare benefits such as Social Security, unemployment insurance, and workers compensation.

By contrast, the standards we have in mind are set not by laws, but rather by norms that have enough weight (and organizing force behind them) to shape employers' decisions about wages and working conditions. At least until the past few decades, such normative standards typically included predictability of schedules, vacation and/or sick leave, annual raises, full-time hours, and, in some industries, living wages and employer-provided health insurance and pensions. Though it may seem utopian to focus on standards at a time when even legally guaranteed rights are frequently abrogated, we argue that both laws and standards are being eroded for similar reasons as employers seek to reduce labor costs. Further, we argue that the existence of strategies to subvert or ignore laws by some employers pulls down labor norms farther up in the labor market.

We do not suggest that *all* U.S. employers have shed the gloves of workplace protection, or that *every* strategy to cut labor costs is inherently "gloves-off." Millions of employers comply with current regulations and do their best to uphold strong labor standards. However, we contend that gloves-off strategies have reached such prevalence that they are leaving their imprint on the broader labor market, creating significant challenges for responsible employers, government, and labor unions and other representatives of civil society. Responsible employers are undercut when unscrupulous employers gain unfair advantage by violating labor laws and standards. Government's mandate to enforce worker protections is stressed by widespread and constantly shifting forms of violation and evasion. Unions and other worker advocates face an uneven playing field. When the floor of labor standards is driven down or dismantled altogether, all of us are affected, not just those at the very bottom.

The goal of this volume is to map the landscape of gloves-off workplace strategies, to connect them to the erosion of norms farther up in the labor market, to identify the workers most vulnerable to these practices, and finally and perhaps most importantly, to identify the ways that the floor under job standards can be rebuilt. In what follows, we first explore conceptual tools for analyzing evasions and breaches of workplace standards and then briefly review evidence about the scope of the problem. We next trace the historical trajectory that first led to the upgrading of workplace protections, then to the partial undoing of the protective web of laws and standards—using this narrative as well to introduce the contents of the volume. We close by considering strategies to "put the gloves back on" in order to re-regulate work.

Beyond the Secondary Labor Market and the Informal Sector

Our focus on evasions and violations of labor laws and standards is related to other concepts, including the secondary labor market (Doeringer and Piore 1971), the underground or undeclared economy (European Commission 2004; Mingione 2000; Venkatesh 2006; Williams 2005), and precarious, marginal, or casualized work (Procoli 2004). Each of these was formulated in research on developed economies. The concept of the informal sector, first used to describe work in the developing world, also belongs on the list, since analysts now widely apply it to Western Europe and the United States (Leonard 1998; Portes, Castells, and Benton 1989; Sassen 1997).

However, these antecedents do not coincide exactly with the phenomenon this volume scrutinizes. For example, discussions of the informal sector and the underground or undeclared economy place primary emphasis on microenterprises and self-employment, whereas we focus on employment relationships in the formal sector, extending even to the very largest employers (including the largest private employer in the world, Wal-Mart, currently facing a spate of overtime violation lawsuits).[1] Peter Doeringer and Michael Piore's notion of the secondary labor market denotes jobs that violate common norms or standards, and subsequent analyses, such as Bulow and Summers (1986) and Dickens and Lang (1985), stretched the concept to encompass a much broader swath of "bad" jobs, defined by wage levels or advancement opportunities. But dual labor market theory did not contemplate direct violations of workplace laws.

Perhaps the concepts that correspond most closely to our gloves-off metaphor are *informal employment* and *unregulated work or employment*. The International Labour Organization (2002) defined informal employment as employment without secure contracts or Social Security coverage, whether in the formal or informal sector. Our gaze is similarly motivated, but both narrower (excluding true self-employment) and broader (including jobs that breach standards other than the contract and Social Security). The term "unregulated work" (or employment) is often used interchangeably with the informal sector, but in recent years researchers, particularly in Europe, have increasingly used it in a way that has much in common with gloves-off employer strategies (Bernhardt, McGrath, and DeFilippis 2007; Dicken and Hall 2003; Esping-Andersen 1999; UN-HABITAT 2004; Williams and Thomas 1996). William Robinson (2003:260) offers a helpful distinction: "Casualization generally refers to the new unregulated work that labor performs for capital under 'flexible' conditions. Informalization refers to the transfer of much economic activity from the formal to the informal economy."

In any case, our chief goal here is not to find the right name for employer evasion and violation of laws and standards, but to explain it. Extending a taxonomy proposed by Avirgan, Bivens, and Gammage (2005), there are four major explanations for the existence and/or growth of unregulated work:

- *Dualist:* Unregulated work is a lingering vestige of precapitalist production.

- *Survivalist:* Unregulated work, including self-employment, is the consequence of family survival strategies in the face of inadequate employment growth.

- *Legalist:* Unregulated work is a response to excessive regulation of businesses and employment (a view advanced forcefully by De Soto 1989).

- *Structuralist:* Unregulated work is generated by capitalist strategies to keep labor costs low.

The structuralist school offers at least two versions of its explanation. Some, such as Piore (1980), maintain that flexible employment is a way to meet fluctuating demands that are an intrinsic feature of capitalism. Others (Castells and Portes 1989; Murray 1983; Sassen 1997) argue that particular circumstances—whether labor surplus, increased competition, or strategic innovation—led businesses in developed countries to seek new ways to avoid labor standards and laws beginning in the 1970s and 1980s. This volume explores the terrain pointed out by the second structuralist camp. While we acknowledge that dualist, survivalist, and legalist forces all contribute to the gloves-off economy, we hold that the main force driving unregulated work consists of new employer strategies growing out of a historically specific conjuncture.

What Do We Know About the Gloves-off Economy?

This volume paints a picture of the ways that workplace protections are increasingly being undermined in many sectors of the U.S. economy. Table 1 provides a useful way to categorize the gloves-off employer strategies that we will examine. This is by no means an exhaustive list. Further, some of the practices described in the table are not invariably gloves-off strategies (though they often are). For example, subcontracting can be used to push down labor standards, but it can also be initiated with other goals in mind, resulting in no degradation of labor standards.

The first row of the table focuses on labor and employment laws. Violation of these laws is straightforward: for example, the employer simply pays less than the minimum wage to her employees, doesn't pay overtime, or blatantly discriminates on the basis of race and gender. Examples of evasion strategies are varied and often more complex, such as using subcontractors, temporary agencies, or other intermediaries to create legal distance between an employer and workers, and using the confusion created by that distance to avoid legal liability.

The second row focuses on the more diffuse concept of the erosion and abandonment of norms in the labor market. Here, the strategies are myriad and, in fact, impact conditions at all levels of the labor market, not just the floor. Declining access to employer-provided health care and defined-benefit pensions is perhaps the most obvious evidence of declining labor market norms. But the expansion of unpredictable scheduling practices and the reemergence of piece-rate or commission pay systems to drive down wages are also in evidence. And increasingly, we also see the outright abandonment of normative standards.

Our focus on what has happened to both legal and normative standards governing the workplace is intentional. In the U.S., employment and labor laws largely set a "floor" of minimum standards (e.g., the minimum wage),

TABLE 1
Examples of Employer Strategies in the "Gloves-off Economy"

	Evasion strategies	Violation strategies
Employment and labor laws	Strategies to evade core workplace laws by creating legal distance between employer and employee, such as these: • Subcontracting on-site and off-site work to outside companies where lower wages are generated via the subcontractor's evasion of labor law • Misclassification of workers as independent contractors • Using temporary, leased, and contract workers to distance and confuse the employment relationship and reduce legal obligations	Outright violation of laws governing the employment relationship, such as these: • Direct violation of core laws: FLSA, OSHA, FMLA, ERISA, Title VII, NLRA, prevailing wage, living wage, etc. • Payment (whole or part) in cash and "off the books" • Failure to contribute to workers' compensation, disability insurance, unemployment insurance, Social Security, etc. • Forced labor and trafficking
	Erosion strategies	**Abandonment strategies**
Normative workplace standards	Strategies that erode normative standards, such as these: • Increases in employee contributions to health insurance and shifts to defined-contribution pensions • Manipulating work hours so that employees do not qualify for benefits • Shift to piece-rate, commission, or project-based pay as a means of lowering wages • Reducing sick days by shifting to package of leave days and/or requiring medical documentation for sick days • Subcontracting and temping out to gain wage and numerical flexibility • Legal union avoidance tactics, such as double-breasting	Outright abandonment of normative standards, such as these: • Wage freezes or outright wage cuts • Failure to provide health insurance and pensions or elimination of programs • Conversion of full-time jobs to part-time • Instituting two-tiered pay systems • Dismantling internal labor markets

while, historically at least, norms have built additional workplace standards on top of that floor (e.g., annual raises, voluntary employer-provided health insurance). Moreover, laws are particularly important in regulating the labor practices of smaller and economically marginal businesses, whereas labor norms are particularly relevant in larger, more profitable enterprises. But laws and norms are inextricably linked. For example, as a growing share of the construction industry moves toward cash payment, the misclassification of employees as independent contractors, and labor brokers (who facilitate violation of wage and hour laws), the more established and higher-wage contractors face increasingly difficult competition, in some cases driving them to dilute or abandon long-established norms. In other industries, subcontracting by large businesses in order to delink some jobs from their core workforce norms may shift employment to subcontractors who compete by skirting or violating the law. Erosions of both legal and normative labor market standards thus move in mutually reinforcing ways.

Finally, a word about the legislative exclusion of a number of occupations from coverage by employment and labor laws (as is the case for certain domestic workers, home care workers, and agricultural workers). These exclusions are widely regarded as historical legacies of the more narrow (and, frankly, racist) legal frameworks for worker protections that existed in the first half of the last century. In fact, these workers are clearly in an employment relationship, and, in what follows, we consider their jobs as squarely within the realm of our analysis.

Violation and Evasion of Workplace Laws

Research on workplace violations is still very much an underdeveloped field, and there are currently few comprehensive estimates of the prevalence of violations. However, the evidence available points to a significant level of violations in some industries. The best evidence we have to date stems from a series of rigorous "employer compliance surveys" conducted by the U.S. Department of Labor in the late 1990s, focusing on minimum wage and overtime violations. For example, the department found that in 1999, only 35% of apparel plants in New York City were in compliance with wage and hour laws; in Chicago, only 42% of restaurants were in compliance; in Los Angeles, only 43% of grocery stores were in compliance; and nationally, only 43% of residential care establishments were in compliance (Department of Labor 2001). Confirming this, Weil (2005), in an independent analysis of Department of Labor administrative compliance data, found that 46% of garment contractors in Los Angeles were in compliance with the minimum wage in 2000. Unfortunately, however, these surveys were largely limited to only a handful of industries and/or regions, and most are no longer being conducted.

As a result, academics and applied researchers have recently begun to generate their own studies of workplace violations, especially of minimum wage and overtime laws. One of the most carefully constructed is a national survey of a random sample of day labor hiring sites across the country; the authors found that 49% of day laborers reported at least one instance of nonpayment of wages and 48% reported at least one instance of underpayment of wages in the preceding two months (Valenzuela et al. 2006). More common are studies relying on convenience samples of workers; while not representative, these often yield suggestive evidence of minimum wage and overtime violations in key industries including restaurants, building services, domestic work, and retail (Domestic Workers United and Datacenter 2006; Make the Road by Walking, and Retail, Wholesale, and Department Store Union 2005; Nissen 2004). For example, in a survey of New York City restaurant employees, researchers found that 13% earned less than the minimum wage, 59% suffered overtime law violations, 57% had worked more than four hours without a paid break, and workers reported a plethora of occupational safety and health violations (Restaurant Opportunities Center of New York and the New York City Restaurant Industry Coalition 2005).

Shifting to other workplace violations, we have recently seen a spate of studies that make innovative use of state administrative data to suggest that 10% or more of employers misclassify their workers as independent contractors (Carré and Wilson 2004; DeSilva et al. 2000; Donahue, Lamare, and Kotler 2007). Breaches of the right to organize unions, guaranteed by the National Labor Relations Act, have become common (Bronfenbrenner 2000). A study by the Fiscal Policy Institute (2007) estimated that between half a million and one million eligible New Yorkers are not receiving workers compensation coverage from their employers, as they are legally due. And while data are rarely available on health and safety violations in the workplace, a study of Los Angeles garment factories in the late 1990s is suggestive, finding that 54% had serious Occupational Safety and Health Administration (OSHA) violations (Appelbaum 1999). As an indirect measure of workers at risk, the Department of Labor has documented that workplace fatalities are disproportionately concentrated in the private construction industry and especially among Latino men (Bureau of Labor Statistics 2006).

The most extreme form of workplace violations is forced labor and trafficking, where the worker is totally controlled by the "employer" and prevented from leaving the situation. Though such practices are very difficult to document, experts estimate that between ten and twenty thousand workers are trafficked into the United States every year and that the average amount of time spent in forced labor as a result of trafficking is between two and five years.[2] One of the most extreme examples is a slave labor operation discovered in 1995 in El Monte, California, where 72 Thai garment workers were forced to work 18 hours a day without pay in a small apartment building enclosed by barbed wire, patrolled by armed guards (Su 1997).

Employer strategies to bend, twist, sidestep, and otherwise evade the laws governing the U.S. workplace are even harder to measure than outright violations, because such strategies are not illegal and so are not monitored by regulatory agencies. Academic researchers have for several decades tracked changes in how employers are reorganizing work and production, but they have often been stymied by the inherent challenges in measuring workplace practices and business strategies (see, for example, Appelbaum et al. 2003; Cappelli et al. 1997; Herzenberg, Alic, and Wial 1998; Kochan, Katz, and McKersie 1989; Osterman 1999). As a result, the best documentation comes largely from in-depth studies focused on particular industries, offering a rich, qualitative understanding of why employers use particular strategies and of the impact they have on workers and job quality; comprehensive quantitative data generally are not available.

Probably the most important evasion strategy is to subcontract certain jobs or functions to outside companies. The workers performing those jobs may still be located on-site (as with subcontracted janitorial workers) or be moved off-site (as with industrial laundry workers cleaning linens for hotels and hospitals). Of course, greater use of subcontracting in and of itself does not necessarily imply an attempt to evade workplace laws—but it certainly can facilitate such evasion. As shown in Table 1, subcontracting can help employers evade responsibility for compliance with employment and labor laws, creating greater legal distance in cases where, for example, a fly-by-night cleaning subcontractor pays less than the minimum wage.

Similarly, for some employers the motivation for using temp, leased, or contract workers is to lessen legal liability for working conditions and social welfare contributions. The deliberate misclassification of employees as independent contractors is perhaps the most extreme version of this strategy, since independent contractors are not covered by most employment and labor laws (Ruckelshaus and Goldstein 2002).

In this row of Table 1 (as in the next), the distinction between violation and evasion strategies is not always clear. For example, an employer may subcontract with the explicit recognition that the contractor will do the dirty work of violating the law by underpaying or failing to make employer unemployment insurance contributions. Still, the distinction between violations and evasions is an important one, not just descriptively but also legally and, by extension, in terms of options for public policy responses.

Erosion and Abandonment of Workplace Standards

The second row of Table 1 deals with workplace strategies that chip away at workplace standards and norms. Each example is of a broadly accepted labor standard that has been eroded or abandoned by some subset of employers.

Some strategies directly erode (nonlegal) normative standards governing wages and working conditions, while still retaining the appearance of compliance. These include the well-documented shift over the last several decades to larger employee contributions to health insurance and to defined-contribution pensions (Boushey and Tilly 2008). Indicative is a recent *Boston Globe* article (Dembner 2007) documenting how a number of Massachusetts businesses evaded that state's new health insurance requirements: A Burger King franchisee extended health coverage but halved the employer contribution so that only three of 27 employees bought in; a large human service provider raised its health insurance eligibility requirement to 30 hours of work per week, disqualifying 100 low-wage employees; another business owner split his company into smaller firms that fell below the 11-employee threshold where the state's requirement kicks in.

Other forms of standards evasion include shifting to methods of payment (such as piece rates or project-based pay) that effectively translate into lower hourly wages. Further, some employers hold the line on hours of employment in order to ensure that workers never qualify for benefits. Included as well are legal tactics to avoid unions, such as doublebreasting and subcontracting to non-union sources.

Above, we discussed subcontracting and temping-out as strategies to evade compliance with employment and labor laws. But more often, these two strategies are used to evade normative standards about wages and job stability—a means of lowering wages and gaining greater staffing flexibility week to week without upsetting the employer's internal structure of decent wages and stable jobs. Again, accurate numbers are difficult to come by, and for subcontracting in particular, the practice varies greatly by industry. But a recent example shows how deeply the practice can penetrate: In the institutional food sales industry, fully 51% of sales come from subcontracted food service providers (Hagerty 2002). Somewhat better data are available on contingent work: The Center for a Changing Workforce and the Iowa Policy Project recently estimated that more than 3.3 million U.S. workers are "permatemps": long-term workers misidentified as "temp" workers, contract workers, or independent contractors (Ditsler and Fisher 2006).

Given their very nature, standards are more often eroded than completely abandoned—but increasingly there is evidence of abandonment. Under that heading we include dropping health or retirement benefits altogether, shifting to a part-time workforce and two-tiered wage systems, and eliminating internal labor markets. Abandonment is most visible as change over time, so we sketch some of the evidence for it in the next section.

Trends in "Gloves-off" Workplace Practices

Above we described the difficulty in obtaining data on the types of workplace strategies shown in Table 1. Even more difficult is identifying *trends* in those strategies—whether they have become more or less prevalent. We know that violations of laws and standards have always been part of the mix, especially in smaller businesses. But by triangulating among different types of data, our assessment is that the erosion and outright rejection of labor standards have become increasingly common, to varying degrees depending on the strategy, industry, and time frame in question. Some of this increase reflects more frequent transgressions by smaller operators as enforcement of existing laws has weakened. A second part stems from shifts of jobs from more-regulated to less-regulated businesses and sectors via subcontracting, the use of temporary agencies, and the like. Yet another portion consists of degradation of standards and in some cases violation of laws by a subset of the large, profitable businesses that previously kept the gloves on.[3]

A few direct measures indicate increases in outright violations of labor law. Françoise Carré and Randall Wilson (2004) reported that the percentage of Massachusetts employers misclassifying workers climbed from 8% to 13% in 1995 to 1997 to 13% to 19% in 2001 to 2003 and that the percentage of employees misclassified by offending employers likewise increased over this period. Researchers have also documented a marked weakening in compliance with the National Labor Relations Act over the past several decades, with a particularly steep rise in the 2000s relative to the last half of the 1990s in illegal firings of pro-union workers (Bronfenbrenner 2000; Human Rights Watch 2000; Mehta and Theodore 2005; Schmitt and Zipperer 2007). For example, recent research has found that almost one in five union organizers or activists can expect to be fired as a result of their activities in a union election campaign, up sharply from the end of the 1990s (Schmitt and Zipperer 2007).

There is also evidence of growing evasion or erosion of labor standards. Employment in temporary help services increased twentyfold between the early 1960s and mid-1990s, an evasion strategy of both normative standards and, potentially, legal liability for working conditions (Carré and Tilly 1998). Hard numbers also document recent shifts in health and pension coverage. Whereas in the 1970s employers typically paid the full cost of health insurance premiums, by 2005, fully 76% of employees were contributing to their individual coverage premiums

(Employee Benefit Research Institute 1986; Mishel, Bernstein, and Allegretto 2007). Similarly, defined-benefit pension plans (which specify the amount of the pension, unlike a 401k) tumbled from covering 84% of full-time workers holding pensions in 1980 to 33% in 2003 (Boushey and Tilly 2008). So while on paper both health and pension benefits are still offered, in reality their cost has become prohibitive for some, with very low take-up rates for low-wage workers in particular.

Significant numbers of employers have crossed the line from erosion to abandonment of standards. For example, the percentage of workers covered by any employer-provided health plan declined from 69% in 1979 to 56% in 2004 (Mishel, Bernstein, and Allegretto 2007). At the same time, the proportion of U.S. workers covered by any retirement plan dropped from 91% of full-time employees in 1985 to 65% in 2003 (Employee Benefit Research Institute 2007, Chapter 10, Table 10.1a). Another instance of standards abandonment is the permanent conversion of full-time jobs to part-time, a practice widespread in retail, where large food stores now typically employ 60% to 80% part-timers (Carré and Tilly 2007; Tilly 1996). More generally, companies that dismantle internal labor markets are walking away from historical job standards (Cappelli 2001; Osterman 1996).

Beyond direct measures of changing employer practices, there is considerable indirect evidence that points to likely increases in gloves-off practices. In particular, to the extent that subcontracting has become more common, we would infer that there is a strong likelihood that evasions or violations of workplace laws and standards have increased as well. Again, while subcontracting in and of itself does not necessarily constitute a gloves-off practice, there is ample evidence that the competitive pressures pushing firms toward subcontracting often encourage the erosion of labor standards. While some industries (e.g., construction and apparel) have incorporated subcontracting for over a century, research on other industries suggests that the practice has spread throughout the U.S. economy. Both the case study literature and aggregate industry and occupational statistics show an increase in contracting and outsourcing (Deloitte Global Financial Services Industry Group 2004; Lane et al. 2003; Mann 2003; Moss, Salzman, and Tilly 2000).[4] In some cases, subcontracting has become so prevalent that entire new industries have been created or dramatically expanded, as with security services, food services, janitorial services, call centers, and dry cleaning and laundry services (serving institutions such as hospitals).

Similarly, to the extent that union density has declined, we would infer a likely increase in gloves-off workplace practices, through two mechanisms. First, in industries that had high union density, loss of union membership typically results in an industry-wide lowering of wage standards and working conditions. Employers compete on the basis of labor costs instead of quality services and products, lowering the wage floor toward the minimum and increasing the likelihood that some employers will go below that floor (or adopt other erosive strategies such as subcontracting or adopting two-tiered wage systems). Second, unions have historically been, and continue to be, key agents in enforcing employment and labor laws, actively monitoring their workplaces for adherence to wage and hour, health and safety, right to organize, and other laws. The decades-long decline in union density in the U.S., therefore, does not bode well. In 1948, almost one in three workers was in a union; by 2005, the fraction had fallen to just one in eight (Schmitt and Zipperer 2007).

Finally, federal capacity to enforce labor standards has waned. The Brennan Center for Justice reports that "between 1975 and 2004, the number of [Department of Labor] workplace investigators declined by 14 percent and the number of compliance actions completed declined by 36 percent—while the number of covered workers grew by 55 percent, and the number of covered establishments grew by 112 percent" (Bernhardt, McGrath, and DeFilippis 2007:31). In similar fashion, the Occupational Safety and Health Administration's budget has been cut by $25 million in real dollars since 2001, and at the same time the agency has shifted resources away from enforcement and deterrence toward "compliance assistance" (AFL-CIO Safety and Health Office 2007). At its current staffing and inspection levels, it would take federal OSHA 133 years to inspect each workplace under its jurisdiction just once (AFL-CIO Safety and Health Office 2007).

Up to this point, we have stayed at a descriptive level, mapping out the types of workplace strategies that constitute the gloves-off economy. But understanding how we got here is critical for understanding how to respond going forward; in what follows, we give a brief tour of the trajectory of labor market regulation that has landed us at the threshold of broken labor standards.

How the Gloves Went On and Came Off Again: The Rise and Fall of the Regulation of Work

The gloves-off economy did not appear out of nowhere. Employers' decisions about how to organize work and production are shaped by competitive forces and institutional constraints, each of which they also influence. Indeed, we see the trajectory toward labor cost reduction progressing along four axes: business has become less inclined toward self-regulation, government regulation of business has increasingly gone unenforced, the decline in unions has limited civil society regulation of business, and government has reduced the social safety net and adopted policies that expand the group of vulnerable workers.

The Gloves Go On: Rising Regulation of Work in the United States, 1890–1975

The first to regulate employment in the United States were businesses themselves. In the late 19th and early 20th centuries, the vertical integration documented by Alfred Chandler (1977, 1990), as well as horizontal integration—for example, at U.S. Steel and General Motors—came to fruition. This had a number of consequences. Oligopoly power shifted competition away from price competition and allowed large corporations to pass on added costs including labor costs (Freeman and Medoff 1984). Companies enjoyed sheltered capital markets, since the major source of finance was retained earnings, and managerial capitalism flourished. To increase control over production processes, businesses standardized their hiring and supervision, rather than leaving them to the whims of individual managers (Jacoby 1985; Roy 1997; Zunz 1990).

The combination of large companies, the importance of firm-specific knowledge, and personnel management oriented toward adding value rather than cutting costs led to widespread development of internal labor markets featuring long-term employment, upward mobility, and company-run training. Of course, labor unrest and union pressure also played a strong role (Gordon, Edwards, and Reich 1982; Jacoby 1997).

At the same time, government regulation of employment began to develop alongside business self-regulation, spurred to action by the muckraking journalists and crusading advocates of the Progressive Era. States led in the innovation, instituting "Workman's Compensation" programs, regulating child labor, and passing safety and women's minimum wage legislation.

In the crucible of the Great Depression, the federal government finally stepped forward in concerted fashion to establish a system of employer regulation via the New Deal legislation of the 1930s. The cornerstone of this system was the 1938 Fair Labor Standards Act (FLSA), which set the floor for wages and overtime. Initially, the FLSA excluded some groups of workers, but it was expanded from the 1940s through the 1980s to include most workers except for employees of state and local government, small-farm workers, and some domestic and home care workers (Department of Labor 2007). The 1935 National Labor Relations Act (NLRA) provided private-sector workers with the right to organize around working conditions, to bargain collectively, and to strike.

Later, Title VII of the 1964 Civil Rights Act prohibited discrimination by covered employers (with a small number of exclusions, such as the federal government itself) on the basis of race, color, religion, sex, or national origin. Legislative and judicial extensions of the act banned sexual harassment and discrimination on the basis of pregnancy, age, or disability. Finally, the regulation of health and safety on the job was established by the 1970 Occupational Safety and Health Act, which is enforced by OSHA.

In step with heightened government regulation of the terms and conditions of employment, civil society expanded its regulatory role as well. Labor unions took the lead. Though unions in the United States date back to the 18th century, the critical turning point for the country's labor movement came with the organizing drives of the Congress of Industrial Organizations (CIO)—and of the American Federation of Labor (AFL) from which it had emerged—in the 1930s and 1940s. In 1935, when the NLRA was passed, the AFL (prior to the CIO's departure) claimed 2.5 million members. By 1945, the AFL and CIO combined claimed 14.8 million workers, over one-third of the nonagricultural workforce (New York Public Library 1997).

A less widely recognized element of civil society regulation of the workplace was launched in 1974 with the federal government's creation of the Legal Services Corporation (LSC). LSC disburses federal funds to independent local groups of public interest attorneys, with a mission to "promote equal access to justice and to provide high-quality civil legal assistance to low-income Americans" (Legal Services Corporation 2008a). While local legal services agencies address a wide range of issues, their portfolio typically includes labor, both through individual lawsuits and through litigation directed more broadly at the implementation of "the unemployment system, wage and hour laws, low wage worker protections, and training for disadvantaged families" (Greater Boston Legal Services 2008).

In addition to direct regulation of employment, government took on a stronger role in regulating labor supply from the 1930s forward. From the 1930s to the 1970s, regulating labor supply chiefly meant limiting the extent to which economically vulnerable workers were forced into taking any job, regardless of the pay, working conditions, or their family's needs. The 1935 Social Security Act was the key law in this regard, creating income streams for several distinct groups—widows and single mothers, the elderly, the disabled, and those unemployed through no fault of their own—to protect them from destitution when they could not work. The net effect of the act was to provide income to vulnerable groups in the workforce, making them less desperate for work.

Immigration policy can also directly expand or contract the number of vulnerable workers in an economy. For example, during a critical two decades, 1942 to 1964, the U.S. Bracero Program managed a large flow of legal, regulated immigrants from Mexico. The program, aimed at limiting illegal immigration and meeting the labor needs of agribusiness (which faced labor shortages during World War II), offered 4.5 million work contracts to Mexicans over its lifetime, about 200,000 per year. *Braceros* had far from full rights as workers: They were temporary and tied to an individual employer, and they often suffered abuse at the hands of farm owners and the U.S. and Mexican governments. Still, the program offered an attractive alternative to illegal immigration, which would have left immigrants even more vulnerable (Gammage, this volume).

Thus, regulation of the U.S. workplace followed an upward arc for the first 75 years of the 20th century. Businesses built rules and bureaucracies that reshaped jobs, and an important subset of companies achieved market dominance and shared some of the resulting "rents" with their workforce. Government took an increasingly active role in mandating and enforcing employment rights and standards; civil society, especially in the form of unions, did the same. Government policies also provided supports and opportunities that moderated the whip of desperation for particular groups of potential workers. American workplaces in the early 1970s were no workers' paradise, but many workers were sheltered by a set of norms and regulations that, from today's vantage point, look quite impressive.

The Gloves Come Off: Declining Regulation of Work in the United States, 1975–Present

Then it all began to unravel. A historical map of the deregulation of work in the United States—and recent attempts at re-regulation—can also serve as a map of the major themes of this volume.

How Employers Take the Gloves Off

Starting in the mid-1970s, business self-organization moved in new directions. Whereas vertical integration characterized most of the 20th century, disintegration has been a business watchword since the 1980s. Corporations are increasingly subcontracting and outsourcing work, creating extended supply chains (Gereffi 2003; Harrison 1994; Moss, Salzman, and Tilly 2000). The public sector as well has turned to subcontracting, in the privatization trend that has swept governments from federal to local in recent decades (Sclar and Leone 2000). Globalization and rapid technological change have rendered market dominance more transitory. Capital has become more mobile, undermining job stability

(Bluestone and Harrison 1982; Silver 2003). Businesses draw increasingly on nonstandard forms of work, often mediated by a third party: even the largest corporations have distanced themselves from lifetime employment (Baumol, Blinder, and Wolff 2003). As AT&T geared up to lay off an estimated 40,000 workers in early 1996, vice president for human resources James Meadows told *The New York Times*, "People need to look at themselves as self-employed, as vendors who come to this company to sell their skills." Instead of "jobs," people increasingly have "projects" or "fields of work," he remarked, leading to a society that is increasingly "jobless but not workless" (Andrews 1996:D10).

The chapters in the next section of this volume, How Employers Take the Gloves Off, highlight key aspects of these shifts in employer behavior. Noah Zatz sets the scene by reviewing the core employment and labor laws protecting workers on the job, then teases out the myriad ways that some employers dodge or violate them. Ruth Milkman, followed by Nik Theodore, Edwin Meléndez, Abel Valenzuela Jr., and Ana Luz Gonzalez, offers related discussion of the role that new forms of business organization play in the degradation of work. Exploring construction, building services, and trucking in southern California, Milkman documents the emergence of business strategies like subcontracting, double-breasting, and converting truckers from employees to "owner-operators" and the direct negative impact these practices have on job quality in these sectors. Theodore and co-authors focus on the growing phenomenon of day labor, especially in construction, and provide evidence from a survey of day laborers in the Washington, DC, area that this work is primed for and riddled with abuse of basic labor standards. Laura Dresser reminds us that caring and cleaning work in the home includes both old and new elements: child care and cleaning work as old as human society as well as the recent explosion in home health care stemming from changes in the family and in the health care industry. An analysis spanning these different occupations, Dresser argues, highlights a shared and structural vulnerability to abuses of labor rights and standards.

At the same time that businesses have restructured over the past three decades, government regulation of employers has declined. The laws and agencies established in the middle of the 20th century to regulate business still exist, and there are more workplace regulations, but there have not been commensurate increases in the government's capacity to investigate and ensure compliance with these laws. According to David Weil (this volume), between 1940 and 1994, the number of workplace regulations administered by the Department of Labor grew from 18 to 189; currently there are nearly 200 statutes to oversee. But as we noted above, federal resources for enforcement have been scaled back considerably. Thus, although regulation may be increasing on paper, in practice there is strong evidence that some of our most basic workplace laws are not being enforced. Noah Zatz, in his chapter in this volume, drives the point home by distinguishing between the reach (coverage) and grasp (enforcement effectiveness) of government workplace regulation. Moreover, the standards set by some of those laws are weaker today than they were several decades ago. The core standards of the FLSA have become weaker as the wage floor provided by the minimum wage has fallen (though recent legislation at the state and federal level has boosted it somewhat), and federal regulatory changes recently reduced the reach of the overtime pay provisions by exempting more workers. In 2003, analysts estimated that this redefinition would remove an added eight million workers (about 6% of the total employed workforce) from eligibility for overtime pay (Eisenbrey and Bernstein 2003).

Part of the deregulation occurred simply by choosing agency directors skeptical of—or even hostile to—the regulation of business. For example, beginning with President Reagan in 1981, Republican presidents making appointments to the National Labor Relations Board began to choose board members opposed to unions, creating an ever-less-favorable terrain for union representation (Miller 2006, Moberg 1998). In some cases, businesses themselves are playing an important role in driving down government-mandated labor standards. For example, it was the restaurant and retail industries, which employ the bulk of low-wage workers, that led the drive to reduce the real value of the minimum wage (Tilly 2005).

Alongside the weakening of governmental institutions regulating employers, civil society's grip has also loosened as unions have lost much of their historic strength. Declining union membership has been driven by a number of factors, but concerted (often illegal) anti-union activity has clearly played a role. For example, Bronfenbrenner (2000) has documented that employers threaten to close all or part of their business in more than half of all union organizing campaigns and that unions win only 38% of representation elections when such threats are made, compared to 51% in the absence of shutdown threats.[5] Research on deunionization in the construction, trucking, and garment industries shows that gloves-off workplace practices increase as a result (Belzer 1994; Milkman 2007; Milkman this volume, Theodore this volume). Finally, about one third of non-union workers in the U.S. would prefer union representation (Freeman and Rogers 1999), another indicator that the decline in private-sector union membership has had more to do with employer strategies than with the preferences of American workers.

With unions on the defensive and reduced to a small corner of the private sector, employers have had a relatively free hand to contain and even reduce wages and benefits in non-union settings. As a result, the gap between union and non-union compensation yawns wide. Full-time workers who are union members earn 30% more per week than their non-union counterparts (Bureau of Labor Statistics 2007). Seventy percent of union workers have defined-benefit pension plans; only 15% of non-union workers do (Labor Research Association 2006). Union members are also 25% more likely to have employer-provided benefits, like health insurance or a retirement plan (Schmitt et al. 2007).

Less momentous than union atrophy, but perhaps more insidious, is the trimming of funds for the Legal Services Corporation. In 2007 dollars, nationwide federal funding for LSC stood at $757 million in 1980, but following deep cuts in 1981 and 1995 had fallen to $332 million in 2007, with the number of clients served dropping from 1.6 million to 1 million (Hoffman 1996; Iowa Legal Aid 2008; Legal Services Corporation 2007; Legal Services Corporation 2008b). Federal legislation also barred use of LSC funds for class-action lawsuits (Hoffman 1996) and limited immigrant representation to permanent residents and a few other selected categories (such as refugees and asylum seekers). These cuts have muted important voices advocating for low-wage workers' rights.

Workers at Risk

Whether intentionally or not, federal and state policy makers have in recent years exacerbated the trend toward deregulation by adopting policies that leave growing numbers of workers increasingly vulnerable to gloves-off practices. This has occurred along multiple dimensions: immigration policy, safety net and welfare policy, and policies affecting ex-offenders. The three chapters making up our section on "Workers at Risk" tell these stories in more detail.

Sarah Gammage leads off in chapter 6 with a history of shifting U.S. immigration policy and a vivid depiction of the shaky labor market position of undocumented—and even some documented—immigrants. Widely regarded as dysfunctional on a host of dimensions, U.S. immigration policy has effectively increased the number of workers vulnerable to gloves-off strategies, because undocumented workers are largely unable to access core rights in the workplace. In particular, the 1986 Immigration Reform and Control Act legalized nearly three million immigrants but simultaneously criminalized the knowing employment of undocumented immigrants. This criminalization, coupled with escalating enforcement of employer sanctions in recent years, consigns undocumented immigrant workers, estimated at 7.2 million in March 2005

(Passell 2006) to a shadowy existence, without status and vulnerable to workplace abuse. The Supreme Court's 2002 *Hoffman Plastic Compounds* decision (discussed both by Gammage and by Amy Sugimori in chapter 9) has only made things worse, as the first recent decision to chip away undocumented immigrants' recourse to formal protection under law.

Other social policies have added to the pool of vulnerable workers. The "welfare reform" of 1996, which essentially ended government financial support for nonworking single mothers, marked the culmination of a long series of state and federal restrictions and benefit reductions of welfare programs through the 1980s and early 1990s, pushing millions of single mothers into employment. The landmark 1996 legislation focused on moving families from welfare into self-sufficiency as quickly as possible and signaled the end of the government's willingness to provide cash assistance to able-bodied adults, regardless of their status as parents or caretakers.[6] In chapter 7, Mark Greenberg and Elizabeth Lower-Basch conclude that most single mothers are better off economically as workers than as welfare recipients; however, many remain trapped in low-wage jobs or struggling to survive without a (reported) job or access to welfare funds—again, a group vulnerable to gloves-off employer strategies.

Other social programs have also been hard hit by the shift toward reducing the social wage. Unemployment insurance today reaches a smaller proportion of the unemployed than it did 30 or 40 years ago: Whereas in 1970, 44% of the unemployed received unemployment insurance, in 2006 that percentage had fallen to 35% (calculated by the authors from Council of Economic Advisors 2007; Employment and Training Administration 2007a, 2007b). Unemployment insurance eligibility depends on reaching certain thresholds of earnings and hours worked in the period preceding unemployment. Ironically, the spread of low earnings has reduced the percentage of unemployed workers who are eligible for support.

Also expanding the stock of vulnerable workers has been the dramatic climb in incarceration rates, which has led to a mushrooming ex-offender population that faces significant formal and informal bars to employment. Over two million persons, disproportionately black and Latino, are currently behind bars, a 500% increase over the last 30 years (The Sentencing Project 2008). The United States has the highest incarceration rate of any nation in the Organisation for Economic Co-operation and Development, much of which stems from the high rates of incarceration for drug offenses.[7] Of the state prison population, African American and Hispanic prisoners are more likely than whites to have been sentenced for drug offenses: 15% of whites, 25% of African Americans, and

27% of Hispanics. According to Maurice Emsellem and Debbie A. Mukamal (chapter 8), many of those now being released from prison were convicted on drug offenses (37%), and nearly two thirds overall served time
for nonviolent offenses (Glaze and Bonczar 2007). As they are released
from prison, ex-offenders face significant challenges integrating into stable
employment, especially since many more sectors of the labor market are
using background checks and limiting employment for felons, pushing yet
another population to the margins of the world of work.

Since most forms of evasion and violation of workplace standards are
not measurable in standard data sets, we cannot definitively say which
workers are touched by such practices. Here we have focused on three
groups of workers whose power in the workplace has been significantly
shaped—and more often than not reduced—by public policy, resulting
in greater vulnerability to substandard working conditions. But it is not
an exhaustive list, and clearly there are many more groups of workers
trapped in the gloves-off economy, whether because of their skill level,
lack of work experience, skin color, gender, or other reasons. From the
standpoint of this volume, however, the key lesson is that the workers
most often impacted by "gloves-off" workplace practices are those that,
for varying reasons, have little or no recourse to either challenge an
employer's behavior or to seek employment elsewhere.

Putting the Gloves Back On

Fortunately, there is more to the story of the gloves-off economy than
unscrupulous employer practices, the loosening of state and civil society
regulation of the workplace, and the policy-fueled expansion of vulnerable
groups of workers and job seekers. Advocates, organizers, and policy makers are increasingly developing new strategies to enforce employment and
labor laws and reestablish standards in the workplace, sometimes with the
cooperation of parts of the employer community. The final section of this
volume, "Putting the Gloves Back On," highlights a number of recent successes and promising directions for re-regulating work.

These drives to put the gloves back on take varied forms, but all
involve reactivating government, unions, or other elements of civil society
to restore worker protections. In chapter 9 Amy Sugimori surveys a wide
range of innovative state and local initiatives to safeguard the rights of
immigrant workers in the context of increasingly punitive policy implementation and escalating numbers of workplace violations. Stephen
Lerner, Jill Hurst, and Glenn Adler, themselves architects of some of the
most successful union organizing strategies of the last two decades,
describe in chapter 10 how the Service Employees International Union
successfully reorganized the building cleaning industry against steep odds

and assess the prospects for a repeat performance with security guards. In chapter 11 Paul Sonn and Stephanie Luce trace the broadening and deepening of the living wage movement, which has stepped up from local to state to national victories, and now is even beginning to go global. David Weil closes the volume in chapter 12 by exploring under what circumstances the business community may accept or even welcome new regulations and under what circumstances it closes ranks to oppose regulation. Weil particularly focuses on potential divergences in perceived self-interest between large and small businesses and between "high road" employers who already exceed proposed standards and their "low road" counterparts who would feel the bite of new regulation.

This volume does not exhaust the full variety of illegal or evasive strategies by employers, the groups of vulnerable workers, or the new solutions being developed on the ground. Instead, our goal is to put the gloves-off economy squarely onto the radar screen of policy makers, researchers, and practitioners, because it is our belief that without intervention, the trend toward unregulated work will only worsen. Given the often hidden nature of these jobs and workplace strategies, researchers will need to apply innovative methods to more accurately map such practices. The search for solutions, too, is at the stage of experimentation. There is no returning to the typical job of 1970 (nor would we want to go there, for any number of reasons). But as the chapters in this volume show, there are promising models for revitalizing job standards in the 21st-century workplace as well as promising examples of the diverse coalitions that are needed to drive change. In the end, the core truth is that workers, government, unions, and responsible employers all have a stake in finding ways to put the gloves of worker protections back on.

Acknowledgments

The authors would like to thank Françoise Carré, Paul Osterman, and the editorial board of the Labor and Employment Research Association for their generous reading of and comments on this chapter. All errors of fact and analysis remain our own.

The editors also acknowledge the researchers who have been contributing to a website created in 2003: "Gloves Off: Bare-Fisted Political Economy." Visit www.glovesoff.org to read more about their organization and their work.

Endnotes

[1] Likewise, informal and underground transactions violate or evade a wide range of laws, notably tax laws, while we limit our attention to avoidance of labor laws and standards.

[2] See Department of State (2004), Bales, Fletcher, and Stover (2004), Clawson et al. (2003), and Department of Justice (2004).

[3] While employment law does provide for the means to hold the original employer accountable, in practice establishing this joint liability can be difficult and time consuming; see Zatz in this volume.

[4] In addition to industry studies, a rare systematic look at subcontracting based on a Bureau of Labor Statistics survey on contracting-out shows an increase in outsourcing of five functions over the 1980s (Abraham and Taylor 1996).

[5] The frequency and credibility of threats to relocate have been boosted by a series of free trade agreements, most notably the North American Free Trade Agreement, which have removed restrictions on U.S. corporate investment abroad as well as trade barriers to goods produced abroad by U.S. companies or their subcontractors.

[6] In a less-noticed change that actually generated most of the savings in the reform, Congress excluded many legal noncitizen immigrants who have entered the United States from federally funded Temporary Assistance for Needy Families (TANF), Medicaid health insurance, food stamps, and SSI disability programs (though states may use their own funds to aid immigrants, and some of these provisions have been pared back since 1996). During the 1990s, the states also phased out or greatly reduced general assistance programs, the income support program of last resort for able-bodied adults without dependent children.

[7] Drug offences accounted for 1 in 4 of those in jail in 2002, and 20% of state and 55% of federal prison inmates in 2001 (Sentencing Project 2008).

References

Abraham, Katharine, and Susan Taylor. 1996. "Firms' Use of Outside Contractors: Theory and Evidence." *Journal of Labor Economics* Vol. 14, no. 3, pp. 394–424.

AFL-CIO Safety and Health Office. 2007. *Death on the Job: The Toll of Neglect—A National and State-by-State Profile of Worker Safety and Health in the United States*. Washington, DC: AFL-CIO. <http://www.aflcio.org/issues/safety/memorial/doj_2007.cfm.> [April 28, 2008].

Andrews, Edmund L. 1996. "Don't Go Away Mad, Just Go Away: Can AT&T Be the Nice Guy as It Cuts 40,000 Jobs?" *New York Times*, February 13, pp. D1–D10.

Appelbaum, Eileen, Annette Bernhardt, and Richard J. Murnane, eds. 2003. *Low-Wage America: How Employers Are Reshaping Opportunity in the Workplace*. New York: Russell Sage Foundation.

Appelbaum, Richard P. 1999. *Los Angeles Jewish Commission on Sweatshops*. Los Angeles, CA: Los Angeles Jewish Commission on Sweatshops.

Avirgan, Tony, L. Josh Bivens, and Sarah Gammage. 2005. *Good Jobs, Bad Jobs, No Jobs: Labor Markets and Informal Work in Egypt, El Salvador, India, Russia, and South Africa*. Washington, DC: Economic Policy Institute.

Bales, Kevin, Laurel Fletcher, and Eric Stover. 2004. *Hidden Slaves: Forced Labor in the United States*. Washington, DC, and Berkeley, CA: Free the Slaves and Human Rights Center, University of California.

Baumol, William J., Alan S. Blinder, and Edward N. Wolff. 2003. *Downsizing in America: Reality, Causes, and Consequences*. New York: Russell Sage Foundation.

Belzer, Michael. 1994. "The Motor Carrier Industry: Truckers and Teamsters Under Siege." In Paula B. Voos, ed., *Contemporary Collective Bargaining in the Private Sector*. Madison, WI: Industrial Relations Research Association, pp. 259–302.

Bernhardt, Annette, Siobhán McGrath, and James DeFilippis. 2007. *Unregulated Work in the Global City: Employment and Labor Law Violations in New York City*. New York: Brennan Center for Justice, New York University.

Bluestone, Barry, and Bennett Harrison. 1982. *The Deindustrialization of America*. New York: Basic Books.

Boushey, Heather, and Chris Tilly. 2008. "Avere un lavoro: i limite del sistema di sostegno sociale contributivo negli Statis Uniti" ("Get a Job: The Limits of Work-Based Social Support in the United States"). *Annali della Fondazione di Vittorio* (Rome). Special issue on "New Poverty, New Priorities: Rethinking Social Inclusion." February, pp. 227–60.

Bronfenbrenner, Kate. 2000. *Uneasy Terrain: The Impact of Capital Mobility on Workers, Wages, and Union Organizing*. Ithaca, NY: New York State School of Industrial and Labor Relations, Cornell University.

Bulow, Jeremy I., and Lawrence H. Summers. 1986. "A Theory of Dual Labor Markets with Application to Industrial Policy, Discrimination, and Keynesian Unemployment." *Journal of Labor Economics* Vol. 4, No. 3, pp. 376–414.

Bureau of Labor Statistics. 2006. *National Census of Fatal Occupational Injuries in 2005*. Washington, DC: Bureau of Labor Statistics. <http://www.pathfndr.com/bls2005fatal.html>. [April 28, 2008].

———. 2007. "Median Weekly Earnings of Full-Time Wage and Salary Workers by Union Affiliation and Selected Characteristics." <http://stats.bls.gov/news.release/union2.t02.htm>. [October 6, 2007].

Cappelli, Peter. 2001. "Assessing the Decline of Internal Labor Markets." In Ivar Berg and Arne Kalleberg, eds., *Sourcebook of Labor Markets: Evolving Structures and Processes*. New York: Plenum, pp. 207–45.

Cappelli, Peter, Laurie Bassi, Harry Katz, David Knoke, Paul Osterman, and Michael Useem. 1997. *Change at Work*. New York: Oxford University Press.

Carré, Françoise, and Chris Tilly. 1998. "Part-Time and Temporary Work: Flexibility for Whom?" *Dollars and Sense*. January/February.

———. 2007. *Continuity and Change in Low-Wage Work in Retail Trade in the United States: A Set of Company Case Studies*. Report to the Russell Sage Foundation. Boston, MA: Center for Social Policy, University of Massachusetts Boston.

Carré, Francoise, and Randall Wilson. 2004. *The Social and Economic Costs of Employee Misclassification in Construction*. Boston, MA: Construction Policy Research Center, Harvard Law School Labor and Worklife Program and Harvard School of Public Health.

Castells, Manuel, and Alejandro Portes. 1989. "The World Underneath: The Origins, Dynamics, and Effects of the Informal Economy." In Alejandro Portes, Manuel Castells, and Lauren A. Benton, eds., *The Informal Economy: Studies in Advanced and Less Developed Countries*. Baltimore: Johns Hopkins University Press, pp. 11–37.

Chandler, Alfred. 1977. *The Visible Hand: The Managerial Revolution in American Business*. Cambridge, MA: Harvard University Press.

———. 1990. *Scale and Scope: The Dynamics of Industrial Capitalism*. Cambridge, MA: Belknap/Harvard University Press.

Clawson, Heather J., Kevonne M. Small, Ellen S. Go, and Bradley W. Myles. 2003. *Needs Assessment for Service Providers and Trafficking Victims*. Fairfax, VA: Caliber. <http://www.ncjrs.gov/pdffiles1/nij/grants/202469.pdf>. [April 28, 2008].

Council of Economic Advisors. 2007. "2007 Report Spreadsheet Tables." *Economic Report of the President*. <http://www.gpoaccess.gov/eop/tables07.html>. [September 26, 2007].

Deloitte Global Financial Services Industry Group. 2004. *The Titans Take Hold: How Offshoring Has Changed the Competitive Dynamic for Global Financial Services Institutions*. Deloitte Research Report. New York: Deloitte Global Financial Services Industry Group.

Dembner, Alice. 2007. "Firms Find Ways around State Health Law." *Boston Globe*. December 23, p. A1.

Department of Justice. 2004. *Report to Congress from Attorney General John Ashcroft on U.S. Government Efforts to Combat Trafficking in Persons in Fiscal Year 2003*. Washington, DC: U.S. Department of Justice.

Department of Justice, Office of Justice Programs. 2006. *Number of Persons under Jurisdiction of State Correctional Authorities by Most Serious Offense, 1980–2004*. <http://www.ojp.usdoj.gov/bjs/glance/tables/corrtyptab.htm>. [April 28, 2008].

Department of Labor. 2001. *1999–2000 Report on Initiatives*. Employment Standards Administration, Wage and Hour Division. Washington, DC: U.S. Department of Labor.

Department of Labor, Employment Standards Administration, Wage and Hour Division. 2007. *History of Changes to the Minimum Wage Law*. <http://www.dol.gov/esa/minwage/coverage.htm>. [September 26, 2007].

Department of State. 2004. *Trafficking in Persons Report: June 2004*. Washington, DC: U.S. Department of State.

DeSilva, Lalith, Adrian Millett, Dominic Rotondi, and William Sullivan. 2000. *Independent Contractors: Prevalence and Implications for Unemployment Insurance Programs*. Report prepared for the United States Department of Labor. Rockville, MD: Planmatics. <http://wdr.doleta.gov/owsdrr/00-5/00-5.pdf>. [April 28, 2008].

De Soto, Hernando. 1989. *The Other Path: The Invisible Revolution in the Third World*. New York: Harper & Row.

Dicken, Linda, and Mark Hall. 2003. "Labour Law and Industrial Relations: A New Settlement?" In Paul K. Edwards, ed., *Industrial Relations: Theory and Practice*. Oxford: Blackwell, pp. 124–156.

Dickens, William T., and Kevin Lang. 1985. "A Test of Dual Labor Market Theory." *American Economic Review*, Vol. 75, no. 4, pp. 792–805.

Ditsler, Elaine, and Peter Fisher. 2006. *Nonstandard Jobs, Substandard Benefits: A 2005 Update*. The Iowa Policy Project. September. <http://www.iowapolicyproject.org/2006docs/060929-nonstd_full.pdf>. [February 20, 2008].

Doeringer, Peter B., and Michael J. Piore. 1971. *Internal Labor Markets and Manpower Analysis*. Lexington, MA: DC Heath.

Domestic Workers United and Datacenter. 2006. *Home Is Where the Work Is: Inside New York's Domestic Work Industry*. New York: Domestic Workers United & Datacenter.

Donahue, Linda, James Lamare, and Fred Kotler. 2007. *The Cost of Worker Misclassification in New York State*. Cornell University, ILR School. <http://digitalcommons.ilr.cornell.edu/cgi/viewcontent.cgi?article=1009&context=reports>. [April 28, 2008].

Eisenbrey, Ross, and Jared Bernstein. 2003. *Eliminating the Right to Overtime Pay: Department of Labor Proposal Means Lower Pay, Longer Hours for Millions of Workers*. Washington, DC: Economic Policy Institute.

Employee Benefit Research Institute. 1986. *Features of Employer Health Plans: Cost Containment, Plan Funding, and Coverage Continuation*. Issue Brief No. 60. November.

————. 2007. *EBRI Databook on Employee Benefits.* <http://www.ebri.org/publications/ books/index.cfm?fa=databook>. [June 20, 2007].

Employment and Training Administration. 2007a. *Unemployment Insurance Financial Data Handbook.* Department of Labor ET Handbook No. 394. <http://ows. doleta.gov/dmstree/handboos/394/link70.html#taxre>. [October 6, 2007].

————. 2007b. *Unemployment Insurance Data Summary.* <http://www.workforce security.doleta.gov/unemploy/content/data.asp>. [October 6, 2007].

Esping-Andersen, Gösta. 1999. "A Welfare State for the 21st Century." In Anthony Giddens, ed., *The Global Third Way Debate.* Oxford: Polity Press, pp. 134–56.

European Commission. 2004. *Undeclared Work in an Enlarged Union: An Analysis of Undeclared Work—An In-Depth Study of Specific Items.* Brussels: European Commission Directorate-General for Employment and Social Affairs.

Fiscal Policy Institute. 2007. *New York State Workers' Compensation: How Big Is the Coverage Shortfall?* New York: Fiscal Policy Institute. <http://www.fiscalpolicy. org/publications2007/FPI_WorkersCompShortfall_WithAddendum.pdf>. [April 28, 2008].

Freeman, Richard B., and James L. Medoff. 1984. *What Do Unions Do?* New York: Basic Books.

Freeman, Richard B., and Joel Rogers. 1999. *What Workers Want.* Ithaca, NY: ILR Press.

Gereffi, Gary. 2003. "The Global Economy: Organization, Governance, and Development." In Neil Smelser and Richard Swedberg, eds., *Handbook of Economic Sociology.* Princeton, NJ: Princeton University Press, pp. 160–82.

Glaze, Lauren E., and Thomas P. Bonczar. 2007. *Probation and Parole in the United States, 2005.* NCJ 215091. Washington, DC: U.S. Department of Justice, Bureau of Justice Statistics.

Gordon, David M., Richard Edwards, and Michael Reich. 1982. *Segmented Work, Divided Workers: The Historical Transformations of Labor in the United States.* New York: Cambridge University Press.

Greater Boston Legal Services. 2008. *Types of Service.* <http://www.gbls.org/ service.htm>. [February 10, 2008].

Hagerty, James R. 2002. "Aramark Aims to Gobble Up Business from Rivals in Europe." *Wall Street Journal,* January 24. <http://online.wsj.com/article/ 0,,SB1011813924401834640.djm,00.html>.

Harrison, Bennett. 1994. *Lean and Mean: The Changing Landscape of Corporate Power in the Age of Flexibility.* New York: Basic Books.

Herzenberg, Stephen A., John A. Alic, and Howard Wial. 1998. *New Rules for a New Economy: Employment and Opportunity in Postindustrial America.* Ithaca, NY: Cornell University Press.

Hoffman, Jan. 1996. "Counseling the Poor, But Now One by One." *New York Times.* September 15, p. 47.

Human Rights Watch. 2000. *Unfair Advantage: Workers' Freedom of Association in the United States Under International Human Rights Standards.* New York: Human Rights Watch.

International Labour Organization. 2002. *Women and Men in the Informal Economy: A Statistical Picture.* Geneva: International Labour Organization.

Iowa Legal Aid. 2008. *A History of Legal Services in the Nation and Iowa.* <http://www.iowalegalaid.org/about/RTF1.cfm?pagename=A%20History%20of% 20Legal%20Services%20in%20the%20Nation%20and%20Iowa>. [February 10, 2008].

Jacoby, Sanford. 1985. *Employing Bureaucracy: Managers, Unions, and the Transformation of Work in American Industry, 1900–1945.* New York: Columbia University Press.

———. 1997. *Modern Manors: Welfare Capitalism Since the New Deal.* Princeton. NJ: Princeton University Press.

Kochan, Thomas A., Harry C. Katz, and Robert M. McKersie. 1989. *The Transformation of American Industrial Relations.* Ithaca, NY: ILR Press.

Labor Research Association. 2006. "The Growing Gap in Benefits." LRA Online. <http://www.workinglife.org>. September 15. [June 10, 2007].

Lane, Julia, Philip Moss, Hal Salzman, and Chris Tilly. 2003. "Too Many Cooks? Tracking Internal Labor Market Dynamics in Food Service with Case Studies and Quantitative Data." In Eileen Appelbaum, Annette Bernhardt, and Richard Murnane, eds., *Low-Wage America: How Employers Are Reshaping Opportunity in the Workplace.* New York: Russell Sage Foundation, pp. 229–69.

Legal Services Corporation. 2007. *Full Senate Votes to Increase LSC's Budget to $390 Million.* <http://www.lsc.gov/press/pr_detail_T7_R43.php>. [February 10, 2008].

———. 2008a. *What Is LSC?* <http://www.lsc.gov/about/lsc.php>. [February 10, 2008].

———. 2008b. *Fiscal Year 2009 Budget Request.* <http://www.lsc.gov/pdfs/budgetrequestfy2009.pdf>. [February 10, 2008].

Leonard, Madeleine. 1998. *Invisible Work, Invisible Workers: The Informal Economy in Europe and the US.* London and New York: Macmillan Press and St. Martin's Press.

Make the Road by Walking, and Retail Wholesale and Department Store Union. 2005. *Street of Shame: Retail Stores on Knickerbocker Avenue.* Brooklyn, NY: Department Store Union (RWDSU/UFCW) and Make the Road by Walking.

Mann, Catherine L. 2003. *Globalization of IT Services and White Collar Jobs: The Next Wave of Productivity Growth.* International Economics Policy Briefs, number PB03-11, December. <http://www.iie.com/publications/pb/pb03-11.pdf>. [April 25, 2008].

Mehta, Chirag, and Nik Theodore. 2005. *Undermining the Right to Organize: Employer Behavior During Union Representation Campaigns.* Chicago: Center for Urban Economic Development, University of Illinois at Chicago. <http://www.americanrightsatwork.org/publications/general/undermining-the-right-to-organize-employerbehavior-during-union-representation-campaigns.html>. [April 25, 2008].

Milkman, Ruth. 2007. *LA Story: Immigrant Workers and the Future of the U.S. Labor Movement.* New York: Russell Sage.

Miller, Congressman George. 2006. "Workers' Rights Under Attack by Bush Administration: President Bush's National Labor Relations Board Rolls Back Labor Protections," *Committee on Education and the Workforce, U.S. House of Representatives.* <http://edlabor.house.gov/publications/NLRBreport071306.pdf>. [July 28, 2008].

Mingione, Enzio. 2000. "Introduction: Immigrants and the Informal Economy in European Cities." *International Journal of Urban and Regional Research,* Vol. 23, no. 2, pp. 209–11.

Mishel, Lawrence, Jared Bernstein, and Sylvia Allegretto. 2007. *The State of Working America 2006–07.* Washington, DC, and Ithaca, NY: Economic Policy Institute and Cornell University Press.

Moberg, David. 1998. "Republicans Warp the Labor Board." *The Progressive.* May.

Moss, Philip, Harold Salzman, and Chris Tilly. 2000. "Limits to Market-Mediated Employment: From Deconstruction to Reconstruction of Internal Labor

Markets." In Francoise Carré, Marianne Ferber, Lonnie Golden, and Steve Herzenberg, eds., *Non-Traditional Work Arrangements and the Changing Labor Market: Dimensions, Causes, and Institutional Responses*. Madison, WI: Industrial Relations Research Association, pp. 95–121.

Murray, Fergus. 1983. "The Decentralization of Production: The Decline of the Mass-Collective Worker." *Capital and Class*, Vol. 19, pp. 74–99.

New York Public Library. 1997. *American History Desk Reference*. New York: Stonesong Press/Macmillan.

Nissen, Bruce. 2004. *Employment Practices and Working Conditions in the Building Services Industry in Miami-Dade County, Florida*. Miami: Center for Labor Research and Studies, Florida International University.

Osterman, Paul, ed. 1996. *Broken Ladders: Managerial Careers in the New Economy*. New York: Oxford University Press.

———. 1999. *Securing Prosperity*. Princeton, NJ: Princeton University Press.

Passell, Jeffrey S. 2006. *The Size and Characteristics of the Unauthorized Migrant Population in the U.S.: Estimates Based on the March 2005 Current Population Survey*. Pew Hispanic Center. March 7. <http://pewhispanic.org/files/reports/61.pdf>. [February 10, 2007].

Piore, Michael J. 1980. "Dualism as a Response to Flux and Uncertainty." In Suzanne Berger and Michael J. Piore, eds., *Dualism and Discontinuity in Industrial Society*. Cambridge: Cambridge University Press, pp. 23–54.

Portes, Alejandro, Manuel Castells, and Lauren A. Benton, eds. 1989. *The Informal Economy: Studies in Advanced and Less Developed Countries*. Baltimore: Johns Hopkins University Press.

Procoli, Angela, ed. 2004. *Workers and Narratives of Survival in Europe: The Management of Precariousness at the End of the Twentieth Century*. Albany, NY: SUNY Press.

Restaurant Opportunities Center of New York and the New York City Restaurant Industry Coalition. 2005. *Behind the Kitchen Door: Pervasive Inequality in New York City's Thriving Restaurant Industry*. New York: Restaurant Opportunities Center of New York and New York City Restaurant Industry Coalition.

Robinson, William I. 2003. *Transnational Conflicts: Central America, Social Change, and Globalization*. London: Verso Books.

Roy, William. 1997. *Socializing Capital: The Rise of the Large Industrial Corporation in America*. Princeton, NJ: Princeton University Press.

Ruckelshaus, Catherine, and Bruce Goldstein. 2002. *From Orchards to the Internet: Confronting Contingent Worker Abuse*. New York: National Employment Law Project and Farmworker Justice Fund.

Sassen, Saskia. 1997. *Informalization in Advanced Urban Economies*. Issues in Development Discussion Paper #20. Geneva: International Labour Office.

Schmitt, John, Margy Waller, Shawn Fremstad, and Ben Zipperer. 2007. *Unions and Upward Mobility for Low-Wage Workers*. Washington, DC: Center for Economic and Policy Research.

Schmitt, John, and Ben Zipperer. 2007. *Dropping the Ax: Illegal Firings During Union Election Campaigns*. Washington, DC: Center for Economic and Policy Research.

Sclar, Elliot, and Richard Leone. 2000. *You Don't Always Get What You Pay For: The Economics of Privatization*. Ithaca, NY: Century Foundation/Cornell University Press.

Silver, Beverly. 2003. *Forces of Labor: Workers' Movements and Globalization Since 1870*. Cambridge, England: Cambridge University Press.

Su, Julie. 1997. "El Monte Thai Garment Workers: Slave Sweatshops." In Andrew Ross, ed., *No Sweat: Fashion, Free Trade, and the Rights of Garment Workers*. New York: Verso, pp. 143–50.

The Sentencing Project. 2008. *Incarceration*. <http://www.sentencingproject.org/IssueAreaHome.aspx?IssueID=2>. [April 28, 2008].

———. 2008. "Facts about Prisons and Prisoners." <http://www.sentencingproject.org/Admin%5CDocuments%5Cpublications%5Cinc_factsaboutprisons.pdf>. July. [July 29, 2008].

Tilly, Chris. 1996. *Half a Job: Bad and Good Part-Time Jobs in a Changing Labor Market*. Philadelphia: Temple University Press.

———. 2005. "Living Wage Laws in the United States: The Dynamics of a Growing Movement." In Maria Kousis and Charles Tilly, eds., *Threats and Opportunities in Contentious Politics*. Boulder, CO: Paradigm Publishers, pp. 143–60.

UN-HABITAT. 2004. *The State of the World's Cities 2004/2005: Globalization and Urban Culture*. London: Earthscan.

Valenzuela, Abel Jr., Nik Theodore, Edwin Melendez, and Ana Luz Gonzalez. 2006. *On the Corner: Day Labor in the United States*. Los Angeles: Center for the Study of Urban Poverty. <http://www.sscnet.ucla.edu/issr/csup/uploaded_files/Natl_DayLabor-On_the_Corner1.pdf>. [April 25, 2008].

Venkatesh, Sudhir Alladi. 2006. *Off the Books: The Underground Economy of the Urban Poor*. Cambridge, MA: Harvard University Press.

Weil, David. 2005. "Public Enforcement/Private Monitoring: Evaluating a New Approach to Regulating the Minimum Wage." *Industrial and Labor Relations Review* Vol. 58, no. 2, pp. 238–57.

Williams, Colin C. 2005. "The Undeclared Sector, Self-Employment, and Public Policy." *International Journal of Entrepreneurial Behavior and Research*, Vol. 11, no. 4, pp. 244–57.

Williams, Colin C., and Rhodri Thomas. 1996. "Paid Informal Work in the Leeds Hospitality Industry: Regulated or Unregulated Work?" In Graham Haughton and Colin C. Williams, eds., *Corporate City? Partnership, Participation, and Partition in Urban Development in Leeds*. Aldershot: Avebury, pp. 171–86.

Zunz, Olivier. 1990. *Making America Corporate, 1870–1920*. Chicago: University of Chicago Press.

Chapter 2

Working Beyond the Reach or Grasp of Employment Law

Noah D. Zatz
University of California, Los Angeles

How well does labor and employment law protect the most vulnerable workers in today's United States? This chapter surveys the field by emphasizing the formal reach and the practical grasp of our system of labor regulation. Employment law[1] reaches out to regulate only specific work arrangements; it does not apply to all firms and all workers. Among those within this reach, many nonetheless slip through the law's grasp as a result of imperfect enforcement.

Public debate about employment law rarely considers these issues of the scope of employment coverage and the effectiveness of employment law enforcement. Instead, it typically focuses on substantive rights: what employers must do for their workers, or not do to them. If workers are mistreated or deprived—if we see the damage inflicted when employers take the gloves off—then the natural legal reform is to strengthen substantive labor rights. The national legislative agenda of the Democratic Party largely reflects this approach: At the top of today's (and yesterday's) list are minimum wage increases, paid sick leave and expanded family leave, and enhanced union organizing rights.

Focusing on gaps in formal rights risks overlooking another mechanism that can lead to substandard labor conditions: workers' exclusion from the benefits of labor protections already on the books. Indeed, one paradox of today's labor market is that working conditions at the bottom have deteriorated (Bernhardt et al. 2008) even as substantive legal rights have expanded or, at worst, stagnated over the past several decades.[2] Some explanation lies in labor practices that exploit these limitations of reach and grasp. An increased minimum wage may do little for a home health aide classified as an independent contractor or a "companion," not an employee, or for a janitor employed by a fly-by-night subcontractor who vanishes at the first sign of legal trouble.

This chapter surveys how workers fall beyond the reach or grasp of the employment law protections most relevant to low-wage workers. I provide a framework uniting what often have been distinct inquiries into, on the one hand, the challenges to employment law coverage posed by new ways of structuring labor and, on the other, problems of employment law enforcement (Barenberg 2003; Foo 1994; Stone 2004). Insofar as employers benefit when these protections do not "stick," one way or another, exploiting limitations in coverage and enforcement may be alternative strategies.[3] Attention to these limits encourages us to analyze employment law as a partial method of regulating work. The chapter also surveys emerging legal strategies that challenge this partiality. Some seek to extend the reach or strengthen the grasp of existing regulatory forms, but others experiment with legal vehicles that rely less heavily on employer–employee relationships as the foundation of worker protection. These innovations in regulating work reinforce the idea that employment law is but one institutional approach to worker protection, and they invite critical reflection on and imagination of an array of reform possibilities that share employment law's substantive goals but not always its traditional means.

Workers Beyond Employment Law's Reach: Limited Coverage

Employment regulation in the U.S. has three basic structural features. First, workers and their employers acquire obligations to one another through legally binding contracts. For the most part, these obligations simply are whatever both parties agree to. If they agree, these obligations can be quite extensive, but they also can be quite minimal if the parties do not agree to more. Second, an array of employment laws passed by legislatures selectively supersede these contractual agreements. A statute may require an employer to pay at least a minimum wage, notwithstanding an employee's agreement to a lower one. When there is no statute directly on point, however, the contract governs.[4] Third, and most important here, these laws apply to a specific type of contract for work, employment contracts between employers and employees.

This chapter addresses these statutes that regulate employment contracts and form the core of "labor and employment law." Rules governing relationships between employers and individual employees generally are known as "employment law," while "labor law" regulates employers' relationships to employees engaged in collective action, most significantly through labor unions that engage in collective bargaining.[5] Broad characterizations of labor and employment law also include employment-based "social insurance" programs like unemployment compensation and Social

practical grasp. Enforcement failures permit substandard conditions to persist and thereby constitute a second general mechanism depriving workers of employment law protections. Enforcement failures arise out of two classes of employer behavior: evasion and defiance. Insofar as employment laws require more of employers than they would otherwise provide, employers have obvious incentives for noncompliance. Economic models weigh the costs of compliance against the expected costs of noncompliance, the latter being a function of both the risks of detection and the costliness of any subsequent remedies (Weil 2005).[10] This framework suggests two employer approaches to noncompliance: evading detection through the manipulation or suppression of record-keeping, and defying legal mandates by simply integrating noncompliance into ordinary business operations and accepting expected remedies as a cost of doing business. The preceding discussion of coverage also can be integrated into this framework: Employer practices that reorganize a labor force to reduce employment law coverage essentially make it cheaper to comply with the fewer employment law obligations that remain.

Evasion and Documentation

Two common forms of evasion undermine systems of documentation that provide the foundation for employment law enforcement. First, employers *misclassify* workers by keeping a full panoply of official documentation that, if accurate, would demonstrate employment law compliance but that instead conceals underlying violations. Second, employers participate in the *informal economy* by failing to incorporate their employment relationships into legally mandated documentation systems, thereby shifting their workers "off the books."

Misclassification and informality both strike at the recordkeeping practices upon which employment law enforcement relies. Documentation maintained by employers and information reported to public entities, especially tax authorities, identify the firm's employees, their periods of employment, and some of the conduct (particularly compensation) regulated by law. The FLSA requires that employers keep records of employees' wages and hours, and less detailed information on employees' earnings must be reported to state and federal tax authorities in the course of complying with payroll tax obligations. Title VII requires certain employers to record and report the race and sex composition of their workforce, and the Occupational Safety and Health Act mandates records on workplace illness, injury, and exposure to hazards. Many employers, especially large ones, maintain personnel records much more extensive than required by law.

Misclassification. The most basic form of evasion is for an employer to deny an employment relationship with a worker and thereby assert that the worker's complaints lie beyond the scope of employment law. The possible forms of misclassification track the limits on employment coverage discussed above.

Again, the most prominent issue is independent contractor misclassification, in which the firm records and reports its payments to the worker for services rendered but nonetheless classifies the relationship as one between customer and contractor, not employer and employee. The firm issues an IRS Form 1099 reporting the income but does not pay or deduct payroll taxes and does not record working hours and hourly wages. Such a practice is not intrinsically suspicious, because legitimate independent contracting relationships are quite common. As a result, a superficial review of company records would not reveal any violations. Moreover, an employee without sophisticated understanding of employment law might well accept the employer's classification as authoritative, especially if it was explicit from the outset and the employee signed documents acknowledging independent contractor status. Available evidence suggests that misclassification of employees as independent contractors is quite common (Donahue, Lamare, and Kotler 2007).

Important forms of misclassification also occur at other boundaries of employment coverage. Recently, lawsuits alleging misclassification under the FLSA white-collar exemptions from overtime premiums have surged in number and prominence, often resulting in very large damages or settlements with major corporations (Levine and Lewin 2006). Employers may also misclassify workers as "trainees," who are not covered under many statutes, as occurred in one prominent recent case involving labor trafficking (*Chellen* v. *John Pickle Co.*, 344 F. Supp.2d 1278 [N.D. Okla. 2004]).

Even when a firm carries workers on the books as nonexempt employees, there remain opportunities for misclassification that relate to substantive compliance rather than the fact of coverage. For instance, compensable time may be recorded incorrectly when employees must perform work "off the clock" that is not reflected in company records, and nominal wages may be inflated when they are offset with illegal "deductions" for transportation, tools, or uniforms provided by the employer (McHugh 2001). These are, in essence, forms of misclassification of time and expenses.

Informality. Firms also may evade detection by failing to keep official records, at least with respect to a particular kind of information. Thus, instead of misclassifying an employee as a contractor and filing a 1099, the employer might simply pay the worker in cash and not report the transaction to government authorities, though it might still keep its own separate set of books.[11] Or, instead of recording an employee as working a 40-hour week and then requiring an additional 8 hours of unrecorded work, an employer might not maintain payroll records at all. Such unrecorded or unreported transactions are characteristic features of the informal economy, though scholars vigorously dispute how best to define and characterize it (Portes and Haller 2005).

Like misclassification, informality stymies detection of labor violations and determination of subsequent eligibility for social insurance protections. For instance, an unemployment insurance applicant may be denied benefits because the administering agency has no record of prior employment. In addition, informality erects evidentiary hurdles in the event that an enforcement agency or individual employee does seek legal redress. No documentation may be available establishing that the employee worked for the employer at all, let alone the precise period of time, or detailing the weekly hours and wages that were paid. The major legal response to this problem is that, at least in the FLSA context, once employers are shown to have violated recordkeeping requirements, a series of presumptions allow employees to establish their working time and wages with very little evidence and place a heavy burden on employers to rebut this evidence.

Defiance

Even when an employer violates labor standards in plain view, the existing system of enforcement may do little to stop it. First, noncompliance in plain view leads to enforcement actions only when someone bothers to look, and then to follow up. Second, enforcement action may lead to a remedial action insufficient to deter the underlying violation, especially when most violations go unremedied. Third, remedies themselves may go unenforced, primarily because they necessarily come after the fact and so may be ineffectual if the employer has dissolved or become insolvent. In all these regards, employer and regulatory conduct must be viewed as of a piece: The feasibility of defiance depends in large part on the intensity of regulatory activity.

Detection and adjudication. Enforcement agencies use two basic methods to detect possible labor violations: proactive monitoring and reactive investigation of complaints. Once a possible violation has been detected, further action is required to obtain a binding legal judgment and accompanying remedy. All of these tasks require substantial time and resources, especially for personnel. These resources generally must come from public budgets. As with police and prosecutors, civil regulatory agencies usually cannot recoup their costs from employers who violate the law, even in situations where private litigants would be able to seek payment of their attorneys' fees. Even as the workforce has grown, as have the number of workplace laws requiring enforcement, enforcement agencies' staffing and budgets have stagnated or shrunk over the past several decades, with shorter-term shifts depending on party control of legislative and executive branches (Bernhardt and McGrath 2005; Occhialino and Vail 2005). These agencies can inspect only a tiny fraction of covered establishments, and when they do, they find violations at high rates, especially with regard to wages and workplace safety (Santos 2005; Weil 2005).

Enforcement by private litigants faces its own distinctive challenges. Litigation usually is too expensive for low-wage workers to finance representation by an attorney. The prospect of recovering $5,000 in lost earnings may be too little to make the expense and hassle of a lawsuit worthwhile, even though it could be half a low-wage worker's annual income.[12] Aggregating small claims into a single lawsuit can change this calculus, and this is the classic function of class action litigation. Recently, however, class actions have faced new restrictions throughout the legal system, and some developments threaten to nearly eliminate them in employment discrimination law specifically. These procedural questions have been central to the massive *Dukes* v. *Wal-Mart, Inc.* pay and promotion sex discrimination lawsuit on behalf of Wal-Mart's low-wage women workers (509 F.3d 1168 [9th Cir. 2007]), and they may yet be resolved by the Supreme Court as the suit proceeds. Additionally, for historically idiosyncratic reasons, the FLSA does not permit class actions at all, instead allowing only a procedurally cumbersome "collective action" that requires each worker to opt into the lawsuit. This restriction does not apply to state wage-and-hour laws, and there has been a sharp growth recently in class actions brought under these state laws, often in combination with more limited FLSA claims (Finkel 2003).

Remedies. Low enforcement rates provide important context for an analysis of remedies. A remedy that fully compensates an individual employee for harm suffered may be grossly inadequate to deter the employer if only a fraction of violations yield such a remedy (Weil 2005). For the most part, the monetary remedies for employment law violations are limited to one or two times the employee's lost wages.[13]

Weak remedies have been identified as an important culprit in underprotection of the NLRA right to organize (Weiler 1990). This is somewhat counterintuitive, because a relatively high proportion of all violations should receive regulatory attention, given that unions have the information and motivation to identify violations and pursue claims beyond that of an individual aggrieved employee.[14] Unlike a wage-and-hour case, however, an employer's gain from firing union activists may far exceed the compensation lost by individual workers fired for organizing. Instead, the employer may successfully disrupt an organizing campaign that might otherwise result in much more costly CBAs or strikes, and that moment will long have passed by the time the individual worker receives a remedy.

Collection. Just as a substantive legal mandate does not automatically lead to compliance, a court judgment awarding damages does not automatically lead the employer to pay. Large, ongoing firms generally do pay, however, because they have substantial, identifiable assets that can be frozen or liquidated to satisfy a judgment. The story may be quite different for smaller, unstable firms, especially ones operating in the informal economy. These firms may have no identifiable assets at all, may enter bankruptcy when facing a judgment, and may simply disappear, possibly to reopen under a new name. This pattern has been especially well documented in the garment industry (Foo 1994).

An Example: Unauthorized Noncitizen Workers

Each topic discussed above bears much richer development, and many of them receive it in other chapters of this volume. By bringing together these different mechanisms through which workers may lack employment protections, an overview facilitates analysis of how these mechanisms interact. Without attempting to be comprehensive, this section suggests some such interactions by analyzing an important illustrative case: employment law protections for noncitizen workers who lack legal authorization to remain in the U.S. and to hold employment here, or "unauthorized noncitizen workers."[15] Unauthorized noncitizen workers disproportionately are low-wage workers and make up a substantial and growing fraction of the low-wage workforce (Capps, Fortuny, and Fix 2007).

Immigration Status and Employment Law Coverage

Under current law, a worker's immigration status is irrelevant to whether that worker is an "employee" covered by employment laws. The Supreme Court directly addressed this issue under the NLRA in the 1980s, and lower courts consistently have extended this precedent to other statutes, including the FLSA (Fisk and Wishnie 2005).

Notwithstanding their coverage, unauthorized noncitizen workers still receive limited employment law protections. Most importantly, the Supreme Court's 2002 decision in *Hoffman Plastic Compounds* (535 U.S. 137) held that an unauthorized worker could not receive the standard NLRA remedy of back pay for lost wages after his employer violated the NLRA by firing him for union organizing. *Hoffman's* exact scope remains uncertain, but unauthorized workers generally still do receive compensation for underpayment of work actually performed, as well as remedies other than lost wages.

Hoffman's reasoning is analogous to the arguments against employment law coverage for prison labor and other "nonmarket" work. The court downplayed the economic relationship between employee and employer and gave precedence to matters of immigration policy, emphasizing the worker's possibly criminal conduct (Fisk and Wishnie 2005). Consistent with the highly racialized history of treating unauthorized workers, especially those from Mexico, as both a second-class labor force and a criminal menace (Ngai 2004), the social status of the workers appears to be driving the scope of employment protections, rather than employment protections responding to workplace vulnerability or recognizing the status claims enabled by work.[16]

Immigration Status and Access to Enforcement

One common argument for granting unauthorized noncitizens full employment rights is that denying them these rights will make them a more attractive workforce for employers and thereby harm authorized workers. This basic point can be generalized to account for other limitations in coverage and enforcement addressed by this chapter. Thus, even if unauthorized status does not itself reduce employment rights, employers might still prefer unauthorized workers if they more easily fall beyond the reach or grasp of employment law for other reasons.

An unauthorized workforce might lead to underenforcement if unauthorized workers are less inclined to participate in enforcement proceedings that involve both confrontation with their employer (or former employer) and exposure to government authorities. That seems plausible because unauthorized workers' immigration status provides employers a ready justification for firing or refusing to hire them and exposes the worker to possible deportation (Bosniak 2006; Shaviro 1997; but cf. Milkman 2006). This hypothesis is borne out by employers' opportunistic invocation of work authorization to fire workers involved in organizing campaigns, retaliatory threats to report to immigration authorities workers who assert employment rights,[17] and, less directly, many employers' perception that recently arrived workers are less likely to resist employer demands, display "attitude," and complain about illegal or unfair treatment (Mehta, Theodore, and Hincapié 2003; Waldinger and Lichter 2003).

Immigration status acquires direct legal significance in the enforcement process when investigation or litigation prompts inquiries into work authorization. Because work authorization affects remedies after *Hoffman Plastic*, employers and enforcement agencies ordinarily would want to ascertain authorization status to determine how much back pay is at issue. Revealing unauthorized status, however, imperils an employment law plaintiff's ability to stay employed and remain in the U.S. Because this danger might deter unauthorized workers from participating in enforcement activities, a number of courts have limited inquiries into immigration status until late stages of litigation; if early success yields a settlement, those inquiries need not ever occur (Cunningham-Parmeter 2008).

Interaction Between Coverage and Enforcement

Employment law coverage and enforcement interact strongly because unauthorized noncitizen workers cannot be employed legally. Employers must document their employees' work authorization and may not employ those who lack it. Therefore, hiring unauthorized noncitizen workers requires either avoiding (or concealing) an employment relationship or evading enforcement through false documentation (that is, misclassifying workers as authorized) or nondocumentation (that is, informality).

This observation sheds light on the ubiquitous subcontracting of labor-intensive services within industries with many unauthorized noncitizen workers. Particularly prominent has been outsourcing of building maintenance services by office buildings and by major retailers like Wal-Mart (Clelland 2000; Greenhouse 2003; Milkman 2006). By severing an employment relationship, subcontracting allows the user firm to utilize a worker's labor without running afoul of employment-based immigration restrictions and labor standards and also without engaging in misclassification or informality. For instance, a small janitorial subcontractor might operate on a cash basis without payroll or work authorization documentation when a large retail chain could not feasibly have an in-house janitorial division operating in the same fashion. In addition, such a subcontractor might maintain assets insufficient to satisfy many judgments against it.

In such circumstances, subcontracting does more than just shift the employment relationship between firms. That would not benefit the user firm if its savings in expected compliance or liability costs would simply reappear as a component of the subcontractor's fee. If, however, employment law enforcement against the subcontractor is more difficult than against the user, then the subcontractor can violate the law more cheaply than the user, and it can offer this savings as a benefit of subcontracting. The same features of small subcontractors that minimize exposure to employment law also limit other aspects of their operations, including maintaining a public reputation, acquiring physical capital, taking on substantial debt, and so on. Not surprisingly, then, small unstable firms of this sort often rely on symbiotic subcontracting relationships with larger, more enduring enterprises.

Directly employing unauthorized workers but misclassifying them as authorized also might seem attractive to large, well-established employers. It is compatible with maintaining extensive recordkeeping and widespread misclassification with respect to independent contractor status and white-collar exemptions appears to have occurred at major corporations like FedEx, Microsoft, and Starbucks (Orey 2007; *Vizcaino* v. *Microsoft Corp.*, 120 F.3d 1006 [9th Cir. 1997]). For firms like these, subcontracting may conflict with organizational imperatives toward high levels of centralized monitoring and control. Misclassification, however, becomes riskier when enforcement authorities can readily detect it with available information. Unlike independent contractor status or a white-collar exemption, work authorization generally fits these conditions because it can be determined based on government records of immigration or citizenship status, without inquiring into how a specific employer organizes its workforce. Immigration enforcement increasingly exploits this point through cross-matching of relevant databases, especially Social Security numbers, despite the serious problems with using a Social Security "no-match" as a proxy for unauthorized status (Mehta, Theodore, and Hincapié 2003). More effective detection of misclassification thus may lead to more subcontracting and informality or to substitution of non-employee workers (such as the Colorado inmates mentioned above), rather than simply to substitution of authorized employees.

New Approaches to Expanding Labor Protections

A number of legal developments, often at the state or local level, respond to the problems of limited coverage and weak enforcement. This section provides a framework for analyzing different approaches. Two strengthen existing employment laws by expanding coverage or intensifying enforcement. Two others, however, implicitly challenge the basic model of government intervention into the relationship between employer and employee. One extends responsibility for an employer's labor standards to the employer's customers. Another places more responsibility directly on the state to address workers' problems that might traditionally have been analyzed as maltreatment by employers.

Expanding Employment Law Coverage

The most obvious way to protect workers who fall beyond the reach of employment law is simply to extend that reach and make them employees. For instance, efforts are under way in Congress to amend the FLSA definition of employment in order to reverse the Supreme Court's recent *Coke* decision excluding many home health care workers. Individual states also often have used state employment law to fill gaps in federal coverage, such as California's enactment in the 1970s of labor law protections for agricultural workers excluded from the NLRA. More recently, California enacted *"Hoffman* fix" legislation to provide full employment protections to unauthorized noncitizen workers, notwithstanding the Supreme Court's *Hoffman Plastic* decision (Cal. Lab. Code §1171.5). Changing the basic definitions of employment, especially the independent contractor/employee distinction, has been the goal of many scholars, government commissions, and activists. The most common reform suggestion is to replace the restrictive common-law test, and its emphasis on control over the production process, with the FLSA's more expansive "economic realities" analysis, which focuses on a worker's economic dependence on the employer (Stone 2006; U.S. Commission on the Future of Worker–Management Relations 1994). There is little indication, however, that such a change is likely in the U.S., though other countries have experimented with intermediate categories such as "dependent contractor."

Another way to expand coverage is to intervene in firm structure and limit the processes of disintegration described above; doing so results in more covered employees using existing definitions of employment. Most notably in home health care and child care, public intermediaries have been established that convert independent contracting into employment relationships (Brooks 2005; Delp and Quan 2002). This government-funded care work occurs in the private home of the person being cared for (especially in the home health aide context) or of the person providing care (especially in the context of family day care providers). These care workers often have been classified either as independent contractors or as employees of the end consumer, not as public employees, despite substantial state influence over compensation levels and other conditions.[18] Recently, several states have created public employers-of-record that receive state funds, pay compensation to care workers, and become entities with which employees can bargain collectively through public sector unions. This model of vertical reintegration rose to prominence with the stunningly successful organization by the Service Employees International Union (SEIU) of more than 70,000 home health care workers in Los Angeles County in 1999 (Delp and Quan 2002).

This intermediary model begins with the goal of establishing an employment relationship and then works backward to create an organizational form with the desired effect. The government's role is essential but also ambiguous. It acts not only as the employer but also as the paying consumer, and the consumer role provides its leverage over organizational form. Notably, the government does not rely on its regulatory power, as evidenced by the fact that privately funded home health care and child care are not required to use these or other employer intermediaries.

Another structural intervention does take a regulatory approach. California's janitorial contractor worker retention law provides that, when a property owner substitutes one janitorial contractor for another, the successor contractor generally must retain its predecessor's employees for 60 days (Cal. Lab. Code §1061). On the surface, this policy provides job security at a moment when layoffs are particularly likely, but, more significantly, it blunts the combined impact of subcontracting (vertical disintegration) and successorship (temporal disintegration) on unionization and collective bargaining (Becker 1996). A building still can shed a CBA negotiated between its contractor and its janitors by switching to a new contractor, but for both practical and legal reasons, workforce continuity makes it much easier for the incumbent union to establish a collective bargaining relationship with the new contractor, rather than having to start from scratch organizing a new workforce.

Strengthening Enforcement

Current efforts to improve enforcement largely focus outside the legislative arena,[19] on intensifying enforcement activity and using more effective tactics (Campaign to End Wage Theft 2006; Weil 2007). For instance, both private attorneys and nonprofit workers' rights organizations have been bringing large-scale lawsuits for wage and hour violations in low-wage industries like garment production, building services, and delivery. Often these cases have been coordinated with active organizing by traditional labor unions or by independent workers' centers (Milkman 2006; Sachs 2008). These cases also have helped develop precedents rejecting misclassification and applying principles of joint employment. A particularly innovative recent enforcement effort is the Maintenance Cooperation Trust Fund (MCTF), the product of a collective bargaining agreement between SEIU and janitorial contractors in California (Estlund 2005). MCTF monitors wage violations by nonunion competitors and both assists workers in litigation and brings the results of its investigations to the attention of public enforcement agencies.

Within public enforcement agencies, targeted campaigns have sought to achieve enforcement levels sufficient to shift labor standards throughout an entire industry. Such campaigns systematically investigate employers in industries with high noncompliance rates, rather than simply responding to worker complaints. In the 1990s, USDOL targeted the garment industry in New York City and elsewhere, and more recently the New York state attorney general's office conducted a well-known greengrocer campaign (Estlund 2005; Weil 2005). Both campaigns used the leverage gained from legal remedies for past violations to garner employer agreement to mechanisms making enforcement easier in the future. Other interesting developments in public enforcement include the use of criminal prosecutions for nonpayment of wages (Verga 2005) and, in cases such as *Chellen* v. *John Pickle Co.* (446 F. Supp.2d 1247 [N.D. Okla. 2006]), the EEOC's pursuit of discrimination claims in tandem with claims for wage and hour violations within low-wage industries highly stratified by race and nationality.

Consumer Power and Consumer Responsibility

Shifting away from direct state enforcement of employer responsibilities, several recent efforts give consumers an important role in setting labor standards. One strategy draws on the high-profile antisweatshop campaigns aimed at U.S. consumers of products manufactured abroad. Such campaigns organize consumer pressure to reward compliance and punish noncompliance with employment law. The reward strategy attracts customers to employers identified as compliant, as the Greengrocer Code of Conduct sought to do by providing labels to participating stores. The punishment strategy targets consumer boycotts or picketing at employers accused of employment law violations, a tactic widely used by workers' centers (Bodie 2003; Gordon 2005).

One way to analyze consumer involvement is as informal sanctions supplementing official enforcement mechanisms. What this analysis leaves out, however, is the burden consumers bear in increased prices, decreased convenience, or other factors. Another way to see these consumer-driven strategies, then, is as spreading responsibility for maintaining labor standards beyond the employer, who shares its costs with consumers. As I noted earlier, the creation of public employer intermediaries has some of this character, too, as the state uses its leverage as a consumer to restructure employment relationships and, crucially, to take on the financial costs of higher labor standards.[20]

Several new approaches to combatting abuse of subcontracted workers go beyond these essentially self-imposed forms of consumer responsibility. They make subcontractors' customers liable for the subcontractors' employment law violations, rather than using joint employment theories to extend the employment relation up the supply chain. For instance, California's AB633 makes garment manufacturers "guarantors" of their subcontractors' wage-and-hour practices. If unpaid wages cannot be collected from the employing subcontractor, they can be collected from the guarantor, without needing to establish an employment relationship (Elmore 2001). California also has a "financially insufficient contracting" law that, in specified industries, holds user firms responsible for subcontractors' violations, but only when the risk of such violations was reasonably apparent from the financial and other terms of the subcontract (Narro 2006). The message of consumer responsibility is quite clear: A user must forgo the lower price it could obtain by doing business with a contractor willing to violate the law. Indeed, such statutes have been called "brother's keeper laws." Shifting responsibility to users of subcontractors can provide a more stable, solvent target from which to seek a remedy when a violation occurs. As David Weil's research shows, extending liability to users also can enlist their capacity for supply-chain monitoring in the service of employment law enforcement (2005).

Furthermore, Illinois recently began applying a customer responsibility model in the area of staffing agencies. The Illinois Day and Temporary Labor Services Act (820 Ill. Comp. Stats. §175) took effect in 2006 and provides extensive protections for nonclerical workers employed by staffing agencies and supplied to user firms known under the statute as "third party clients." Although these user firms might sometimes be joint employers under general employment law principles, the act bypasses such questions and simply declares that the user "shall share all legal responsibility and liability" for wage and hour violations, without otherwise treating the user as an employer (§175/85).

These consumer-focused approaches build upon an employment-based model but take an important additional step. A user firm is never liable to a worker unless that worker has an employment relationship with another employer (the subcontractor or staffing agency) and that employer violates an employment law. But once such a violation is established, the user firm may bear legal responsibility for the working conditions in question despite not having its own employment relationship to the worker. As a practical matter, these laws treat users as themselves part of the problem when they allow subcontractors to compete for the user's business by employing illegal labor practices. Doing so places the employer–employee relationship in a broader context in which substandard working conditions are not simply the product of an employer's power over its employee.

State Provision of Worker Benefits

In principle, the government rather than consumers could act as a "guarantor" of labor standards and provide recompense when employees cannot recover directly from their employers. One element of California's AB633 antisweatshop statute provides an isolated example of this approach (Elmore 2001). It uses a portion of garment industry registration fees to create a fund designed to cover unpaid wages that cannot be collected from either employers or guarantors. Although uncommon in employment law, this government payor-of-last-resort role is routine in the social insurance context. Even if an employer fails to pay the required payroll tax, an eligible employee can still receive benefits based on the untaxed employment; the costs are made up through general tax revenues. The difference appears to turn on whether the employer's role is understood as funding a government benefit (the social insurance case) rather than fulfilling its own obligation to a worker (the minimum wage case), even though this distinction may be more formal than real (Shaviro 1997).

When the government or a consumer guarantees the availability of a remedy, it shifts the costs of employer *non*compliance away from workers themselves. An additional step away from employer responsibility shifts the costs of *compliance* from the employer to the state. Many expansions in worker protections are taking just this form. The federal Earned Income Tax Credit (EITC) now supplements a minimum wage worker's annual income by up to about $4,500, depending on family composition. This additional income is equivalent to roughly a $2.30 hourly raise for a full-time, full-year hourly worker, but it is a raise delivered and funded by the government rather than an employer. California's new paid family and medical leave program also relies on public funding and benefit delivery.

This chapter's concerns with coverage and enforcement add a new dimension to the important debate over whether the costs of various worker protections, especially any new ones, ought to be placed initially on employers (as with the minimum wage) or the state (as with the EITC). That debate usually assumes that employer-based protections reach all workers. Instead, many workers already fall outside existing protections due to limited coverage or enforcement, and these workers are unlikely to receive the benefits of any expanded employer-based protections. Moreover, some employers might respond to new responsibilities not by cutting jobs or raising prices, as employment law's critics usually argue, but by taking action to narrow their workers' coverage or to evade or defy enforcement. Government-funded protections might mitigate these problems.

Placing compliance costs on the state also opens up the possibility of spreading coverage beyond employment. Indeed, the EITC and many social insurance programs specifically cover independent contractors and other self-employed people in addition to employees (Linder 1999; Zatz 2006). Further extensions to include unpaid household work have been proposed (Staudt 1996). Such expansions are administratively feasible because the programs do not rely on employers as a funding or delivery mechanism.[21]

These same administrative features also can facilitate shrinking coverage to a subset of employees. Although details vary greatly by program, benefits paid to workers by the state often carry greater restrictions on eligibility for noncitizens. While unauthorized noncitizen workers are entitled to minimum wages from employers, they cannot supplement that income with the EITC, and there have been serious proposals to deny the EITC to many authorized immigrant workers, something currently inconceivable for the minimum wage.

The Future of Worker Protections

This chapter has surveyed how workers come to fall beyond the reach or grasp of employment law protections and the varied ways those protections might be extended. The breadth of available responses should provide cause for some optimism by suggesting new avenues of attack on stubborn problems, such as the difficulties of achieving employment law enforcement against small, informal subcontractors. This flexibility, however, also generates a challenge: How are we to choose among strategies that, were they successful, might yield similar results? This question becomes pressing whenever we consider adopting a new policy, but of course it also applies to existing institutions that might benefit from change.

At a minimum, the preceding discussion makes clear that those of us concerned about how workers fare in a gloves-off economy cannot afford simply to focus on the unjust outcomes and seek to legislate or litigate or organize against them. In a world of shifting organizational forms and imperfect enforcement, issues of institutional design must be front and center. The questions include these:

- Which workers receive the benefit or protection, and how are they identified?
- Who delivers the worker protection or benefit, and who pays for it?
- Who pays to remedy noncompliance, and how does it compare to the cost of compliance?
- Who monitors for noncompliance, and how easy is it to detect?
- Who can seek a remedy, and how?

Although these issues often seem purely pragmatic in nature, sometimes they implicate the most basic questions about why we have employment laws in the first place. This is particularly true for questions about coverage: Who receives and who provides protections? The controversies surrounding the proper balance between employer and state provision of worker protections illustrate this point.

With regard to the entity responsible for providing worker protections, consider current campaigns for Fair Share Health Care statutes. This policy would mandate that employers either provide a minimum level of health care benefits to their employees or provide an equivalent level of funding to state health care programs that cover low-income workers. One of proponents' rallying cries is that these public programs are "subsidizing" employers' failure to provide health care (Contreras and Lobel 2006). Analogous criticisms have been leveled at the EITC (Bluestone and Ghilarducci 1996).

Such critiques beg the question of who is subsidizing whom. Implicitly, they assume a minimum package of economic resources that workers ought to receive from their employers. When the state supplies that package itself rather than requiring employers to do so, the state subsidizes employers. But what if providing that package (at least to workers) was the primary responsibility of some other entity, such as consumers or fellow citizens? If so, then minimum wage laws would be requiring *employers* to "subsidize" the rest of us who are permitted to evade our responsibility for workers' well-being. Obviously, the analysis might vary by type of protection and by degree. I find, for instance, that my students are taken aback when I suggest that a public education system improperly "subsidizes" employers who fail to pay for their workers' children's schooling, even though the same students often have expansive conceptions of employers' obligations to provide living wages, health care, and paid leave.

Similar questions arise with regard to which workers are covered. When worker protections rest on employers, the problem of unprotected workers reduces to how we distinguish employees from independent contractors or from volunteers, the reach of joint employment doctrine, and so on. Once we consider other vehicles for protecting workers, however, these questions may be reframed: Perhaps the problem is overreliance on employment relationships to target and deliver the protections at issue?

The minimum wage/EITC debate again is instructive. Critics of the minimum wage often claim that the EITC has higher "target efficiency" because it targets workers living in low-income households while the minimum wage applies to low-wage workers regardless of other household resources (Shaviro 1997). One defense simply accepts the targeting as good enough when balanced against other considerations (including who bears the costs). A more fundamental response, though, is that the target efficiency critique begs the question of who should be targeted. If the minimum wage is not simply an antipoverty device but also, for instance, a means of protecting from exploitation workers who occupy a weak bargaining position in the labor market, then a targeting analysis would look quite different. Even so, one might still go on to ask whether employees are the only workers subject to exploitation, whether employers are the only ones who carry it out, and whether markets for paid labor are the only institutions that create the requisite vulnerability (Folbre 1982; Zatz 2008).

Answering such questions requires engaging the most basic issues of what labor and employment law is for. It is not enough to say that all workers deserve certain protections or to focus only on what those protections should be. We need to understand exactly what makes someone a "worker" and why that matters, exactly how and by whom that protection should be provided, and what should happen next when the protection fails. Paying attention to the full range of ways in which protections already are provided, and avoided, makes clear the need to confront these problems and can both stimulate and discipline our attempts to solve them. In particular, we must face the limitations of employment law and consider responses that lie both inside and outside that familiar framework.

Acknowledgment

I am grateful to Annette Bernhardt, Andrew Elmore, and Catherine Ruckelshaus for their very helpful comments on prior drafts of this chapter.

Endnotes

[1] For reasons I go on to explain, I will use "employment law" as shorthand for "labor and employment law."

[2] Relatively new federal statutes include the Worker Adjustment and Retraining Notification (WARN) Act of 1988 addressing mass layoffs and plant closings, the Americans with Disabilities Act of 1990, and the Family and Medical Leave Act of 1993. The Civil Rights Act of 1991 also substantially strengthened existing protections against employment discrimination, as have court decisions developing protections against sexual and racial harassment.

[3] A third strategy, not addressed here, is placing work beyond the reach of the U.S. law by locating production in another country.

[4] For this reason, substantive labor standards can fall without either a change in law or a violation of existing law. Cutting a worker's wage from $25 to $10 per hour does not run afoul of a legal minimum wage well below $10 per hour.

[5] Workers' collective action outside of unions also is protected both by the National Labor Relations Act and, in narrower ways, by other statutes (Estlund 2005; Sachs 2008).

[6] The two major exceptions are in labor law and federal regulation of employer-provided pension and health care benefits, both of which generally preempt any state regulation in the area. State law also typically creates a floor beneath local law but no ceiling above it.

[7] Guy Davidov has developed the most sophisticated purposive theory in this area, one that builds on the conceptions of control present in the case law (2002).

[8] Courts and commentators sometimes attempt to square the idea of joint employment with the paradigm of a single integrated employer by identifying joint employment with situations in which subcontracting is a sham, or at least an attempt to evade employment law responsibilities (*Zheng* v. *Liberty Apparel*, 355 F.3d 61 [2d Cir. 2003]).

[9] The Family and Medical Leave Act is a notable exception. Not only is coverage dependent on job tenure but the right conferred—reinstatement—is worthless if the firm no longer exists at the end of the leave period.

[10] Although clearly useful, such models do not account for consequences of noncompliance outside the formal legal system—including public, consumer, and labor perceptions of the firm—and for other ways in which legal mandates may affect organizational behavior, including through workers' and employers' beliefs about legitimate or desirable conduct (Albiston 2007). Employers may shape what behavior workers and regulators perceive as compliant, arguably providing a third way to blunt enforcement, one that I do not address here but that is the subject of a burgeoning literature on organizational response to civil rights law (Edelman, Uggen, and Erlanger 1999; Marshall 2005).

[11] Employers may later claim that the worker was an independent contractor, making such cases a variant on misclassification.

[12] Mitigating this problem are provisions, common in employment statutes that permit private lawsuits, requiring employers to pay successful plaintiffs' attorneys' fees.

[13] An important but narrow exception is the FLSA "hot goods" provisions, which essentially permits the USDOL to impound goods produced under substandard conditions. David Weil's research shows how aggressive use of this remedy can produce significantly higher compliance levels (2005).

[14] Researchers typically take the number of reinstatements ordered by the NLRB as a reasonable proxy for the actual number of workers illegally terminated by an employer for union activity (Schmitt and Zipperer 2007). Worker organizations also play an important role in catalyzing enforcement of other employment rights (Sachs 2008).

[15] Using "noncitizen" rather than "immigrant" conveys that those who migrate into the U.S. to work do not necessarily seek to remain permanently (Lopez 1981). "Unauthorized" rather than "undocumented" focuses attention on legal status; unauthorized workers often possess identity documents that do not establish work authorization. "Unauthorized" also avoids linking overly expansive connotations of "illegal" to individuals who, for instance, may legally work outside of an employment relationship.

[16] In this regard, stripping meaningful employment rights from today's unauthorized noncitizen workers resembles the large-scale exclusion of African Americans from New Deal labor protections through statutory excision of agricultural and domestic workers from the category of "employee".

[17] More generally, retaliation against workers for asserting employment rights is another important form of evasion. Employment laws almost always include separate protections against retaliation, but these too are only as effective as their enforcement.

[18] These factors led to an employment classification in one influential case under the FLSA's broad definition of employment (*Bonnette* v. *California Health and Welfare Agency*, 704 F.2d 1465 [9th Cir. 1983]).

[19] Organized labor's federal legislative priority, the Employee Free Choice Act, is a partial exception. One section of the bill would prioritize investigations into and enhance remedies for unfair labor practices during organizing drives and between union recognition and a first contract.

[20] A similar dynamic underlies "living wage" laws that selectively raise the wage floor for government contractors and some other recipients of public support (Sonn 2006). These laws are more politically successful than analogous increases in the broader "minimum wage" applicable to all employers. One reason seems to be that the government is acting principally as a consumer. It binds itself, but no one else, to do business only with firms that meet certain labor standards and to accept any increased costs, just like a shopper who only patronizes stores certified as employment-law compliant. Notably, living wage laws typically do not attempt to stop contractors from passing any increased costs back to the government customer.

[21] Other protections that are more difficult to monetize—like job security—may be hard to deliver in this fashion (Lester 2005).

References

Albiston, Catherine. 2007. "Institutional Perspectives on Law, Work, and Family." *Annual Review of Law and Social Science*, Vol. 3, no. 1, pp. 397–426.

Barenberg, Mark. 1994. "Democracy and Domination in the Law of Workplace Cooperation." *Columbia Law Review*, Vol. 94, no. 3, pp. 753–983.

———. 2003. "Workers: The Past and Future of Labor Law Scholarship." In P. Cane and M. Tushnet, eds., *The Oxford Handbook of Legal Studies*. New York: Oxford University Press, pp. 563–92.

Becker, Craig. 1996. "Labor Law Outside the Employment Relation." *Texas Law Review*, Vol. 74, no. 7, pp. 1527–62.

Bernhardt, Annette, and Siobhán McGrath. 2005. "Trends in Wage and Hour Enforcement by the U.S. Department of Labor, 1975–2004." New York: Brennan Center for Justice. September.

Bernhardt, Annette, Heather Boushey, Laura Dresser, and Chris Tilly. 2008. "An Introduction to *The Gloves-Off Economy*." In Annette Bernhardt, Heather Boushey, Laura Dresser, and Chris Tilly, eds., *The Gloves-Off Economy*. Urbana-Champaign, IL: Labor and Employment Relations Association, pp. 1–29.

Billings, Deborah. 2004. "DOL Scales Back Overtime Regulations Changes, Says 6.7 Million Low-Wage Workers Will Benefit." *Labor Relations Reporter*, Vol. 174, no. 13 (April 26) p. D24.

Bluestone, Barry, and Teresa Ghilarducci. 1996. *Making Work Pay: Wage Insurance for the Working Poor*. Annandale-on-Hudson, NY: Jerome Levy Economics Institute of Bard College.

Bodie, Matthew T. 2003. "The Potential for State Labor Law: The New York Greengrocer Code of Conduct." *Hofstra Labor and Employment Law Journal*, Vol. 21 (Fall), pp. 183–207.

Bonnette v. *California Health and Welfare Agency*, 704 F.2d 1465 [9th Cir. 1983].

Boris, Eileen, and Jennifer Klein. 2006. "Organizing Home Care: Low-Waged Workers in the Welfare State." *Politics and Society*, Vol. 34, no. 1, pp. 81–108.

Bosniak, Linda. 2006. *The Citizen and the Alien: Dilemmas of Contemporary Membership*. Princeton. NJ: Princeton University Press.

Brooks, Fred P. 2005. "New Turf for Organizing: Family Child Care Providers." *Labor Studies Journal*, Vol. 29, no. 4, pp. 45–64.

Cal. Lab. Code §1061.

Cal. Lab. Code §1171.5.

Campaign to End Wage Theft. 2006. *Protecting New York's Workers: How the State Department of Labor Can Improve Wage-and-Hour Enforcement*. December.

Cantor, David, Jane Waldfogel, Jeffrey Kerwin, Mareena McKinley Wright, Kerry Levin, John Rauch, Tracey Hagerty, and Martha Stapleton Kudela. 2001. *Balancing the Needs of Families and Employers: Family and Medical Leave Surveys*. Washington, DC: Westat.

Capps, Randolph, Karina Fortuny, and Michael E. Fix. 2007. *Trends in the Low-Wage Immigrant Labor Force, 2000–2005*. Washington, DC: Urban Institute. March.

Chellen v. *John Pickle Co.*, 344 F. Supp.2d 1278 [N.D. Okla. 2004].

———. 446 F. Supp.2d 1247.

Clelland, Nancy. 2000. "Heartache on Aisle 3: Sweatshop for Janitors." *Los Angeles Times*, July 2, p. A1.

Contreras, Julia, and Orly Lobel. 2006. "Wal-Martization and the Fair Share Health Care Acts." *St. Thomas Law Review*, Vol. 19, no. 1, pp. 105–36.

Cunningham-Parmeter, Keith. 2008. "Fear of Discovery: Immigrant Workers and the Fifth Amendment." *Cornell International Law Journal*, Vol. 41, no. 1, pp. 27–81.

Davidov, Guy. 2002. "The Three Axes of Employment Relationships." *University of Toronto Law Journal*, Vol. 52, no. 4, pp. 357–418.

———. 2004. "Joint Employer Status in Triangular Employment Relationships." *British Journal of Industrial Relations*, Vol. 42, no. 4, pp. 727–46.

———. 2006. "The Reports of My Death Are Greatly Exaggerated: 'Employee' as a Viable (Though Over-Used) Legal Concept." In G. Davidov and B. Langille, eds., *Boundaries and Frontiers of Labour Law*. Portland, OR: Hart Publishing, pp. 133–52.

Davidov, Guy, and Brian Langille. 2006. "Introduction: Goals and Means in the Regulation of Work." In G. Davidov and B. Langille, eds., *Boundaries and Frontiers of Labour Law*. Portland, OR: Hart Publishing, pp. 1–10.

Delp, Linda, and Katie Quan. 2002. "Homecare Worker Organizing in California." *Labor Studies Journal*, Vol. 27, no. 1, pp. 1–23.

Donahue, Linda H., James Ryan Lamare, and Fred B. Kotler. 2007. *The Cost of Worker Misclassification in New York State*. Ithaca, NY: School of Industrial and Labor Relations, Cornell University.

Dukes v. *Wal-Mart, Inc.*, 509 F. 3d 1168 [9th Cir. 2007].

Edelman, Lauren B., Christopher Uggen, and Howard S. Erlanger, 1999. "The Endogeneity of Legal Regulation." *American Journal of Sociology*, Vol. 105, no. 2, pp. 406–54.

Elmore, Andrew. 2001. "State Joint Employer Liability Laws and Pro Se Back Wage Claims in the Garment Industry." *UCLA Law Review*, Vol. 49, no. 1, pp. 395–445.

Equal Employment Opportunity Commission. 1997. *Application of EEO Laws to Contingent Workers Placed by Temporary Employment Agencies and Other Staffing Firms*. Enforcement Guidance 915.002.

Estlund, Cynthia L. 2005. "Rebuilding the Law of the Workplace in an Era of Self-Regulation." *Columbia Law Review*, Vol. 105, no. 2, pp. 319–404.

Fabrizio, Elizabeth J., and Susan J. McGolrick. 2006. "In Landmark 3-2 Ruling, NLRB Issues Guidelines on Supervisory Status for Nurses and Other Workers." *Labor Relations Reporter*, Vol. 180, no. 12, p. D29.

Finkel, Noah A. 2003. "State Wage-and-Hour Law Class Actions." *Employee Rights and Employment Policy Journal*, Vol. 7, no. 1, pp. 159–82.

Fisk, Catherine L., and Michael J. Wishnie. 2005. "The Story of Hoffman Plastic Compounds, Inc. v. NLRB: Labor Rights without Remedies for Undocumented Immigrants." In L.J. Cooper and C.L. Fisk, eds., *Labor Law Stories*. New York: Foundation Press, pp. 399–438.

Folbre, Nancy. 1982. "Exploitation Comes Home: A Critique of the Marxian Theory of Family Labour." *Cambridge Journal of Economics*, Vol. 6, no. 4, pp. 317–29.

Foo, Lora Jo. 1994. "The Vulnerable and Exploitable Immigrant Workforce and the Need for Strengthening Worker Protective Legislation." *Yale Law Journal*, Vol. 103, no. 8, pp. 2179–212.

Frosch, Dan. 2007. "Inmates Will Replace Wary Migrants in Colorado Fields." *New York Times*, March 4, p. 25.

Fudge, Judy. 2006. "The Legal Boundaries of the Employer, Precarious Workers, and Labour Protection." In G. Davidov and B. Langille, eds., *Boundaries and Frontiers of Labour Law*. Portland, OR: Hart Publishing, pp. 295–315.

General Accounting Office. 1999. *Fair Labor Standards Act: White-Collar Exemptions in the Modern Workplace*. [Washington, DC: General Accounting Office.

Goldstein, Bruce, Marc Linder, Laurence E. Norton II, and Catherine K. Ruckelshaus. 1999. "Enforcing Fair Labor Standards in the Modern American Sweatshop." *UCLA Law Review*, Vol. 46, no. 4, pp. 983–1163.

Gonos, George. 1997. "The Contest Over 'Employer' Status in the Postwar United States: The Case of Temporary Help Firms." *Law and Society Review*, Vol. 31, no. 1, pp. 81–110.

Gordon, Jennifer L. 2005. *Suburban Sweatshops: The Fight for Immigrant Rights*. Cambridge, MA: Harvard University Press.

Greenhouse, Steven. 1998. "Many Participants in Workfare Take the Place of City Workers." *New York Times*, April 13, p. A1.

———. 2003. "Illegally in U.S., and Never a Day Off at Wal-Mart." *New York Times*, November 5, p. A1.

Higgins, John E. Jr., Peter A. Janus, Barry J. Kearney, W.V. "Bernie" Siebert, and Kenneth L. Wagner, eds. 2006. *The Developing Labor Law: The Board, the Courts, and the National Labor Relations Act*. 5th ed. Washington, DC: Bureau of National Affairs.

Hoffman Plastic Compounds, Inc. v. N.L.R.B., 535 U.S. 137 [2002].

Illinois Day and Temporary Labor Services Act, 820 Ill. Comp. Stats. §175.

Kalleberg, Arne L. 2000. "Nonstandard Employment Relations: Part-Time, Temporary and Contract Work." *Annual Review of Sociology*, Vol. 26, no. 1, pp. 341–65.

Lester, Gillian. 2005. "A Defense of Paid Family Leave." *Harvard Journal of Law & Gender*, Vol. 28, no. 1, pp. 1–83.

Levine, David I., and David Lewin. 2006. "The New 'Managerial Misclassification' Challenge to Old Wage and Hour Law or What Is Managerial Work?" In D. Lewin, ed., *Contemporary Issues in Employment Relations*. Ithaca, NY: Cornell University Press, pp. 189–222.

Linder, Marc. 1987. "Farm Workers and the Fair Labor Standards Act: Racial Discrimination in the New Deal." *Texas Law Review*, Vol. 65, no. 7, pp. 1335–93.
———. 1999. "Dependent and Independent Contractors in Recent U.S. Labor Law." *Comparative Labor Law and Policy Journal*, Vol. 21, no. 1, pp. 187–230.
Long Island Care at Home v. *Coke*, 127 S. Ct. 2339 [2007].
Lopez, Gerald P. 1981. "Undocumented Mexican Migration: In Search of a Just Immigration Law and Policy." *UCLA Law Review*, Vol. 28, no. 4, pp. 615–714.
Lung, Shirley. 2003. "Exploiting the Joint Employer Doctrine." *Loyola University Chicago Law Journal*, Vol. 34, no. 2, pp. 291–358.
Marshall, Anna-Maria. 2005. "Idle Rights." *Law and Society Review*, Vol. 39, no. 1, pp. 83–124.
McHugh, Rick. 2001. "Recognizing Wage and Hour Issues on Behalf of Low-Income Workers." *Clearinghouse Review* (September-October), pp. 289.
Mehta, Chirag, Nik Theodore, and Marielena Hincapié. 2003. "Social Security Administration's No-Match Letter Program: Implications for Immigration Enforcement and Workers' Rights." Chicago: Center for Urban Economic Development, University of Illinois at Chicago.
Milkman, Ruth. 2006. *L.A. Story: Immigrant Workers and the Future of the U.S. Labor Movement*. New York: Russell Sage Foundation.
Narro, Victor. 2006. "Impacting Next Wave Organizing: Creative Campaign Strategies of the Los Angeles Worker Centers." *New York Law School Law Review*, Vol. 50, no. 2, pp. 465–513.
Nationwide Mutual Insurance Co. v. *Darden*, 503 U.S. 318 [1992].
Ngai, Mae M. 2004. *Impossible Subjects: Illegal Aliens and the Making of Modern America*. Princeton, NJ: Princeton University Press.
Oakwood Care Center, 176 L.R.R.M. [BNA] 1033 [2004].
Occhialino, Anne Noel, and Daniel Vail. 2005. "Why the EEOC (Still) Matters." *Hofstra Labor and Employment Law Journal*, Vol. 22, no. 2, pp. 671–708.
Orey, Michael. 2007. "Wage Wars: Workers—from Truck Drivers to Stockbrokers— Are Winning Huge Overtime Lawsuits." *BusinessWeek*, October 1, pp. 50–60.
Portes, Alejandro, and William Haller. 2005. "The Informal Economy." In N.J. Smelser and R. Swedberg, eds., *The Handbook of Economic Sociology*. Princeton, NJ: Princeton University Press, pp. 403–25.
Sachs, Benjamin I. 2008. "Employment Law as Labor Law: Toward a New Model." *Cardozo Law Review*, Vol. 29, no. 6, pp. 2685–2748.
Santos, Fernanda. 2005. "Study Finds Lax Safety Standards at Construction Sites." *New York Times*, October 18, p. B3.
Schmitt, John, and Ben Zipperer. 2007. "Dropping the Ax: Illegal Firings During Union Election Campaigns." Washington, DC: Center for Economic and Policy Research. January.
Schultz v. *Capital International Security, Inc.*, 466 F.3d 298 [4th Cir. 2006].
Shaviro, Daniel. 1997. "The Minimum Wage, the Earned Income Credit and Optimal Subsidy Policy." *University of Chicago Law Review*, Vol. 64, no. 2, pp. 405–81.
Silbaugh, Katharine. 1996. "Turning Labor into Love: Housework and the Law." *Northwestern University Law Review*, Vol. 91, no. 1, pp. 1–86.
Smith, Peggie. 1999. "Regulating Paid Household Work." *American University Law Review*, Vol. 48, no. 4, pp. 851–924.
Sonn, Paul K. 2006. *Citywide Minimum Wage Laws: A New Policy Tool for Local Governments*. New York: Brennan Center for Justice. May.

Stanley, Amy Dru. 1998. *From Bondage to Contract: Wage Labor, Marriage, and the Market in the Age of Slave Emancipation*. New York: Cambridge University Press.

Staudt, Nancy C. 1996. "Taxing Housework." *Georgetown Law Journal*, Vol. 84, no. 5, pp. 1571–1647.

Stettner, Andrew, Rebecca Smith, and Rick McHugh. 2004. "Changing Workforce, Changing Economy: State Unemployment Insurance Reforms for the 21st Century." New York: National Employment Law Project.

Stone, Katherine V.W. 2004. *From Widgets to Digits: Employment Regulation for the Changing Workplace*. New York: Cambridge University Press.

———. 2006. "Rethinking Labour Law: Employment Protection for Boundaryless Workers." In G. Davidov and B. Langille, eds., *Boundaries and Frontiers of Labour Law*. Portland, OR: Hart Publishing, pp. 155–79.

Tomlins, Christopher. 1995. "Subordination, Authority, Law: Subjects in Labor History." *International Labor and Working-Class History*, Vol. 47 (Spring), pp. 56–90.

U.S. Commission on the Future of Worker–Management Relations. 1994. *Final Report*. Washington, DC: U.S. Departments of Labor and Commerce.

Valenzuela, Abel Jr. 2001. "Day Laborers as Entrepreneurs?" *Journal of Ethnic and Migration Studies*, Vol. 27, no. 2, pp. 335–52.

Verga, Rita J. 2005. "An Advocate's Toolkit: Using Criminal 'Theft of Service' Laws to Enforce Workers' Right to Be Paid." *New York City Law Review*, Vol. 8, no. 1, pp. 283–310.

Vizcaino v. Microsoft Corp., 120 F.3d 1006 [9th Cir. 1997].

Waldinger, Roger, and Michael I. Lichter. 2003. *How the Other Half Works: Immigration and the Social Organization of Labor*. Los Angeles: University of California Press.

Weil, David. 2005. "Public Enforcement/Private Monitoring: Evaluating a New Approach to Regulating the Minimum Wage." *Industrial and Labor Relations Review*, Vol. 58, no. 2, pp. 238–52.

———. 2007. "Crafting a Progressive Workplace Regulatory Policy: Why Enforcement Matters." *Comparative Labor Law and Policy Journal*, Vol. 28, no. 2, pp. 125–54.

Weiler, Paul C. 1990. *Governing the Workplace: The Future of Labor and Employment Law*. Cambridge, MA: Harvard University Press.

Weiss, Robert P. 2001. "'Repatriating' Low-Wage Work: The Political Economy of Prison Labor Reprivatization in the Postindustrial United States." *Criminology*, Vol. 39, no. 2, pp. 253–92.

Western, Bruce, and Katherine Beckett. 1999. "How Unregulated Is the U.S. Labor Market? The Penal System as a Labor Market Institution." *American Journal of Sociology*, Vol. 104, no. 4 (January), pp. 1030–60.

Zatz, Noah D. 2006. "What Welfare Requires from Work." *UCLA Law Review*, Vol. 54, no. 2, pp. 373–464.

———. 2008. "Working at the Boundaries of Markets." *Vanderbilt Law Review.*, Vol. 61, no. 3, pp. 857–958.

Zheng v. Liberty Apparel, 355 F.3d 61 [2d Cir. 2003].

CHAPTER 3

Putting Wages Back into Competition: Deunionization and Degradation in Place-Bound Industries

RUTH MILKMAN
University of California, Los Angeles

This chapter analyzes employment restructuring in three major place-bound industries: residential construction, short-haul trucking, and building services.[1] I draw on fieldwork and other data from southern California, a region that often typifies or anticipates national trends. In all three industries, unionization was extensive in both the region and the nation during the postwar period. As a result, high wages and extensive fringe benefits were well established, although most workers in these fields had little or no postsecondary education. By the early 1980s, however, all three industries had been utterly transformed by successful employer-driven efforts to weaken or eliminate unions: wages plummeted, benefits evaporated, and working conditions sharply deteriorated as union density collapsed.

In all three industries, subcontracting became a key arena for employers' restructuring strategies. In the case of construction, starting in the mid-1970s, newly created non-union subcontractors began to penetrate the residential sector of the industry, and soon they were regularly undercutting union subcontractors with lower bids. During the recovery that followed the steep recession of the early 1980s, when construction activity ground to a halt, this transition was firmly consolidated. The region's residential construction industry was reconstituted on an entirely non-union basis, with dramatic effects on wages, benefits, and working conditions.

Deunionization was equally rapid in the regional trucking industry. The Teamsters' once-formidable strength collapsed almost overnight as deregulation swept the industry in the early 1980s, and sweatshop-like pay and conditions soon became the norm. Here too subcontracting was a central feature of restructuring, although it took a different form in this case than in construction. In the deregulated environment of the 1980s, trucking employers abandoned the practice of hiring drivers as hourly workers and instead began to set up arrangements with owner-operators and other independent contractors who rapidly took over the work.

Unions also declined among building service workers in the early 1980s, as population growth and changing real estate ownership patterns in the region spurred restructuring. Here too subcontracting was the wedge by means of which the union was increasingly undercut. Just as developers had done in residential construction, now building owners increasingly turned to non-union cleaning contractors to service their buildings. Some had hired their own janitors before; others had used union subcontractors. Now more and more turned to the non-union firms, which rapidly undercut their unionized competitors.

Labor costs make up a large proportion of total costs in all these industries, and with the collapse of the union-based (and in the case of trucking, regulation-based) system taking wages out of competition, cut-throat competition among subcontractors and the intensive labor exploitation classically associated with it rapidly reemerged. Fringe benefits and job security disappeared along with the union wage premium, and once-stable jobs soon were replaced by increasingly precarious employment arrangements. Under the newly fashionable banner of "flexibility," labor practices of questionable legality began to flourish. Reports of all-cash wages, lack of overtime compensation, substandard pay for "training periods," and other such practices had become commonplace in all three cases by the 1980s.

Subcontractor-driven deunionization was the motor driving change in these industries, but the dynamics most commonly cited in scholarly and popular accounts of union decline were conspicuously absent. None of these cases involved deindustrialization or a shift in employment from union to non-union sectors (see Farber and Western 2001). On the contrary, employment *grew* during the 1980s in southern California (and many other regions as well) in these three industries, and all three had been union strongholds before the restructuring began. Nor was union decline caused by globalization or job relocation offshore, for construction, trucking, and building services are all place-bound industries that are invulnerable to outsourcing. The lack of "demand" for unions among non-union workers, which some commentators suggest can help account for the broader decline of union density in this period (see Farber and Krueger 1993), cannot explain these cases either, since all were previously highly organized industries.

Southern California, moreover, does not fit the dominant narrative of union decline, which is rooted in the rustbelt experiences of deindustrialization and outsourcing. The region did lose manufacturing jobs in the 1970s and 1980s (most notably in aerospace), but it nevertheless experienced rapid economic growth in the late 20th century. In residential construction, short-haul trucking, and building services, that growth provided a safety valve, as once-desirable jobs deteriorated in this period. Rather than trying to swim against the tide of union decline, many of the workers affected moved horizontally into other high-wage (and often, still-unionized) positions. Some could do this without even changing occupations. Thus construction workers migrated from the residential sector into the booming (and still highly unionized) commercial sector; truckers moved from local, short-distance jobs to long-haul work, where unions hung on and conditions were better; and janitors moved from the private to the still-unionized public sector. Those able to make such transitions were overwhelmingly native-born workers, most of them white males, except in the janitorial case, where African Americans and women were also employed.

Meanwhile, the region had become a magnet for the new immigration that gathered speed after 1965. As native-born workers abandoned their formerly unionized jobs in industries like trucking, residential construction, and building services, employers turned for replacements to the newcomers, mostly from Mexico and Central America. In the residential building trades, labor recruitment (formerly organized by the unions) was increasingly taken over by opportunistic "labor barons" with ready access to newly arriving immigrants. In trucking, restructuring led to an independent contracting system, and immigrant owner-operators, paid by the truckload rather than by the hour, poured into the field. Finally, in janitorial work, contract-cleaning firms—freed of union restrictions—increasingly turned over labor recruitment and supervision to Latino foremen and crew leaders. Although at the time, many observers, and even some union leaders, blamed immigrants for the decline of organized labor's influence, in fact deunionization *preceded* the influx of foreign-born workers into these industries. Thus the shift to immigrant labor was a consequence more than a cause of employment restructuring, a dynamic the last section of this chapter exposes in more detail.

The main driver of transformation in these three industries, nationally and in southern California, was not deindustrialization or a sectoral shift in employment, not globalization and outsourcing, not immigration. Rather it was a broader change in the power balance between labor and capital, with non-union subcontractors as the driving wedge. All three industries were destabilized by the surge in anti-unionism in the late 1970s and early 1980s that commentators like Freeman and Medoff (1984), Freeman (1988), and Goldfield (1987) have documented. Equally important, union organizing efforts were few and far between in the transitional period (see Farber and Western 2002; Freeman and Medoff 1984), a problem exacerbated in southern California by the "safety valve" effect of economic expansion noted above. A decade later, the new immigrant workforce in all three industries would actively seek to unionize, but in the late 1970s and 1980s, restructuring was unconstrained by any serious resistance from organized labor.

The Anti-Union Offensive in Construction

The transformation began in the construction sector. As Linder (2000) has shown in detail, the national corporate anti-union assault generally associated with the 1980s was foreshadowed by developments in the construction industry during the Vietnam War years. Wage demands from building trades unions escalated in the late 1960s, stimulated by low unemployment in the absence of wage and price controls. In response, the nation's major construction firms, along with their largest industrial customers, launched a full-scale anti-union offensive in the early 1970s. Nonunion "merit shop" contractors began aggressively bidding on jobs, not only in suburban and southern markets where unions were weak but also in highly unionized areas like southern California. They benefited from new construction technologies that facilitated employment of fewer skilled workers, as well as a key NLRB decision in 1973 that sanctioned the use of "double-breasted" firms with both union and non-union subsidiaries (Palladino 2005:176). As the mid-1970s recession further eroded labor's bargaining power, open-shop firms began to boldly underbid their unionized competitors, and they increasingly put the building trades on the defensive. The unions responded by reopening contracts and "giving back" past gains, paving the way for the wave of concession bargaining that rippled across the nation in industry after industry in the 1980s.

The employers' attack on the building trades unions proved highly effective. Nationally, union density in construction was cut in half between 1970 and 1990 (falling from 42% to 22%), with the residential sector particularly hard hit (Allen 1994). Leading the open-shop offensive were the Associated Builders and Contractors (ABC), whose largest chapter was in Los Angeles (Bourdon and Levitt 1980; Galenson 1983). The ABC explicitly targeted Los Angeles as the "proving ground" for its efforts; by the late 1970s, some 300 contractors in that city had withdrawn from collective bargaining agreements and announced plans to subcontract work to non-union firms (Palladino 2005).

Construction in southern California had been completely unionized in the mid-1960s, and density remained high through the late 1970s. In 1965, there were 119,200 building trades union members in the region, more than the number of wage and salary workers (104,200) in the construction industry at that time (California Department of Industrial Relations 1965; *Union Labor in California* 1966).[2] As an L.A. carpenters' union official declared in 1969, "There isn't a nail driven in this area that isn't driven by a union man with a union card in his pocket" (Haggerty 1976:25). A master labor agreement governed wages in this era, and the building trades unions carefully monitored construction sites to ensure that premium rates were paid for especially difficult jobs. Union members had extensive benefits, including pensions, health insurance, and paid vacations. "For every dollar that we paid a man, we were paying another 65 cents between the taxes and the benefits and the workers' comp," one contractor recalled. "Most of it was in the union benefit package."[3] The unions also ran formal apprenticeship programs and hiring halls on which many employers relied for their labor supply.

But construction union membership in the region had slipped to 93% of wage and salary employment by 1975, down from more than 100% a decade earlier.[4] By 1987, union density in construction had plummeted to 53% (*Union Labor in California* 1989). The turning point was the deep recession of the early 1980s, when the region's building industry came to a standstill. During the subsequent recovery, the open-shop sector gained the upper hand: A 1984 survey found that non-union general contractors accounted for fully three fourths of residential and one third of commercial construction in the 11-county southern California region (Berkman 1986).

Nationally, construction was an early battleground in the broad corporate assault on unionism that would come to fruition in the late 1970s and 1980s. The open-shop movement was orchestrated by the industry's big players; smaller contractors often preferred to remain in the union fold as long as they could. "There's no union contractor I know of that by choice would go open shop for the hell of it," the president of the Associated General Contractors stated in 1981. "It's a lot easier for him to stay union as long as he can compete," since the union provides a reliable supply of trained workers and sets uniform wage scales. "But the minute he starts to lose work and his business is threatened, he will go double-breasted or open shop. That's all there is to it. He has to" (*Engineering News-Record* 1981:26). Thus as the non-union sector grew, "the prices dropped out from underneath the union contractors," one employer recalled in an interview, "and so they were unable to compete. . . . Some double-breasted and went nonunion, but most of them went out of business."

The open-shop contractors initially profited handsomely by bidding against union firms, but later, as the union sector shrunk, they too had to face intense competition from other open-shop operations. Initially, the building trades unions offered little resistance to the employer attacks, especially in the residential sector. "Residential construction was not a primary battleground between unions and antiunion employers, but rather was abandoned to nonunion employers by default," Linder (2000:180) concludes. The AFL-CIO's national Building and Construction Trades Department did launch a pilot organizing campaign in 1978 that focused on Los Angeles and claimed some success (Palladino 2005). Yet many building trades union leaders in the region were reticent about this effort. Insofar as they maintained their grip on commercial construction, they did not perceive the triumph of the ABC-led open-shop movement in the residential sector as a major threat, especially if their members readily found new work in the booming commercial sector. "In the 1980s, we had tremendous growth in the commercial industry," a local union official recalled. "We were building twenty, thirty-story buildings, it was just work for us and that's all we cared about. [Residential] is a lost industry, we'll just concentrate on commercial."

Not surprisingly, deunionization led to rapid deterioration in wages, conditions, and benefits in the residential sector. Pay rates were cut by as much as half over the 1980s, overtime work remained common but was often not properly compensated, and fringe benefits became a dim memory. "Once the union was actually broken out of the business," a contractor frankly stated, "these guys were taking a screwing, it was as simple as that."

Unscrupulous and illegal practices that had been rare in the union era emerged as competition among contractors spun out of control. There were reports of workers being paid on an all-cash basis, and even accounts of payment in drugs. At a 1988 hearing, a union contractor laid out the economic logic underlying such practices to the Orange County Human Relations Commission (1989:16):

> The average $10-an-hour employee may take home $8 out of that $10 that he earns after the taxes and the FICA and so on is deducted. Well, the typical cash-paying employer will say, "Look, I'll pay you $8.50 in cash, you're going to be $.50 better off." That saves him $1.50 right off the bat. That's just the tip of the iceberg. What else is he saving? He saves all his share of the payroll taxes that go on top of that: workers' compensation insurance and the other legal requirements, easily another $2.50. By not putting this work on the books, he's saving his obligation to the State and Federal taxes that he owes, easily another $1.00. You're talking $6.00 an hour in savings. I want

to ask any subcontractor out there if he can work on 60% of his
labor payroll . . . obviously, you cannot compete with him.

Under these conditions, union workers began to leave the residential
trades; indeed, most never returned after the recession at the beginning
of the 1980s.

With the union marginalized, residential contractors transferred the
tasks of labor recruitment, training, and deployment to a cadre of "labor
barons" (also known as labor brokers, *coyotes, contratistas,* or *patrons*).
These were Latino entrepreneurs, experienced craft workers themselves, who moved into the vacuum created by the union's collapse and
began to recruit immigrant workers into the industry, drawing on extensive social and kinship networks in the immigrant community. "They
[immigrant workers] didn't speak English, or very little," one contractor
explained in an interview.

> You had the rise of the Hispanic that was bilingual, was a little
> sharper than the rest of them, and he very quickly realized that
> he could put himself in the position of being a labor baron and
> not have to touch a tool and make a lot more money than
> anybody working. So he was the guy that would contact the
> drywall contractor and say, "Gee, I control fifty drywall hang-
> ers, you know. I'll run your work for you.". . . I have no respect
> for them [labor barons]. They cheat their people, they cheat
> the drywall contractor, they cheat everybody. In many cases
> they will add people to the payroll that don't even exist, just
> put dead men on the payroll. And then they just take the check
> down to the local check cashing place where they'll cash any-
> body's check and, you know, pay the small fee, and they'll cash
> five or six checks in different names. Other times they'll have
> guys take a check for x number of dollars, cash the check and
> give them back a certain amount of it in cash. It's very hard to
> control. Obviously we cannot follow a man down to cash his
> check and make sure he puts the money in his own pocket.

A union staffer described similar abuses that became common in this
period:

> They were controlling pools of thirty and forty people, living
> off these guys. They would give them twenty, thirty bucks a
> day. They could get away with this, because in Mexico you're
> lucky if you were making $30 a week. And to come here and
> make $30 a day, you're a king, you know. And some of these
> patrons had a big house and he had them live with him and
> he'd charge them rent. So he's whacking 'em twice. He charges
> 'em gas to go to work and he charges 'em for living with him.

The labor baron system in construction was not really new; such arrangements had been common in the preunion era (see Montgomery 1987, chapter 2), and persisted on the margins of the industry even when the workforce was largely native-born and white (see Haber 1930). But starting in the 1980s, with the virtual collapse of the union and the ensuing shift to immigrant labor, these practices became pervasive in the mainstream of residential construction. If southern California was in the vanguard, other regions soon followed.

The whole setup had many advantages from the contractors' point of view. Not only were they spared the tasks of labor recruitment, but all the headaches of union work rules, grievances, and bureaucratic bottlenecks were gone, plus costs were lower and market risks externalized. As a contractor explained, "If you're going to bid so much money to do an operation and you don't use a labor baron, and you pay out these dollars, you may run over cost. Where if you just put it out as so much money and let them worry about getting it done, you've already locked in your margin."

In an industry where labor accounts for more than half of total production costs, the potential savings to employers were enormous. To be sure, with the labor barons acting as middlemen, the contractors themselves became increasingly "disconnected from the people that were actually doing the work," as one contractor put it in an interview. But a more flexible system of labor deployment was difficult to imagine, and it quickly became institutionalized as unionism was effectively eliminated from the residential sector. Meanwhile, changes in immigration policy—specifically the introduction of employer sanctions in 1986—made this arm's-length approach to labor recruitment even more attractive to employers (Massey, Durand, and Malone 2002).

If employers benefited, workers paid a heavy price for this new regime. Not only were their earnings sharply reduced, but they also were forced to absorb the industry's market-related risks to an unprecedented degree, without any of the advantages unionism had previously secured. Residential construction had effectively reverted to the age of cutthroat competition, with predictable consequences for workers. Although the underlying mechanisms were different, a similar process was under way in other industries as well in this period.

Deregulation and the Restructuring of Trucking

The same organized corporate interests that led the open-shop offensive in the construction industry also lobbied successfully to reconfigure the nation's political and legal environment during the 1970s. Among the most far-reaching of the changes they were able to put into place was deregulation, especially in the transportation and communications sectors.

In the trucking industry, deregulation had devastating effects on unions and workers, reducing wages sharply and precipitating rapid deterioration in working conditions. The modes of worker recruitment, compensation, and deployment were radically transformed as much of the trucking industry came to resemble what Michael Belzer (2000) has aptly labeled "sweatshops on wheels."

Advocates of trucking deregulation included the National Association of Manufacturers (also a player in the earlier effort to deunionize the construction industry) and major industrial shippers. Their initial successes took shape as a series of administrative actions in the late 1970s and then culminated in the Motor Carrier Act of 1980, the key legislation deregulating the trucking industry. Advocates of deregulation explicitly targeted unions as an obstacle to market efficiency. Trucking employers, however, along with the Teamsters union, strongly opposed deregulation (Moore 1986).

In the post–World War II period, thanks in part to regulation as well as to the surge in labor organizing that marked the 1930s and 1940s, trucking was among the nation's most unionized industries. In southern California, by the 1950s this key transportation sector was unionized "wall to wall." (Disaggregated figures are not available, but the 1955 data collected by the California Department of Industrial Relations [California Department of Industrial Relations 1956; *Union Labor in California* 1956] found 68,900 union members in "transportation and warehousing," a category that also included bus drivers, pilots, and other transportation workers. With a total of 75,700 wage and salary workers in this sector in 1955, clearly union density in trucking was extremely high.) The trucking firms that serviced the Los Angeles–Long Beach port, among others, were all under contract with the Teamsters. "You had to be union to get in on those docks," one trucker recalled.

Trucking wages were impressive in this era of high union density. Nationally, truckers' average earnings were 38% higher than those of manufacturing workers as late as 1980 (Perry 1986); at the Los Angeles–Long Beach port during the 1960s and 1970s, truckers earned even more than the famously militant longshore workers with whom they interfaced daily. Although they were exempt from the minimum wage and overtime provisions of the Fair Labor Standards Act, since the vast majority of truckers were Teamsters members in this period, they were protected by contractual rules governing hours and pay practices. They were paid by the hour and guaranteed 40 hours' work per week. The union contracts also guaranteed extensive benefits, including paid holidays, paid vacations, health insurance, and seniority rights, as well as grievance procedures.

Even before deregulation, non-union trucking had begun to expand throughout the United States during the postwar decades. The legal prohibition on secondary boycotts under the Taft-Hartley Act of 1947 and the Landrum-Griffin Act of 1959 made it difficult for the Teamsters to organize new non-union carriers, while rapid increases in union wage levels in this period deepened trucking employers' motivation to avoid unionization and helped stimulate greater use of owner-operators (Levinson 1980). In southern California's transportation and warehousing sector, union density fell from 91% in 1955 to 70% 20 years later.

But the decline accelerated sharply with deregulation, along with rising fuel costs and the deep recession of the early 1980s. Now "trucking changed from an almost completely unionized industry, following a centrally-bargained pattern, to a partially unionized industry" (Belzer 1994:260). Nationally, unionization fell from 60% of the nation's truckers in 1980 to only 25% by century's end (Belzer 2000). The decline was especially rapid in the early 1980s, by one estimate falling by half between 1981 and 1985 alone (Perry 1986; Rose 1987). In southern California, union density in the industry fell to 46% by 1985—half the level of 30 years before. Even within the long-distance segment of the industry, where unions maintained a foothold, wages and benefits were deeply eroded in the early 1980s by national-level concession bargaining, while many employers dropped out of the National Master Freight Agreements entirely, extracting even greater givebacks at the local level (Rose 1987).

Short-haul trucking soon came to be dominated by non-union owner-operators who labored long hours for low pay without any of the extensive fringe benefits that had once been standard features of Teamster contracts. With wages no longer taken out of competition, "low wages, long hours, and unsafe and unsanitary working conditions returned to trucking" (Belzer 2000:7). As deregulation advocates promised, ground shipping prices did decline as the basis of competition in the industry shifted from quality of service to price. But the vast bulk of these savings—an estimated 80% (Belzer 2000)—came not from increased efficiency but instead from sharply reduced wages and the elimination of fringe benefits. Costs and risks were increasingly transferred to workers in the deregulated environment, as small firms contracting work out to owner-operators began to replace the larger, unionized trucking companies that once dominated the industry.

The segment of the trucking industry servicing the port of Los Angeles and Long Beach followed this pattern to the letter. Prior to deregulation, a few large firms had dominated drayage in the harbor area, and virtually all their employees had been Teamsters. After 1980, however, mid-sized and small companies began competing for the work. As a trucking firm executive explained:

> In 1980, a lot of middle to upper management employees of trucking companies lost their jobs because their companies went out of business. So they decided, "Hmm, I'll just start hiring owner-operators, independent contractors, and I'll get myself a license to operate and I'll cut the going rates by twenty percent." With deregulation, you could start a trucking company and operate out of a phone booth. All these people needed, the entrepreneurial people here, was "How do I get enough drivers to buy enough trucks—used trucks, actually, because they put them all in used trucks, okay?"

At the same time, paralleling developments in construction, the large unionized firms soon began "double-breasting," that is, setting up non-union subsidiaries, and many encouraged workers to become independent contractors. The owner-operator idea had widespread appeal among workers. "You had people coming into the industry who saw this as an opportunity," one trucker recalled. "They thought, 'Hey, I'll be my own boss . . .' So everybody got their trucks. Everybody's mother got their trucks." Moreover, as a trucking executive noted, this arrangement also had considerable appeal for employers:

> The advantage of the owner-operator independent contractor for a company who hires those drivers is that it becomes a non–asset based company. They do not own the equipment. They do not have employees that they have to guarantee work for. And if that employee doesn't have work, you're not responsible for unemployment insurance and so forth, because he's not an employee, okay?

Thus the large unionized firms rapidly disappeared from the Los Angeles and Long Beach ports. The Teamsters did attempt to reorganize port truckers in the early 1980s under these changed conditions, but after a few years they abandoned the effort.

The rates paid by steamship companies to have cargo containers trucked from the harbor to various local destinations fell sharply with this transition—by as much as half according to some industry insiders. These savings came largely at the expense of the truckers themselves, who now were paid by the load rather than hourly and received no income while they waited for work, often for as long as half a day, in huge queues at the shipping terminals. "They would contract that particular work out to a driver and he would be paid a set amount of money for taking that can [freight container] from Los Angeles to the harbor," a former union truck driver recalled. "Whereas [before] we got paid for dead time, we got an hourly rate. [After 1980,] we just couldn't compete. We were getting chewed up. I mean, why I am going to pay a union carrier 'X' amount of money when I could get a guy for half the amount?"

Although costs for shippers declined, far from illustrating the virtues of unfettered market competition, the harbor trucking industry in the aftermath of deregulation is a spectacular example of the *inefficiencies* that can result. Trucking congestion has grown steadily worse with the rapid increases in the volume of goods flowing through the port (the nation's largest) and is a grave concern for shippers, trucking employers, and drivers alike. But despite periodic appeals for rationalization (like a centralized dispatching system), market anarchy persists. The deregulated industry depends on the truckers themselves absorbing the costs of inefficiency in the form of unpaid hours waiting for jobs.

As independent contractors, the drivers also bear a disproportionate share of the market risks. They not only incur all the costs associated with owning and maintaining a truck, but they also are vulnerable to unpredictable fluctuations in fuel prices, fines for overweight containers, and other such factors beyond their control. The health insurance, pension plans, sick pay, and paid vacations that unionized truckers enjoyed before 1980 have since become a distant dream. Once they have purchased a truck (which involves monthly loan payments as well as insurance, repairs, fuel, and so forth), most owner-operators can only make ends meet by working excessively long hours, often compromising safety in the process. Even with the long hours, by the mid-1990s port truckers' net incomes had declined to about $20,000 a year, once all the expenses for which they were responsible were met. In this regard they are like truck drivers in the non-union sector nationally, who, as Belzer (2000) reports, typically earn little more than the minimum wage.

At the Los Angeles and Long Beach ports, trucking firms have been accused in recent years of taking advantage of immigrant drivers with limited proficiency in English, imposing hefty charges for liability insurance, workers compensation, and other such items as payroll deductions, even though the workers are owner-operators (Mongelluzzo 1994). Some trucking firms depend on Latino middlemen, who play a role similar to that of the labor brokers in construction, recruiting immigrant drivers and helping them purchase trucks, obtain insurance, and so forth in exchange for a substantial portion of their pay.

Like their counterparts in residential construction, today the trucking firms—and more importantly, their clients, the commercial shippers and retailers who dominate the port—obtain highly flexible labor at greatly reduced costs under this new regime. Immigrant truck drivers, nominally independent contractors but tied to their de facto employers through elaborate arrangements that involve loans, insurance, and other business necessities, absorb the costs of the new flexibility. Far from the postindustrial utopia imagined by some early apostles of the "new economy," then, trucking deregulation has instead heralded a return to classic sweatshop conditions (see also Bonacich and Wilson 2007).

"Flexibility" and Restructuring in Building Services

Even when unionization was at its peak, density was never quite as high in the building service industry as it was in the construction and trucking sectors, but organized labor had captured a substantial share of the janitorial market in cities around the country by the 1950s. Before World War II, janitors in Chicago, New York, and San Francisco had been organized, along with those in Seattle, St. Louis, Boston, Philadelphia, Milwaukee, Minneapolis, and Portland. The Building Services Employees International Union (BSEIU, as it was called until 1968, when it dropped the "B") had 40,000 members by 1937, and it continued to grow steadily thereafter. It gained 130,000 members during the 1940s alone, recruiting janitors in cities across Canada as well as the United States. By 1960, BSEIU's total membership had grown to 275,000, although by then it had begun to recruit in other industries outside building services as well (Beadling et al. 1992).

Los Angeles was among the cities BSEIU organized in the aftermath of the war. A 1956 management survey found that service workers in 35% of Los Angeles's major office buildings were unionized (Building Service Employees International Union, *Report to Locals*, June 1956). BSEIU Local 399 had over 7,000 members in 1957, about half of whom were employed by building maintenance contractors (3,225) or directly by office building owners (385), while another large group (1,050) cleaned theaters and supermarkets ("Local Composition Form," July 24, 1957, SEIU Archives, Wayne State University, SEIU Research Department Historical Files Collection, Box 14, Folder "Local 399: General"). By the late 1960s, most janitors cleaning large office buildings in downtown Los Angeles were unionized, as were many of those in outlying areas (Mines and Avina 1992).

The largely African American building service workers in the region never earned as much as their counterparts in construction or trucking, but by 1975 unionized janitors in Los Angeles averaged $3.75 an hour—double the rates paid a decade earlier and well above the minimum wage (then $2.10). Wages for the city's unionized janitors continued to rise over the next few years by about 50 cents an hour, reaching an all-time high of $12 an hour in 1982. In response to BSEIU demands, the city's cleaning contractors also had agreed to employ janitors on a full-time basis, eliminating the part-time arrangements that prevailed during the preunion era. Janitors' benefits included 11 paid holidays, full medical coverage (Mines and Avina 1992), and access to grievance and arbitration procedures.

By 1973 the flagship SEIU local in Los Angeles, Local 399, had nearly tripled its membership over the 1957 level. Much of this growth was due to extensive new organizing among hospital workers, but the local also had 5,300 members in its building maintenance division in 1973 (up from 3,225 in 1957) and another 2,000 or so performing janitorial jobs in supermarkets, industrial facilities, and other commercial buildings ("Breakdown of Local 399 Membership by Division," July 31, 1973, SEIU Archives, Wayne State University, George Hardy Collection, Box 42, Folder: "Local 399 June–July 1973").

Deunionization began a bit later in building services than in construction and trucking, taking off in the 1980s. Although the union's founding locals in New York and Chicago held their ground, between 1979 and 1984, according to the union's official history, 15 of the SEIU's 22 building services locals suffered "drastic declines in membership" (Beadling et al. 1992:74). Los Angeles was typical in this regard. Despite an office building boom in the region in the aftermath of the recession that opened the 1980s, by 1985 Local 399's building services membership had fallen to 1,800 workers, only about 8% of the city's growing janitorial workforce. The union contract signed in 1983 included major wage concessions, reflecting a desperate effort to hold on to the remaining membership in building services (Mines and Avina 1992).

The combination of expansion of the non-union sector and concessions in the union sector sent real wages for the city's janitors into a tailspin: they fell 36% from 1983 to 1988 alone (Bernstein 1989). Total office space in Los Angeles doubled over the decade that ended in 1994, but the number of janitors increased only by 25% (Service Employees International Union 1995). Thus janitors found themselves cleaning more space for less pay. Cleaning costs declined from $1.87 per square foot per year in 1979 for the city's downtown buildings to $1.08 in 1993 (in constant dollars), even as cleaning contractors' revenues rose (Service Employees International Union 1995).

For firms that specialize in janitorial services, direct labor is the single largest component of total operating costs—more than 50% for the larger cleaning contractors, which enjoy economies of scale on overhead and other expenses (Building Service Contractors Association International 1995). In contrast to industries like construction, where the small enterprises have the greatest incentives to reduce labor costs, in building services the largest firms are in such a position. In the 1970s and 1980s, as national and even international firms came to dominate the building services industry, efforts to cut costs by avoiding union contractors began to emerge. Non-union building maintenance firms surfaced around the country in the 1970s, undercutting the unionized cleaning contractors with discounted prices, especially in outlying areas of major cities. As the non-union sector grew, it put growing competitive pressure on the unionized firms, whose costs were inevitably higher. These trends were apparent as early as 1971 in Los Angeles, when the president of a union firm complained to Local 399.

> We have a serious problem in the city of Los Angeles. It is grow-ing in intensity and becomes more alarming every week. I am referring again to nonunion competition over which, it appears, the union has no control. So that makes two of us. We have esti-mated that we have lost about $1,000,000 a year to non-union competitors. (A.H. Wittenberg, Jr. to Michael McDermott, July 30, 1971, SEIU Archives, Wayne State University, George Hardy Collection, Box 41, Folder: "Local 399, Aug. 1971").

Foreshadowing later developments, the non-union cleaning companies in Los Angeles were already beginning to hire immigrants in the 1970s and were "delegating a great deal of decision-making power to Hispanic crew leaders, who typically recruit, hire, fire and pay workers" (Mines and Avina 1992:432; see also Johnston 1994: 160).

Entering the market for office cleaning requires minimal capital, and indeed, there are many small "mom-and-pop" companies in the busi-ness. But few owners of major buildings are willing to entrust their valu-able properties to such firms. Rather they tend to contract with larger, more reputable companies. After a group of midsized non-union clean-ing firms aggressively moved into the market in the late 1970s and early 1980s, disrupting the old equilibrium whereby unionization had taken wages out of competition, more and more of the unionized firms set up non-union "double breasts." Faced with this, Local 399 was forced to grant concessions to hold on to its remaining janitorial membership, by now reduced to a small core group in downtown Los Angeles.

The union did launch some efforts to organize the new non-union firms in the early 1980s, but it made little headway. Even when the SEIU was able to win NLRB elections among janitors (it won three in Los Angeles between 1981 and 1985), its efforts were constantly stymied, for building owners could simply terminate their contracts with the newly unionized cleaning firms (such contracts typically have 30-day cancellation clauses) and arrange to obtain services from a non-union firm instead (Mines and Avina 1992; Waldinger et al. 1998). The strike weapon was also undermined. As one Local 399 staffer put it, "We used to walk out to settle our differences, but now if we go out, we don't get back in" (Mines and Avina 1992).

Freed of the constraints that had accompanied unionization, cleaning contractors increasingly turned responsibility for hiring and firing and for day-to-day operations over to first-line supervisors. As in the construction and trucking cases, Latino intermediaries now emerged as key players, prized for their ability to tap into and control the immigrant labor supply that rapidly came to dominate the janitorial workforce. As in those other cases, the absence of union regulation combined with a relatively informal and decentralized form of management soon gave rise to unscrupulous and often illegal practices that exploited the vulnerability of the new immigrant workforce.

In 2000, the *Los Angeles Times* published an exposé of such practices in the segment of the industry comprised of non-union subcontractors hired to clean supermarkets and other large retail establishments:

> He works the midnight shift seven nights a week, stripping, waxing and buffing the floors. . . . He says he earns far less than the minimum wage, and just laughs when asked about overtime pay for his 56-hour weeks. Strong chemicals make his nose bleed, burn his fingers and eat the soles of his cheap sneakers. He operates powerful, potentially dangerous machines but isn't protected by workers' compensation insurance. . . . Not only are many janitors earning subminimum wages—about $550 to $750 twice a month for 56-hour weeks—they are also untaxed. Typically paid in cash or personal checks, with no deductions for Social Security, Medicare or federal and state income tax, they are part of a thriving underground economy that robs billions of dollars from U.S. and California treasuries every year. . . . [None of the workers interviewed] could name the company for whom they worked. They knew only the subcontractor, who showed up twice a month to pay them in personal checks. They told of wrapping steel wool pads around their sneakers when stripping floors, to keep from slipping on the slick chemicals. They told of weeks they went unpaid, of arbitrary schedule changes (Cleeland 2000:1).

Another case that came to public attention involved an office cleaning company firm that pleaded guilty in court to failing to pay overtime and to keep legally required records. One of the employees involved complained that he was forced to work up to 19 hours without a break and was paid neither the minimum wage nor overtime (Fausset 2001).

One common practice was to demand that newly hired janitors turn over their first month's pay to the supervisor to secure their jobs. Some supervisors reportedly extracted sexual favors from female janitors on the same basis. Health and safety protection was non-existent for janitors working with dangerous chemicals and heavy machinery, and unpaid overtime was common (Gardetta 1993). One janitor told the *Los Angeles Times* in 1988 that he had worked for five weeks full-time for no pay in a "training program." After that, when he refused his supervisor's demand of a $150 payoff out of his first paycheck to keep the job, he was summarily fired (Ybarra 1988).

Cynthia Cranford (2001:97) describes other employment practices, most of them illegal, used by cleaning firms:

> Working for more hours than one was paid, and earning less than the minimum wage, was very common in this industry and was achieved in multiple ways. Cleaners often worked by the piece, rather than by the hour. . . . Cleaners were also encouraged to bring family members to "help" with the work without being paid. And many janitors worked for weeks without pay, to "practice" in order to get a "recommendation." . . . Cleaners were also pressured to prepare their supplies before they clocked in and to work different split shifts, clocking in under different names at each shift. Cleaners were often paid in cash or by personal check in order to avoid detection of such violations, to avoid having to pay social security.

Thus in janitorial work as in residential construction and trucking, classic sweatshop conditions became endemic in the wake of deunionization. In addition to sharply reduced wages and the disappearance of benefits, janitors were subjected to a variety of illegal and exploitative practices, similar to those facing others in the growing deregulated, non-union low-wage labor market. Meanwhile, first in southern California, and later in many other parts of the nation, employers in those labor markets were rapidly recruiting foreign-born workers into these newly degraded jobs.

Incorporating Immigrant Labor

Some commentators have attributed the precipitous decline of unionism during the late 1970s and early 1980s to the increased availability of "cheap" immigrant labor. In this view, a large influx of foreign-born workers—particularly those with limited education who seek relatively low-skilled jobs—inevitably depresses wages, especially for the less-educated and for ethnic and racial minorities. Economist Vernon Briggs (2001:174), for example, argues that "unskilled and poor" immigrants, "by their presence . . . impoverish similarly situated native-born workers and their families in the same local labor markets." George Borjas (1999) takes a different approach but comes to a similar conclusion, attributing a large share of the recent growth in U.S. income inequality to immigration. Noting that the sharp decline in union density took place in the very same period as the surge in immigration, Briggs (2001) suggests that "the revival of mass immigration is likely to be a contributing factor to the decline in unionism."

The strong correlation between declining union density and increasing immigration does not, however, mean that the causal arrow should be drawn in the way that these commentators presume. On the contrary, there is evidence to suggest that it operated in precisely the opposite direction: that deunionization—which, as we have already seen, leads to deterioration in wages, benefits, and working conditions—provokes native-born workers to abandon no-longer-desirable jobs, at which point immigrants fill the vacancies. That is precisely what appears to have happened in the cases examined here. Apart from the qualitative evidence summarized above, the timing of the immigrant influx, together with selected comparisons between the labor market in southern California and in other parts of the nation, provides support for this interpretation.

When deunionization took off in the late 1970s and 1980s, it affected many parts of the United States that lacked any significant supply of immigrant labor. Southern California attracted a disproportionate share of immigrants in this period, and most of the rest were concentrated in a few other regions (Massey, Durand, and Malone 2002; Portes and Rumbaut 1990). But in all three of the industries considered here, union decline, and the accompanying deterioration in compensation and working conditions, was by no means confined to such immigrant-rich labor markets. That alone casts doubt on the notion that the increased availability of immigrant labor was an important cause of deunionization.[5]

Moreover, in some areas of the United States where a large supply of immigrants *was* available in this period, such as New York City, union decline was relatively modest in some of the very same industries where rapid deunionization had radically transformed labor conditions in southern California. In the janitorial case, for example, deunionization was geographically uneven: The SEIU maintained its grip on building services in its historic strongholds of New York, Chicago, and San Francisco even as it collapsed in Los Angeles and many other cities. But immigrants moved into the New York building services workforce to almost the same degree as they did in Los Angeles. By 1990, 57% of New York City's janitors were foreign-born, compared to 64% of those in the Los Angeles region.[6] Yet because the vast majority of both native- and foreign-born janitors in New York were union members, in 1990 they earned $7,000 more annually than their Los Angeles counterparts

(Waldinger et al. 1998). The influx of immigrants in this case had no apparent effect on the strength of the union.

In construction and trucking, too, union decline was well under way in regions all across the nations at a time when immigration was still highly concentrated in a few gateway cities. In construction, as discussed above, rapid deunionization began in the 1970s and accelerated in the early 1980s. At this point, however, major urban immigrant receiving areas like New York and Chicago were *more* likely to retain a significant union presence in construction, relative to the Sunbelt or the booming suburban and exurban areas, where immigration flows had not yet appeared. And in terms of race, ethnicity, and nativity, the construction workforce was surprisingly stable during these years. Nationally, 90.6% of unionized construction workers were white in 1977–78, and the figure was only slightly lower—89.0%—in 1989. In the non-union sector, too, whites made up 91% of the workforce at both the beginning and the end of this period of rapid union decline (Allen 1994). These data are difficult to reconcile with the hypothesis that immigration was a key driver of union decline.

In the trucking industry, similarly, there was minimal change in the ethnic and racial makeup of the workforce at the national level prior to the rapid deunionization that followed deregulation in the 1980s. In 1970, 80.9% of truckers in the United States were native-born whites; in 1980, the figure was virtually unchanged at 81.0%. Only *after* 1980 did immigrants (as well as African Americans) enter trucking in significant numbers. In the Los Angeles area, 10.5% of truckers were foreign-born Latinos in 1980; 10 years later the figure had skyrocketed to 26.1%, and during that same decade the total number of truckers in the region rose by more than a third (Milkman 2006).

Even if the availability of immigrant labor accelerated the shift to low-road employment practices, the sequence of events for both construction and trucking suggests that immigrant employment was more a consequence than a cause of the change. The janitorial case is more ambiguous, since there was substantial growth in immigrant janitorial employment in southern California as early as the 1970s. This early immigrant influx probably reflected the initial emergence of the non-union sector during the 1970s, for (as noted above) unionized building service employers had complained about undercutting by non-union contractors as early as 1971. Other qualitative evidence suggests that new non-union contractors relied on immigrant labor from the outset, especially in outlying areas of Los Angeles's sprawling metropolis (Mines and Avina 1992).

In all three industries, the increase in immigrant employment occurred earlier and was more extensive in southern California than in the nation as a whole. This is not surprising, given the region's prominence as an immigrant gateway and the later dispersion of immigrant flows throughout the United States (see Frey 2002; Massey, Durand, and Malone 2002). By the time immigrants became a significant presence in the nation as a whole, union decline was already ancient history. Meanwhile, employers rapidly came to view immigrants as highly desirable workers. "You know, the good old days of the Anglo-Saxon worker, there were good sides to it and there were bad sides to it. Communication was good. Work ethic was bad," one drywall contractor declared.

> The drywall trade, being a piecework operation, it has always been a haven for people who cannot get to work at eight o'clock every day. The white guys, you had no communication problem. But unfortunately there was a higher than desirable percentage of the alcoholics, the drug users, the problem personalities. When John Smith wanted to show up at nine, ten o'clock and then miss two days during the week, the Hispanics were there wanting to work. Willing to work. Showing up early. Working all day. Drug use is almost nonexistent. Drinking on the job: in the drywall trade they like their beer, but generally speaking you don't find them drinking during working hours and they don't stick around the jobs and drink. Those two issues I think are much better under Hispanic labor than they ever were under the white Anglo. A lot of the so-called white Anglos that worked in the trade, not all of them, but a great percentage of them, were not the most desirable. So you really got the bottom of the work status in the white Anglos. Where in the Hispanic, you're getting mainstream, you're getting more of the family-oriented. For them it was a good job. It was a much better job than picking strawberries. So you got a better class of worker.

Managers in other immigrant-employing industries expressed similar views. "If I could find another labor force as reliable . . . as Mexicans, I would use it," an executive in the building services industry remarked in the early 1990s. "But I can't." And a manager at a unionized janitorial firm complained that "there are plenty of people on the union benches, but they are rejects" (Mines and Avina 1992; see also Waldinger and Lichter 2003).

Thus all three industries were radically transformed in the final decades of the 20th century. In an earlier era, thanks to unionization, native-born white male truckers and construction workers with limited formal education earned high wages and extensive fringe benefits, and had good working conditions as well. Janitorial workers were several notches below those labor aristocrats on the occupational ladder, and they included more women as well as African Americans. But even their jobs had provided superior wages, benefits, and working conditions in the glory days of organized labor.

In the 1970s and early 1980s, however, everything changed. Employers relentlessly attacked unionism and extracted cost savings and "flexibility" from the workforce—both directly, by means of wage and benefit cuts, and indirectly, by introducing new organizational forms that forced workers to absorb more market risk. In all three industries, subcontracting was at the center of the transformation process. In residential construction (where subcontracting had always been ubiquitous) and in building services (where it had been commonplace as early as the 1950s), employers increasingly shifted work to non-union subcontractors, and this became the key wedge undermining unionism. In trucking, reliance on subcontractors was a more radical break with the past, facilitated by deregulation.

Although subcontracting per se did not necessarily produce labor degradation, it facilitated the process of externalizing market risks and of decentralizing management. Some risks were shifted to workers themselves, as in the shift from hourly pay systems to job-based payment in trucking. At the same time, the labor barons that took over in construction, the independent trucking contractors, and the newly empowered crew leaders in the janitorial industry turned increasingly to more casualized forms of labor recruitment and management. In combination with growing competitive pressures, these organizational shifts soon generated new forms of labor degradation. In residential construction, trucking, and building services alike, the result was the same: Wages fell sharply, benefits were eliminated, and working conditions deteriorated, in many instances regressing to levels reminiscent of pre–New Deal sweatshops.

Faced with these circumstances, native-born workers abandoned these employment fields, and immigrants rapidly replaced them. Upper-level managers looked the other way while the "labor barons" and supervisors to whom they had transferred responsibility for labor recruitment and management engaged in a variety of unsavory and often illegal labor practices. The immigrant newcomers at first appeared—to friend and foe alike—"willing" to tolerate such practices. Virtually no one expected them to mount an organized response. Starting in the late 1980s, they would surprise everyone by doing precisely that. But that is another story (see Milkman 2006, chapter 4).

Endnotes

[1] This chapter includes material adapted from chapter 2 of my book, *L.A. Story: Immigrant Workers and the Future of the U.S. Labor Movement* (New York: Russell Sage Foundation, 2006). Reprinted with the publisher's permission.

[2] The discrepancy is due to the fact that substantial numbers of building trades union members were unemployed, working in other industries, in the military, on strike, and so on. As a result, union density often exceeded 100% in this period.

[3] This quote is from an interview conducted in the course of my fieldwork; unless otherwise indicated, such interviews are the source for other unattributed quotes in the rest of the chapter.

[4] The fact that 1975 was a recession year, when unemployment was at a peak level, means that the actual density drop was even sharper than these data indicate: The 1975 denominator (the number of wage and salary workers) was at an unusually low point in this cyclically sensitive industry, whereas the numerator remained high since many unemployed building trades workers retained their union membership.

[5] Borjas (1999) points out the complexity of distinguishing cause and effect in analyzing the relationship between immigration and wages, since native-born workers can "vote with their feet" in response to an influx of immigration. This is one possible interpretation of the out-migration of native-born workers from California to other states in the 1980s, which in Borjas's view enlarged the labor supply in the receiving regions and thus depressed wages there as well. Borjas neither examines the relationship of immigration to deunionization nor considers the possibility that deunionization was an intervening variable precipitating both increased demand for immigrant labor and the observed decline in wages for relatively low-skilled jobs.

[6] Note that these figures include immigrants of all racial and ethnic groups. The makeup of New York's immigrant population is far less homogenous than that of Los Angeles. In 1990, foreign-born Latinos made up 33% of New York's building service workers, whereas in Los Angeles the figure was 56%. (These figures are for the New York metropolitan area, which includes the five boroughs of New York City as well as Putnam, Rockland, and Westchester counties.)

References

Allen, Steven G. 1994. "Developments in Collective Bargaining in Construction in the 1980s and 1990s." In Paula B. Voos, ed., *Contemporary Collective Bargaining in the Private Sector*. Madison, WI: Industrial Relations Research Association.

Beadling, Tom, Pat Cooper, Grace Palladino, and Peter Pieragostini. 1992. *A Need for Valor: The Roots of the Service Employees International Union, 1902–1992*. Washington, DC: Service Employees International Union.

Belzer, Michael H. 1994. "The Motor Carrier Industry: Truckers and Teamsters Under Siege." In Paula B. Voos, ed., *Contemporary Collective Bargaining in the Private Sector*. Madison, WI: Industrial Relations Research Association.

———. 2000. *Sweatshops on Wheels: Winners and Losers in Trucking Deregulation*. New York: Oxford University Press.

Berkman, Leslie. 1986. "Construction Unions Try to Stem Job Losses." *Los Angeles Times*, March 16, p. D1.

Bernstein, Harry. 1989. "While Building Owners' Profits Soar, Janitors Get Poorer." *Los Angeles Times*, August 15, p. D1.

Bonacich, Edna, and Jake B. Wilson. 2007. *Getting the Goods: Ports, Labor and the Logistics Revolution*. Ithaca, NY: Cornell University Press.

Borjas, George J. 1999. *Heaven's Door: Immigration Policy and the American Economy.* Princeton, NJ: Princeton University Press.

Bourdon, Clinton C., and Raymond E. Levitt. 1980. *Union and Open-Shop Construction.* Lexington, MA: Lexington Books.

Briggs, Vernon M. 2001. *Immigration and American Unionism.* Ithaca, NY: Cornell University Press.

Building Service Contractors Association International. 1995. *1994 Financial & Operating Ratios Survey.* Privately published.

Building Service Employees International Union. 1956. *Report to Locals.* Privately published.

California Department of Industrial Relations. 1956. *California Labor Statistics Bulletin, Area Supplement.*

California Department of Industrial Relations. 1965. *California Labor Statistics Bulletin, Area Supplement.*

Cleeland, Nancy. 2000. "Heartache on Aisle 3: Sweatshop for Janitors." *Los Angeles Times,* July 2, p. 1.

Cranford, Cynthia. 2001. *Labor, Gender and the Politics of Citizenship: Organizing Justice for Janitors in Los Angeles.* Ph.D. dissertation, University of Southern California, Los Angeles.

Engineering News-Record. 1981. "Union Construction in Trouble." Special Report. November 5, p. 26.

Farber, Henry S., and Alan B. Krueger. 1993. "Union Membership in the United States: The Decline Continues." In Bruce E. Kaufman and Morris M. Kleiner, eds., *Employee Representation: Alternatives and Future Directions.* Madison, WI: Industrial Relations Research Association.

Farber, Henry S., and Bruce Western. 2001. "Accounting for the Decline of Unions in the Private Sector, 1973–1998." *Journal of Labor Research,* Vol. 22, no. 3 (Summer), pp. 459–85.

———. 2002. "Ronald Reagan and the Politics of Declining Union Organization." *British Journal of Industrial Relations,* Vol. 40, no. 3 (September), pp. 385–401.

Fausset, Richard. 2001. "Employer Pays Janitor Part of Wages Owed." *Los Angeles Times,* June 13, p. B5.

Freeman, Richard B. 1988. "Contraction and Expansion: The Divergence of Private Sector and Public Sector Unionism in the United States." *Journal of Economic Perspectives,* Vol. 2, no. 2 (Spring), pp. 63–88.

Freeman, Richard B., and James L. Medoff. 1984. *What Do Unions Do?* New York: Basic Books.

Frey, William H. 2002. *Census 2000 Reveals New Native-Born and Foreign-Born Shifts Across U.S.* Research Report no. 02-520. Ann Arbor: Population Studies Center, Institute of Social Research, University of Michigan.

Galenson, Walter. 1983. *The United Brotherhood of Carpenters: The First Hundred Years.* Cambridge, MA: Harvard University Press.

Gardetta, Dave. 1993. "Clocking Time with Janitors Organizer Rocio Saenz." *L.A. Weekly,* August 5, p. 16.

Goldfield, Michael. 1987. *The Decline of Organized Labor in the United States.* Chicago: University of Chicago Press.

Haber, William. 1930. *Industrial Relations in the Building Industry.* Cambridge, MA: Harvard University Press.

Haggerty, Cornelius J. 1976. "Labor, Los Angeles, and the Legislature." Oral history interview, conducted by Amelia R. Fry in November 1969. Berkeley: Earl Warren

Oral History Project, Regional Oral History Office, Bancroft Library, University of California, Berkeley.

Johnston, Paul. 1994. *Success While Others Fail: Social Movement Unionism and the Public Workplace*. Ithaca, NY: ILR Press.

Levinson, Harold M. 1980. "Trucking." In Gerald G. Somers, ed., *Collective Bargaining: Contemporary American Experience*. Madison. WI: Industrial Relations Research Association.

Linder, Marc. 2000. *Wars of Attrition: Vietnam, the Business Roundtable, and the Decline of Construction Unions*. Iowa City: Fanpihua Press.

Massey, Douglas S., Jorge Durand, and Nolan J. Malone. 2002. *Beyond Smoke and Mirrors: Mexican Immigration in an Era of Economic Integration*. New York: Russell Sage Foundation.

Milkman, Ruth. 2006. *L.A. Story: Immigrant Workers and the Future of the U.S. Labor Movement*. New York: Russell Sage Foundation.

Mines, Richard, and Jeffrey Avina. 1992. "Immigrants and Labor Standards: The Case of California Janitors." In Jorge A Bustamante, Clark Reynolds, and Raul Hinojosa-Ojeda, eds., *U.S.–Mexico Relations: Labor Market Interdependence*. Stanford, CA: Stanford University Press.

Montgomery, David. 1987. *The Fall of the House of Labor*. New York: Cambridge University Press.

Mongelluzzo, Bill. 1994. "L.A. Attorney Alleges Blacklisting of Drivers." *Journal of Commerce*, January 3, p. 2B.

Moore, Thomas Gale. 1986. "Rail and Trucking Deregulation." In Leonard W. Weiss and Michael W. Klass, eds., *Regulatory Reform: What Actually Happened*. Boston: Little, Brown.

Orange County Human Relations Commission. 1989. *Zero Dollars per Hour: A Report on Labor Exploitation in Orange County*. Mimeographed copy. Santa Ana, CA: Orange County Human Relations Commission.

Palladino, Grace. 2005. *Skilled Hands, Strong Spirits: A Century of Building Trades History*. Ithaca, NY: Cornell University Press.

Perry, Charles R. 1986. *Deregulation and the Decline of the Unionized Trucking Industry*. Philadelphia: The Wharton School, Industrial Research Unit.

Portes, Alejandro, and Rubén G. Rumbaut. 1990. *Immigrant America: A Portrait*. Berkeley: University of California Press.

Rose, Nancy L. 1987. "Labor Rent Sharing and Regulation: Evidence from the Trucking Industry." *Journal of Political Economy*, Vol. 95, no. 6, pp. 1146–78.

Service Employees International Union, Local 399. 1995. *A Penny For Justice: Janitors and L.A.'s Commercial Real Estate Market*. Mimeographed copy. Los Angeles: Service Employees International Union, Local 399.

Union Labor in California. 1956. California Department of Industrial Relations, Division of Labor Statistics and Research.

———. 1966. California Department of Industrial Relations, Division of Labor Statistics and Research.

———. 1989. California Department of Industrial Relations, Division of Labor Statistics and Research.

Waldinger, Roger, and Michael Lichter. 2003. *How the Other Half Works: Immigration and the Social Organization of Labor*. Berkeley: University of California Press.

Waldinger, Roger, Chris Erickson, Ruth Milkman, Daniel J.B. Mitchell, Abel Valenzuela, Kent Wong, and Maurice Zeitlin. 1998. "Helots No More: A Case

Study of the Justice for Janitors Campaign in Los Angeles." In Kate Bronfen-brenner, Sheldon Friedman, Richard W. Hurd, Rudolph A. Oswald, and Ronald L. Seeber, eds., *Organizing to Win: New Research on Union Strategies*. Ithaca. NY: Cornell University Press.

Ybarra, Michael J. 1988. "Janitors Claim Cleaning Companies Mistreat Them." *Los Angeles Times*, December 30, p. A3.

CHAPTER 4

Day Labor and Workplace Abuses in the Residential Construction Industry: Conditions in the Washington, DC, Region

NIK THEODORE
University of Illinois at Chicago

EDWIN MELÉNDEZ
The New School

ABEL VALENZUELA JR.
University of California, Los Angeles

ANA LUZ GONZALEZ
University of California, Los Angeles

On September 14, 2007, the town of Herndon in northern Virginia bowed to pressure from anti-immigrant groups (principally those affiliated with the Minuteman Civil Defense Corps) and shuttered its day labor worker center (Aizenman and Dwyer 2005; Altamirano 2007). The center, which had been in operation for less than two years, provided a place for construction contractors, landscaping companies, and private households to hire day laborers for a variety of manual-labor jobs. On a typical day, approximately 100 to 120 laborers assembled at the site in the hope of getting work (Barakat 2007). Prior to the opening of the center, day laborers in Herndon gathered outside a local convenience store and along major thoroughfares in the town. With the center's closing, many workers vowed to return to the streets to search for work (Bruillard 2007).

Elsewhere in Virginia, day laborers have been experiencing the effects of a slowing national economy and the downturn in the housing market. "I have never seen so many men out here before or so few trucks," said Vicente Crespo, 37, a laborer from El Salvador. "A year ago, I was working all month and getting $15 an hour. Now, if I'm lucky, I get a job for a few hours and they pay $10" (quoted in Constable and Sanchez 2007:A01). Layoffs in other sectors of the economy have increased the numbers of day laborers gathering in public spaces dramatically, leading to intense competition for scarce jobs. "There's no time to negotiate. You just grab the door handle and jump in," Crespo added. On the street "it's every man for himself."

Each morning, hundreds of day laborers in the Washington, DC, area assemble in parking lots, at major intersections, and in other public spaces to search for work. They wait, often for hours, in the hope that a construction contractor, homeowner, landscaping company, or small business will hire them for the day. Those fortunate enough to be hired will work as construction helpers, movers, demolition haulers, painters, cleaners, and gardeners or perform other manual labor. Those less lucky will continue their search until mid-afternoon, when they will leave the hiring site until returning the following morning.

By most accounts, day labor work is on the rise in the United States. Once largely confined to major urban areas—primarily gateway cities, such as Chicago, Los Angeles, and New York City, with historically high levels of international migration—the practice of searching for work in public spaces has spread to smaller towns, suburbs, and newly developing exurban areas. In many respects, day labor is the epitome of the type of flexible employment arrangements that increasingly are favored by employers. Workers are employed strictly as needed, employers avoid and evade responsibility for unemployment and workers' compensation insurance, and gross earnings are low. In this chapter we examine the phenomenon of day labor in the Washington, DC, area by documenting the employment conditions faced by the laborers. Reporting results from the Washington, DC, subsample of the first national survey of day laborers, we examine the characteristics of the supply of and demand for casually employed laborers in the region. The next section situates day labor within a restructuring residential construction industry and explores the relationship between casualized employment arrangements and the "mainstream" economy. We then consider the methodological challenges of surveying day laborers and describe our approach to conducting this workforce survey. This is followed by a presentation of survey findings on day laborer demographics, as well as the terms of employment, wages, and health and safety conditions associated with day labor. In the final section we consider the most promising policy intervention to restore the floor under the day labor market—worker centers—where day labor hiring is more formalized and transparent and where labor standards are better protected.

Unregulated Work in the Residential Construction Industry

Over the past three decades, the construction industry has become bifurcated, with one segment offering high-wage, relatively stable, unionized work (primarily on industrial, government, and infrastructure projects) and the other offering poorly paying, contingent, non-union work (mainly on residential and, to some extent, commercial projects). The factors that have led to the divergence of employment practices in the industry are many, including legal and regulatory changes that have restricted the ability of building trades unions to organize workers in the industry, the exclusion of large segments of the labor force from unionized training and employment opportunities, the increasing capacity of non-union contractors to carry out high-quality work, and concerted efforts on the part of end users to reduce the influence of unions at construction worksites (Erlich and Grabelsky 2005; Weil 2005). As a result, over the course of the last 30 years, not only has union density in the construction industry fallen from approximately 40% to less than 15%, but "large and growing segments of the industry are outside the union sphere of influence even in the large urban markets where overall union presence remains relatively strong" (Erlich and Grabelsky 2005:424–5). Echoing this point, David Weil (2005:448) notes that "this decline in union density masks the virtual elimination of unionized building trades in some metropolitan areas."

Declining union presence has had serious consequences for both the non-unionized and unionized segments of the industry. The influence of unions on wages and working conditions in the construction industry extends well beyond those workers covered by collective bargaining agreements and the contractors that employ them. When union density is high, non-union contractors are compelled to raise wages and improve working conditions in an effort to remain competitive with their unionized counterparts. Even those workers who are not employed under a union contract thus enjoy some of the benefits of a strong union presence in the industry. However, when density falls to very low levels, the "union effect" on wages across the local labor market all but disappears. This in turn sets in motion processes of labor market adjustment. Unionized workers leave the jurisdiction for areas where prevailing wage rates are higher, resulting in labor shortages in low-union labor markets. "With wages too low to attract the industry's traditional demographic base of recruits, contractors [turn] to immigrants to fill the vacuum. . . . [Today,] undocumented immigrants are clearly the industry's backbone in many areas and even in subsectors like residential and light commercial in still strong union markets" (Erlich and Grabelsky 2005:426; see also Milkman 2006, 2008).

Changes in the organization of construction industry labor markets have had far-reaching effects on employment arrangements in the industry, particularly for practices in the sector's residential segment (which accounts for more than half of the entire industry and nearly three quarters of the private-sector market [Weil 2005]). In an effort to bolster profit margins as well as to contend with fluctuating demand for their services, many residential construction contractors are devising tactics to contain labor costs by radically remaking employment arrangements. They are cutting the wages of some workers and deepening their dependence on contingently employed labor by adopting various flexible work arrangements, including misclassifying independent contractors, employing workers through temporary staffing agencies, increasing their reliance on subcontractors, and hiring casual laborers who are hired "off the books." The destabilization of standard employment contracts (which were based on the expectation of continuing employment) is typically justified in terms of achieving long-run competitiveness—holding the line on prices by making previously fixed costs variable. However, in the construction industry, these restructuring tactics have produced a vicious cycle of cost cutting and labor exploitation as firms in segments of the industry have attempted to achieve short-run profitability by sweating labor, cutting back on workplace safety provisions, and pursuing other low-road forms of competition. As cost-cutting measures based on the externalization of work and the segmentation of the labor force take hold in an industry, the balance of competition shifts in the direction of low-road firms, leading to further downgrading of employment conditions across the industry. When processes of labor sweating go unchecked and employers are allowed to reap the benefits of low-cost, flexible labor, the competitive dynamics of entire industry segments can be transformed (see Rubery and Wilkinson 1981; Theodore 2003).

Within residential construction labor markets, "the growing use of immigrant workers meshes with the structural trend toward subcontracting. As general contractors/construction managers shift on-site labor responsibilities to an array of mobile subcontractors, intermediaries such as temporary employment agencies or individual labor brokers emerge that seek to provide non-union firms some of the referral services offered to unionized contractors by a union hiring hall"

(Erlich and Grabelsky 2005:428). Such intermediaries have prolifer-ated in the construction industry, their presence associated with low wages and workers' heightened exposure to substandard working con-ditions (see Bernhardt et al. 2005; Bernhardt, DeFilippis, and McGrath 2007; Gordon 2005; Mehta and Theodore 2006; Peck and Theodore 2007; Theodore, Valenzuela, and Meléndez 2006). One aspect of the bifurcation of the construction sector, then, is the emer-gence of new forms of labor market segmentation brought on by a diminished role of general contractors in directly structuring employ-ment arrangements. As employment arrangements are increasingly left to the market (e.g., to suppliers of contingent workers like temp agencies and informal day labor hiring sites), the relative importance of internal labor markets is reduced, reservation wages have fallen, and the reliance on subcontracting has grown (see Peck 1995; Sassen 2002). "The increased use of undocumented workers also comple-ments the growing presence of the underground economy in con-struction. It is a small step for an unscrupulous employer to move from hiring undocumented workers to operating entirely off the books—or vice versa. . . . Legitimate employers—union or non-union—that provide a living wage and benefits for their employ-ees are constantly looking over their shoulders at the legions of sub-contractors that play by a different set of rules" (Erlich and Grabelsky 2005:428–9).

The highly casualized segments of the residential construction industry do not exist as an independent labor market that is entirely separate and distinct from the more regulated, "mainstream" con-struction labor market. Rather, the dynamics of the more casualized segments are conditioned by the restructuring strategies of the enter-prises that employ these workers and by three decades of shrinking union presence in the industry, which has ushered back in a range of employer practices associated with the "gloves-off" economy. The principal function of the day labor market and of other highly precari-ous, casualized employment arrangements is to absorb the most intense cost pressures of industries undergoing deep restructuring. The residential construction industry is the primary employer of day laborers in the Washington, DC, area. As has been the case in many other industries, residential construction contractors have adapted to leaner and more cost-conscious strategies. Cost pressures have led contractors to adopt alternative hiring practices, and many have turned to contingent workers from day labor hiring sites as a way to hold down wages and circumvent U.S. labor and employment laws. It is these contractors who frequent the open-air labor markets in Virginia, Maryland, and elsewhere in the Washington, DC, area to secure their eager, hard-working, inexpensive, and flexible work crews.

Methodology

To document the conditions under which day laborers in the Washington, DC, area are employed, a survey was administered in July 2004 among workers at 16 hiring sites in Maryland, Virginia, and Washington, DC. These interviews were completed as part of the National Day Labor Survey, which surveyed workers at 264 hiring sites across 20 states and the District of Columbia. In total, 476 in-person surveys were completed in the Washington, DC, region. Interviews included questions regarding worker demographics, occupational characteristics, wages, and working conditions. The surveys were administered in English, Spanish, and French. Each survey took approximately 45 minutes to complete, and respondents were paid $10 for their participation.

The research design included procedures to overcome four methodological challenges. First, day labor (looking for work day-to-day in public spaces and at worker centers) is not an easily defined occupation that conforms neatly to established occupational classification schemes. Moreover, because day laborers may undertake tasks associated with multiple construction trades, as well as other manual-labor occupations, during a given work week, even the identification of a primary occupation is often problematic. It is not uncommon for day laborers to perform a variety of jobs during the course of a week or month.

Second, day laborers usually are hired by many different employers for a variety of assignments ranging in length from a few hours to several weeks. As a result, the employment status of a given worker may fluctuate among job seeker, informal day laborer, and employee hired in a standard employment arrangement. This means that simple counts of workers congregating at day labor hiring sites, depending on the season, time of day, or current demand for day laborers, may not provide an accurate measure of the size of the market.

Third, hiring sites, although often visible to passersby, are nevertheless difficult to keep track of in their totality. New sites emerge, old sites disappear, and some sites are difficult to identify. This adds to the difficulty in generating an accurate count of the workers in this labor market.

Fourth, at any given time, who is and is not a day laborer is in flux. For some workers, day labor is a full-time occupation and primary source of income. For others it is a temporary occupation or second job. Still others use day labor as a stepping stone to full-time work in the formal economy.

This dynamic reality makes day labor difficult to track, since workers move in and out of this segment of the job market. Surveys of workers at hiring sites miss those who have moved on to permanent or short-term employment and even those hired on the day of the survey. The day-to-day operations of this labor market complicate systematic exploration. The inability to assess the mobility of day laborers is an unfortunate shortcoming of point-in-time surveys like the one presented here.

To account for these methodological challenges we identified as many day labor hiring sites as possible and developed a random sampling frame for the selection of survey participants. Prior to administering the survey, we worked closely with day laborers, staff from community organizations, the National Day Laborer Organizing Network, and government representatives to identify 16 area hiring sites. Sites included ones located close to construction supply and home improvement stores; others in public spaces, such as major thoroughfares; and day labor worker centers operated by community-based organizations and municipalities. At each hiring site, workers were randomly selected to be interviewed. The survey adapted conventional sampling techniques based on selection counts for each site according to the number of job seekers present. The rejection rate for participation was less than 10%.

Profile of Day Laborers in the Washington, DC, Area

On a typical day in the Washington, DC, area an estimated 8,887 workers are either employed as or searching for work as a day laborer.[1] Day laborers gather at 16 hiring sites in the region. The size of sites varies, with small sites attracting several dozen job seekers and large ones drawing several hundred (Table 1). The overwhelming majority of the area's day laborers are migrant workers from Mexico, Central America, South America, and Africa (Figure 1), suggesting that day labor hiring sites are an important entry point for migrants into the region's construction industry. Of the migrant day laborers surveyed, 25% have

TABLE 1
Size of Day Labor Work Sites in the
Washington, DC, Area

Size (no. of workers)	Frequency	Average no. of workers
Small (5–29)	5	16
Medium (30–69)	6	42
Large (70+)	5	123

Source: National Day Labor Survey, 2004.

FIGURE 1
Country of Origin of Day Laborers in the Washington, DC, Area

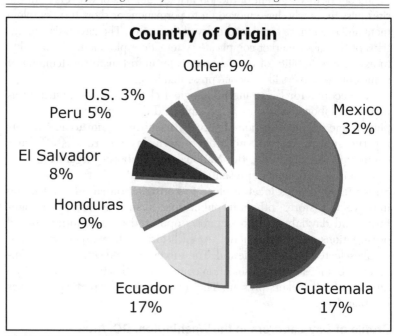

Source: National Day Labor Survey, 2004.

lived in the United States for less than one year, 30% for five years or longer, and 19% for more than 10 years. Seventy-seven percent of the day laborers surveyed are undocumented immigrants, 98% are men, and nearly half are age 35 or older (Table 2). These varied characteristics suggest a workforce that defies stereotypes of being uniformly young, recently arrived, undocumented immigrants.

Occupations, Wages, and Earnings

Day laborers in the Washington, DC, area are employed primarily by construction contractors and other companies. Sixty-nine percent of workers interviewed reported that the employer that hired them most often was a contractor or company. The remaining 31% indicated that private households were their main employers. Day laborers perform a variety of manual-labor jobs, mainly related to the construction industry (Table 3). Workers were asked about the types of jobs they have performed as a day laborer. Top occupations include construction laborer, material mover, gardener/landscaper, painter, and drywall installer. The

TABLE 2
Demographic Characteristics of Day
Laborers in the Washington,
DC, Area

Characteristic	%
Male	98
Female	2
Foreign-born	98
Undocumented immigrant	77
Years in the U.S.	
<1	25
1–5	45
6–10	11
11+	19
Age	
<25	20
25–34	33
35–44	27
45+	19
Mean age	35

Source: National Day Labor Survey, 2004.

diversity of occupations identified reflects both the broad range of generalist (and some specialist) skills possessed by day laborers as well as the wide variety of tasks that employers turn to them to complete.

The earnings of day laborers tend to be extremely volatile and dependent on a range of labor market factors as well as on conditions

TABLE 3
Top Tasks Performed by Day
Laborers in the Washington,
DC, Area

Task	%
Construction labor	88
Moving/hauling	85
Gardening/landscaping	81
Painting	75
Drywall installation	58
Roofing	54
Plumbing	33
Electrician	18

Source: National Day Labor Survey, 2004.

in the construction industry (and overall economy) more generally. The overwhelming majority of workers (89%) surveyed indicated that day labor is their sole source of employment. More than half (51%) search for work seven days a week, and an additional 31% seek work five or six days a week. Despite the fact that searching for work is a full-time activity for most day laborers, securing work is difficult. A study of day laborers in New York City found that more than three quarters of day laborers who seek work every day indicated that during a "good week" they are able to secure employment at least five days (Theodore, Valenzuela, and Meléndez 2006). But for day laborers, few weeks can be classified as "good." During slow periods, or "bad weeks," they are employed, on average, just two days a week, despite seeking work every day. During bad weeks, one third of workers are employed one day or less, and just 1% are employed five days during the week. The instability of day labor is related directly to high levels of worker impoverishment, despite hourly wages that are relatively high when compared to federal and state minimum wage rates.

The hourly wages of day laborers in the Washington, DC, area follow a right-skewed bell-shaped distribution, with wages clustering at $10 (the median wage) and to a lesser extent around $12.[2] Survey respondents were asked to report their daily wages and earnings for each job worked during the previous week (a total of 977 jobs across the sample). From these responses, it is possible to ascertain the wage pattern of day laborers in the Washington, DC, area. At the low end of the hourly wage distribution, less than 2% of day-labor jobs paid under $7 an hour (Figure 2). Slightly more than 14% of assignments paid between $7 and $9.99 an hour. At the upper end of the wage distribution, nearly 54% of jobs paid between $10 and $11.99 an hour, and just over 30% paid $12 or more.[3]

Despite these relatively high wage levels, the annual earnings of most day laborers place them among the working poor. Typical earnings are low both because the work is unstable and because workers are regularly subjected to wage theft (the nonpayment or underpayment by employers of wages for work completed). The erratic nature of day labor combined with even modest variations in daily wages can lead to dramatic swings in workers' monthly earnings.

Among the workers who search for day labor jobs full-time (five or more days a week), the median monthly earnings in the previous month was $800. However, approximately 32% of full-time day laborers earned $500 or less in that month. On the upper end of the earnings scale, just under 8% of respondents reported earnings of more than $2,000 that month. But the volatility in earnings can best be seen when comparing earnings during peak periods (good months) and slack periods

FIGURE 2
Hourly Wages of Day Labor Jobs in the Washington, DC Area

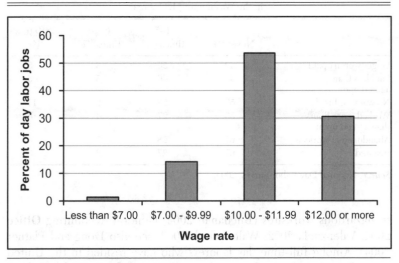

Source: National Day Labor Survey, 2004.

(bad months). Although day laborers reported median earnings in the prior month of $800, they also indicated that in a good month median earnings reach $1,500. However, during periods of weak labor demand, median monthly earnings fall to just one third of peak, or $500. So even in cases where Washington, DC, area day laborers experience more good months than bad, they are unlikely to earn annual incomes of more than $15,000. Multiplying the more realistic median monthly earnings during the time of the survey (July) by 12 months yields an annual income of just $9,600, an amount close to the federal poverty threshold and one inadequate for coping with the high cost of living in or near Washington, DC.

Working Conditions

Employer violations of labor and employment rights are common in the Washington, DC, day labor market. These conditions exacerbate the problem of low and volatile earnings of day laborers. Eighty percent of respondents reported that they had suffered some type of abuse by their employer while working as a day laborer (Table 4). The violations that have been experienced by the most day laborers are nonpayment of wages (58%), being underpaid (57%), and being denied water or breaks at the worksite (43%).

In addition to the nonpayment of wages and other employer abuses, day laborers endure a high incidence of workplace injury and exposure

TABLE 4
Frequency of Employer Abuses Reported by Day Laborers
in the Washington, DC, Area

	Never (%)	1–5 times (%)	6–10 times (%)	>10 times (%)
Wages weren't paid	42	50	3	5
Paid less than agreed upon	43	46	5	5
No water or breaks	57	28	5	11
Worked more hours than agreed upon	63	27	4	6
Abandoned at worksite	67	28	2	3
Insulted	67	27	2	3

Source: National Day Labor Survey, 2004.

to hazardous worksites (Buchanan 2004; General Accounting Office 2002; Valenzuela 2002; Walter et al. 2002; see also Dong and Platner 2004). Among full-time day laborers who have resided in the United States for at least one year, exposure to unsafe conditions at the worksite is a common occurrence. Nearly one quarter (24%) of day laborers in the Washington, DC, area have suffered one or more injuries requiring medical attention while on the job. The median number of days missed seeking work was 15.[4] In most cases, day laborers reported that they did not receive the medical attention they needed following a workplace injury. In the rare instances where an injured worker received professional medical attention for a workplace injury, the day laborer or their family paid for the costs of treatment 33% of the time, the employer 41% of the time, Medicaid 15% of the time, private insurance 3% of the time, and workers' compensation insurance 9% of the time.

By any measure, day labor is a difficult and hazardous occupation. More than 79% of day laborers in the Washington, DC, area indicated that their work is dangerous. Day labor has developed into an exploitive and hazardous labor market niche whose substandard conditions are reinforced by the willingness of unscrupulous employers to take advantage of workers' pressing need for daily employment. The one aspect of this market that is most promising, its wages, is nullified by the infrequency of employment and the high incidence of underpayment and nonpayment of wages. Other abuses such as the lack of breaks and water, as well as occupational safety hazards, further define day labor as substandard work. Nevertheless, day laborers continue to endure the hazards of dangerous worksites, mainly because they fear that if they speak up, complain, or otherwise challenge unsafe conditions, they will be fired, not paid for work completed, or reported to immigration officials (Mehta and Theodore 2006).

Protecting Labor Standards: Day Labor Worker Centers

The growth of day labor in the United States is related to changes in the construction industry more generally. The loss of union density in residential construction and the concomitant rise of a non-union industry segment that competes principally on price has created strong incentives for contractors to achieve cost savings wherever possible. The problem for day laborers, however, is that employers' reliance on casualized employment arrangements is associated with other cost-saving moves, such as cuts in training and safety equipment and, too often, a breach of basic labor standards. Again, while attempts to contain labor costs have been made throughout the industry, they have had the greatest traction in the non-unionized segment that is involved primarily in residential construction. The unionized sector of the construction industry has for years focused on large-scale infrastructure, government, and industrial projects, leaving to non-union contractors a robust but volatile market for new home construction and remodeling. Small construction contractors undertaking a home remodeling, a room add-on, or a landscaping project have devised numerous ways to hold down their costs in order to remain attractive to clients. One way to control labor costs is to hire day laborers.

Day labor work in the Washington, DC, area is characterized by routine violations of labor laws, while working-time instability and systemic underemployment are endemic features of the occupation. During a typical work week, day laborers usually are hired for a day or two, employers take few precautions to ensure worker safety, nonpayment of wages is common, and workers are treated as if they are entirely substitutable. These conditions prevail, in part, because even during periods of relatively strong demand, most day laborers are unable to secure steady employment; at best, one third to one half can expect to secure employment on any given day. As a result, competition for jobs is intense, and unscrupulous employers stand ready to take advantage of that fact.

In some cases, workers have devised systems of wage setting and other strategies for coping with employers that might be given to abusive behavior. For example, workers may informally agree on hourly or daily wage rates, and through this type of collective action establish reservation wages at hiring sites (see Valenzuela and Meléndez 2003). In cases where worker solidarity at an informal hiring site is strong, these wage rates effectively become the minimum wage for the site. This probably explains why reported hourly wages in the Washington, DC, area cluster around $10 to $12. In other instances, workers will communicate with one another to issue warnings about abusive employers, thereby informally attempting to place a floor under working conditions. However, given the desperation for work and the constant influx of new arrivals at informal hiring sites, unscrupulous employers often find willing workers, despite the warnings of more experienced day laborers.

To address day labor workplace abuses, community organizations, workers' rights advocates, and municipalities in the region have established day labor worker centers in an attempt to reduce violations in the day labor market. Several of these worker centers are managed by Casa de Maryland and are affiliated with the National Day Laborer Organizing Network (see http://www.ndlon.org/), a network of organizations dedicated to improving conditions in the day labor market, including by creating formalized hiring sites that can safeguard the rights and well-being of workers. Day labor worker centers are sites where day laborers can safely congregate and employers are encouraged to find workers. In some cases these sites are no more than an enclosed, open-air venue with seats or benches. In their more developed form, these centers are full-service community organizations that operate a hiring hall, coordinate workers' rights activities, and foster the incorporation of day laborers into the formal economy. Many also offer educational courses and other activities to better integrate the workers into the regional economy.

Worker centers are now widely seen as the most immediate and effective response to the challenges faced by day laborers (Theodore, Valenzuela, and Meléndez 2008). On the demand side of the labor market they offer a way to monitor the practices of employers and to curtail abuses such as wage theft and exposure to unsafe working conditions. On the supply side, they organize and normalize the hiring of day laborers, monitor worker quality, and provide opportunities for worker incorporation into the mainstream economy through employment assistance and, in some cases, skills training. Finally, in the wider community in which day laborers work and live, these centers participate as key stakeholders in the resolution of neighborhood conflicts around day labor, such as the regulation of seemingly disorderly hiring sites and assisting with local policing matters related to day labor. Through being anchored in local communities, worker centers become key community partners that aid in humanizing day labor work and demystifying day laborers and the families they support.

Data for the Washington, DC, area allow us to provide a perspective on the role of worker centers in shoring up wages in the day labor market. Table 5 presents wages and time worked by type of site. Workers interviewed at worker centers reported a weekly earnings premium of 23%, or an additional $68, when finding work through a center ($362) compared to the weekly earnings of those interviewed on street

TABLE 5
Average Wages by Type of Day Labor Site
in the Washington, DC, Area

	Street	Center	Total
Wages per week	$294.12	$362.11	$308.35
Wage per hour	$10.62	$13.26	$11.18
Hours per day	8.61	8.82	8.66
Days per week	2.18	1.95	2.13

Source: National Day Labor Survey, 2004.

corners ($294). This premium is primarily the product of a higher average hourly wage of $13.62 for workers participating in the centers in contrast to the $10.62 reported by those seeking work on street corners.

As the data presented indicate, the creation of day labor worker centers marks a significant step forward in defending labor standards in the residential construction industry. "Labor centers are the most cost-effective investment of government money I can imagine," said Thomas E. Perez, Maryland's Secretary of Labor, Licensing and Regulation. "We're providing employment, addressing public safety by creating an orderly process, keeping people from street corners and protecting workers" (quoted in Brewington 2007). However, worker centers, along with other attempts to contend with the problems of unregulated work in U.S. cities (see Fine 2006; Gordon 2005; Jayaraman and Ness 2005; Narro 2005/06; Ness 2005; Sugimori 2008), face stiff challenges. Foremost among them is the need to confront pernicious problems of worker disorganization that arise from the systemic marginalization of undocumented immigrants and other workers who are employed in the growing casualized labor markets in the United States. Yet there have been notable successes in the region, by both day labor worker centers and other workers' rights advocates. Determined grassroots organizing efforts, leadership from within the ranks of the day laborer workforce, and the actions of effective community groups have made significant strides in shoring up conditions in the day labor market. Still, important local efforts to hold employers accountable for violations of employment laws, to establish and maintain wage standards, and to help day laborers transition from the informal to the formal economy, ultimately collide with a national immigration policy that deems undocumented migrants to be "illegal immigrants"—thereby driving them and their employers underground, back into the informal economy where workplace abuses go largely unchecked (Theodore 2007). It seems, then, absent a significant policy shift regarding the legal status of undocumented immigrants, that informal day labor markets will continue to expand in Washington, DC, and elsewhere as growing numbers of enterprises pursue a low-road path to competitiveness and increasing numbers of workers are drawn into the web of informal employment practices created by these employers.

Acknowledgments

The research presented in this chapter draws on a project funded by the Ford Foundation, the Rockefeller Foundation, and the Washington Area Partnership for Immigrants, a funding collaborative of the Community Foundation for the National Capital Region. Thanks to Maribeth Bandas, Francisco Cartagena, Jacinta Carvallo, Yecenia Castillo, Amy Langrehr, Lucia Martinez, Rosa-Denise Ortega, Ronald Vega Pardo, and Adriele Robles for their assistance in carrying out this research. Thanks also to Laura Dresser for her comments on an earlier draft of this paper.

Endnotes

[1] Methodological note on estimation procedures for determining the size of the day laborer population in the Washington, DC, area: The number of day laborers included in the survey count is assumed to be less than the entire day laborer population that is accessing day labor hiring sites. The formula used to estimate the size of the day laborer population is based on two assumptions: an individual worker did not use more than one site to access day labor jobs during the time of the survey, and workers might secure multiple-day assignments and therefore not be at the hiring site every day. In addition, the number of job seekers identified in the survey count likely underestimates the day laborer population because it includes only those day laborers who were seeking work at the time interviewers visited each site and because interviewers may have missed several hiring sites in the area because those sites were not known to the day laborers interviewed or to the key informants contacted during the site-identification phase of the project. Finally, since the Washington, DC, area was part of a national study following a complex design in which the researchers divided the country into five strata based on the proportional presence of Latinos and immigrant populations, the estimation of the weights also depends on the size of the area and the number of interviews of the area in relation to the size and the number of interviews in all other areas in the strata.

The weight for a case from the Washington, DC, area (i.e., an interviewed worker) is defined as the inverse of the probability of selection. In this case, the probability of selection is affected by four factors: the likelihood that an SMSA (Standard Metropolitan Statistical Area) was selected from the stratum, the likelihood that a site within an area was identified and visited during the period of the study, the likelihood that the worker was at the site the day and time of the data collection, and the likelihood that a worker was selected for an interview from those who were at the site the day of the visit. Mathematically, these factors can be expressed as:

$$Wi = 1/[Pa°Ps°Pn°Pi]$$

Where:

Wi = weight for interviewed worker i,

Pa = probability of selection of an SMSA from the strata,

Ps = probability of selection of a site within the SMSA,

Pn = probability of a worker being present at the site, and

Pi = probability a worker is selected for an interview the day of the site visit.

Given that:

Pa = selected areas / eligible areas in stratum = 2

Ps = sites visited / sites found = 16 / 16

Pn = workers counted at the site / total workers in the area = 1,361 / 4,442

Pi = interviewed workers / highest count of workers at the site during visit = 476 / 1,361

where:

TDLj = total workers in the area = ODLj + NDLj

ODLj = on-site day laborers = highest count of workers at the site during the visit

NDLj = not-on-site day laborers = ODLj ° (DLW − DWW) / (DLW)

DLW = average days looking for work in a week = 5.84

DWW = average days worked in a week = 3.23

Thus, each job seeker at a site on any given day represents:

Wi = 2 ° 1 ° 2.86° 3.26 = 18.67

And the estimated total day labor population of the area is

T = Wi ° 476 = 8,887.

The estimates do not take into account the many reasons why a day laborer might not be at a hiring site on a given day (e.g., illness or injury, looking for permanent work). In addition, it is likely that other, unidentified sites exist in the region yet were unknown to the research team and its informants.

[2] Workers were asked to report their pay as well as the number of hours worked for each day during the previous week. Hourly wages were then computed using this information.

[3] Because the survey was administered during a peak month (July), it is likely that these wage rates tend toward the upper bound of typical wage rates for day laborers.

[4] Responses were top-coded at 30 days.

References

Aizenman, N.C., and Timothy Dwyer. 2005. "Words Fly at Day-Laborer Center in Herndon: Contested Site Opens with Few Jobs but Much Debate." *Washington Post*. December 15, p. B01.

Altamirano, Natasha. 2007. "Laborer Center Draws a Crowd." *Washington Times*. September 15.

Barakat, Matthew. 2007. "Herndon Closes Day Laborer Center." Associated Press, September 15.

Bernhardt, Annette, James DeFilippis, and Siobhan McGrath. 2007. *Unregulated Work in the Global City: Employment and Labor Law Violations in New York*

City. New York: Brennan Center for Justice at New York University School of Law.

Bernhardt, Annette, James DeFilippis, Nina Martin, and Siobhan McGrath. 2005. "Unregulated Work and New Business Strategies in American Cities." *Proceedings of the 57th Annual Meeting*. Champaign, IL: Labor and Employment Relations Association, pp. 188–96.

Brewington, Kelly. 2007. "Day-Labor Center Opens." *Baltimore Sun*, December 20.

Bruillard, Karin. 2007. " 'What We Had Here Was a Family.' " *Washington Post*, September 15, B01.

Buchanan, Susan. 2004. "Day Labor and Occupational Health: Time to Take a Closer Look. *New Solutions: A Journal of Environmental and Occupational Health Policy*, Vol. 14, pp. 253–60.

Constable, Pamela, and Marcela Sanchez. 2007. "Day Laborers Squeezed on Two Sides: Legal Crackdown, Job Slump Coincide." *Washington Post*, October 10, p. A01.

Dong, Xiuwen, and James W. Platner. 2004. "Occupational Fatalities of Hispanic Construction Workers from 1992 to 2000." *American Journal of Industrial Medicine*, Vol. 45, no. 1, pp. 45–54.

Erlich, Mark, and Jeff Grabelsky. 2005. "Standing at a Crossroads: The Building Trades in the Twenty-First Century." *Labor History* Vol. 46, no. 4, pp. 421–45.

Fine, Janice. 2006. *Worker Centers: Organizing Communities at the Edge of the Dream*. Ithaca, NY: Cornell University Press.

General Accounting Office. 2002. *Worker Protection: Labor's Efforts to Enforce Protections for Day Laborers Could Benefit from Better Data and Guidance*. Washington, DC: General Accounting Office.

Gordon, Jennifer. 2005. *Suburban Sweatshops: The Fight for Immigrant Rights*. Cambridge, MA: The Belknap Press of Harvard University Press.

Jayaraman, Sarumathi, and Immanuel Ness, eds. 2005. *The New Urban Immigrant Workforce: Innovative Models for Labor Organizing*. Armonk, NY: M.E. Sharpe.

Mehta, Chirag, and Nik Theodore. 2006. "Workplace Safety in Atlanta's Construction Industry: Institutional Failure in Temporary Staffing Arrangements." *Working USA*, Vol. 9, no. 1, pp. 59–77.

Milkman, Ruth. 2006. *L.A. Story: Immigrant Workers and the Future of the U.S. Labor Movement*. New York: Russell Sage Foundation.

———. 2008. "Putting Wages Back into Competition: Deunionization and Degradation in Place-Bound Industries." In Annette Bernhardt, Heather Boushey, Laura Dresser, and Chris Tilly, eds., *The Gloves-off Economy: Workplace Standards at the Bottom of America's Labor Market*. Urbana-Champaign, IL: Labor and Employment Relations Association, pp. 65–89.

Narro, Victor. 2005/6. "Impacting Next Wave Organizing: Creative Campaign Strategies of the Los Angeles Worker Centers." *New York Law School Law Review*, Vol. 50, pp. 465–513.

Ness, Immanuel. 2005. *Immigrants, Unions, and the New U.S. Labor Market*. Philadelphia: Temple University Press.

Peck, Jamie. 1995. *Work-Place: The Social Regulation of Labor Markets*. New York: Guilford.

Peck, Jamie, and Nik Theodore. 2007. "Flexible Recession: The Temporary Staffing Industry and Mediated Work in the United States." *Cambridge Journal of Economics*, Vol. 31, no. 2, pp. 171–92.

Rubery, Jill, and Frank Wilkinson. 1981. "Outwork and Segmented Labour Markets." In Frank Wilkinson, ed., *The Dynamics of Labour Market Segmentation*. London: Academic Press, pp. 115–32.

Sassen, Saskia. 2002. "Deconstructing Labor Demand in Today's Advanced Economies: Implications for Low-Wage Employment." In Frank Munger, ed., *Laboring Below the Line: The New Ethnography of Poverty, Low-Wage Work, and Survival in the Global Economy*. New York: Russell Sage Foundation, pp. 73–94.

Sugimori, Amy. 2008. "State and Local Policy Models Promoting Immigrant Worker Justice." In Annette Bernhardt, Heather Boushey, Laura Dresser, and Chris Tilly, eds., *The Gloves-off Economy: Workplace Standards at the Bottom of America's Labor Market*. Urbana-Champaign, IL: Labor and Employment Relations Association, pp. 217–42.

Theodore, Nik. 2003. "Political Economies of Day Labour: Regulation and Restructuring of Chicago's Contingent Labour Markets." *Urban Studies*, Vol. 40, no. 9, pp. 1811–28.

―――. 2006. "Closed Borders, Open Markets: Immigrant Day Laborers' Struggle for Economic Rights." In Helga Leitner, Jamie Peck, and Eric S. Sheppard, eds., *Contesting Neoliberalism: Urban Frontiers*. New York: Guilford Press, pp. 250–65.

Theodore, Nik, Abel Valenzuela Jr., and Edwin Meléndez. 2006. "*La Esquina* (The Corner): Day Laborers on the Margins of New York's Formal Economy." *Working USA*, Vol. 9, no. 4, pp. 407–23.

―――. 2008. *Day Labor Worker Centers: New Approaches to Protecting Labor Standards in the Informal Economy*. Chicago: Center for Urban Economic Development, University of Illinois at Chicago.

Valenzuela, Abel Jr. 2002. "Working on the Margins in Metropolitan Los Angeles: Immigrants in Day Labor Work." *Migraciones Internacionales*, Vol. 1, pp. 5–28.

Valenzuela, Abel Jr., and Edwin Meléndez. 2003. *Day Labor in New York: Findings from the NYDL Survey*. Los Angeles and New York: Center for the Study of Urban Poverty, UCLA and Community Development Research Center, Milano Graduate School of Management and Urban Policy, New School University.

Walter, Nicholas, Philippe Bourgois, H. Margarita Loinaz, and Dean Schillinger. 2002. "Social Context of Work Injury among Undocumented Day Laborers in San Francisco." *Journal of General Internal Medicine*, Vol. 17, pp. 221–29.

Weil, David. 2005. "The Contemporary Industrial Relations System in Construction: Analysis, Observations and Speculations." *Labor History*, Vol. 46, no. 4, pp. 447–71.

Chapter 5

Cleaning and Caring in the Home: Shared Problems? Shared Possibilities?

Laura Dresser
University of Wisconsin, Madison

This paper focuses directly on some of the nation's most invisible workers: those who work each day to clean homes and care for the people in them. Whether providing hands-on health care and support for the frail, direct childcare for the young, or housekeeping services for the busy, these workers share more than a common worksite. Home-based cleaning and caring workers also earn exceedingly low wages, suffer generally weak labor standards, and hold jobs that remain some of the worst in our economy. In many ways, in-home work is a sector where the gloves of labor and job quality standards were never really put on.

Despite longstanding status as quintessential low-wage work, in the last 10 years, home-based cleaning and caring jobs have generated significant and inspiring innovations to improve job quality. Unionization of home health and family daycare has provided some of the labor movement's most significant membership increases in recent years, delivering substantial wage and benefits improvements for at least 300,000 workers. Co-op models have emerged for all types of in-home work, proving that better wages and working conditions are possible in home-based cleaning and caring jobs. And advocacy campaigns for childcare, domestic, and home health workers have increased awareness of these jobs and won significant policy victories to help promote the interests of the workers doing them.

However, despite the poor conditions and surprising innovation shared by these in-home workers, significant differences separate them as well, especially regarding strategies to improve the jobs. Probably the most important difference is who pays for the work. Private household workers who clean homes, cook meals, and/or take care of children are paid by the homeowners; home health workers who support and care for

TABLE 1
Occupations with a Substantial In-Home Workforce

	Inside the home	Outside the home
Childcare workers	Family childcare provider (in provider's home) Nanny, au pair, babysitter (in child's home)	Daycare workers and preschool teachers (in child daycare centers, preschool programs, etc.)
Hands-on health care	Home health aides and personal home care workers	Nursing aides, orderlies, attendants (in nursing homes, hospitals, etc.)
Maids and housekeepers	Domestics, maids, and housekeepers	Maids and housekeepers (in hotels, hospitals, etc.)

the frail, disabled, and elderly in their homes are often paid by federal medical assistance or other insurance programs; childcare providers who care for children in the employer's home generally work for more well-off families; and family childcare providers who give that care in their own homes are paid by parents (and sometimes, indirectly, by state subsidies) and care for children across the income spectrum. Strategies to improve the jobs, then, must connect to very different funding structures. Focusing instead on *the home as a worksite* illuminates both the real differences and the surprising similarities that these home-based workers share.

Throughout this paper, I discuss workers whose worksite is the home. Table 1 shows these key in-home occupations. To help draw a more complete picture of these jobs, the table compares key in-home occupations to more visible counterparts in out-of-home settings. In terms of childcare, this chapter focuses on workers who provide childcare in homes, either their own or that of the client. This universe includes nannies, au pairs, babysitters, and family daycare providers. While the most common mental image of a childcare worker may be of a teacher in a daycare center, nearly half of the national childcare workforce is actually home-based. The in-home workforce also includes home health workers providing hands-on care and support to the elderly, frail, or disabled, allowing them to live in their own homes. Home health covers both home health attendants (providing hands-on care for the old, the frail, and the disabled), and personal care workers (who assist with daily living, including getting up and dressed, laundry, cooking, and cleaning). In institutional settings (principally nursing homes and hospitals), hands-on health care is delivered by nursing aides, orderlies, and attendants. The hands-on home health care workforce comprises just under one third of the total frontline hands-on health care workforce. Finally, in-home workers also include housekeepers who work directly in homes as "maids" or "domestic workers" for private household employers. While "maids" and "housekeepers" are found in many sectors outside of homes, they are especially evident in hotels and other lodging places as well as hospitals. One third of all maids and housekeepers work in homes.

Explicitly excluded from the in-home workforce identified here are the many people who care and clean in the home without pay.[1] The large numbers of people doing in-home cleaning and caring work for "free" have direct and negative effects on wages and standards for workers in the paid sector. However, the focus in this chapter is directly on the workers who do this work for wages.

Grouping these disparate occupations makes clear a series of problems that define these in-home cleaning and caring jobs. First, in terms of work organization, work in the home is inherently isolated and intimate. The isolation and intimacy generate similar challenges for workers regardless of specific occupation. Further, work tasks are strikingly similar across some occupations (some personal care workers are doing exactly what a housekeeper does, but the titles differ because the type of client differs). While distinctions may seem clear, in fact the occupational lines (e.g., maids, health aides, childcare workers) and industrial lines (e.g., health care, private service, childcare) in these jobs can be quite difficult to discern; grouping helps make their similarities clear. Finally, across occupations the home-based workforce shares many demographic characteristics, and anecdotal evidence suggests that many workers move fluidly through these occupations and industries (Brooks 2005); grouping the occupations acknowledges that reality as well.

But when we turn to options for improving the jobs, differences between them reemerge as critical. The lessons generated by policy and program innovation in some occupations are impossible to extend to others. Funding source differences are especially relevant in trying to fund enhancement of job quality. Strategies to improve jobs in a private pay market will always differ from strategies where public dollars dominate, even if the work content is identical. So while it is clear that disparate in-home workers have much in common—from challenges of work organization to poor wages and benefits, to name just two, it is equally clear that there is no single silver bullet strategy to improve these jobs.

The next section of this chapter draws a more complete picture of in-home jobs, the wages and benefits they offer, and the women who hold them. I discuss the shared traits of in-home work and why those traits matter. Given that foundation, the subsequent sections explore key elements of strategies to improve in-home cleaning and caring jobs and the ways that the in-home subsectors differ, especially with regard to strategies for improving the jobs. The final section describes some strategies that have worked to improve in-home cleaning and caring jobs and the promise and limits of those strategies.

Getting a Handle on Work in the Home

The work of caring and cleaning in the home is as old as the home itself. The work is also inherently domestic—a maid doesn't face ruinous wage competition from Singapore—and immune to outsourcing. The jobs have not been fundamentally reorganized by technological change over the last 20 years. While globalized capital and technological change often shoulder the blame for poor labor standards, these jobs stand as a reminder that other forces are at work as well.

Why care about work in the home? These jobs are with us and, taken together, will grow in the foreseeable future. These jobs also consistently provide very low wages, volatile hours, and few, if any, benefits. Further, significant numbers of them are explicitly and effectively outside the basic labor protections that are the presumed framework for workers in this nation. The demographics and vulnerability of the workforce also encourage attention to in-home workers. Finally, many of these jobs provide badly needed service of great social value. Their social importance requires that we find ways to improve the jobs as well.

Size of the Workforce and Forces Behind Growth in Jobs

In-home jobs are notoriously invisible, and surveys almost certainly underreport the size of the total workforce, both because the work often verges toward "under the table" arrangements that individuals are less likely to report and because a major segment of the workforce—immigrants—is almost certainly underrepresented in national surveys (General Accounting Office 1998). Given this, it is reasonable to assume that the current American Community Survey count of 1.8 million in-home cleaning and caring workers almost certainly understates the total employment in these jobs.

Table 2 provides the 2005 employment breakdown for the key in-home occupations. The largest employment subsector is in-home health workers (both personal care workers and home health aides)—some 680,000 in 2005. These workers are found principally in the home health services industry, but a substantial number are in the private household services industry. Those who work in home health services are employed by agencies, while those in private households typically are hired directly by one or more clients. Home health aides generally deliver hands-on

TABLE 2
Employment, Wages, and Benefits of In-Home Workers, 2005

Occupation	Industry	No. of workers	Median wage (2005 $)	Employee health insurance (CPS; %)	Participation in pension (CPS; %)
Home health workers	Home health services	560,570	8.30	22.9	12.2
	Private household services	119,736	9.06	13.9	2.0
	Total home health	680,306	8.40	21.9	11.1
Childcare workers	Private household services	199,563	6.95	8.3	3.2
	Family childcare providers	449,652	5.79	8.5	4.3
	Total childcare	649,215	6.12	8.4	4.0
Maids and housekeepers	Private household services	426,614	8.49	4.8	1.3
Total in-home		1,756,135	7.75	13.2	6.4
National, all workers			14.95	54.8	46.4

Note: For tabulations on health care and pensions, only workers working more than half-time all year are included.
Source: Author's analysis. Number of workers and median wage from 2005 American Community Survey; health and pension benefits from March 2006 Current Population Survey.

health care: moving, bathing, dressing, and otherwise physically assisting clients. Personal care workers provide supportive services in the home: cooking, cleaning, and attending to clients' needs. These jobs will continue to post strong growth in the face of an aging U.S. population and increasing pressures to move more care work from nursing homes into homes and communities (Hecker 2006).

In 2005, another 649,000 workers provided childcare in homes, split across the child daycare and private household service industries. Childcare providers in private households include both those who "live in" with employers and those who live in their own homes but work in employers' private residences. In private households, childcare workers most often provide care for the child or children of a single family. Identifying in-home providers in the "child daycare" sector (which includes center-based care) is a bit more difficult. To do so, we select those child daycare providers who report being self-employed (excluding center- and preschool-based staff). These workers generally have children from more than one family in their own homes. Identified this way in the 2005 American Community Survey, we find some 450,000 family-based providers. Again, it is very likely that this substantially undercounts the family provider sector; some researchers estimate that as many as 650,000 individuals provide family childcare services (Burton et al. 2002).[2]

Finally, in 2005, some 427,000 maids and housekeepers cleaned, cooked, and provided other domestic maintenance for private households. The housekeepers in private households have a one-to-one relationship with at least one employer/homeowner, many workers having more employers. In-home cleaning is very often informal, and the workforce of maids and housekeepers in private household services is almost certainly underreported and undercounted.

Taken together, these in-home occupations are growing rapidly. The growth is driven largely by the strong trajectory of home health employment. According to the U.S. Bureau of Labor Statistics, health care support occupations are projected to grow dramatically over the next decade: Personal and home care aide employment is projected to grow by 41% by 2014; the base of home health aides will expand some 56%, making it *the fastest-growing occupation* in the economy (Hecker 2006). What's more, these two occupations are among those with the largest numerical job growth and are projected to add nearly 650,000 jobs to the economy by 2014 (Hecker 2006). Projected expansion results from the aging of the Baby Boom generation and the continuing move toward home-based rather than institutional care (preferred often for both cost and quality reasons). The childcare workforce is projected to grow by 38% between 2004 and 2014 (Smith and Baughman 2007).

One clear contributor to the growth in these jobs is the increasing labor force participation of women. Women have long done most of the caring, cooking, and cleaning for their own families, including their own parents as they aged. But as they work in the paid labor market, families turn to other women to do the tasks they once did. A second important contributor over the last 20 years may be growing income inequality in the nation. As Milkman, Reese, and Roth (1998:485) point out, inequality feeds home work both because it implies that there are a number of very poor individuals for whom work in the home will present the best option and because income at the top allows for increasing demand from rich households for domestic help: "The elite corps of professional and managerial women, whose ranks have expanded so dramatically in recent years, can now purchase on the market much of the labor of social reproduction traditionally relegated to them as wives and mothers." The continuing growth of inequality in the U.S. may fuel growth in these jobs. However, the modest declines of the domestic work sector may suggest that market alternatives (meals out, for example) are also part of the picture.

Low Job Quality

Poor job quality is indisputable for in-home workers: Wages are extremely low and benefits non-existent, and even basic labor standards do not effectively cover many of these workers. Table 2 summarizes wage and benefit data for the in-home workforce.

Workers cleaning and caring in the home earn some of the lowest wages in the economy. In 2005, the median wage for these 1.8 million workers was $7.60, just barely above the 10th percentile wage ($7.20 per hour; Mishel, Bernstein, and Allegretto 2007) and essentially half the national median ($14.60 per hour). Providing just over $15,000 in annual income (in the unlikely case where the job offers full-time year-round employment), these jobs can't keep a family of three out of poverty. These are exceedingly low wages, even within the low-wage labor market. And self-employed childcare workers are the worst off, reporting a median wage of just $5.68 per hour, a rate attesting to the long hours and low pay that childcare consistently delivers.

Such low wages combined with concerns about data quality and representativeness for this group may lead to some skepticism regarding these wages. However, comparison with wages in the same occupations in industries more "on the books" suggests that these reports are quite consistent. For example, the median hourly wage of maids and housekeepers in traveler accommodation is $7.82, slightly below but roughly in line with the $8.33 median for maids and housekeepers in private service. The in-home care workers actually face an "in-home" penalty: family providers earn roughly $2 less an hour than center-based childcare workers, and home health workers earn between $1 and $2 less than nursing home attendants and orderlies.

Low and chronically unstable hours combine with low wages to generate low income for the workforce. When clients leave town or don't want services, most workers, in all three occupations, simply don't work. The median worker gets some 30 or 35 hours of work per week, though family daycare providers work longer hours than any other group.

Few in-home workers receive health insurance from their employers; just 13% of in-home workers with half-time year-round work or more get health insurance, compared with 55% of the national workforce. Home health providers working for home health agencies have the highest access to employer health insurance; one in five workers reports having employer-provided health insurance. Just 8% of in-home childcare providers and less than 5% of private maids and domestics receive health insurance through their employers.

The pension picture is even grimmer, again even for the workers with year-round employment at least half time. Home health is again the strongest; just over one in 10 home health workers participates in an employer pension plan. The participation is lower among childcare workers (6%). Only 1% of private household maids and housekeepers participate in employer-provided pension plans. The benefits levels for these in-home workers are rock bottom. Paid vacation, holiday time, and sick leave are also rare (Families and Work Institute 2006).

Basic Labor Standards

The basic labor protections for these workers are also weak, for a number of reasons. First, labor laws contain explicit exemptions and exceptions that target specific in-home workers (Bernhardt, McGrath, and DeFilippis 2007). In-home workers in private household services, both those that clean and those that care for children, are explicitly excluded from coverage of many labor protections, including OSHA, and from the right to organize unions (Bernhardt, McGrath, and DeFilippis 2007; Domestic Workers United and DataCenter 2006). "Part-time babysitting" services are explicitly exempted from federal minimum wage and overtime law (Bernhardt, McGrath, and DeFilippis 2007). Likewise, minimum wage and overtime requirements of the Fair Labor Standards Act exclude some home health workers, an exclusion upheld in a June 2007 federal Supreme Court ruling.[3]

Labor regulation is also weak for some in-home workers who are truly independent contractors and for others who are misidentified as self-employed. Independent contractors have no standing for basic labor protections like minimum wage, overtime, workers' compensation (Bernhardt, McGrath, and DeFilippis 2007), and unemployment insurance (Shulman 2003). For an in-home worker to be an independent contractor she must be found to be running her own business. Determination of employment status is complex and decided case by case depending on the facts of the particular relationship. Factors to be considered vary depending on what law is being enforced; wage and hour laws have the broadest definition of who is a covered employee, and workers' compensation and some antidiscrimination laws have a narrower one. Thus, many family daycare providers are self-employed and run their own businesses. (The notable exception is family daycare providers working with children whose families receive public subsidies; rates and important working conditions for these care providers are determined by subsidy policy.) Some housekeeping workers may also be independent contractors, but only in cases where they have substantial control over the terms of their work (with rate schedules, their own equipment, and multiple clients). Finally, some states have established home care systems that define home health workers as independent contractors as well. Such definition is contentious, as home health workers are not running their own businesses and do not control the terms of their work. Though they are misidentified as independent contractors, the effect of the definition is to exclude home health workers from basic labor protection. (Many of the successful strategies to improve in-home work hinge on the definition of the employer; these strategies are discussed later in greater detail.)

But perhaps most important, the *effective* protection of these workers is even weaker than the formal legal protection. In part this is due to the invisible, informal, and "under the table" nature of these jobs. Formal labor protections mean very little for workers who are working off the books, because successful enforcement of these protections depends on workers' willingness to come forward to complain with evidence of the mistreatment. In this context, the rights of workers and the responsibilities of employers are routinely ignored, if they are even understood. And while financial advantages can accrue to both employer and employee if the work stays "off the books," the informality of the work relationship makes it ripe for neglect, evasion, and violation of basic labor standards.

Demographics of the Workforce

Table 3 makes it clear that these jobs are fundamentally women's jobs: 95% of the workforce is female. The childcare workforce is slightly more feminized, the home health workforce slightly less, but no occupational group falls below 90% female.

Further, these jobs are also dominated by women of color and immigrants. Though Latinos/as make up 13% of the national workforce, they comprise more than 50% of maids and housekeepers. And while blacks make up 11% of the national workforce, fully 3 in 10 home health workers are black. Noncitizens make up just 9% of the national labor force, yet 45% of in-home maids and domestics are noncitizens. In the overall in-home workforce, more than 25% are Hispanic; another 17% black; and fully 20% noncitizens.

Finally, more than 25% of the workers who hold these jobs have not completed high school degrees. This is more than double the national share for working people. Ironically, childcare workers have both the highest educational attainment *and* the lowest wages for any of these in-home occupations.

TABLE 3
Demographics of In-Home Workers, 2005

Occupation	Industry	Female (%)	Hispanic (%)	Black (%)	Noncitizen %	High school degree or more (%)
Home health workers	Home health services	92.2	19.1	30.0	13.6	74.4
	Private household services	90.0	16.8	20.5	16.7	76.2
	Total home health	91.8	18.7	23.0	14.1	74.8
Childcare workers	Private household services	96.1	21.3	7.5	20.8	80.3
	Family childcare providers	97.4	20.0	15.3	13.4	82.5
	Total childcare	97.0	20.4	12.9	15.7	81.8
Maids and housekeepers	Private household services	95.0	52.1	6.5	45.5	58.2
Total in-home		94.5	27.4	17.3	22.3	73.3
National, all workers		47.1	13.5	11.0	9.0	88.6

Source: Author's analysis, 2005 American Community Survey.

High Social Value

In spite of miserable pay and benefits, much of the work that goes on inside homes has a very high personal and social value. This is obvious across the range of care work that happens in the home. Indeed, work in the home may conjure up the image of the maid working for a very rich family in urban America, and while that is an important part of the picture, in fact many of these workers are working directly with children and adults who need support and care to develop and maintain independence. Many are providing a critical social service. Their jobs deserve attention because of the high value of the service they provide, even in the context of very low rewards for it.

Shared Traits of In-Home Work

There are at least three defining features of in-home work: the work is inherently isolated and autonomous; the work is inherently intimate; and the work is socially perceived as inherently "women's" work, and often the provenance of women of color with few alternatives.

In the Home = Isolated/Autonomous

Work in the home is inherently isolated and autonomous, and much of both the good and the bad of this work finds its roots in that truth. For many of these workers, the isolation is evident before a job is secured, as the negotiation and agreement on the terms of work require a one-to-one deal with the employer. Indeed, for many of these workers, each new negotiation basically starts from scratch. From the time a job connection is established, working in the home is essentially a solitary endeavor. If co-workers or supervisors exist at all, they are remote. There is no "water cooler," or the relationship building and problem solving that can happen at a more standard worksite. There is no natural community for support, for checking on what's reasonable, for seeing a pattern of problems. Perhaps more important, there is no one there to observe the situation and defend the worker if a client accuses her of something, makes unreasonable demands, or treats her unacceptably. These women workers, many without the resources provided by years of education or native facility with English, face their employer one-on-one, and the employer can have a very strong hand.

But for many workers, "isolation" is also "independence and autonomy." Many in-home workers prefer the autonomy and self-reliance of individual work. There are no co-workers to slow you down, no supervisor to stare over your shoulder, no one to second-guess your decisions or approaches. And there's no office gossip or in-fighting. Home health workers with prior experience in nursing homes state a preference for the autonomy and relationships they can build in home health settings (Dresser, Lange, and Sirkus 1999). Within broad parameters, they can decide what order to do tasks in, stay a bit longer, or provide extra service. Indeed, a 1999 study in the area around Dane County, Wisconsin, documented lower rates of both pay and turnover in home health compared to nursing homes (Dresser, Lange, and Sirkus 1999). Clearly, for some, autonomy and independence in home health more than made up for the lower wages.

Some domestic workers appreciate autonomy in terms of controlling their own schedules and being able to bring their children to the job site (very hard to do at a traditional worksite; Romero 1992). There may be more space for negotiation between employer and employee in domestic work because of its one-on-one character, leading, at times, to flexibility for the workers.

While all these jobs are isolated in ways, there is substantial variation in the isolation. At one extreme is the domestic worker or nanny who actually lives with the client family. These "live-in" workers quite literally cannot escape work when they sleep. Their jobs can be extremely stressful; interview and survey evidence from New York City makes it clear that they can be the worst jobs in the industry (Domestic Workers United and DataCenter 2006). This level of isolation, especially for workers with little English and no connections outside of the client family, can lead to abuse of the worker and violation of basic labor and human rights.[4]

As this example suggests, one factor that reduces worker isolation is having multiple clients. Such a structure provides a more diverse base of demand and allows the worker to check standards in one situation against another. Multiple employers also minimize the financial impact of a loss of a client and income. But multiple clients can also come with heavy costs. Scheduling, transportation, and other logistical issues are often stressful and costly. (See Dawson and Surpin 2001 for discussion of these issues in home health work.)

Workers employed by a third-party agency or assigned by a "broker" or "matching" service may be (but are not necessarily) less isolated as well. They may get training, assignments, and supervision from a central source. But this connection can often be quite weak, with the worker never hearing from the agency unless the schedule changes. And, in fact, written assignments or job descriptions are often disregarded once the worker is engaged with a client.

In the Home = Intimate

In-home work is also inherently intimate, as the lines between workplace and the private are consistently crossed. This is especially true for the workers who enter their clients' homes. Whether the worker is cleaning or providing care or support, she is often presumed to be or treated as "a part of the family." The workers develop a deep store of information about clients' lives; many develop strong affection for their clients.

Like isolation, intimacy is a double-edged sword. For many care and support providers, the relationship to the client is a critical element of job quality. Workers, especially those providing direct care to the old or young, develop strong connections to their clients. The bond makes the work rewarding, and the quality of care received can be higher when relationships are stronger.

Even so, intimacy raises many problems for workers. Being "part of the family" can be both fulfilling and demeaning. First, while the worker may be a "part" of many client families, she is a more central part of her own family. The expectations and presumptions of clients can often creep and expand, leaving the worker hard pressed to draw a boundary (Domestic Workers United and DataCenter 2006). Exact distinctions about what should and should not be included in the work are hard to discern and difficult to navigate. While a home health aide may know that she is not supposed to do laundry, saying no to a frail client can be very difficult, especially when the bond between client and care provider is strong. Family childcare providers can find it nearly impossible to refuse care to a child when parents have no money to pay for the care.

Again, while this work is all intimate, some is substantially more so. In general the more hours with a single client, the more intimate the relationship. Live-in domestic workers are clearly inextricably connected to the client family, as are full-time workers with just one client. But even less-intensive hours with a family can create deep intimacy. Caring for a frail or dying person, even just a few hours a day, may be the most deeply intimate work, requiring the client, the client's family, and the care provider to develop a strong relationship of trust. Caring for children also brings up intimate and essential issues about the family's priorities for child rearing. Housekeeping comes with an intimacy of knowledge of the client's private life (from phone calls to underwear), but in general the work does not require the emotional connection and investment that the provision of good care generally requires. And housekeeping for multiple clients (rather than one) is clearly less intimate than cleaning only for one.

For many workers, the fact that this work is autonomous and intimate is one of its rewards. But the isolation and the intimacy can also lead to higher levels of exploitation and instability in the jobs.

In the Home = "Women's Work" and Work Done by Women of Color

These jobs also share a legacy of low status. In part, this has to do with the fact that women, usually mothers, have always done this work, and done it for free. Care work within the home is not seen as "real work" and therefore is not paid as such. Sexism and the consistently low social value placed on women's work is clearly a core issue in wage setting. Indeed, it is hard to drive up the wage for workers who have such an active "free" alternative.

Additionally, and equally important and clear from the demographic data, this work, when paid, has been systematically and predominantly the domain of women of color and immigrants (Rollins 1985). In the 20th century, domestic work was a key occupation of black women in the U.S. North and South: In 1940, 60% of employed black women worked in domestic service. Today, domestic work is dominated by Hispanics and other immigrant women: More than half of maids and housekeepers in private household services are Hispanic. Blacks are dramatically over-represented in home health jobs. Like sexism, discrimination against people of color has also fundamentally structured the presumed value of and rewards offered for this work.

Discrimination pushes wages down twice here. First, the work is considered to be of very low worth and is paid as such. Second, the women workers who hold the jobs—women of color and immigrants—have fewer opportunities outside these in-home jobs. Anecdotally, at least, when women can get out of these jobs (either because they have a better grasp of English or a better understanding of external options) many of them do so (see, for example, Gordon 2005). As with day labor for many new male immigrants, women immigrants often try to move out of in-home work in order to get into better pay and/or working conditions.

Why These Shared Traits Matter

Though the in-home workforce is often divided along industrial and occupational lines, the characteristics identified here apply to all of them. Another way to note just how much these workers share is to think a bit harder about what really is the difference between the work of a "maid/domestic" (in private household services) and a "personal care worker" (in home health). The federal definition of both jobs includes cleaning the home, laundry, cooking, and shopping for food. In private household services, most (but certainly not all) workers are paid with private dollars, whereas in home health many workers are paid through public or private insurance. And the home health worker is always working with someone who is frail or needy in some way, and the domestic may not be. But these concerns of pay and or client base don't change the fact that the actual content of the work can be very similar. We know also that these jobs can shift across occupations: A worker is hired to do childcare and then discovers she is expected also to clean and do laundry; a home health aide is approached by the family to do a few hours of cleaning and cooking to assist the client; a full-time domestic worker works with a family over the years, shifting from childcare to cleaning to elder care. The divisions between these jobs aren't always easy to establish. Workers themselves report moving across the occupations in a California study of home health workers that found that many in-home workers had "always worked in caring professions" such as home care, childcare, and housecleaning (Howes et al. 2002:3–4).

The shared traits of isolated, intimate, and undervalued work go a long way toward explaining why these jobs can be extremely hard to improve. Extremely low wages and poor job quality invariably lead to high turnover. Indeed, childcare and home health are riddled with high turnover (Smith and Baughman 2007), and, at least anecdotally, domestic work is as well. The workforce has only weak professional identity; the worker may identify more with her client than with other in-home workers. And worksites are not only isolated but also widely dispersed. Collective action to improve wages of in-home work requires building collective identity, but several factors stand directly in the way of building collective voice: extremely small work units (most often a unit of one), very low social value and little professional identity, and high turnover.

Strategies for Improving In-Home Work

Any successful strategy to improve in-home job quality will necessarily have two elements. First, the solution will bring a set of workers together and build some collective sense and awareness among them. Second, those workers will need to identify some source of money or other resources to raise the standard in the job. In some ways, improving in-home work is both as straightforward and as difficult as that.

Collective action requires a collective identity for workers. The very isolation of the workers pushes squarely against collective identity. But it is only in conversation and connection with others that these in-home workers can begin to understand their own situation in the larger context. Further, given their often strong connection to clients, in-home workers need some collective connection both to remind them that their project is not only about their own position and to help them think more broadly about how improving the conditions of their work could actually improve their service to the client. Collective action can also make visible this otherwise socially invisible work and force the issues of value and wages into public discourse. Without collective action, the work is too easily discussed in terms of (often positive) anecdotal experience rather than collective reality. But building some collective framework only begs the question of money.

The second obvious and necessary ingredient is finding some money. The low social value of the work, and the relatively weaker external opportunities for many of the workers who do it, mean that the collective consciousness needs to be directed at raising wages—and that takes money. But a central problem here, especially in family childcare and home health care, is that many clients simply cannot pay more for the services they receive. So the search for money does not always end with the client, it can extend beyond, to the public sector, especially when attention can be drawn to the connection between the quality of the care provided and the quality of the job.

Important Differences in These Occupations

From low job quality to work in isolation, in-home jobs share many fundamental characteristics, regardless of industry and occupation. Even key steps to improve in-home jobs are similar. But focusing on the means of taking those steps—how to create a collective organization or voice and where to find the money—reveals very real differences that separate these in-home workers.

In-home jobs cannot be improved without finding more money to improve them. Because the fundamental issue to improving the jobs is money, probably the most salient strategy to create a collective identity is carefully targeting the employer in it. Though obviously a straightforward question—who is the employer?—in fact, for many in-home workers the very simple first step of trying to identify the employer may be one of the most confounding. For housekeepers and maids with a single client, the employer is unambiguous. For home health workers with one client who are paid privately and childcare workers who work for one family, the same is true. For maids and housekeepers, private health care, and childcare workers with multiple clients, however, there is no single employer. In these situations, the employers actually far outnumber the workers. Further, family daycare providers are certainly self-employed, and some maids and housekeepers (with substantial control over the terms of their work) are also self-employed.

Once public money enters the system, however, even these answers on exactly who the employer is become yet more complex. In the case of home health work, much of the money coming into the system is, in fact, public money: The majority of financing of long-term care comes from Medicaid and Medicare (see Dawson and Surpin 2001 for 1998 data). In some localities, the client is able to select and hire the care worker, while the state or local unit of government directs Medicaid and/or Medicare money to the care worker. In some instances, the payment for work goes directly from the state to the care worker; in others the client receives and redirects the money to the care worker (Boris and Klein 2006). Other insurance providers may also work this way, providing payment while still allowing consumer choice in hiring. Given the very heavy public investment in home health care, these workers have the most to gain from finding ways to identify the public sector as their employer.

There is public money in childcare, but not as much as in home health, and the money follows an indirect route to childcare providers.

Public subsidies to childcare are extended to specific low-income work-ing parents; the government covers some or all of the cost of care while the parent has the ability to choose the desired childcare arrangement (Child Care Bureau 2006). A family daycare provider with five or six children in her care may or may not have publicly subsidized children in her client base. And many family providers will see the number of children with subsidies shift dramatically over time, not only because their client base shifts but also because family eligibility for subsidies (or willingness to put up with the bureaucratic system of getting those subsidies) will change over time as well. That means that family providers, clearly self-employed, may have a partial relationship with public funds, but also that the depth of the reliance on state subsidies can be low and quite variable.

Family providers and other self-employed in-home workers also face an antitrust barrier to their collective action. Federal and state antitrust laws actually prohibit family childcare providers, as providers of services in a competitive market, from meeting to discuss rates. Such a prohibi-tion extends to any set of self-employed or small-business owners who meet to discuss and raise rates. So not only family childcare providers but also housekeepers with multiple clients are actually prohibited from taking the first step identified for raising rates, which is to create and build a collective organization and agenda.

Public money is one measure of public commitment to these in-home jobs, and the variation in public money in the different jobs is extreme. Another important question when it comes to creating identity and leveraging money is related but distinct: Is there a significant public good being produced by the in-home workers? Home health workers have a strong positive argument here. The shift from institutional to home-based care for the frail and elderly over the last generation has clearly promoted better health and well-being for clients, while saving the state money in medical assistance budgets. The home health workers who make such a shift possible are the point at which these larger public medical systems touch the client, and the quality of the care provided is directly and clearly related to the quality of jobs the system supports. Finding more money for these home health workers, whether employed through agencies or as independent contractors, hinges not only on find-ing the public money already in the system but also on making argu-ments and coalitions around the public good that the workers produce.

As I have noted, the actual public money flowing to family childcare providers is significantly more constrained. But the argument for the public good they provide is equally strong. The system of early child-hood education and care in the U.S. is nearly entirely privatized in the first four years of life and then shifts dramatically onto the public sector when children head to kindergarten. The public interest in children doesn't simply begin on the first day of kindergarten, however. Indeed, the quality of care and education leading up to their first day in school has very direct effects on how well they can do in schools and how intensively schools need to deal with them. The ever-expanding number of states committed to universal four-year-old kindergarten is just one testament to the strength of the public-good argument and its political salience. When childcare providers, in homes and in centers, make clear their contribution to the public good through quality care, they begin to build the coalitions and political will that make finding money possible.

The in-home workers with some of the strongest strategies for job improvement are those who can identify public money and public good to support the demands. In-home workers in private markets, working directly for one or multiple clients, are in a much more difficult but not impossible space. Strategies on the purely private side of the market still require stronger collective voice and finding money for building better jobs. But the money in these instances is with the employer/householder base, and the movement needs to build not only regulatory but also social infrastructure. Putting regulations on the books for a market that is, in many ways, largely off the books cannot change the industry without an accompanying broad and strong social movement.

What Has Worked to Improve In-Home Work?

In-home jobs have been "bad" jobs for a very long time in the U.S. But new thinking in the last 20 years about how to organize and improve these jobs has begun to produce meaningful results. Unions, co-ops, and legal and advocacy campaigns have all found ways to take on the project of improving these jobs.

Unions and Public Authority Strategies

The development of the public authority model is the most influential innovation in in-home work. The roots of the model go back to the 1980s, when SEIU (Service Employees International Union) was first trying to organize home health workers in California's home care program. In 1987, the court found that neither the state nor the county was an "employer" for the home care workers. At that point, SEIU began pursuing a legislative and advocacy strategy to establish a public authority to serve as "employer of record" for purposes of bargaining. The county-based public authorities finally redefined the home health providers as workers and established a legal employment relationship between the county and them. As Boris and Klein (2006:84) point out in their review of these strategies, "[t]he public authority, which made the local or state government into an employer to bargain with, became the mechanism to end the fiction of the home care worker as independent contractor and cut through obfuscations stemming from home care's place within the welfare state."

The public authority model in home health has had some dramatic successes (see Schneider 2003 for a very accessible summary). Most famously, in 1999, 74,000 home care workers joined SEIU in Los Angeles, the largest union organizing victory since the 1940s. The model in California has spread to nearly all counties in the state. Oregon and Washington also have public authorities, and all together at least 300,000 workers on the Pacific Coast are now union members and employees of public authorities. Wage and benefits gains for many (but not all) of these home health workers have been substantial. Home care workers have also gained the right to organize also in Illinois, Michigan, Massachusetts, and New York.

These public authority strategies leverage both the public dollars in home health and the public good produced by it. Labor has played a leading role in developing the model, but it has been joint work with consumer advocates that has made the progress possible. In the public authority states, consumer and worker advocates have joined together because of the strong links between job and care quality. Their common interest in decent standards for the jobs and their influence on public policy has secured a new model in this previously invisible sector of work.

The public authority model has been adapted now to family daycare providers, though the logic shifts slightly. As competitors in the market providing daycare services, family daycare providers are prohibited from meeting to discuss and establish rates. In most states, the process starts with an executive order, issued by the governor, that allows providers to organize and negotiate with the state on a specific set of issues. These executive orders allow the family daycare providers to work together in a union, but they do not establish the state as an employer of record as in home health. Indeed, the orders always explicitly state that family providers are not employees of the state (Chalfie, Blank, and Entmacher 2007).

Illinois is the leader in the family childcare public authority. In Illinois, a union of all 49,000 family daycare providers that receive (via parents) subsidies from the state negotiates with the state over reimbursement rates, health benefits, and administrative policy. The negotiations have led to substantial increases in subsidy rates, the development of a health insurance option, and formalization of grievance procedures. Similarly, family childcare providers in Washington State are organized and have negotiated with the state over the same sorts of issues. Organizing in this model is also ongoing in Oregon, Iowa, New Jersey, New York and Michigan, where governors have all signed executive orders (or, in Michigan, an "interlocal agreement") that have started the organizing and bargaining processes (Chalfie, Blank, and Entmacher 2007).

Public authority strategies have been truly powerful for promoting the interests of in-home care workers, but they have run into multiple and sometimes surprising road blocks. Indeed, spreading the model within California to in-home workers who assist the independent living of the developmentally disabled has been extremely slow-going because the independent contractor model is not as prevalent in that sector in California. Public authority strategies work best where in-home health care work is all arranged through independent contracting. In many states, however, agencies hire home health workers to provide in-home care. If work is organized through agencies, then there is no need for a public authority to serve as the employer of record; the agency already holds the title. The public authority model also requires political support from a strong labor and consumer coalition. In some states, that coalition may not have sufficient leverage to secure the executive orders and/or legislation required to get the process going.

Worker Cooperatives

As SEIU was developing the public authority strategy in Illinois and California, another project to improve home health jobs was established in the Bronx. Cooperative Home Care Associates (CHCA) was established as part of a community-based economic development program to create jobs through worker-owned firms. Since its genesis in 1985, CHCA has grown in both scale and advocacy ambition. The organization "anchors a national cooperative network generating over $60 million annually in revenue and creating quality jobs for over 1,600 individuals" (Cooperative Home Care Associates 2007). Worker cooperatives have proved that better jobs can be economically viable in other parts of in-home work as well. Philadelphia has Childspace Cooperative Development, Inc. (CCDI), which works with its affiliated worker-owned childcare centers and pursues advocacy for stronger job quality in childcare.[5] Domestic worker cooperatives have been established in California and Long Island. In rural Wisconsin, a worker-owned home care cooperative has improved quality of care and the quality of jobs (Bau 2006).

These enterprises alone do not approach the scale of impact that the public authority models do. But they are critical in at least three ways. First, the very existence of an in-home business with different priorities and higher-quality jobs proves that a different way of designing and

rewarding in-home jobs is possible. Second, and probably more important, these co-ops, especially CHCA and CCDI, have entered directly
into advocacy and policy making, bringing the voice and needs of workers more centrally into debates on job quality in their industries. Third,
in their advocacy, the care-focused co-ops have continued to help build
the consumer–worker coalitions that better jobs require.

Alone, worker co-ops cannot transform the quality of jobs in in-home
work. This is due, in part, to the vagaries of the competition that co-ops
face. Like other businesses, some worker co-ops will thrive while others
fail. The Day Care Justice Co-op in Rhode Island faded away as foundation and state budget support dried up (Roder and Seavey 2006). If the
business is competitive, then it can stand as a model for a new way to
treat in-home workers. But even then, proving that a competitive higher
wage and a more worker-focused model are possible does not mean that
others will follow suit. Some may, but many will continue with business
as usual. That is why systemic advocacy in these industries is important
in addition to the demonstration projects that co-ops provide.

Advocacy Campaigns

Bringing workers together around an agenda of job improvement is
another approach to improving the jobs. The advocacy must capture
public attention and make issues of compensation explicit. Most public
authority campaigns start out with a labor–consumer coalition and advocacy agenda, before they secure the changes needed to build the public
authority model. But many coalitions have been formed around a more
general agenda of job quality and have pursued other strategies as well.

Domestic workers in Long Island, New York, pursued an advocacy
campaign to change the behavior of the placement firms through which
many domestics and clients are connected (Gordon 2005). Placement
firms agreed to provide domestics with a detailed description of their
rights in their jobs and to provide both domestics and clients with a written job description including wages. These changes were important
innovations, both to prove to the domestic workers that they could
secure changes through organizing and to provide better information on
jobs to domestics. However, as Gordon points out, this policy was insufficient to really change the domestic's experience on the job; after the
placement agency makes a connection, it steps out of the picture, and at
that point the job description and statement of rights can be easily over-
looked by clients.

A key next step in advocacy for domestic workers has been the work
in New York to pass a "domestic workers' bill of rights." (See Sugimori in
this volume for a description of the bill and campaign.) It is clear that

such a campaign needs to promote both a legislative and social agenda. Given that the substantial majority of these jobs are held off the books, a purely legislative strategy to secure formal rights is insufficient. Only in the context of a broad social movement of domestic workers themselves, and their mutual commitment to upholding stronger labor standards in the private domestic market, can such regulations gain the foothold they need to reform the structure of jobs and pay.

Conclusion

The in-home work of home health workers, childcare workers, and maids and housekeepers shares many fundamental characteristics. In-home workers earn exceedingly low wages, face volatile hours, rarely receive benefits, and are often effectively or explicitly excluded from basic labor protections. Further, the home *as a worksite* creates similar problems for these diverse workers. Their work is isolated, making it difficult, even impossible, to determine functional norms and standards for the work. The work is intimate, often building strong bonds between worker and employer but few connections to other workers. The work is dominated by women of color and immigrants, with fewer external options and less knowledge of their own rights and standing in the American labor market. Finally, and given these problems, the strategies to improve any of these jobs require development of collective identity and money to support the wage and benefit increases that would make such jobs family-supporting. Though the workers are diverse in occupation, the shared problems of the in-home cleaning and caring workforce are striking.

Turning to the question of shared possibilities for improving jobs, however, restores some complexity to the picture of in-home work. Success in unionizing home health workers illustrates this most clearly: Creating a public authority to serve as employer of record moves the workforce, en masse, from independent contractor to worker status. Negotiations with the state over rates and benefits then lift the wages for these in-home workers. The strategy, requiring the aggregation of workers and negotiations with the state, has been successful only when strong coalitions around the quality of care have also supported the change. Essentially, the success in home health care, and in family childcare as well, has hinged on both the public authority model to aggregate the workforce and the public-good argument about the importance of improving the quality of jobs in order to improve the quality of care. This strategy has led to the development of more significant and systematic approaches to improving the jobs.

On the private-pay side of the in-home workforce, the public-dollars and public-good arguments evaporate, and the prospects for systematically changing the structure of the industry diminish. Changing private-pay in-home jobs requires both sweeping regulatory change and, perhaps more important and difficult, the development of a broad understanding and support of those regulations on the part of both private householders and the in-home workers they employ. With the jobs so consistently off the books, with arrangements made generally one-to-one with workers who often have little understanding of American labor market standards and few options outside of in-home work, regulatory changes are a necessary but insufficient first step to improving jobs. The second step is to develop the sort of collective voice and solidarity on the workforce side, and the social awareness among the public and employers, that would make stronger regulations enforceable.

For all in-home workers, the shared lesson is clear. These jobs will not be improved without increasing collective identity and finding the money (in private or public pockets) to substantially improve wages and benefits. And in spite of the isolation of these workers across the country, in-home cleaning and caring workers are building the awareness, the coalitions, and the policy models that can do just that.

Acknowledgments

Thanks to Annette Bernhardt for discussions and detailed comments on drafts, to Adrienne Pagac for research assistance, and to Adam Slez for data work. Thanks also to Heather Boushey, Ruth Milkman, Chris Tilly, and Wade Rathke for comments and suggestions on previous drafts of the paper.

Endnotes

[1] I also exclude those who run businesses or have home offices or otherwise work on external projects inside the home.

[2] Burton et al. (2002:8–9) note the "available data sources and estimates . . . of the U.S. childcare workforce [are] . . . unreliable," particularly for home-based childcare workers, for a few reasons. The Department of Labor does not track self-employed workers and therefore does not include home-based providers in its surveys or data. Though the national census does track the self-employed through its Current Population Survey, it is highly likely that family childcare providers are undercounted as a result of respondents' failure to disclose their occupation.

[3] *Long Island Care at Home, Ltd.* v. *Coke*, No. 06-593, 127 S. Ct. 2339, decided 06/11/07. Note also that coverage under state laws varies, but some states do provide minimum wage and overtime for domestic workers. The National Employment Law Project actively monitors state-level policies on this issue.

[4] Indeed, the most extreme "live-in" cases are actually victims of human trafficking. For example, The Break the Chain Campaign of Washington, DC, a coalition of more than two dozen organizations that litigates, proposes legislation, and negotiates with the U.S. and other foreign governments on behalf of domestic workers, details the recent cases of such abuse it has worked with on its website

(http://www.ips-dc.org/campaign/stories.htm). For other examples of human rights violations in domestic work, see Zarembka (2002).

[5] To learn more about Childspace Cooperative Development, Inc., go to http://www.childspacecdi.org/about.cfm [October 22, 2007].

References

Bau, Margaret. 2006. "Wisconsin Leads the Way in Caregiving Co-ops." <http://www.agri-view.com/articles/2006/12/28/capitol_news/producer01.txt>. [October 22, 2007].

Bernhardt, Annette, Siobhan McGrath, and James DeFilippis. 2007. "Unregulated Work in the Global City: Employment and Labor Law Violations in New York City." *Brennan Center for Justice Report.* New York, NY: Brennan Center for Justice, pp. 1–116.

Boris, Eileen, and Jennifer Klein. 2006. "Organizing Home Care: Low-Waged Workers in the Welfare State." *Politics and Society,* Vol. 34, no. 1 (March), pp. 81–107.

Brooks, Fred P. 2005. "New Turf for Organizing: Family Child Care Providers." *Labor Studies Journal,* Vol. 29, no. 4 (Winter), pp. 45–64. <http://muse.jhu.edu/journals/labor_studies_journal/toc/lab29.4.html>. [February 23, 2007].

Burton, Alice, Marcy Whitebook, Marci Young, Dan Bellm, Claudia Wayne, Richard M. Brandon, and Erin Maher. 2002. "Estimating the Size and Components of the U.S. Child Care Workforce and Caregiving Population." Center for the Child Care Workforce, pp.1–46. <http://www.ccw.org/pubs/workforceestimatereport.pdf>. [September 13, 2007].

Chalfie, Deborah, Helen Blank, and Joan Entmacher. 2007. "Getting Organized: Unionizing Home-Based Child Care Providers." National Women's Law Center, pp. 1–35. <http://www.nwlc.org/pdf/GettingOrganized2007.pdf>. [August 12, 2007].

Child Care Bureau. 2006. "Child Care and Development Fund Fact Sheet." *U.S. Department of Health and Human Services—Administration for Children and Families.* October 2006. <http://www.acf.hhs.gov/programs/ccb/ccdf/factsheet.htm>. [September 13, 2007].

Cooperative Home Care Associates. 2007. *About Us.* <http://www.chcany.org/index-1.html>. [October 22, 2007].

Dawson, Steven L., and Rick Surpin. 2001. *Direct-Care Health Workers: The Unnecessary Crisis in Long-Term Care.* The Aspen Institute, pp. 1–33. <http://www.paraprofessional.org/publications/Aspen.pdf>. [September 13, 2007].

Domestic Workers United and DataCenter. 2006. *Home is Where the Work Is: Inside New York's Domestic Work Industry.* July 14, pp. 1–42. <http://www.domesticworkersunited.org/homeiswheretheworkis.pdf>. [April 2, 2007].

Dresser, Laura, Dori Lange, and Alison Sirkus. 1999. *Improving Retention of Frontline Caregivers in Dane County.* Center on Wisconsin Strategy, pp. 1–31. <http://www.cows.org/pdf/rp-jwf-retent.pdf>. [September 13, 2007].

Families and Work Institute. 2006. "What Do We Know About Entry-Level, Hourly Employees?" *Supporting Entry-Level, Hourly Employees—Research Brief No. 1.* pp. 1–8. <http://familiesandwork.org/site/research/reports/brief1.pdf>. [September 12, 2007].

General Accounting Office. 1998. *Immigration Statistics: Information Gaps, Quality Issues Limit Utility of Federal Data to Policymakers: Report to Congressional Requesters.* Washington, DC: General Accounting Office.

Gordon, Jennifer. 2005. *Suburban Sweatshops: The Fight for Immigrant Rights.*
Cambridge, MA: Belknap Press of Harvard University Press.
Hecker, Daniel E. 2006. "Occupational Employment Projections to 2014." *Monthly
Labor Review.* U.S. Department of Labor, Bureau of Labor Statistics, pp.
70–101 <http://www.bls.gov/opub/mlr/2005/11/art5full.pdf>. [May 29, 2007].
Howes, Candace, Howard Greenwich, Lea Grundy, and Laura Reif. 2002. "Struggling
to Provide: A Portrait of Alameda County Homecare." East Bay Alliance for a
Sustainable Economy (EBASE) and Center for Labor Research and Education
(CLRE), pp. 1–13. <http://laborcenter.berkeley.edu/homecare/homecare.pdf>.
[September 13, 2007].
Long Island Care at Home, Ltd. v. *Coke.* 2007. 127 S. Ct. 2339.
Milkman, Ruth, Ellen Reese, and Benita Roth. 1998. "The Macrosociology of Paid
Domestic Labor." *Work and Occupations*, Vol. 25, no. 4 (November),
pp. 483–510.
Mishel, Lawrence, Jared Bernstein, and Sylvia Allegretto. 2007. "Table 3.4: Wages for
All Workers by Wage Percentile, 1973–2005 (2005 Dollars)." *The State of
Working America 2006/2007.* Ithaca, NY: ILR Press.
Roder, Anne, and Dorie Seavey. 2006. "Investing in Low-Wage Workers: Lessons from
Family Child Care in Rhode Island." *Public/Private Ventures*, pp. 1–48.
<http://www.ppv.org/ppv/publications/assets/206_publication.pdf>. [May 5, 2007].
Rollins, Judith. 1985. *Between Women: Domestics and Their Employers.* Philadelphia:
Temple University Press.
Romero, Mary. 1992. "Women's Work Is Never Done." *Maid in the U.S.A.* New York:
Routledge, Chapman and Hall.
Schneider, Stu. 2003. "Victories for Home Health Care Workers." *Dollars & Sense*
(September/October), pp. 25–27. <http://www.paraprofessional.org/
publications/Victories_for_home_health_care_workers.pdf>. [October 12, 2007].
Shulman, Beth. 2003. *The Betrayal of Work: How Low-Wage Jobs Fail 30 Million
Americans.* New York: New Press.
Smith, Kristin, and Reagan Baughman. 2007. "Low Wages Prevalent in Direct Care
and Child Care Workforce." *Carsey Institute Policy Brief No. 7* (Summer),
pp. 1–12. <http://carseyinstitute.unh.edu/documents/PB_caregivers.pdf>.
[September 12, 2007].
Zarembka, Joy M. 2002. "America's Dirty Work: Migrant Maids and Modern-Day
Slavery." In Barbara Ehrenreich and Arlie Russell Hochschild, eds., *Global
Woman: Nannies, Maids, and Sex Workers in the New Economy.* New York: Met-
ropolitan Books, pp.142–53.

CHAPTER 6

Working on the Margins: Migration and Employment in the United States

SARAH GAMMAGE
Economic Commission for Latin America and the Caribbean

A patchwork quilt of immigration regulations in the United States conspires to criminalize the undocumented, limit worker agency, and diminish voice. These immigration policies and laws interact with an eroding set of labor market institutions and regulations that protect worker rights. Outsourcing, subcontracting, and declining workplace enforcement of labor rights create a fertile environment for employers to evade their obligations. Additionally, a host of intermediaries and labor brokers insulate employers from prosecution, fostering predatory hiring and securing indentured workers—many of whom owe money to these same intermediaries for their undocumented passage to the United States.

It is 20 years since the Immigration Reform and Control Act (IRCA) was passed in 1986, and the United States is facing another wrenching period of immigration policy reform. Only this time, the multiple regulations and loopholes are being revised in the context of a seemingly endless and untenable war on terrorism at home and abroad, amid a heightened sense of insecurity and punitive nationalism.

Without a doubt, current immigration policy in the United States is inadequate and outdated. Furthermore, as the complex and frequently contradictory regulations are implemented, they have been deployed in increasingly restrictive and repressive ways, rendering immigrants more vulnerable in the workplace and in the community.

Migration is a livelihood strategy of last resort for many individuals and households throughout the world. Yet, increasingly, the combined pressures of underemployment, economic stagnation, conflict, persecution, and environmental disaster compel millions to migrate. The global flow of migrants has more than doubled since the 1970s, rising to almost 175 million in 2000 (International Organisation for Migration 2005).

Migrants are overwhelmingly from the developing countries where their economies are in transition or experiencing the complex processes of stabilization, adjustment, and liberalization. Recent figures reveal that more than 60 percent of those who have relocated in search of work and a better life are from the developing world (International Organisation for Migration 2005).

The United States is a major receiver of immigrants, and since the 1960s, the numbers of foreign-born residents in the country have increased substantially. The Migration Policy Institute (2005) notes that "in terms of absolute numbers, this number is at its highest point in history." According to U.S. Census Bureau Current Population Survey data for 2003, 33.5 million foreign-born individuals lived in the US, representing about 11.7% of the entire population (U.S. Census Bureau 2004). Yet this percentage remains well below the historic peaks of almost 15% that occurred in 1890 and 1910.

The majority of new foreign-born residents are from Latin America. Although documented and undocumented migrants enter the United States through a variety of channels by land, sea, and air, a primary site for labor migration is the U.S.–Mexico border. The porous border is increasingly being penetrated by an array of individuals seeking economic opportunity to the north, human traffickers profiting from desperation, transnational labor brokers recruiting workers, and family members hoping to reunite with those who have been separated by time and distance.[1]

Upon entering the United States, migrants are particularly vulnerable, facing contingent rights to secure employment, housing, health care, and other state transfers. Migrants tend to cluster in informal and insecure employment, and they are frequently considered flexible and often expendable labor. Many find themselves working in sectors that are poorly regulated and where statutory labor law does not apply or is inadequately enforced. Furthermore, those without documents are disproportionately vulnerable to predatory recruitment in the informal economy for low-paying and often dangerous work.

In this chapter I examine labor migration from Latin America to specific sectors such as construction, meat packing and processing, and hotels and restaurants. The analysis draws on interviews with Salvadoran migrants in greater Washington, DC, between 2002 and 2006[2] and on secondary data from the Bureau of Labor Statistics and the Department of Homeland Security. The research presented links a growing body of work that examines how immigration law has interacted with eroding labor market standards and regulation to strip migrant workers of bargaining power in the workplace.

Immigrant Latino Workers in the U.S. Economy

The United States Census 2000 reported that approximately 12.5% of the country's labor force was made up of foreign-born workers. A rapidly growing proportion of that group is Latino. Data from the 2006 Current Population Survey reveal that Hispanics[3] comprise about 50% of the foreign-born labor force, compared with approximately 7% of the native-born labor force. It is estimated that Latinos make up more than 80% of the undocumented workforce (Lowell, Gelatt, and Batalova 2006). Their immigration status notwithstanding, it is clear that most of those who come to the United States do so to work. Participation rates for foreign-born men are comparatively higher than rates for their native-born counterparts. A little less than 82% of all male foreign-born and 55% of female foreign-born over the age of 16 were either working or actively seeking work in 2006.[4] This compares with 72% of male native-born and 60% of female native-born.

Table 1 reports the distribution of native and foreign-born workers by industry. Foreign-born workers cluster in wholesale and retail trade,

TABLE 1
Distribution by Industry of Native and Foreign-Born Workers in 2004

Industry	Native-born (%)	Foreign-born (%)	
		All	Hispanics
Agriculture, forestry, fishing, and mining	2.0	2.2	3.8
Construction	7.2	10.6	17.0
Manufacturing, durable goods	7.3	8.1	7.9
Manufacturing, nondurable goods	4.1	6.0	7.9
Wholesale and retail trade	15.2	13.6	12.3
Transportation and warehousing	4.2	4.2	3.9
Utilities	0.9	0.3	0.2
Publishing/broadcasting/ communication/ information services	2.6	1.5	0.9
Finance, insurance, and real estate	7.1	5.1	3.1
Professional and other business services	11.7	12.9	12.5
Educational services	9.3	5.2	3.1
Hospitals and other health services	10.1	9.1	4.4
Social services	2.1	1.7	1.6
Arts and entertainment	2.0	1.4	1.3
Eating, drinking, and lodging services	5.9	10.4	12.3
Repair and maintenance services	1.4	2.0	2.5
Personal and laundry services/ private household services	1.8	3.8	4.0
Public administration	5.0	1.9	1.0

Source: Kochhar (2004), Table 6. Pew Hispanic Center. Data from the Current Population Survey.

professional and other business services, construction, and eating, drinking, and lodging services. Hispanic foreign-born workers demonstrate similar patterns of employment by industry, with the addition of agriculture. They also cluster in a number of occupations (not shown) including construction, production work, building and grounds cleaning and maintenance, food preparation and serving, office and administrative support, and sales-related work. Some of these occupations are among the fastest-growing in the U.S. labor market (Lowell, Gelatt, and Batalova 2006).

Although Latino immigrants are heterogeneous and have varying levels of education, they possess lower levels of education than other foreign-born populations. Approximately 49% have completed high school or have higher education qualifications.[5] Moreover, recent immigrants from Mexico and Central America, who make up the majority of the Latino foreign-born population, appear to have comparatively lower levels of education than those from Southern Cone countries. Approximately 70% of Mexican immigrants, 65% of Salvadoran immigrants, and a little over 50% of all Dominican immigrants documented in the 2000 Census had not completed high school (Gammage and Schmitt 2004). These figures are consistent with a population of largely rural immigrants who have had limited access to formal education. Disproportionately, these immigrants find work in the service sector with the top 10 occupations for Mexican, Dominican, and Salvadoran immigrants being construction workers, cooks, grounds and maintenance workers, janitors and building cleaners, maids and housekeeping cleaners, miscellaneous agricultural workers, truck drivers, production workers, and carpenters.

As can be seen from Table 2, foreign-born workers earn less than their native-born counterparts (Kochhar 2006). Foreign-born Latinos also earn far less than other non-native workers. This may reflect the fact that the composition of the Latino labor force appears to be changing. Kochhar reports that approximately eight out of every 10 new jobs landed by Latinos in 2005 and 2006 went to foreign-born Latinos. Foreign-born Hispanics/Latinos also accounted for nine of every 10 new Latino workers in the labor force. Indeed, foreign-born Latinos currently dominate the Latino labor force. Unfortunately, the number of years of formal education completed appears to be declining over time, particularly for Mexican and Central American migrants (Gammage and Schmitt 2004). This decline in formal education levels may contribute to greater labor market segmentation and depress wages in sectors densely occupied by recent Latino immigrants.

Thus, the terms and conditions of employment for immigrants, particularly recent arrivals, appear to be generally poorer than those for the native-born. For immigrants without documents, they may be even worse.

TABLE 2
Earnings by Race and Foreign-Born Status

	Median weekly earnings ($)
All workers	577
Hispanics	431
Native-born	487
Foreign-born	389
Non-Hispanic whites	623
Native-born	623
Foreign-born	657
Non-Hispanic blacks	487
Native-born	487
Foreign-born	521
Non-Hispanic Asians	662
Native-born	655
Foreign-born	674

Note: Data are reported for the first six months of 2006 in 2005 dollars. Non-Hispanic Asians include Native Hawaiian and Pacific Islanders. Those without pay, unincorporated self-employed, and those with a wage less than $50 per week are excluded. The median wage divides workers into two equal groups, with one-half earning more than the median wage and the other half earning less. All numbers and percentages are rounded after year-to-year changes have been computed.
Source: Kochhar (2006), Table 14. Pew Hispanic Center tabulations of Current Population Survey, 2005.

A recent report on informal or precarious employment in Los Angeles estimated that there were approximately 679,000 informal workers in Los Angeles County earning annualized wages of about $12,000 (Flaming, Haydamack, and Joassart 2005). These authors estimate that 65% of these workers in the city of Los Angeles and 61% in the county are undocumented. The authors measure the informal economy, calculating the number of jobs that do not show up in formal data sources and that operate outside of established labor laws. These are jobs that would otherwise be considered legal but are not effectively regulated. In Los Angeles County, the majority of these workers are Latino and foreign-born. Their employers pay low wages and no benefits. Flaming, Haydamack, and Joassart estimated that as a result of such workers being paid "off the books," the public sector is shortchanged each year by approximately $2 billion in unpaid employee benefits and insurance that is mandated by law for underwriting the public's costs in providing a minimal social safety net for workers. The authors assert that "these costs are not avoided simply because the responsible parties fail to pay them. Instead, costs are shifted to other segments of society and the social safety net becomes more precarious" (Flaming, Haydamack, and Joassart 2005:18).

Another prominent study of informal or precarious work in the United States was conducted by Valenzuela et al. (2006). These authors conducted a national survey of 2,660 day laborers at 264 hiring sites in 139 municipalities in 20 states and the District of Columbia. They found that the overwhelming majority of day laborers comprise undocumented immigrants from Latin America: Almost 60% were Mexican, another 28% were Central American, and 6% were from South America and the Caribbean. Approximately 40% of day laborers have lived in the United States for more than 6 years. Despite the length of residence, 75% of day laborers were undocumented migrants.[6] These authors also observe that the day-labor market "is rife with violations of workers' rights" (2006:2). Day laborers are regularly denied payment for their work, many are subjected to hazardous job sites, and most endure insults and abuses by employers. Valenzuela et al. concluded that "the growth of day-labor hiring sites combined with rising levels of workers' rights violations is a national trend that warrants attention from policy makers at all levels of government" (2006:2).

A similar study of undocumented workers in Chicago in 2002 explored the wages, working conditions, and economic contributions of these immigrants. Mehta et al. (2002) found that undocumented workers seek employment at extremely high rates; almost 91% of undocumented migrants of working age in their sample were employed, most in low-wage service and laborer occupations. Approximately 30% were working in food-service and restaurant-related enterprises, undertaking hand-packing and assembly in warehouses and retail outlets, or engaged in janitorial and cleaning jobs. The undocumented Latin American men and women experienced significant wage penalties, being paid on average 22% and 36% less than their documented counterparts. Undocumented immigrants consistently reported working in unsafe conditions and complained of frequent wage and hour violations. The majority lacked access to health insurance and did not receive benefits under government safety-net programs, despite approximately 70% of all workers having taxes deducted from their paychecks.

Fences and Coyotes: The High Cost of Passage to the United States

Immigration to the United States is a complicated affair, particularly for the undocumented. A series of events has changed the nature of the border and of the regulations that apply to temporary or permanent immigrants. The signing of the North American Free Trade Agreement (NAFTA) in 1994 spurred vigorous investment in border policing and security. The smoother flow of goods and services secured by NAFTA was countered with stricter means of restraining the flows of people across the border. Concessions were made to an increasingly vocal public demanding harsher immigration policies. This restrictionist approach was highlighted by the passage of Proposition 187 in 1994 in California, which sought to bar undocumented immigrants from receiving social services. Operation "Hold the Line" in El Paso, Texas, and Operation "Gatekeeper" in San Diego saturated the border with patrol officers, adding more technology and firepower, night-vision scopes, and newer and stronger barriers. The Immigration and Naturalization Service budget nearly tripled between 1993 and 1999, rising from $1.5 billion to $4.2 billion (Andreas 2000).

In the wake of September 11, the immigration discourse in the United States continues to change. The 2007 budget for border patrol and enforcement rose to $7.8 billion (Department of Homeland Security 2006). The recent House Resolution 4437, "Border Protection, Anti-Terrorism, and Illegal Immigration Control Act," embodies these tectonic shifts in policy. The bill proposes significant increments in enforcement and an extensive investment in border fencing. On October 4, 2007, President Bush signed into effect a law that will finance hundreds of miles of new fences along the U.S.–Mexico border. By May 2008, an additional 361 miles of fencing should be built along the border between Calexico, California, and Douglas, Arizona, and a further 30 miles of fencing along the Laredo, Texas, border crossing (Associated Press 2006).

As the fencing rises, so too does the cost of undocumented passage to the United States. Costs vary depending on the type of passage, the origin of the migrant, the services offered for transport, the provision of "safe houses" and employment connections, and whether the potential migrant chooses to purchase falsified documents. While some migrants from Mexico may pay as little as $500 to $2,000 for passage across the desert, other migrants from Central America can pay as much as $5,000 to $10,000.

Roberto, a migrant from El Salvador, paid $6,000 for his own passage in 2002. He went with a trusted *coyote* and was caught and held at the border and subsequently deported. Since some agreements with coyotes entitle the migrant to three attempted crossings, he was able to return with the same coyote and successfully made the crossing in 2003. In 2006, Roberto paid $9,500 to another coyote to bring his son Nacho across the border. Both Nacho and Roberto work in a meat-packing factory in the Midwest, earning between $8 and $12 an hour. Their shifts vary, but they regularly work between 10- and 12-hour days. On one shift Roberto and Nacho enter the plant at about 4 a.m. and leave at 6 p.m.; on another they start work by 8 a.m. and leave at 7 p.m. They work between 60 and 80 hours a week without benefits, although they do receive overtime; holidays and sick leave are not paid. After two years, they continue to repay part of the loans acquired for their undocumented passage.

The cost of undocumented immigration indebts households and entire kinship networks. Many migration loans are often shared transnationally between relatives in the United States and in the home country. Gloria, a young woman from San Miguel, El Salvador, who contributed to bringing her brother to the United States, continues to contribute to paying off the $6,500 debt that her family incurred to bring him here. Gloria's family members in the United States and in El Salvador are obligated to make debt payments on the loan and repay what is owed to the coyote.

However the migrant chooses to repay his or her debt, many people are usually invested in the outcome. José came to the United States from El Salvador in 2001. He has been relatively successful in finding work and now has Temporary Protected Status. Despite having been here for several years, he stills owes money to brothers and cousins. "My family helped me out. By the time I had finished paying what I owed down there, I paid almost $4,000. My brothers and sisters up here helped me out with the remaining $5,300."

But even after having paid that much money, José was not able to ensure an easy crossing. He traveled with others, initially by air and then overland across the desert, walking in subzero temperatures for miles without water or even a flashlight. The travelers had no idea where they were; the group was large, and several people were left behind. José has no idea what happened to them.

The escalating cost of undocumented entry to the United States responds to and is reflected in the number of deaths on the border. In 2005 a record-breaking 473 migrant deaths occurred at the border, more than 260 of them on the border with Arizona (Migration Policy Institute 2006). Yet at the same time as the death toll mounts, the numbers of people apprehended while crossing the border have not changed significantly since 1993, even though the border patrol has tripled in size. Prior to the dispatch of the U.S. National Guard to the U.S.–Mexico border in 2006, there were an estimated 9,790 border patrol agents guarding the border. As federal agencies have tightened border security in urban areas, smugglers and traffickers have increasingly funneled their charges onto more perilous trails. There is evidence that coyotes or smugglers are resorting to drugs such as pseudoephedrine, Tylenol, amphetamines, and herbal supplements such as ephedra (a precursor of amphetamines) to keep border crossers wakeful and to suppress their appetites (Pomfret 2006). Unfortunately, such drugs accelerate dehydration and fatigue and place migrants at even greater risk.

Although small-scale coyotes are still active, as human trafficking becomes more complex, larger-scale operations are entering the business of ferrying migrants northward. These enterprises are transnational, sophisticated, and ruthless, with members and networks extending across the border. Increasingly, groups that ferried drugs and contraband goods across the border are conveying people also. A multiplicity of gangs operate across the border, smuggling people and passing them on to affiliates or selling them to buyers and intermediaries. A prospective migrant may not know the extent of these exchanges and may end up being sold to several buyers and labor brokers in the course of his or her passage (Jordan 2001). As the cost of passage rises, migrants are increasingly being locked into contracts with labor brokers because of their debts. Where family members in the home country have given up title to assets such as land and housing, these intermediaries may have even greater leverage over the migrant.

Labor Brokers and Intermediaries

Many coyotes also act as labor brokers, ensuring the repayment of the escalating cost of undocumented passage. The recruitment networks are extensive and effective, spanning communities and countries. Unscrupulous employers are benefiting from predatory traffickers who are delighted to convey willing workers from Zacatecas, Mexico, to carpet factories in Georgia, or from La Unión, El Salvador, to construction sites, asbestos abatement, and landscaping firms in Virginia.

A well-known coyote from eastern El Salvador is famous in his hometown for providing workers to a variety of construction firms in Annapolis, Maryland (Aizenman 2006). The coyote recently campaigned for and won the mayoral election. He has publicly boasted that he has found jobs for more than 200 people from his town, securing the well-being of several hundred families and ensuring the flow of remittances to his community in El Salvador. While the coyote is publicly liked and revered, he has also profited from his work, buying several houses and plots of land and attaining a position of power and influence with local government.

It is not only small companies that employ intermediaries to recruit workers. The 2001 indictment of Tyson Foods for conspiring to transport illegal Mexican immigrants across the border and obtain counterfeit work papers for jobs at more than a dozen poultry plants across the country highlights how widespread the practice of predatory hiring has become. The use of employment agencies and labor market intermediaries as well as traffickers and coyotes who ferry undocumented people across the U.S.–Mexico border enables large firms like Tyson to employ undocumented workers.

Tyson, like most meat processors, used the Immigration and Naturalization Service (INS) Basic Pilot Program to verify the right to work of newly hired workers. This system requires that employers submit the alien registration numbers of newly hired non-U.S. citizens to the INS for verification. However, the suit against Tyson Foods Inc. alleges that the company employed workers who were hired and provided by temporary service agencies that did not use the Basic Pilot Program. These workers were apparently hired with Tyson's full knowledge that most were unauthorized for employment in the United States.

Tyson admitted that it used temporary employment agencies to obtain foreign workers, but it denied responsibility for the immigration violations committed by the agencies. Employment agencies acting as intermediaries recruited across the border using coyotes and labor brokers who received between $200 and $500 for each worker delivered to the plants. In the confusion of immigration regulations, temporary protected status, deferred enforced departure, and short-term agricultural work visas, undocumented workers were hired.

The meat processing and packing industry is emblematic of the constellation of forces that fosters informal and precarious work. Companies seeking to evade negotiations with unions relocated meat packing and processing to rural areas, hiring immigrants and densely recruiting the foreign-born. Turnover is high in the industry; hours are long, and injury rates are rising precipitously. To maximize profits, meat processors have continually increased the speed of production. Twenty years ago, meatpacking plants slaughtered about 175 cattle an hour; today that number can be as high as 400 (Schlosser 2001). These accelerated production-line speeds threaten the safety of the food supply and endanger slaughterhouse workers.

Yet these hiring practices are not visible only in the Dickensian environments of meat processing and packing in the exurban and rural Midwest. Castañeda (2002) cites the case of a Maryland landscaper who cheated 23 Mexican workers out of more than $100,000 due them for working in parks in the District of Columbia. These workers paid a Mexican recruitment agency to be brought to the United States on guest-worker visas. The men were provided substandard housing, and $175 per month was subtracted from their pay for the privilege of sleeping on the floor with the use of only one bathroom. They were underpaid, and overtime was not honored. They worked long hours and had a number of other unspecified and illegal deductions taken from their wages. When they tried to complain to the authorities, they were let go by the landscaper. The case remains disputed, and to date compensation has not been paid to these workers.

Other types of guest workers with full rights to work in the United States also face poor and substandard working conditions, with few guarantees or protections. For example, guest workers hired by major retail and hotel chains have also been recruited as contingent labor to serve clients, cook meals, and clean rooms in ritzy neighborhoods and central urban kitchens. Eighty-two guest workers from Bolivia, Peru, and the Dominican Republic recently filed a suit against recruiting firms working for Decatur Hotels (Cass 2006). These workers paid between $3,500 and $5,000 to recruiting firms applying for H-2B visas that enable employers to hire non-native workers because they cannot find native workers to fill their positions. Under immigration law, these workers are bound to the employer that obtained the H-2B visa and cannot work for another company or employer. Mary Bauer, an attorney for the Immigrant Justice Project of the Montgomery, Alabama–based Southern Poverty Law Center, explained that "their debt makes them desperate to work—but Decatur doesn't give them enough hours. And if they switch jobs, they're breaking the law. They are captive workers in a situation of virtual debt peonage" (Cass 2006:A11).

History of Immigration Law and Labor Markets

To understand how employers can evade responsibilities and recruit workers at arm's length, we have to also understand how immigration law itself has changed, rendering immigrant workers more vulnerable to deportation and, as a result, to exploitation. Immigration law is beset by an accretion of policies and programs that create opportunities for certain groups of migrants and employers. For example, the recent history of Latin American migration to the United States has been shaped by the Bracero Program (1942–1964), which institutionalized large-scale migration from Mexico to the United States. The Bracero Program was created to meet the needs of agribusiness, which was facing labor shortages during World War II. It was also intended to curb illegal migration. The program provided employers with a cheap source of labor, offering more than 4.5 million individual contracts for temporary employment in agriculture. Andreas (2000:33) observes that during the decades in which this program existed, "an interdependent relationship between employers and migrants became firmly established." One consequence of this program was a steady increase in labor migrants seeking and obtaining employment by bypassing formal hiring and cross-border recruitment procedures.

Although recruitment was supposed to be arranged prior to migration, large numbers of workers made their way across the border informally, finding employment under the Bracero Program on arrival. The state sanctioned and managed these flows, with the border patrol capturing undocumented migrants, returning them to Mexico, and frequently allowing their readmission the same day under the Bracero Program in order to meet the needs of employers clamoring for workers and field hands (Calavita 1994).

Immigrant workers were encouraged and recruited across the U.S.–Mexico border, subject largely to the fluctuating demands from agribusiness. When public opinion shifted and fewer workers were required, the numbers admitted would decline. Efforts were made to clarify immigration and labor policy in the early 1950s by developing tougher legislation to limit "illegal" migrants. In 1952, Congress passed an act that made it illegal to "harbor, transport, or conceal illegal entrants." Interestingly enough, employment was excluded from the category of "harboring" in response to the Texas proviso amendment as a concession to agribusiness (Calavita 1994). This law contributed to criminalizing undocumented migrants while exempting employers from any responsibility. The state, therefore, became complicit in shifting the burden of responsibility to the migrants and implicitly encouraging flows of undocumented migrants northward.

Andreas (2000:35) maintains that under this system, the "incentives for clandestine entry were further reinforced by the 1965 Immigration Act," which imposed a limit of 120,000 immigrant visas for the Western Hemisphere. Despite this limit's representing an increase from earlier quotas, the rise in demand for immigrant visas, coupled with the ending of the Bracero Program, promoted an overflow of immigrants and escalated the numbers of those seeking clandestine entry. The 1965 act was followed by the 1976 decision to limit visas to 20,000 per year per individual country in the Western Hemisphere—creating a vast backlog of applicants from Mexico who were allowed to remain in the U.S. on extended temporary work visas or who slipped into illegality as their temporary work permits expired.

Over this period, border enforcement was weak and sporadic, even though apprehensions increased from approximately 71,000 in 1960 to more than a million in 1978 (Andreas 2000). Although the U.S–Mexico border is almost 2,000 miles long, the border patrol's budget in 1980 was less than that of the Baltimore police department in the same year (Teitelbaum 1980, cited in Andreas 2000). Interior enforcement was virtually non-existent, enabling employers to continue to employ undoc-umented workers with little or no threat of discovery and in the event of discovery, with no employer sanctions.

As the flows of undocumented labor migrants increased and the hikes in oil prices of the 1970s induced recession, there was a renewed focus on immigration in the media. Conflict and scorched-earth policies in Central America contributed to the flows of refugees and asylees northward. Yet the nature of U.S. involvement in those conflicts pre-vented many Central Americans from gaining refugee status. Those who were displaced by civil war and repression were labeled economic migrants, and concerns about their presence in the United States prompted a new round of legislation in the mid-1980s.

In 1986, Congress passed the Immigration Reform and Control Act (IRCA). The act's legalization provisions conferred legal status on nearly 3 million undocumented immigrants, the vast majority of Mexican and Central American origin. The stated goal of the act was to stem the flow of undocumented immigrants across U.S. borders by imposing fines on employers who knowingly hired undocumented workers. At the same time as the law incorporated an amnesty provision, employer sanctions were imposed and increased appropriations were made for enforcement. The employer-sanctions provision designated penalties for employers who hired aliens not authorized to work in the United States. Under the amnesty provision, illegal aliens who had lived continuously in the United States since before January 1, 1982, could apply to the INS for legal resident status by May 4, 1988, the application cutoff date. IRCA provided many Central Americans and Mexicans the opportunity to reg-ularize or legalize their immigration status. The uncertainty of this period afforded loopholes in what Mahler (1995) describes as the "lucra-tive liminal law" that enabled a multitude of profiteers and purveyors of legal services to obtain fees for processing "deferred enforced depar-tures" for clients—enabling them to work until such time as they might be proven eligible or ineligible for amnesty. The net effect was a system that enabled many ineligible immigrants to prolong their residency and obtain temporary or interim work permits.

On the heels of the IRCA came a series of Temporary Protected Status (TPS) measures. Salvadorans were among the first group to be eligible for such status in 1990, and they continue to make up the great-est proportion of TPS visa holders (Bailey et al. 2002). Temporary Protected Status grants select foreign-born nationals residence and access to employment for a period of 6 to 18 months (which may be extended depending on the specifics of the individual case). TPS does not confer permanent rights to residency or to work in the United

States. Those granted TPS receive work authorization but are ineligible for public cash or medical assistance. However, all TPS recipients can apply for deferred-enforced-departure status (DED), which also enables them to maintain temporary residence and work privileges. TPS and DED status have been offered periodically to Central Americans throughout the 1990s and more recently in response to a series of emergencies including Hurricane Mitch in 1998 and the earthquakes in 2001.

Finally, the Nicaraguan Adjustment and Central American Relief Act, signed into law on November 19, 1997, provided special rules regarding applications by certain Guatemalan, Salvadoran, and some former Soviet-bloc nationals for suspension of deportation and cancellation of removal.

Immigration law is not all-encompassing. Like trade agreements, special status is negotiated for different national groups reflecting their country's engagement with the United States or in response to specific needs expressed by foreign governments and nationally based employers. A sudden environmental or economic disaster such as Hurricane Mitch can open up opportunities to renegotiate Temporary Protected Status for the undocumented residing and working in the United States. An apparent dearth of qualified workers in specific subsectors, such as information and communications technologies, can spur an increase in requests for H1-B visas from high-tech firms in California and Virginia. Most of these visa categories can be used to obtain the right to work as a non-immigrant temporary worker.

The U.S. Citizenship and Immigration Services website lists 21 different types of temporary employment categories for non-immigrant workers that allow workers to stay for a period spanning a few months to several years. In 2005, there were 1.6 million non-immigrant temporary workers registered in the United States. More than half of these visas were used for temporary workers from Europe and Asia (54%), 32% were from Africa, and a little under 10% were from Latin America.

There is a marked regional disparity in the source of these temporary workers that reflects the skill sets, educational qualifications, and economic niches that workers from different regions tend to occupy. Figure 1 reveals that the overwhelming majority of seasonal agricultural and non-agricultural workers in 2005 were from Latin America (and the Caribbean) with the preponderance of these visas being given to Mexican and Central American workers. In contrast, the greatest proportion of professional specialty occupation visas (H1-B), intra-company transfer visas (L1), and treaty traders and investor visas (E1-E3) were allocated to workers from Asia and Europe.

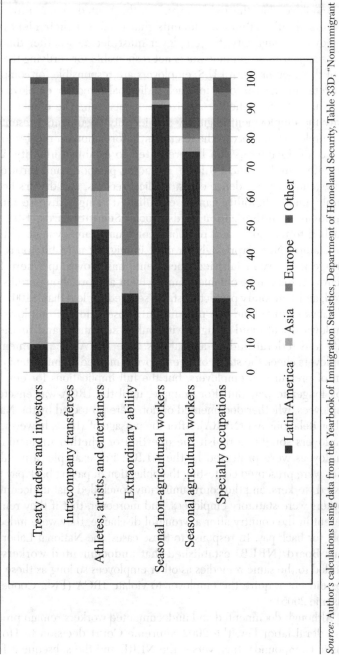

FIGURE 1

Distribution of Temporary Work Categories for Internationals, by Region of Origin, 2005

Source: Author's calculations using data from the Yearbook of Immigration Statistics, Department of Homeland Security; Table 33D, "Nonimmigrant Temporary Worker Admissions (1-94 Only) By Region and Country of Citizenship: Fiscal Year 2005."

Legally, the onus is on the employer to establish whether a prospective employee has the right to work in the United States. Prospective workers should submit documents that establish their identity and employment eligibility; the employer must decide whether the documents appear to be genuine but is not responsible for verifying the validity of the documents. All U.S. employers are responsible for completing and retaining an I-9 form for each individual hired for employment in the United States, whether a citizen or noncitizen. The employer must verify the employment eligibility and identity documents presented by the employee and record the document information on the I-9 form. A variety of documents can be presented to establish identity; 22 are currently listed on the I-9 form, including passports and birth certificates, temporary residence cards, medical records, and driver's licenses. Employment eligibility can be established using a diverse range of employment authorization cards, Social Security cards, I-94 forms attached to passports, and passports containing employment authorization stamps. Not surprisingly, in most immigrant neighborhoods a vast cottage industry in falsified documents has grown up where Social Security cards can be obtained, employment authorization permits replicated, and temporary protective status secured for less than $100.

Laws change, and the pursuit and prosecution of employers and employees peaks and troughs with public sentiment and revisions in state and federal budget allocations. The IRCA's requirement that employers check the status of all employees marked an important escalation of pressure on employers, but the full implications for employees took longer to play out. For example, until the IRCA was enacted, all employees, whether documented or not, were protected by the National Labor Relations Act (NLRA). After the passage of IRCA, however, some employers sought to revisit the question of whether undocumented employees were protected by the NLRA. For example, a number of cases were presented contesting the obligation of paying back pay to dismissed workers, and the courts uniformly concluded that undocumented workers were statutory employees, and moreover, that if they remained present in the country after a wrongful discharge, they were indeed eligible for back pay. In response to these cases, the National Labor Relations Board (NRLB) established that undocumented workers were entitled to the same remedies as other employees so long as these remedies did not require the employer to violate IRCA (Fisk, Cooper, and Wishnie 2005).

Although documented and undocumented workers remain protected by federal labor law, the 2002 Supreme Court decision in Hoffman Plastic Compounds, Inc., versus the NLRB and the subsequent federal and state court decisions interpreting Hoffman have changed the landscape regarding immigrant workers' labor and employment rights. This ruling means that undocumented immigrants are no longer eligible for back pay in the case of unfair dismissal but that they continue to be considered statutory employees. Since this ruling, remedies that were previously available to undocumented workers to protect their labor rights are being continually challenged in court. In a circumstance where documented and undocumented workers' rights are complex and subject to change, it is hardly surprising that those whose language ability is limited face insurmountable barriers asserting and defending their rights.

The shift to more punitive approaches to immigration and the derogation of migrants' rights has been particularly visible since September 11, 2001. The deadlock on immigration law reform that culminated in scuppering the McCain-Kennedy immigration bill in 2007 is part of an ongoing crisis within the Republican Party right to define a nationalist and security-focused discourse that is also friendly to capital and agricultural interests. The internal turmoil that this provokes within the Republican Party has the potential to alienate America's fastest-growing electoral bloc and may eventually force a more conciliatory approach to immigration policy.

Captive Workers

The multiplicity of visa categories, temporary work permits, and deferred enforced departure status fosters a continuum of worker rights, with those workers who have full rights being permanent residents and citizens and those with fewer rights being temporary workers or the undocumented. Natives are immediately differentiable from non-natives, citizens and permanent residents from noncitizens. Temporary work visa categories are transferable only in very rare cases where a new employer offers a job of a similar visa category status and is willing to apply for a conversion or extension of the existing visa category on behalf of the worker. There are ceilings and quotas for these visa categories. Conversion is rare, and workers are usually bound to particular jobs by their visa. Typically, a temporary worker obtains the visa through the employer and has no freedom to move jobs or look for employment elsewhere.

The immigration laws and employment regulations create windows of opportunity for migrants and employers alike. Verification of documents is rarely undertaken, and plausible deniability cloaks many immigrant hires, sheltering both employers and employees. A worker with H-1B or H-2B status is unlikely to file complaints against an employer, since residency depends upon that employer and the right to work is not transferable. A worker with TPS has a window of 18 months to work, within which time he or she can renew status if eligible or seek to convert immigration status, filing for residency or initiating an asylum case. During the time that a case is pending, the individual can obtain temporary work authorization. A migrant can then try one of many avenues to regularize status or obtain a new category of deferred enforced departure status. One of the most common avenues for obtaining a green card or residency permit is for an employer to agree to "sponsor" someone by filing a petition on his or her behalf.

If you owe significant amounts of money to a coyote or labor broker, and your migration status is at best conditional and at worst undocumented, you may be more predisposed to withstand poor treatment and substandard working conditions.

Marco is a young man in his late 20s from eastern El Salvador. He was among the few young men in his rural community who had finished high school and gone to university. His three brothers were in the United States living in Boston; he lived alone with his aging mother and aunt in a two-room house in a coastal village on the Gulf of Fonseca. Despite having gone to university and graduating with a degree in economics, he was unable to find work in El Salvador. After much soul-searching, he and his brothers decided that it would be better were he to come to the United States. In 2004, they paid a coyote $6,000; Marco was taken to Nogales, Mexico, and then across the border into Texas. Once in Texas he was picked up by the border patrol, held briefly, and then let go. After registering with the authorities and agreeing to present himself for a deportation hearing, he got a bus to Virginia. Owing half the money to a coyote, he agreed to work in construction. His first job was hard; the hours were long and his wages were docked by as much as a third for the payment to the coyote and another third for housing. Marco and his undocumented crew members finished work in Virginia and were transferred by the coyote to a construction site in Maryland. Things appeared to be going well until there was an accident on the site. One of the other young men fell more than 30 feet from the scaffolding. The construction foreman called an ambulance, but he let everyone on the crew know that they would have to leave, because he was concerned that the site would be inspected and the workers' undocumented status discovered. As a result all the undocumented workers were let go.

Marco called his brothers in Boston, concerned that he was not going to be able to pay what he owed the coyote. They collectively decided to pay off the remaining debt to the coyote and bring Marco up to Massachusetts. The debt was paid off by taking out more loans.

Marco's brothers used payday loans and borrowed from friends and relatives to pay off the remaining $2,000 and purchase Marco's bus ticket to Boston.

While the situation of the undocumented may be particularly bad, professional non-immigrant employees may also be tied to their employers. This is the case for temporary workers with a visa status such as that conferred by the H-1B, H-1C, H2, H3, and L-1 programs.[7] These workers are granted non-immigrant visas to perform specific jobs that are considered to be temporary. The employer must petition for the right to have a worker enter the country under an H or L visa. In the case of an H-1B visa for a specialty worker, the employer must file a labor condition application with the Department of Labor and then petition for the worker's entry if the worker resides outside the United States at the time of hiring. Work authorization for H-1B foreign specialty workers is employer-specific and limited to employment with the approved employer. A change of employer requires a new H-1B petition.

Because the visa is linked to the specific job, employees may be particularly vulnerable to abuse and less likely to register a complaint against their employer. A Federation for American Immigration Reform (2003) report quotes Fadi Bishara, the president and founder of techVenture, a specialty recruitment firm for Silicon Valley: "The employer is getting more productivity and cheaper labor. Because many H-1B applicants are willing to do whatever it takes to get into the country, they will work day and night and they won't complain. They're willing to compromise some of their salaries. They're a special breed" (*Wired News*, April 2006, quoted in Federation for American Immigration Reform 2003:8).

Certainly a number of studies have concluded that wages for some H-1B visa holders are significantly less than for their native-born counterparts—despite the fact that these jobs are higher status and higher skilled (Federation for American Immigration Reform 2003; Government Accountability Office 2005; Miano 2005). Miano (2005) finds that wages for H-1B workers in computer programming occupations are overwhelmingly concentrated at the bottom of the U.S. pay scale. Wages reported on labor condition applications for 85% of H-1B workers were lower than the median U.S. wage in the same occupations and state.

Linguistic Isolation and Worker Rights

Even those immigrants who have full papers and rights to work frequently encounter language and literacy barriers or regulations that prevent them from practicing their chosen professions in the United States. These indviduals may also find themselves with limited bargaining

TABLE 3
Percentages of Foreign-Born Persons Reporting That They Do Not Speak English,
by Year of Arrival (17 Years of Age and Older)

Year of arrival	Born in Mexico		Born in El Salvador		Born in the Dominican Republic	
	Women	Men	Women	Men	Women	Men
Reported in 1990						
Before 1959	38.4	31.1	28.8	31.6	29.1	15.3
1960–1969	38.5	34.8	33.3	19.9	44.8	34.0
1970–1979	49.7	41.9	42.8	32.1	50.1	37.8
1980–1990	71.0	64.0	63.0	53.4	66.2	60.3
1991–2000	—	—	—	—	—	—
Reported in 2000						
Before 1959	37.6	37.0	28.6	20.2	35.4	25.0
1960–1969	39.1	37.8	37.8	22.5	43.3	41.1
1970–1979	43.7	37.9	39.0	29.4	45.1	38.0
1980–1990	56.4	47.0	48.1	38.8	46.8	39.4
1991–2000	76.0	71.2	67.3	65.3	61.7	53.5

Source: Gammage and Schmitt (2004). Analysis of 1% Public Use Micro Sample of the 2000 Census. Annex, Table 20.

power and seeking employment at the bottom of the labor market. The language barrier, however, is likely to be more significant for those with little or no education. Table 3 reports for Mexico, El Salvador, and the Dominican Republic the percentages of the foreign-born who do not speak English. Alarmingly, these percentages are rising, a finding that is consonant with the rising numbers of immigrants from rural communities among this population. Women are consistently more likely to report that they do not speak English with any proficiency.

It is not just the undocumented who are vulnerable to substandard working conditions. Liliana holds a permanent residency card that she obtained through the American Baptist Church class action suit. In 1991, the U.S. government and attorneys settled the American Baptist Churches (ABC) versus Thornburgh class-action suit, which alleged that the government engaged in discriminatory treatment of asylum claims made by Guatemalans and Salvadorans fleeing conflict during the civil war. As a result, Guatemalans and Salvadorans who were present in the United States before October 1, 1990, and September 19, 1990, respectively, were granted new interviews and asylum decisions, irrespective of any prior decisions on their asylum claims. Liliana is among the more privileged of the Salvadoran immigrants who fled the civil war, because she was able to have her asylum petition reviewed and granted. Yet even Liliana does not feel protected in the workforce. She is not represented by a union and feels that she has little opportunity to negotiate with her employer for benefits that she should be entitled to. Lacking fluency in English and with inadequate knowledge of her rights, she is reluctant to press for better working conditions.

Liliana has a son in El Salvador, and she sends money back to her mother and her son. She sends $350 a month in remittances to El Salvador for rent, food, medicine, and school books. Liliana works in a kitchen for a major chain of hotels and restaurants and is paid $10 an hour. Her shifts vary and are determined by her employer; as a result, she is rarely able to work a 40-hour week. She is concerned about money and is constantly trying to make ends meet. Any unanticipated expenditure poses great strain on her finances and well-being.

> Savings. I had savings, yes. But not any more. I worked really hard—but this job that I currently have with [name omitted] is dreadful. You can never tell how many hours you will get. It is in a university—so they let you go at the end of each semester. They pay $10 an hour—but it is really hard work. I work in the kitchen. Both my thumbs are broken or sprained. I can barely lift anything now. Do you think I can get compensation? No, no they won't even apply for it. I earn $200 a week, my rent is $600 a month and I send back $350 a month. All my savings are gone. There is nothing left. I am in debt. I have to get another job (Gammage 2004).

Declining Enforcement and Weakening Labor Protections

U.S. immigration policies have failed workers and immigrants alike. But it isn't just the immigration system that is broken—the labor market needs fixing too. Labor market protections are eroding, and attempts to prevent the predatory hiring of undocumented workers focus largely on dismissal, employer fines, and deportation of those who are found to be without papers. Unfortunately, the body of evidence to date reveals that sanctions disproportionately hurt workers and rarely penalize employers. From 1999 to 2004, the number of criminal employer cases where employers knowingly recruited undocumented workers referred for prosecution by the federal government fell from 182 to 4, and the amount of fines collected dropped from $3.7 million to $212,000 (Hsu and Lyderson 2006). In combination, these two trends indicate a significant reduction in the government's capacity to ensure that employers are complying with the most basic workplace laws.

Cuts in funding and legislative revisions have hampered most worker protection agencies. Bernhardt and McGrath (2005:1) report that "over the past three decades, enforcement resources and activities of the U.S. Department of Labor have either stagnated or declined, at the same time that the number of workers and workplaces in the country has expanded." Funding cutbacks in the Occupational Safety and Health Administration (OSHA) have reduced Department of Labor worker protection programs substantially. Similarly, the number of labor inspectors per worker has declined significantly over the last half century. Gordon reports in an analysis of American sweatshops that in the 1950s, the Wage and Hour Division of the Department of Labor had one inspector for every 46,000 workers. By the 1990, this ratio had dropped to one inspector for every 150,000 workers (Gordon 2005).

Simultaneously, as state- and federally funded institutions that protect worker rights become more embattled, union membership is also declining. Farber (2005) explores the reasons for the decline in union density and finds that union density is significantly higher where unions are allowed to negotiate union security provisions (e.g., in agency shops) and where employers have a legal duty to bargain with labor unions. Disproportionately, informal jobs fall in the private sector or are outsourced to private contractors. Consequently, the decline in union membership in the private sector diminishes voice protections across a number of sectors that may be particularly vulnerable to poor and eroding terms and conditions of employment.

Conclusions

As the institutions and bodies that protect and advocate for labor rights wane in importance in the United States, a multiplicity of immigration laws and practices that criminalize undocumented immigrant workers contribute to their contingent rights and claims on employers and accelerate the eroding terms and conditions of employment. The immigration system in the United States has given rise to a confusing array of visa categories and work permits that enables employers to discriminate between native and nonnative workers. These visa categories in combination with declining labor enforcement and weakening labor protections conspire to create a fertile ground for worker abuse and exploitation. A plethora of intermediaries have emerged that recruit outsourced labor and provide workers for employers. Many of these intermediaries fail to observe labor rights, and they insulate employers from prosecution. Enforcement is ineffective, and employers seldom face sanctions for paying below statutory minimums or failing to observe labor obligations.

Greater investment should be made in ensuring that native and nonnative workers are treated equally. Wages, hours, and benefits should be carefully tracked in industries employing temporary and contingent workers and in those sectors where temporary work visas are frequently sought and obtained. Protecting workers whether they are native or non-native, documented or undocumented requires policies and programs that do not differentiate between workers or allow employers to do so. Innovative initiatives in states such as California to require employers with 10 or more employees who choose not to offer health coverage to contribute an amount equal to 4% of payroll toward the cost of employee health coverage have the potential to reduce informality and to reduce discrimination in the labor market.

Finally, in a fashion similar to the prosecution of human trafficking, judicial and legal procedures need to be developed to allow migrants to bring cases against employers for worker abuse. Protecting migrants during these cases, enabling them to obtain visa extensions and work permits to ensure that they are not penalized by deportation, could increase the number of cases against employers failing to adhere to current labor law and reduce the incentives to treat non-natives as second-class workers.

Acknowledgment

I would like to thank Eileen Appelbaum, Marty Chen, Chris Tilly, and Joann Vanek for their comments on my chapter.

Endnotes

[1] Human traffickers are typically only engaged in transporting people across the border or trading human cargo. Labor brokers are those intermediaries who facilitate hires and receive a portion of the worker's pay or a fee for finding employment. Increasingly, however, these distinctions are becoming blurred.

[2] This work was funded by the Ford Foundation and the Inter-American Foundation. The names of interviewees and places of residence in the home and host countries have been changed to protect their anonymity.

[3] The term *Hispanic* is used here because it is the one used in the Current Population Survey to describe people of Latin American origin.

[4] Data from Table 1, "Employment Status of the Foreign-Born and Native-Born Populations by Selected Characteristics, 2005–06, Annual Averages," Current Population Survey, Bureau of Labor Statistics.

[5] Data from the 1% Public Use Micro-Sample of the United States 2000 Census.

[6] About 11% of undocumented day laborers have pending applications for adjustments of their immigration status.

[7] The H categories apply to aliens coming temporarily to perform services in a specialty occupation or a temporary worker to meet the need of a specific employer. U.S. employers may petition for skilled or unskilled alien workers to meet temporary or seasonal needs in positions for which qualified U.S. workers are not available. It is important to note that the employer's need for such services must be temporary. Caps are set on these visa categories. For example, the cap on H1-B admissions in

2001, 2002, and 2003 was 195,000 workers. In 2007 there was an annual cap of 66,000 visas for H-2B workers, though there was no annual cap on visas for H-2A workers. See the Department of Homeland Security (www.uscis.gov) and Immigration and Naturalization Service (2002) for definitions and qualifications for each of these visa categories.

References

Aizenman, Nurith. 2006. "The Migrants' Mayor: Salvadoran's Path to Politics Built on Reputation for Smuggling People North." *Washington Post,* June 2, p. A13.

Andreas, Peter. 2000. *Border Games: Policing the U.S.–Mexico Divide*. Ithaca and London: Cornell University Press.

Associated Press. 2006. *Fence Proposal Marks Death of Immigration Reform*. <http://news.propeller.com/story/2006/09/20/fence-proposal-marks-death-of-immigration-reform/>. [March 2007].

Bailey, Adrian J., Richard A. Wright, Alison Mountz, and Ines M. Miyares. 2002. "(Re)producing Salvadoran Transnational Geographies." *Annals of the Association of American Geographers* Vol. 92, no. 1, pp. 125–44.

Bernhardt, Annette, and Siobhán McGrath. 2005. "Trends in Wage and Hour Enforcement by the U.S. Department of Labor, 1975–2004." *Economic Policy Brief* No. 3, September. New York: Brennan Center for Justice.

Calavita, Kitty. 1994. "U.S. Immigration Policy and Responses: The Limits of Legislation." In Wayne A. Cornelius, Philip L. Martin, and James Hollifield, eds., *Controlling Immigration: A Global Perspective*. Stanford, CA: Stanford University Press.

Cass, Julia. 2006. "Guest Workers Sue New Orleans Hotel Chain: Immigrants Say Decatur Group Failed to Deliver on Promised Employment," *Washington Post*, August 17, p. A11.

Castañeda, Ruben. 2002. "D.C. Awards Contract Despite Labor Probe: Allegations That Landscaping Firm Cheated Mexican Workers Called Irrelevant." *Washington Post*, April 15, p. B3.

Department of Homeland Security. 2006. "President Bush's FY 2007 Budget for U.S. Customs and Border Protection (CBP) Totals $7.8 Billion." Department of Homeland Security, Customs and Border Patrol. <http://www.cbp.gov/xp/cgov/newsroom/fact_sheets/budget/>.

Farber, Henry S. 2005. *Union Membership in the United States: The Divergence between the Public and Private Sectors*. Working Paper Number 503. Princeton University, Industrial Relations Section, September.

Federation for American Immigration Reform. 2003. *Deleting American Workers: Abuse of the Temporary Foreign Worker System in the High Tech Industry*. Washington, DC: Federation for American Immigration Reform.

Fisk, Catherine, Laura Cooper, and Michael Wishnie. 2005. "The Story of Hoffman Plastic Compounds v. NLRB: Labor Rights without Remedies for Undocumented Immigrants." *Duke Law School Legal Studies*. Research Paper Series, Research Paper No. 82, September.

Flaming, Daniel, Brent Haydamack, and Pascale Joassart. 2005. *Hopeful Workers, Marginal Jobs: LA's Off-The-Books Labor Force*. Prepared for the Los Angeles Economy Project under the auspices of the City of Los Angeles. <http://www.economicrt.org/pub/hopeful_workers_marginal_jobs/hopeful_workers_marginal_jobs.pdf>. [February 2008].

Gammage, Sarah. 2004. Personal interviews with Salvadoran migrants in greater Washington, DC.

Gammage, Sarah, and John Schmitt. 2004. "Los Inmigrantes Mexicanos, Salvadoreños y Dominicanos en el Mercado Laboral Estadounidense: Las Brechas de Género en los Años 1990 y 2000." *CEPAL*, June.

Gordon, Jennifer. 2005. "American Sweatshops, Organizing Workers in the Global Economy." *Boston Review*, Vol. 30, no. 3 (Summer), pp. 11–5.

Government Accountability Office. 2005. *H-1B Foreign Workers: Better Tracking Needed to Help Determine H-1B Program's Effects on U.S. Workforce.* United States General Accounting Office, Report to the Ranking Minority Member, Subcommittee on Environment, Technology, and Standards, Committee on Science, House of Representatives, September 2003.

Hsu, Spencer S., and K. Lyderson. 2006. "Illegal Hiring Is Rarely Penalized: Politics, 9/11 Cited in Lax Enforcement." *Washington Post*, June 16, p. A1.

Immigration and Naturalization Service. 2002. *Characteristics of Specialty Occupation Workers (H-1B).* Immigration and Naturalization Service, July.

International Organisation for Migration. 2005. *World Migration Report 2005.* Geneva: International Organisation for Migration.

Jordan, Mary. 2001. "Smuggling People Is Now Big Business in Mexico." *Washington Post*, May 17, p. A1.

Kochhar, Raklesh. 2004. *Latino Labor Report, 2004: More Jobs for New Immigrants But at Lower Wages.* Washington, DC: Pew Hispanic Center.

———. 2006. *Latino Labor Report, 2006: Strong Gains in Employment.* Washington, DC: Pew Hispanic Center.

Lowell, B. Lindsay, Julia Gelatt, and Jeanne Batalova. 2006. *Labor Force Trends: The Future, Past, and Present.* Task Force Insight, No. 17 (July). Washington, DC: Migration Policy Institute.

Mahler, Sarah J. 1995. *American Dreaming: Immigrant Life on the Margins.* Princeton, NJ: Princeton University Press.

Mehta, Chirag, Nik Theodore, Iliana Mora, and Jennifer Wade. 2002. *Chicago's Undocumented Immigrants: An Analysis of Wages, Working Conditions, and Economic Contributions.* University of Illinois at Chicago, Center for Urban Economic Development. February.

Miano, John. 2005. *Bottom of the Pay Scale: Wages for H-1B Computer Programmers.* Washington, DC: Center for Immigration Studies. December.

Migration Policy Institute. 2005. *A New Century: Immigration and the US.* Washington, DC: Migration Information Source.

Migration Policy Institute. 2006. *The US–Mexico Border.* Washington, DC: Migration Information Source.

Pomfret, John. 2006. "An Increasingly Deadly Trail: Tighter Border Has Illegal Immigrants Risking More Perilous Routes." *Washington Post*, June 6, p. A1.

Schlosser, Eric. 2001. *Fast Food Nation.* New York: Houghton Mifflin.

Teitelbaum, Michael. 1980. "Right versus Right: Immigration and Refugee Policy— The United States," *Foreign Affairs*, Vol. 59, no. 1, pp. 21–59.

U.S. Census Bureau. 2004. *The Foreign-Born Population in the United States 2003: Population Characteristics.* U.S. Census Bureau, August. <http://www.census.gov/prod/2004pubs/p20-551.pdf>. [June 2007].

Valenzuela, Abel, Jr., Nik Theodore, Edwin Meléndez, and Ana Luz González. 2006. *On The Corner: Day Labor in the United States.* Los Angeles: UCLA Center for the Study of Urban Poverty.

Chapter 7

Single Mothers in the Era of Welfare Reform

Elizabeth Lower-Basch
Center for Law and Social Policy

Mark H. Greenberg
Center for American Progress

In the 1990s, the United States' welfare system went through a dramatic transformation from a program that provided ongoing, if meager, support to unemployed and very-low-income parents to a far more restrictive program, providing only temporary assistance and emphasizing rapid employment. Several million low-income parents, principally single mothers, were encouraged and pressured to take any available job, and they often faced loss of welfare assistance for failure to do so. In most states, neither participating in education and training activities nor caring for even very young children was an acceptable alternative to work.

While the welfare changes were pushing single mothers toward low-wage employment, two other developments were affecting the conditions for low-wage work and workers. First, during the late 1990s, there was a near-full-employment economy with high demand for low-wage labor. Second, a set of federal and state policy initiatives—including a large expansion of the earned income tax credit, a tripling of childcare funding, broadened health care coverage for low-income families, and an increased minimum wage—worked together to increase the financial rewards of even low-wage jobs.

Taken together, the effects of these changes on single mothers' employment patterns were dramatic. Employment among single mothers overall grew from 55% in 1993 to 73% in 2000. Employment among never-married mothers—the group most affected by the changes—climbed from 43% in 1992 to 66% in 2000 (Department of Health and Human Services 2007). However, claims that low-income parents would make steady progress into better jobs and careers turned out to be largely incorrect. Over time, most families leaving assistance remained mired in low-wage or unstable employment or fell out of the labor market altogether. And those who were unemployed, or remained poor despite employment, were less likely to receive income support through the welfare system. Moreover, the gains in employment reached their peak in 2000: Since that time, employment among single mothers has fallen and poverty has grown, although neither has returned to its previous level. Meanwhile, welfare caseloads continue to decline.

Low-wage workers who receive the full set of work supports clearly have higher incomes than their counterparts of a decade ago. However, many eligible workers do not receive these supports, and many struggle to make ends meet even with the aid of public benefits (Albelda and Boushey 2007). In addition, as more public benefits are conditioned on paid work, the safety net for those who are unable to obtain or sustain employment has become significantly frayed.

This chapter examines the policy changes of the 1990s and since along with the subsequent employment and earnings outcomes for single mothers. It considers how the policy changes affected both employment levels and job quality and discusses implications for next steps for federal and state policies. These policy changes triggered an increase in the supply of low-skilled workers, but they did little, if anything, to improve the quality of the jobs that the workers eventually found. Less-educated single mothers remain part of a low-wage labor market that is prone to the kinds of "gloves-off" strategies described in the other chapters of this volume.

Employment of Single Mothers Before the Mid-1990s

In 1995, prime-age single mothers were nearly as likely to be employed as were married mothers. The employment rate for mothers aged 25 to 44 was 65% for married mothers and 63% for single mothers. When single mothers worked, they worked on average more hours than married mothers (National Research Council and Institute of Medicine of the National Academies 2003). However, single mothers' earnings for full-time work were only about 80% of the earnings of married mothers (Bureau of Labor Statistics 1999). Moreover, the aggregate employment rate for single-mother families actually reflected differing stories for different groups. The employment rate for divorced mothers was higher than that for married mothers, while the employment rate for never-married mothers was lower (Department of Health and Human Services 2007). Divorced mothers tend to be older and better-educated and to have older children than never-married mothers; each of these factors is associated with higher rates of employment.

A range of factors contributed to the lower employment rates of the least-skilled single mothers. The jobs most available to individuals with limited education paid the least, and lower-wage jobs were also least likely to provide employer-based health care, paid sick or vacation days, employer-provided education assistance, or other employer-based benefits (Center for American Progress 2007). Subsidized childcare was available to only a small share of working families, and health care coverage was often unavailable for low-income families not receiving welfare. When work expenses and benefit reductions were combined, less-skilled single mothers often could not earn enough to leave them financially better off than they were on welfare (Edin and Lein 1997).

Moreover, poor unemployed single mothers were more likely to face a range of additional challenges and barriers: physical and mental health difficulties, illness, and disabilities—for themselves, their children, and other family members; lack of transportation alternatives and physical isolation; current and past domestic violence and sexual abuse; drug and alcohol difficulties; extremely poor basic skills; and others (Olson and Pavetti 1996). Over the next decade, welfare and work support policies would address some of these barriers to employment, while at the same time reducing the availability of ongoing assistance to families with non-employed single parents.

Employment Strategies for Single Parents: Welfare and Welfare Reform

Until 1996, Aid to Families with Dependent Children (AFDC) provided cash assistance for very-low-income families with children. Two-parent families were eligible for benefits under limited circumstances, but the vast majority of participating families were headed by single mothers. While AFDC had included for years some features designed to encourage and support employment, promoting work became a major focus of welfare policy in the 1990s.

When AFDC was created in 1935, there was little expectation of mothers being employed outside the home. But between 1950 and 1995, labor force participation among women with children under 18 increased from 22% to 70% (Committee on Ways and Means 2004). Over time, the basic idea of providing income support to enable single mothers to stay out of the workforce came to be seen by many as anachronistic and unfair. In the decades before the 1996 welfare law, policy makers repeatedly enacted requirements and provided for services intended to strengthen the focus on work for families receiving assistance.

Over time, the AFDC program became increasingly controversial. The program's political support was fragile, both because it was perceived by many as a program for minorities and because the share of recipient parents that were widowed, divorced, and separated declined as the share of never-married mothers increased. The share of families working while receiving assistance declined during the 1980s—in part because federal law was changed to make it harder for working families to receive assistance. A large caseload increase between 1988 and 1994, during which the number of families receiving assistance grew from 3.8 million to 5 million, added to concerns that the program was "out of control."

In 1992, Bill Clinton made welfare reform a major campaign theme with his proposal to "end welfare as we know it." The original Clinton pledge spoke of requiring participation in a work program after a time limit, and it tied welfare reform to an expanded minimum wage, health care coverage, and increased funding for childcare. In the 1994 elections, Republicans took majorities of both houses of Congress, and the political climate around welfare reform changed sharply. Republican leadership proposed to repeal AFDC and provide states instead with block grants to develop programs of time-limited assistance. President Clinton vetoed two versions of the proposal before Congress passed and Clinton signed into law the Personal Responsibility and Work Opportunity Reconciliation Act (PRWORA) in August 1996.

PRWORA eliminated the requirement that states assist eligible families and replaced AFDC with Temporary Assistance for Needy Families (TANF) block grants to states. Where before the federal government had matched state spending for cash assistance, under the new block grants, states received a fixed amount of federal money whether their caseloads increased or decreased, with wide discretion given in the use of funds. States were permitted to reduce their own spending on cash assistance and related programs serving needing families by 20% to 25% below spending levels of the 1994 to 1995 period. This meant that as caseloads declined, sums that had previously been spent on cash assistance could be used for other activities.

States were given broad flexibility to determine many parameters of their cash assistance programs, such as work requirements, time limits, and sanction policies. However, the law established a five-year lifetime limit on the use of federal funds to provide assistance, restricted use of federal funds for immigrants in their first five years in the United States, and imposed additional restrictions on when assistance could be provided. To avoid a federal penalty, states were required to achieve an annual "work participation rate." The participation rate rules did the following:

- Sharply restricted the conditions under which education and training could count toward work participation requirements;
- Counted families in the base from which participation rates were calculated even if states determined they should be exempt; and
- Provided for required rates that would eventually reach 50% for all families and 90% for two-parent families for states with no caseload declines, but allowed states a "caseload reduction credit" (i.e., a downward adjustment in the required participation rate) if a state's caseload fell for reasons other than just changing eligibility rules.

The combination of the block grant structure and the caseload reduction credit provided strong incentives for states to take steps to reduce their caseloads whether or not families entered employment.

While there was substantial variation among states in their policy responses to PRWORA, some general patterns emerged. All states reduced or eliminated exemptions from work-related requirements, including those applicable to parents of very young children. Most states made greater attempts to identify individuals with "barriers to employment" such as substance abuse habits or mental health problems, although states have struggled with providing effective services and in engaging all families (Loprest et al. 2007). Virtually all states liberalized earnings rules so as to provide for continued assistance when families entered low-wage employment. Most states limited the degree to which recipients could count participation in education or training activities toward their work requirements, and states encouraged recipients to seek paid employment as soon as possible. States strengthened the penalties for nonparticipation, with many states terminating all cash assistance for failure to comply with program rules. Almost all states adopted the federal five-year lifetime limit on welfare receipt or shorter state limits (Rowe 2006).

Most states also adopted strategies designed to change the "culture of welfare offices" to emphasize work. Most states required applicants to begin searching for work as a condition of application. Some states offered formal diversion programs where applicants were offered lump sum payments to address immediate needs in lieu of ongoing assistance. Some states informally discouraged potential applicants from receiving TANF benefits. Potential recipients may have been dissuaded from applying for welfare because of the complex and burdensome requirements or in order to "bank" limited periods of eligibility for a time of greater need, or they may have not needed to turn to welfare because they were better able to sustain employment because of work supports.

Building a Structure of Work Supports: Preliminary Steps in the 1990s

While the replacement of AFDC with TANF was the most dramatic social policy shift in the 1990s, other policy changes during the decade significantly changed the landscape and broadened the supports available for low-earning families. While the resulting structure was uneven in many key respects, the net result was to substantially strengthen the supports available to low-income working families outside welfare and to increase the rewards of even low-wage work.

Earned Income Tax Credit. During the 1990s, the Earned Income Tax Credit was transformed from a modest refundable tax credit into the largest federal source of income support and asset-building assistance for low-income working families. The EITC provides low-income working families with a tax credit representing a portion of their earnings. If the amount of the credit exceeds the family's tax liability, the excess amount is paid to the family, typically in an annual lump sum. In 1990, the maximum value of the EITC was $953, with the credit fully phased out once earnings passed $20,264. By 1996, the maximum value of the tax had risen to $2,152 for families with one child and $3,556 for families with two or more children. A family with two or more children could continue to receive benefits until its earnings exceeded $28,495. Before the expansions, the EITC provided a credit of 14% of initial earnings for families with children. After the 1990 and 1993 expansions, a low-earning parent with one child received a credit equal to 34% of initial wages, and a low-earning parent with more than one child received a credit equal to 40% of initial wages. These expansions effectively ensured that parents who worked steadily, even in very low-wage jobs, would have higher incomes than they had on welfare.

Childcare. Single parents who work outside the home need childcare. Quality childcare is expensive and usually far out of reach for low-income families without subsidies. Before 1988, dedicated federal funding for childcare had been minimal. The 1988 Family Support Act provided funding for childcare for families receiving welfare and leaving welfare due to employment, and the 1990 Child and Development Block Grant and At-Risk Child Care programs provided childcare funding for other low-income families, but funding was capped and limited for families not receiving or leaving welfare.

The 1996 law increased federal funding for childcare and consolidated the separate programs. While families on and leaving welfare generally continued to receive priority for services, the consolidation simplified access, and the new resources expanded the availability of childcare to nonwelfare families. In addition, as welfare caseloads declined and the share of the TANF block grant used for basic assistance fell, states increasingly devoted TANF funds to childcare in the initial years of TANF implementation. Between 1996 and 2000, combined federal and state spending for childcare tripled, the number of children receiving childcare subsidies nearly doubled, and states were able to initiate a set of new initiatives to promote childcare quality. Approximately 1 million additional children received childcare assistance as a result of the initial expansions. However, even with these expansions, childcare subsidies only reached about one in seven children eligible under federal law (Mezey, Greenberg, and Schumacher 2002).

Health insurance. Congress took action before, during, and after 1996 to broaden health care coverage for families and children outside of welfare. Originally, with limited exceptions, Medicaid coverage for families was limited to those receiving AFDC, so loss of AFDC meant a risk of lost medical coverage for parents and children. Less than a third of low-income children receive health insurance through their parents' jobs, because their employers do not offer insurance coverage; because they are not employed for a long enough period, or for enough hours, to qualify for benefits; or because they can not afford the employee share of the premium even when they are eligible for coverage (Ku, Lin, and Broaddus 2007).

Between 1986 and 1991, Congress extended Medicaid eligibility to more low-income children, regardless of their families' welfare status. While these provisions were gradually phased in over time, by 2002 states were required to cover all children in families with incomes below the federal poverty level, and all children under 6 and pregnant women in families with incomes below 133% of the poverty line. States are allowed, but not required, to use Medicaid to cover children in families with incomes up to 185% of the poverty line (Committee on Ways and Means 2004).

Policy makers widely recognized that the risk of losing health insurance coverage was a significant obstacle preventing low-income families from leaving welfare. This was one reason that Clinton chose to try to enact health care reform before turning to welfare. In the absence of comprehensive health care reform, the 1996 welfare law "delinked" Medicaid eligibility from receipt of cash assistance, basing it on low-income status instead. Moreover, federal law now gave states options to further broaden coverage for low-income families by allowing flexibility in how income and resources were defined. However, in spite of these policy changes, studies found that large numbers of families leaving welfare were not receiving Medicaid (Dion and Pavetti 2000). After these findings were widely disseminated and the federal government applied a combination of pressure and technical assistance, most states revised their processes to reduce the number of families losing coverage due to administrative obstacles.

Meanwhile, the 1997 creation of the State Children's Health Insurance Program (SCHIP) provided states with funding to cover additional low-income children above Medicaid eligibility levels at an enhanced matching rate (Committee on Ways and Means 2004). Between 1997 and 2005, the fraction of low-income children (below 200% of poverty) who were uninsured fell from 23% to 14%, even as the fraction of low-income children covered by employer-sponsored insurance also declined. The increased coverage was due both to SCHIP and increased enrollment in Medicaid as a result of enhanced outreach activities under SCHIP (Ku, Lin, and Broaddus 2007).

Minimum wage. Congress raised the minimum wage from $4.25 an hour to $4.75 in 1996 and to $5.15 in 1997. Among the policy changes, this is the only one that directly attempted to improve the quality of jobs, rather than providing supplemental benefits that improved the well-being of families with children where the adults were employed in low-wage work.

While the minimum wage increase raised the wages of low-earning workers in the short term, it was soon overtaken by the tight labor markets of the late 1990s, which pushed wages for most workers, even those with low skills, above the statutory minimum. By 2006, only 1.5% of workers 16 and older with less than a high school degree earned exactly the minimum wage (Bureau of Labor Statistics 2007).

A partial system of work supports. Thus, in a relatively short period, the policy context for less-educated single parents and other low-income workers had changed dramatically, with AFDC replaced by TANF, while a range of supports—EITC, childcare, health care, minimum wage— were all substantially enhanced. In addition, a set of changes enacted as part of the 1996 law resulted in substantial improvements in the performance of the nation's child support enforcement system. While most states continued to retain child support collected on behalf of families currently receiving welfare, more funds were distributed to families who had left welfare. Child support paid to families provided additional income to single-parent families, and made it more possible for them to make ends meet when in low-wage jobs. Moreover, in the first years after 1996, food stamp participation fell, but in subsequent years, the federal and state governments made a set of changes intended to make the program more accessible to working households and part of the overall structure of work supports.

However, in a range of ways, the new structure of work supports fell short of being comprehensive. The EITC was typically provided only in a once-a-year lump sum rather than as ongoing income support. Childcare, though expanded, remained unavailable to most of the eligible population. The health care expansions principally benefited children, while substantial numbers of low-income parents went without coverage. Most legal immigrants were denied access to federal public benefits, including TANF and food stamps. Nevertheless, the expansions were significant. Further, the populations affected by the work support expansions are far larger than the universe of welfare recipients and former welfare recipients—by tax year 2004, the EITC reached 22.3 million tax filers, and an estimated 15 million children were considered potentially eligible for childcare subsidies.

What Happened? Employment Growth and Low-Wage Employment

We now turn to the employment experiences of single parents in and after the mid-1990s and to the extent to which their experiences were affected by the changed policy environment. These questions have been most extensively studied with respect to families who received and left welfare. However, the policies also affected the broader universe of single mothers, including those who never received welfare. (While our focus here is single mothers, we note that the broadening of supports also extended to single custodial fathers, and in some cases to two-parent families, though very little of the broadened assistance was provided to adults without children.) We first present descriptive information about trends in employment and job quality for low-income single mothers, and then we consider the impact of the welfare and work support policies of the 1990s.

The Economic Context of the 1990s

The new policies were implemented in a period of strong and widely distributed economic growth, in which there were significant improvements in the employment prospects and wages of lower-wage workers. The nation's unemployment rate fell from 7.5% in 1992 to 4.9% in 1997, and then remained under 5% until August 2001. Between 1993 and 2000, the number of employed Americans grew by 20 million. While growth occurred throughout the economy, demand for low-wage workers was particularly high. Real wages for workers at the 10th percentile grew from $6.54 in 1994 to $7.35 in 2000, making up almost the entire decline in wages that had occurred for such workers between 1979 and 1994. Real wage growth for low-wage workers was so strong that workers at the 10th percentile actually gained ground compared to the median worker and even workers at the 90th wage percentile (Congressional Budget Office 2006). With greater demand for low-wage workers, employers became more willing to hire more disadvantaged workers (Holzer, Raphael, and Stoll 2003).

The Increase in Single Mothers' Labor Force Participation

In these exceptionally favorable labor market conditions, there was a historic increase in employment among single mothers. Between 1993 and 2000, employment among single mothers grew from 57.3% to 72.8%, and the number of employed single mothers grew by 1.5 million. Employment growth for single mothers far exceeded that of married mothers, whose employment increased from 63.9% to 68.4% (Gabe 2007). In fact, the employment rate for single mothers has surpassed that of married mothers since 1999. (See Figure 1.)

During this period, employment growth was most dramatic for never-married mothers. Between 1993 and 2000, their employment rate increased by 23 percentage points, compared with 12.5 points for divorced, separated, and widowed mothers, and 4 points for married mothers. (See Figure 2.) Similarly, when considering educational status, single mothers with less than a high school diploma experienced the largest gains in employment, from 48.7% in 1995 to 61.4% in 2002 (Blank and Shierholz 2006).

A significant part of the growth in employment among single-parent families occurred among families leaving welfare. Between 1994 and 2000, the number of families receiving AFDC/TANF declined from 5 million to 2.4 million. National data indicate that in the early years of welfare reform, half or more of families leaving welfare were employed in the quarter and year after leaving assistance (Loprest 1999, 2001). State and local studies of families that left welfare tell a similar story. Acs and Loprest (2001) summarized the findings from a set of state and county studies from the early welfare reform period, funded by the Department of Health and Human Services, that used a consistent set of definitions and measures. They reported that between half and two thirds of families were employed in the quarter after exit, a majority were employed in each quarter of the year after exit, and about three fourths worked at some point during the year after exit. However, only about a third were employed during every quarter in the year after exit. These employment rates are not dramatically higher than those achieved by welfare leavers during the years prior to welfare reform (King and

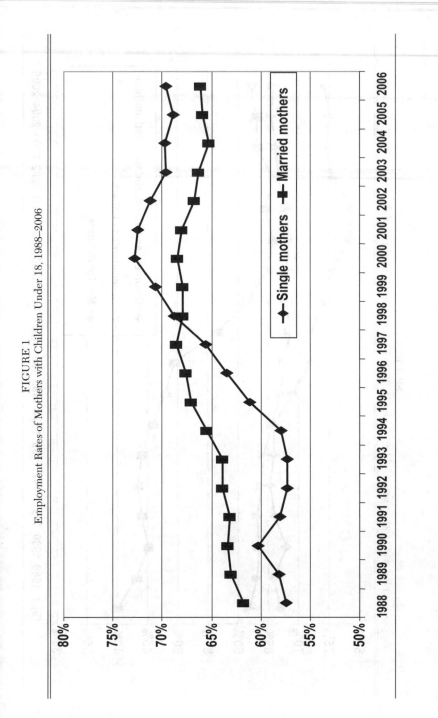

FIGURE 1
Employment Rates of Mothers with Children Under 18, 1988–2006

173

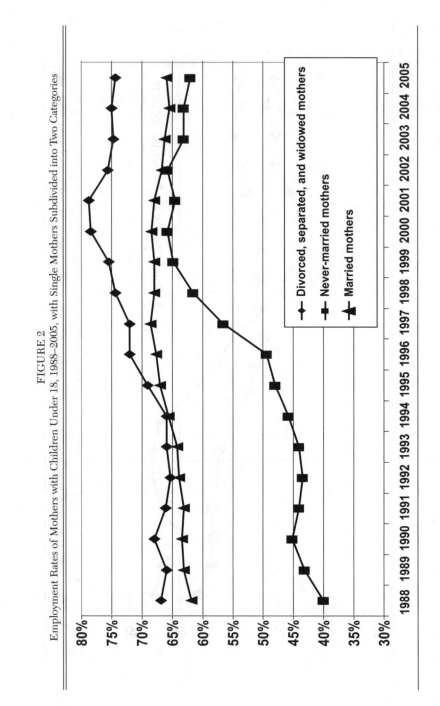

FIGURE 2
Employment Rates of Mothers with Children Under 18, 1988–2005, with Single Mothers Subdivided into Two Categories

174

Mueser 2005), but it is notable that employment rates of leavers increased somewhat while caseloads were falling sharply.

As suggested above, the decline in welfare caseloads was much larger than the number of welfare leavers entering employment. During this period, there was also an increase in the share of low-income single mothers who were not in work and not receiving welfare, a group that now comprises up to one fourth of all low-income single mothers (Blank and Kovak 2007). These single mothers were disproportionately likely to be disabled, and many did not receive disability benefits either (Cohen 2006). The expansion of the "disconnected" population has been one of the troubling consequences of the welfare reform experience.

The dramatic growth in employment among single mothers ended around 2000. The nation entered into recession in 2001, and total employment fell. After 2000, employment rates fell for both single and married mothers. Despite the decline in employment, the TANF caseload continued to fall, albeit at a slower rate, reaching 2.1 million in 2005 (Department of Health and Human Services 2007). Evidence from three national surveys suggests that more recent welfare leavers are less likely to be employed than those who left during 1996 to 2000, with data from the Current Population Survey (CPS) showing a 15 percentage point decline from 2000 to 2005. Both survey and administrative data also show declines in employment following 2000 among current welfare recipients (Acs and Loprest 2007). However, even with the recent declines, the employment rate for single mothers remains well above its level before the growth in the 1990s (Gabe 2007).

What Kinds of Jobs?

In 2005, 20% of all jobs in the United States paid $9 an hour or less, and 10% paid $7.44 an hour or less. Low-wage jobs are more likely to be deficient with respect to all aspects of job quality, including earnings, benefits, job security, advancement opportunity, work schedule, health and safety, and fairness and worker voice (Lower-Basch 2007). Low-wage jobs are concentrated in a handful of industries. Of jobs paying less than $9 an hour, 42% are in just six sectors: food service and drinking places, agriculture, private households, personal and laundry services, accommodation, and retail trade (Congressional Budget Office 2006).

Most of the information about job characteristics for low-income single mothers in the 1990s concerns welfare leavers. Overwhelmingly, leavers entered low-wage jobs, earning above minimum wage but below wages needed to support a family above the poverty line. The average wage rate earned by employed leavers was between $7 and $8 an hour. Leavers reported working close to full time, averaging 35 or more hours a week. Nonetheless, administrative data showed that median earnings of employed welfare leavers were only about $2,700 per quarter, suggesting that many were not working full-time every week. Most often welfare leavers entered jobs lacking basic benefits such as health coverage, sick leave, pensions, and vacation. In the studies that asked about both the availability of health insurance through an employer and enrollment, only about half of those who were potentially eligible for the benefit were enrolled, presumably due to high costs (Acs and Loprest 2001).

Most of the industries where welfare leavers found jobs have high concentrations of low-wage jobs. Loprest (1999) reported that 70% of early leavers were employed in service (46%) or wholesale/retail trade (24%) industries. In 2000, more than half of jobs in eating and drinking places, childcare, and food stores paid poverty-level wages—less than $8.40 an hour. Nonfood retail, hotels and lodging places, and nursing and personal care facilities had only slightly smaller shares of poverty-level jobs, between 40% and 43%. Another 25% to 30% of jobs in these industries pay low wages—between $8.40 and $12.60 an hour in 2000 (Mitnik and Zeidenberg 2007).

While leavers' jobs were concentrated among low-wage industries and occupations, their experience in this respect seemed similar to that of other low-earning single mothers. Overall, wages are low in the United States for single mothers with less than a high school degree ($7.20 an hour) or with a high school degree but no college ($9.17 an hour). Moreover, during 1999 to 2001, 48% of single mothers were employed in services and 18% in retail trade (Levitan and Gluck 2002). Welfare leavers were more likely to be in service occupations than all single mothers (38% versus 23%), slightly less likely to be in administrative/clerical jobs (19% versus 24%), and equally likely to be in sales (12% for both;) (Levitan and Gluck 2002; Loprest 1999).

It comes as little surprise that single mothers who entered employment during the 1990s were at the bottom of the labor market, in jobs with low wages, unsteady hours, and few benefits. However, a key question is the degree to which these workers made progress over time. Some research suggests that irregular work histories are a primary reason why less-skilled workers experience lower wage gains over time, and that when actual work histories are tracked, less-educated workers receive the same percentage returns to experience as more educated workers (Gladden and Taber 1999). However, many low-wage jobs are characterized by inherently unstable schedules and high levels of worker turnover. While some low-wage workers do experience significant increases in earnings, many low-income workers experience modest growth or show no overall upward trend in their earnings. One study that tracked individuals who combined welfare and work in 1999 and were employed in 2001 found that they were just as likely to experience earnings decreases as earnings gains from 2000 to 2001 (Andersson, Lane, and McEntarfer 2004). Moreover, for workers who are starting from the lowest levels of earnings, even significant increases in earnings (on a percentage basis) are often not enough to allow them and their families to escape low-income status.

Longitudinal tracking of former welfare recipients finds that some former recipients did move into better jobs over time, but many did not. In one of the few studies that tracked welfare recipients over multiple years, 19% of a sample of Wisconsin women who began receiving TANF the first year it was implemented (1997–98) were earning at least $15,000 a year six years later (Wu, Cancian, and Meyer 2006). In another study that followed a group of women who received welfare in an urban county in Michigan in 1997, the share of respondents who were working in "good jobs" (defined by a combination of wages, hours, and health benefits) increased from 8.3% in 1997 to 29% in 2001. As would be expected, the probability of holding a good job is higher for former recipients who worked steadily. However, even exceptionally regular employment did not guarantee progression to a good job; of the small fraction of respondents who had worked in every month of the past five years, only 55% were employed in good jobs in 2001 (Johnson and Corcoran 2003).

For both welfare leavers and other low-earning single mothers, one explanation for their limited progression over time is their heavy concentration in low-wage firms and industries. One recent study looked at factors affecting whether single mothers who left poverty in 2001 stayed out of poverty over time. Among those who left poverty due to an employment or earnings increase, those who were able to stay out of poverty were more likely to have held professional/technical jobs or administrative/clerical jobs at the time of poverty exit, and less likely to have held a service job, compared to those who temporarily or permanently returned to poverty. Those who cycled in and out of poverty were more likely to have sales/retail jobs, perhaps reflecting the inherently unstable nature of many retail jobs (Moore, Rangarajan, and Schochet 2007).

Employer characteristics are an important factor in affecting workers' wage progression over time. For example, food stores pay their workers less than comparable workers make elsewhere, while electric, gas, and sanitation services pay their workers more than such workers make elsewhere. Similar variations exist across employers within industries. Where a standard regression involving only worker characteristics can account for only about 30% of the variation in wages across workers, researchers using Longitudinal Employer-Household Dynamics (LEHD), a data set that tracks both workers and employers over time, have been able to explain about 90% of wage variation (Andersson, Holzer, and Lane 2006).

The best predictor of a low-skilled worker's ability to escape low earnings is employment in a high-wage firm or industry. Large firms and low-turnover firms are also associated with earnings gains (Andersson, Holzer, and Lane 2006). The LEHD data confirm that in many cases the types of jobs that characterize the employment experiences of welfare leavers and other low-earning single mothers are "bad jobs" in the sense that they pay less than average even after controlling for the characteristics of the workers. For example, only 6% of welfare recipients who began working in an eating and drinking place in 1999 earned more than $15,000 in both 2000 and 2001, compared with 24% of those who began working in health services in 1999 (Andersson, Lane, and McEntarfer 2004).

Explaining the Results: The Role of Welfare Reform and Work Supports in Promoting Employment, Job Quality, and Advancement

Over the last 10 years, research has sought to explore the role of the TANF and other policy changes in affecting the growth of employment among single mothers in the 1990s. An extensive literature attempts to divide responsibility among welfare reform (both in general and specific policies), the EITC expansion, the economy, and other factors. The research does not answer these questions with a high level of certainty. The fact that employment grew far more for single mothers than married mothers, and that employment growth was greatest for never-married and least-educated single mothers, strongly suggests that the economy was not the only factor affecting the results. In a careful survey of the literature, Blank (2005, 2007) concludes that welfare reform had a significant effect on caseloads and employment but did not explain the majority of these changes. Blank emphasizes that the fact that a set of policies was implemented essentially simultaneously and in an interactive manner makes it virtually impossible to precisely specify the respective role of each component.

Researchers who have attempted to sort out the effects using econometric methods have generally attributed a larger share of the increased employment among single mothers to the EITC than to welfare reform, narrowly defined (Grogger 2003; Meyer and Rosenbaum 1999). By contrast, most studies suggest that welfare reform was the largest contributor to the sharp decline in welfare caseloads. A number of studies suggest that increased availability of childcare subsidies contributed to increased employment among low-income single mothers (Lawrence and Kreader 2006). One study using instrumental variables and a nationally representative sample found that receipt of a childcare subsidy increased the probability of maternal employment by about 15% (Tekin 2005). By contrast, researchers have generally failed to find any impact of the Medicaid and SCHIP expansions on single mothers' employment (Ham and Shore-Sheppard 2005; Meyer and Rosenbaum 1999). This may be because the parents who most valued health insurance coverage, due to having children with chronic conditions, still had difficulty maintaining employment because of their caregiving responsibilities.

Any explanation of the changing employment patterns must also account for the fact that the growth in employment ended around 2000 and appears to have leveled off below its peak but above pre-1993 levels. Considerably less research has been devoted to explaining this plateau. The 2001 recession and subsequent weak recovery likely played an important role. This explanation is supported by the fact that employment rates for married mothers, who were less affected by the policy changes, have also declined modestly from their prerecession peaks.

It is also possible that the impacts of the mid-1990s policies have run their course and that new initiatives will be needed to generate new policy impacts. TANF allocations have remained essentially flat since the program began, and the TANF block grant in 2006 represents less than 80% of its 1997 value. Many observers believe that the families receiving assistance after the large caseload decline have more barriers to employment and will require more intensive services in order to obtain and retain employment, although a set of studies finds no significant changes in a number of recipient characteristics. The share of single mothers who are not working and not receiving welfare has grown, and presumably such families will be less affected by changes in welfare policies. Stagnation in other policies may have played a role as well. The federal minimum wage remained unchanged between 1996 and 2007. Spending on childcare subsidies ceased growing rapidly around 2001, and it fell from $12.3 billion in FY 2003 to $11.7 billion in FY 2005 (Matthews and Ewen 2006). The reauthorization of TANF enacted in early 2006 ultimately focused principally on the mechanics of the participation rate calculations for families receiving TANF assistance, rather than expanding services or supports for low-wage workers or placing a stronger emphasis on job quality for families entering employment.

Having concluded that it is likely that welfare reform and expanded work supports contributed to higher employment levels, it is appropriate also to ask whether they affected job quality for welfare leavers or single-parent families. Just as it is impossible to fully disentangle the effects of individual policies in accounting for employment growth, it is also impossible to disentangle the factors that may have contributed to the generally low job quality for welfare leavers and other low-earning single mothers. Certainly, their background education, work experience, and other characteristics played a crucial role. But did policy also lead to either better or worse jobs than might have been expected by these women's background characteristics? Unfortunately, little of the research of the past decade has addressed this question. This section presents the theoretical reasons why welfare reform and the work supports expansion might have affected the quality of the jobs welfare recipients obtained, and we consider the limited evidence available on the subject. We conclude by examining whether a different set of policies might have had more positive effects on job quality.

First, before the 1996 law was enacted, a number of people suggested that the addition of a large number of welfare recipients to the low-wage labor market would, in itself, reduce job quality by pushing down wages. As noted above, however, the growth in supply occurred at the same time that there was a very strong growth in demand. Ultimately, the growth in demand was so strong that real wages for low-wage workers grew despite the increase in workers. One simulation estimates that over the 1996 to 2000 period, real wages for entry-level workers grew by 8% but would have grown even more, by 10.3%, but for the growth in employment among TANF and food stamp recipients (Hanson and Hamrick 2004).

As noted previously, many states adopted "work first" strategies under welfare reform, in which most recipients were assigned to job search as their primary work-related activity. Some recipients searched for jobs on their own, but many states assigned large numbers of recipients to participate in organized job search activities, often called "job clubs," run by welfare agencies, workforce one-stops, or private contractors. To the extent that these organizations helped link recipients to jobs that were better than the ones they could have found on their own, they might have improved the quality of job matches, even in the absence of allowing recipients to participate in education, training, or other skill-building activities. Given the evidence already presented on the key role of employer characteristics in determining both initial wages and long-term advancement, such improved matches can have significant impacts on workers' well-being (Andersson, Holzer, and Lane 2006). And the argument has been made that simply expediting labor force entry will result in improved job quality in the long run. This could particularly be the case if rapid job entry was combined with work supports that promoted retention and stable employment.

Other aspects of state strategies may have resulted in reductions in job quality. Most states required recipients to accept the first job that was offered to them; turning down a job offer was grounds for termination of benefits. Time limits also put pressure on recipients to leave welfare as soon as possible in order to reserve months of welfare eligibility for future need. Because low-quality jobs often have very high turnover rates and are relatively nonselective in hiring, the first available job is often not the best job that a given individual could obtain. Thus recipients may have accepted jobs that were worse than the jobs they could have found if given more time to search. Moreover, the existence of the EITC and other work supports may have lowered "reservation wages," that is, may have increased the willingness of workers to take jobs that paid less than the jobs workers might have found with more careful searching or after investment in upgrading skills. The net effect of policies depends on the balance between these factors.

In order for job clubs and other job search activities to have increased the quality of recipients' jobs, the agencies must have been involved in actually placing recipients in jobs. There appears to have been significant variation across states and localities in the degree to which this occurred. For example, when welfare leavers in Cleveland were asked to describe the primary way that they found their current or most recent job, only 15% reported being placed in a job or told of a specific job by an employment or welfare agency. Some 78% reported that they had found their job through their own efforts or a referral from a personal contact (Coulton et al. 2004). By contrast, in Detroit, half of Work First contractors indicated that they were directly involved in three quarters or more of all job placements, and 85% of the contractors took credit for more than half of the job placements. These reports were correlated with participant outcomes, supporting the contractors' claims that they were substantially involved in the job placements (Autor and Houseman 2007).

Even where welfare agencies and their contractors were substantially involved in placing recipients in jobs, there is little evidence that these were better jobs than the recipients could have gotten on their own. During the 1990s, welfare agencies increasingly moved toward performance-based contracts with private job placement organizations, both nonprofit and for-profit. In these contracts, the majority of the payments were provided at job placement, typically with additional payments for 30- or 90-day retention targets. Payments were often not tied to wage levels or long-term earnings gains, so many placement agencies had incentives to get recipients into jobs as fast as possible, not necessarily to match them with good jobs. By contrast, one of the few welfare-to-work programs that has been shown to connect recipients to better jobs without upgrading their skills—the Portland, Oregon, site in the National Evaluation of Welfare to Work Strategies (NEWWS)—did so by encouraging participants to be selective about jobs and to seek ones that were full-time, paid well above the minimum wage, and included benefits and potential for advancement (Scrivener et al. 1998). In the absence of such strategies, it appears unlikely that welfare agencies significantly improved the quality of the jobs that most recipients obtained.

Is there evidence that work requirements, time limits, and financial incentives affected the quality of the jobs that welfare recipients obtained? One study of a voluntary earnings supplement program in Canada that increased employment among experimental group members found that they were taking jobs that looked very similar to the jobs found by control group members. This suggests that the supplement increased employment without causing people who would have worked anyway to accept less desirable jobs (Foley and Schwartz 2003). Note, however, that this program provided only "carrots"—financial incentives for recipients who stopped receiving assistance and started work within 12 months. Most welfare programs in the United States included far more "sticks," such as sanctions and time limits. Such policies could be expected to increase the likelihood that participants might be induced to accept less desirable jobs.

Some indirect evidence of an adverse effect of welfare time limits on job quality is offered by Grogger (2003). Based on CPS data from 1979 to 2000, he finds that for single mothers with children under age 12, welfare time limits significantly increased the probability of employment but not the number of weeks worked or the total annual earnings. Grogger suggests that this pattern could be explained if, under the pressure of time limits, single mothers accepted less stable jobs and jobs at lower wage rates than they would have taken otherwise.

For proponents of "work first" strategies, a principal argument was not that initial jobs would be good, but rather that work experience and advancement strategies could help low-wage workers once they were established in the labor market. Recognizing that large numbers of families had entered employment but often in unstable, low-wage jobs, and that they did not seem to be advancing out of poverty on their own, a number of states and localities initiated explicit efforts to promote retention and advancement (National Governors' Association 1998). A mid-1990s study of postemployment services found that case management services offered after individuals left welfare with jobs had had little impact on improving employment retention or earnings (Rangarajan and Novak 1999). Seeking to go further, a multisite demonstration of various employment retention and advancement strategies for families receiving or leaving welfare sought to test a range of approaches. To date, only four of the 11 sites have shown statistically significant impacts on employment or earnings, and the impacts have been quite modest. These findings suggest that retention bonuses may have a positive impact on employment, and they reinforce the importance of close provider connections with employers but do not provide detailed guidance as to a model that should be replicated. Most of the sites found it far more difficult than they expected to engage former welfare recipients in postemployment services (Hamilton 2007).

As noted previously, the 1996 law discouraged states from allowing participation in skill-building activities. In part, this simply reflected a political interest in reducing caseloads rapidly. However, it was also based, at least in part, on findings from NEWWS and earlier experimental research that found that welfare recipients who were assigned to education and training activities did not experience earnings gains large enough to offset their lower earnings in the early years. Education and training were also more expensive than a job search. Researchers from MDRC, the policy organization that conducted the NEWWS evaluation, concluded that few recipients in education- and training-focused programs received enough instruction to gain either literacy skills or a GED. They also noted that a mixed strategy that focused on employment *and* a range of services—including education and training—specifically designed to address recipients' barriers to employment was more successful than either human capital development or labor force attachment in helping parents work more consistently and increasing earnings over the long run (Ganzglass 2006). However, in the heat of welfare reform, this nuanced message was drowned out by those who said that "education and training don't work."

While the 1996 law did allow some recipients to be counted toward the participation rate based on education and training, it placed strict limits on such counting. In practice, almost no states were constrained by the precise definitions of which activities counted toward participation rate requirements, because most states fully met participation rate requirements through caseload reduction and the numbers of low-earning workers receiving assistance. Nevertheless, the federal restrictions on counting education and training sent a strong message that many states were quite willing to receive and implement. As a result, participation in education and training activities among families receiving assistance plummeted when the 1996 law was implemented. The resetting of the caseload reduction credit in the reauthorization of TANF as part of the 2005 Deficit Reduction Act, and the subsequent regulations defining the work activities, have posed additional challenges to states that wish to permit recipients to engage in education and training (Parrott et al. 2007).

This reduced support for skill-building activities may have affected the quality of both initial job entries and progress over time. In a Michigan study, having some postsecondary schooling (relative to being a high school dropout) was estimated to increase the likelihood of transitioning into a good job by 40%. Employers report that they provide more on-the-job training to workers in positions that require reading, writing and computer skills and that these jobs have more potential for wage growth (Johnson and Corcoran 2003).

Would higher participation in education and training have made a difference? Ultimately, that would have depended on how the programs were designed and implemented. Some states have designed innovative education and training programs that learn from the weaknesses of the human capital development programs evaluated under NEWWS. These programs are designed to help participants to obtain career-focused credentials, not just to improve basic skills. They do this by connecting basic skills classes more closely to vocational education, in some cases bringing them into the same classroom. A study by Kentucky's Legislative Research Committee found that welfare recipients who participated in a second year of vocational education had the most successful employment outcomes, with four out of five entering employment, and 30% of participants remaining employed for four consecutive quarters. This group also had the highest earnings for steady workers, about $3,500 more than any other component (Hager et al. 2004).

Conclusion

This volume outlines how employers have been able to lower labor standards by using a wide array of strategies and practices that involve breaking or evading laws and standards. Welfare reform did not cause this trend, but it is clear that single mothers newly entering into low-wage jobs were vulnerable to these kinds of employer practices. While the EITC and other work supports that were expanded during the 1990s increased the effective wages of single parents, they did not protect them from the nonmonetary aspects of weakened labor standards.

The combination of work mandates through the welfare system, expanded work supports within and outside of TANF, and the strong economy clearly resulted in a large movement of single mothers, especially less-educated, never-married mothers, into the labor force. Most typically, these new workers entered into low-wage, unstable jobs with limited opportunity for advancement. There is little evidence that these jobs are worse than those obtained by other similar women, but there is also little evidence that welfare offices helped many recipients find jobs that they could not have found on their own.

In particular, the claim by supporters of welfare reform that taking any job would lead to better job and a career was largely unfulfilled. Less-educated women rarely experience such advancement in the ordinary operation of the labor market, and public policy interventions to help those in low-wage jobs move up were small and largely ineffective. This is a story of missed opportunities. There is evidence that low-wage workers can be helped both through education and training programs that lead toward employment-focused credentials and through programs that provide specific job leads with higher-quality employers. But such programs were the exception rather than the rule in the years following welfare reform.

While restoring skill development activities as a component of TANF programs would be a valuable first step, far more is needed to support skill acquisition by low-wage workers. As TANF now serves only a fraction of low-income single mothers, any programs restricted to welfare recipients would have limited impact on the broader population. A range of policies is needed to expand access to adult education and training, to improve the connections between noncredit and for-credit workforce education at community colleges and other providers, and to make college more affordable and accessible for working adults (Strawn 2007).

The expansion of work supports during the 1990s was not designed to increase the quality of jobs that single-mothers could obtain, but to make it possible for them to obtain the necessities of life in spite of working at low-wage, low-benefit, often irregular jobs. A new set of tools would be needed if the United States were to make a commitment as a society to improving the quality of jobs for low-wage workers. These tools include a level playing field for union organizing; strengthened regulatory mechanisms, such as minimum wages, mandated paid leave, and improved enforcement of health and safety requirements; leveraging of government spending through contracts and economic development activities; and support and technical assistance to sectoral initiatives (Lower-Basch 2007).

In short, a set of policies designed to raise workforce participation can be effective, at least in strong economic conditions, in raising such participation. However, if the goal is also to affect the quality of jobs in the low-wage labor market, a new set of efforts with a range of additional policies must be brought into the mix.

References

Acs, Gregory, and Pamela Loprest. 2001. *Final Synthesis Report of Findings from ASPE's "Leavers" Grants.* Washington, DC: U.S. Department of Health and Human Services.

————. 2007. *TANF Caseload Composition and Leavers Synthesis Report*. Washington, DC: U.S. Department of Health and Human Services.

Albelda, Randy, and Heather Boushey. 2007. *Bridging the Gaps: A Picture of How Work Supports Work in Ten States*. Washington, DC: Center for Economic and Policy Research and the Center for Social Policy.

Andersson, Fredrick, Harry Holzer, and Julia I. Lane. 2006. *Moving Up or Moving On: Who Advances in the Low Wage Labor Market*. New York: Russell Sage Foundation.

Andersson, Fredrick, Julia Lane, and Erika McEntarfer. 2004. *Successful Transitions Out of Low-Wage Work for Temporary Assistance for Needy Families (TANF) Recipients: The Role of Employers, Coworkers and Location*. Washington, DC: Urban Institute.

Autor, David, and Susan Houseman. 2007. "Temporary Agency Employment: A Way out of Poverty?" In Rebecca M. Blank, Sheldon H. Danziger, and Robert F. Schoeni, eds., *Working and Poor: How Economic and Policy Changes Are Affecting Low-Wage Workers*. New York: Russell Sage Foundation, pp. 312–37.

Blank, Rebecca M. 2005. *What Did the 1990s Welfare Reform Accomplish?* Unpublished paper, University of Michigan. <http://www.econ.jku.at/papers/2005/wp0514.pdf>. [April 21, 2008].

————. 2007. *What We Know, What We Don't Know, and What We Need to Know about Welfare Reform*. NPC Working Paper #07-19. Ann Arbor, MI: National Poverty Center.

Blank, Rebecca M., and Brian Kovak. 2007. *Providing a Safety Net for the Most Disadvantaged Families*. NPC Working Paper #07–28. Ann Arbor, MI: National Poverty Center.

Blank, Rebecca M., and Heidi Shierholz. 2006. "Exploring Gender Differences in Employment and Wage Trends among Less-Skilled Workers." In Rebecca M. Blank, Sheldon H. Danziger, and Robert F. Schoeni, eds., *Working and Poor: How Economic and Policy Changes Are Affecting Low-Wage Workers*. New York: Russell Sage Foundation, pp. 23–58.

Bureau of Labor Statistics. 1999. "Highlights of Women's Earnings 1998." Washington, DC: U.S. Department of Labor. <http://www.bls.gov/cps/cpswom98.htm>. [April 21, 2008].

Bureau of Labor Statistics. 2007. *Characteristics of Minimum Wage Workers: 2006*. Washington, DC: U.S. Department of Labor.

Center for American Progress. 2007. *From Poverty to Prosperity: A National Strategy to Cut Poverty in Half*. Washington, D.C.: Center for American Progress.

Cohen, Philip N. 2006. *Not All Boats: Disability and Wellbeing among Single Mothers*. Chapel Hill, NC: Center on Poverty, Work and Opportunity. <http://www.law.unc.edu/documents/poverty/publications/cohenpolicybrief.pdf>. [April 21, 2008].

Committee on Ways and Means. 2004. *2004 Green Book: Background Material and Data on the Programs within the Jurisdiction of the Committee on Ways and Means*. WMCP 108-6. Washington, DC: House of Representatives.

Congressional Budget Office. 2006. *Changes in Low-Wage Labor Markets Between 1979 and 2005*. Washington, DC: Congressional Budget Office.

Coulton, Claudia, Sarah Lickfelt, Nina Lalich, and Thomas Cook. 2004. *How Are They Managing? A Retrospective of Cuyahoga County Families Leaving Welfare*. Cleveland, OH: Center on Urban Poverty and Social Change, Case Western Reserve University.

Department of Health and Human Services. 2007. *Indicators of Welfare Dependence: Annual Report to Congress, 2007.* Washington, DC: Office of the Assistant Secretary for Planning and Evaluation.

Dion, Robin, and LaDonna Pavetti. 2000. *Access to and Participation in Medicaid and the Food Stamp Program: A Review of the Recent Literature.* Washington, DC: Administration for Children and Families, Health and Human Services.

Edin, Kathryn, and Laura Lein. 1997. *Making Ends Meet: How Single Mothers Survive Welfare and Low-Wage Work.* New York: Russell Sage Foundation.

Foley, Kelly, and Saul Schwartz. 2003. "Earnings Supplements and Job Quality among Former Welfare Recipients." *Relations Industrielles/Industrial Relations* Vol. 58, no. 2, pp. 258–86. <http://www.erudit.org/revue/ri/2003/v58/ n2/007304ar.pdf>. [May 7, 2007].

Gabe, Thomas. 2007. *Trends in Welfare, Work and the Economic Well-Being of Female-Headed Families with Children: 1987–2005.* RL30797. Washington, DC: Congressional Research Service.

Ganzglass, Evelyn. 2006. *Strategies for Increasing Participation in TANF Education and Training Activities.* Washington, DC: Center for Law and Social Policy.

Gladden, Tricia, and Christopher Taber. 1999. *Work Progression Among Less Skilled Workers.* Chicago: Joint Center for Policy Research.

Grogger, Jeffrey. 2003. "The Effects of Time Limits, the EITC, and Other Policy Changes on Welfare Use, Work, and Income Among Female-Headed Families." *Review of Economics and Statistics.* Vol. 85, no. 2, pp. 394–408.

Hager, Greg, Tom Hewlett, Lynn Aubrey, and Van Knowles. 2004. *Improving Fiscal Accountability and Effectiveness of Services in the Kentucky Transitional Assistance Program.* Frankfort, KY: Legislative Research Committee.

Ham, John C., and Lara D. Shore-Sheppard. 2005. "Did Expanding Medicaid Affect Welfare Participation?" *Industrial and Labor Relations Review,* Vol. 58, no. 3, pp. 452–70.

Hamilton, Gayle. 2007. *Increasing Employment Stability and Earnings for Low-Wage Workers: Promising Programs in the Employment Retention and Advancement (ERA) Evaluation.* <http://www.acf.hhs.gov/programs/opre/wrconference/ presentations/HamiltonGayle.ppt>. [April 21, 2008].

Hanson, Kenneth, and Karen S. Hamrick. 2004. *Moving Public Assistance Recipients into the Labor Force, 1996-2000.* Washington, DC: Economic Research Service, U.S. Department of Agriculture.

Holzer, Harry, Steven Raphael, and Michael A. Stoll. 2003. *Employers in the Boom: How Did the Hiring of Unskilled Workers Change During the 1990s?* Washington, DC: Urban Institute.

Johnson, Rucker C., and Mary E. Corcoran. 2003. "The Road to Economic Self-Sufficiency: Job Quality and Job Transition Patterns after Welfare Reform." *Journal of Public Policy Analysis and Management,* Vol. 22, issue 4, pp. 615–29.

King, Christopher T., and Peter R. Mueser. 2005. *Welfare and Work: Experiences in Six Cities.* Kalamazoo, MI: Upjohn Institute for Employment Research.

Ku, Leighton, Mark Lin, and Matthew Broaddus. 2007. *Improving Children's Health: A Chartbook about the Roles of Medicaid and SCHIP.* Washington, DC: Center on Budget and Policy Priorities.

Lawrence, Sharmila, and J. Lee Kreader. 2006. *Parent Employment and the Use of Child Care Subsidies.* Washington, DC: Child Care Bureau, Department of Health and Human Services.

Levitan, Mark, and Robin Gluck. 2002. *Mothers' Work: Single Mothers' Employment, Earnings, and Poverty in the Age of Welfare Reform.* New York: Community Service Society of New York.

Loprest, Pamela. 1999. *Families Who Left Welfare: Who Are They and How Are They Doing?* Washington, DC: Urban Institute.

———. 2001. *How Are Families That Left Welfare Doing? A Comparison of Early and Recent Welfare Leavers.* Washington, DC: Urban Institute.

Loprest, Pamela, Pamela A. Holcomb, Karin Martinson, and Sheila R. Zedlewski. 2007. *TANF Policies for the Hard to Employ: Understanding State Approaches and Future Directions.* Washington, DC: Urban Institute.

Lower-Basch, Elizabeth. 2007. *Opportunity at Work: Improving Job Quality.* Washington, DC: Center for Law and Social Policy.

Matthews, Hannah, and Danielle Ewen. 2006. *Child Care Assistance in 2005: State Cuts Continue.* Washington, DC: Center for Law and Social Policy.

Meyer, Bruce D., and Dan T. Rosenbaum. 1999. *Welfare, the Earned Income Tax Credit, and the Labor Supply of Single Mothers.* NBER Working Paper 7363. Cambridge, MA: National Bureau of Economic Research.

Mezey, Jennifer, Mark Greenberg, and Rachel Schumacher. 2002. *The Vast Majority of Federally-Eligible Children Did Not Receive Child Care Assistance in FY 2000.* Washington, DC: Center for Law and Social Policy.

Mitnik, Pablo, and Matt Zeidenberg. 2007. *From Bad to Good Jobs? An Analysis of the Prospects for Career Ladders in the Service Industries.* Madison, WI: Center on Wisconsin Strategy. <http://www.cows/org/pdf/rp-bad-good.pdf>. [April 21, 2008].

Moore, Quinn, Anu Rangarajan, and Peter Schochet. 2007. *Economic Patterns of Single Mothers Following their Welfare Exits.* Washington, DC: Office of the Assistant Secretary for Planning and Evaluation, Health and Human Services.

National Governors' Association. 1998. *Working Out of Poverty: Employment Retention and Career Advancement for Welfare Recipients.* Washington, DC: National Governors' Association.

National Research Council and Institute of Medicine of the National Academies. 2003. *Working Families and Growing Kids: Caring for Children and Adolescents.* Washington, DC: National Research Council and Institute of Medicine of the National Academies.

Olson, Krista, and LaDonna Pavetti. 1996. *Personal and Family Challenges to the Successful Transition from Welfare to Work.* Washington, DC: Urban Institute.

Parrott, Sharon, Liz Schott, Eileen Sweeney, Allegra Baider, Evelyn Ganzglass, Mark Greenberg, Elizabeth Lower-Basch, Elisa Minoff, and Vicki Turetsky. 2007. *Implementing the TANF Changed in the Deficit Reduction Act: "Win-Win" Solutions for Families and States,* 2nd ed. Washington, DC: Center on Budget and Policy Priorities and Center for Law and Social Policy.

Rangarajan, Anu, and Tim Novak, 1999. *The Struggle to Sustain Employment: The Effectiveness of the Postemployment Services Demonstration.* Princeton, NJ: Mathematica Policy Research.

Rowe, Gretchen. 2006. *The Welfare Rules Databook: State Policies as of July 2004.* Washington, DC: Urban Institute.

Scrivener, Susan, Gayle Hamilton, Mary Farrell, Stephen Freedman, Daniel Friedlander, Marisa Mitchell, Jodi Nudelman, and Christine Schwartz. 1998. *National Evaluation of Welfare to Work Strategies: Implementation, Participation Patterns, Costs, and Two-Year Impacts of the Portland (Oregon) Welfare-to-Work*

Program. Washington, DC: Department of Health and Human Services and Department of Education. <http://www.mdrc.org/publications/121/full.pdf>. [April 21, 2008].

Strawn, Julie. 2007. *Strategies to Promote Adult Education and Postsecondary Alignment*. Washington, DC: National Commission on Adult Education.

Tekin, Erdal. 2005. "Child Care Subsidy Receipt, Employment, and Child Care Choices of Single Mothers." *Economics Letters,* Vol. 89, no. 1, pp. 1–6.

Wu, Chi-Fang, Maria Cancian, and Daniel Meyer. 2006. *Standing Still or Moving Up: Evidence from Wisconsin on the Long-Term Employment and Earnings of TANF Participants*. Unpublished paper, University of Illinois at Urbana-Champaign.

Zedlewski, Sheila R., Pamela A. Holcomb, and Pamela J. Loprest, 2007. *Hard to Employ Parents: A Review of Their Characteristics and the Programs Designed to Serve Their Needs*. Washington, DC: Urban Institute. <http://www.urban.org/url.cfm?ID=411504>. [April 21, 2008].

CHAPTER 8

The New Challenge of Employment in the Era of Criminal Background Checks

MAURICE EMSELLEM
National Employment Law Project

DEBBIE A. MUKAMAL
John Jay College of Criminal Justice, CUNY

Americans value hard work and its redemptive power to help transform lives, especially for those who have lost their way. In his 2004 State of the Union address, President Bush called forth these core values in making the case for new federal funding to assist those leaving prison and returning to their communities, stating that "America is the land of second chances, and when the gates of the prison open, the path ahead should lead to a better life" (Bush 2004).

Unfortunately, the reality for people leaving prison is far different from the nation's promise of economic opportunity for those who work hard and play by the rules. As a result of private screening firms that reap profit from our nation's obsession with crime, the politics of incarceration and punishment, and legitimate concerns for workplace safety, 20% of adult Americans—those with a criminal record—too often find themselves stigmatized and shut out of viable employment opportunities.

While criminal background checks often serve a necessary and important function in today's workplace, the integrity of their use has been undermined by several factors. New laws resulting from September 11 disqualify a large category of workers and job seekers based on their past convictions, and blanket policies of private employers deny employment to anyone with even a minor criminal record. Given the rush to judgment, policy makers have also failed to confront the poor quality of federal and state criminal records, which prejudiced the employment prospects of large number of workers. As a result, African American men, urban youth, and others who face significant barriers to employment and limited access to good-paying jobs find themselves even further disadvantaged in today's labor market. Without viable employment options, they will end up being more marginalized and driven deeper into the unregulated and underground economy.

However, thanks to a growing prisoner reentry movement and new public awareness of the costly failures of the "war on crime," an opportunity exists to create a more fair and effective criminal background check process that also promotes job options for people with criminal records and helps reduce recidivism. What follows is a detailed analysis of the major forces driving the proliferation of criminal background checks in employment and a discussion of promising new initiatives championed by public officials, advocates, and unions that offer a meaningful second chance for those with criminal records to connect and contribute to their communities.

Forces Driving Criminal Background Checks on the Job

A number of forces have converged to create the record numbers of workers subject to criminal background checks and now threatened with the loss of their livelihood and future prospects of employment. These factors, described below, include the growing industry of unregulated private screening firms, the results of three decades of mass incarceration, the role of racism in the criminal justice system and employment decisions, and the response of employers and policy makers to legitimate security threats arising from the September 11 attacks.

Mass Incarceration of the Last Three Decades Has
Produced a New Underprivileged Workforce

Over the past generation, our rate of incarceration has more than quadrupled, rising every year since 1972 until it now exceeds 735 per 100,000 people (Harrison and Beck 2006). The United States incarcerates more people per capita than any other country in the world (Walmsley 2005). Specifically, more than 2.2 million men and women are currently incarcerated in federal and state prisons and local jails (Sabol, Minton, and Harrison 2007). A recent study forecasts that the state and federal prison population will increase by 13% (or nearly 200,000 individuals) in the next five years (JFA Institute 2007). This year alone, more than 700,000 people will return home from state or federal prison (Office of Justice Programs n.d.), and another nine million will cycle in and out of local jails (Osborne and Solomon 2006). Nearly two thirds of those being released from prison have served time for nonviolent offenses, including property crimes (25%) and drug offenses (37%; Glaze and Bonczar 2007). The average time a person spends in prison is 30 months (Bonczar 2007), long enough to become disconnected from family and other important networks. As a result of the mass incarceration policies of the last three decades, an estimated one in five adults now has a criminal record on file with a state repository that will appear on a routine criminal background check.[1]

When individuals are released from prison or jail, many return to some of the most impoverished neighborhoods in our country. They face difficulties in finding stable employment and affordable housing, obtaining state identification and necessary physical and mental health services and drug treatment, and connecting to other supports necessary to become productive members of society. Many face substantial financial obligations, including child support orders and past arrearages, supervision fees, court costs, and victim restitution (McLean and Thompson 2007). Given these challenges, many unfortunately return to criminal activity. Nationally, two thirds of prisoners are re-arrested, and nearly 52% are reincarcerated for a new crime or a violation of their release supervision requirements within three years of release (Langan and Levin 2002).

The Growing Industry of Unregulated Private Screening Firms Generates Employer Bias

Also significant, access to criminal records has increased through both public and private sources for civil, particularly employment, purposes. In the past, official state repositories released criminal records only to the subject of the record, the criminal justice system, and a handful of employers and licensing agencies with statutory authority to access them. Now, most states make criminal record information widely available to the public on the Internet (Legal Action Center 2004). Information is often free and does not require the consent of the subject of the record.

Another new trend, and perhaps more troubling, is expanded access to criminal records through private sources. The private background check industry has exploded in recent years. More than 472 private background check companies now advertise their services on the Internet (Bushway et al. 2007). Choicepoint, one of the largest private screening firms, conducted 3.3 million background checks in 2002, most of which included a criminal background check (SEARCH 2005). The 1997 Economic Census reported the existence of 5,077 investigative firms and 1,588 credit bureaus. Federal income tax records showed that the industry generated nearly $2 billion of receipts (Bushway et al. 2007). Information is cheap and available quickly. The cost of a search from a private source ranges between $13.50 and $50, and the information is made available to the purchaser within a week, a significantly shorter period than if the record is accessed through a state repository.

The federal Fair Credit Reporting Act (FCRA) protects workers against abuses associated with background checks by private screening firms, such as the failure to verify the accuracy of the criminal records reported. However, the Federal Trade Commission, which is in charge of enforcing FCRA, has failed to enforce the law as applied to the issue of criminal background checks.[2] Among the more flagrant violations include reporting arrest information that is older than seven years and failing to give applicants an opportunity to dispute the accuracy of the record. Moreover, sealed and expunged information routinely appears on background checks purchased through a private source, because the source of the information is county and state court records rather than the official state repository. Despite a record 400,000 cases of identity theft a year in the United States, commercial background screeners fail to take adequate precautions to identify and correct the privacy violations generated by their reports (Bureau of Justice Statistics and SEARCH 2005).

The growing use of background checks for employment purposes is problematic for a number of reasons, not least of which is the fact that federal and state criminal records are often inaccurate and misleading. A 1995 study in New York State found that 87% of criminal records contained at least one error. The most common type of mistake is missing disposition information, meaning that the record reveals the range of arrest charges but does not include the final outcome of the case, which is often a conviction for a single, less serious offense (Legal Action Center 1995). Moreover, it can be complicated to interpret and appreciate the significance and appropriate use of criminal record information. Thus, employers' reliance on background checks may prematurely foreclose employment opportunities to qualified job seekers.

According to the U.S. Attorney General, rap sheets from the Federal Bureau of Investigation (FBI) are "still missing final disposition information for approximately 50% of its records" (Department of Justice Office of the Attorney General 2006:3). Mostly, the missing information results from arrest information that appears on the rap sheet after the individual has been fingerprinted but is never updated electronically by the state. In more than half of the states, 40% of the arrests in the past five years have no final dispositions recorded. As a result, the FBI's records are similarly incomplete (Bureau of Justice Statistics 2006). Despite the serious limitations of the FBI's rap sheets, the U.S. Attorney General has recommended that Congress expand their availability to private employers and screening firms, not just those that employ workers in selected safety-sensitive industries now authorized by federal and state laws to access these records (Department of Justice Office of the Attorney General 2006).

Race and Racism Play Significant Roles in the Criminal Justice System

The impact of incarceration does not occur evenly across race in the United States, as 60% of federal and state prisoners now belong to racial or ethnic minorities (Harrison and Beck 2006). The incarceration rate for African American men is significantly higher than for white and Hispanic men; African Americans are eight times more likely to be incarcerated than whites (Western 2006). In 2004, the rate of incarceration among African American men was 3,218 (per 100,000), compared to 1,220 for Hispanic men and 463 for whites (Harrison and Beck 2005). One in three African American men has the chance of spending a year in prison during his lifetime (Bonczar 2003).

Research also documents that African Americans with criminal records are disproportionately disadvantaged compared with whites when seeking employment, a reflection of both the effects of racial discrimination and employment bias against people with criminal records. In testing studies that control for the individual's criminal record, African Americans are far more likely than whites to be denied an interview. Indeed, white applicants are three times more likely to get callbacks than similarly credentialed African Americans (Pager 2003). Even more disturbing, a white with a felony conviction is more likely to receive a call-back for a job interview than an African American applicant without a criminal record (Pager 2003).

Recognizing the potential for these inequities, the Equal Employment Opportunity Commission (EEOC) ruled two decades ago that employment decisions based on an arrest or conviction record may indeed violate Title VII of the Civil Rights Act of 1964. That is because such policies disproportionately exclude minorities, in light of statistics showing that they are arrested and convicted at rates significantly in excess of their representation in the population. According to the EEOC, exclusion on the basis of conviction records violates Title VII unless there is a "business necessity" for the employment decision. To establish this defense, the employer must show that it considered three factors in making the exclusionary employment decision: (1) the nature and gravity of the offense(s); (2) the time that has passed since the conviction and/or completion of the sentence; and (3) the nature of the job held or sought (Equal Employment Opportunity Commission 1987). For example, a blanket policy that disqualifies anyone with a criminal record from employment will, more than likely, violate Title VII. A similar EEOC policy governs the use of arrest records, although employers are far more likely to violate Title VII when they rely on arrest records alone without an especially compelling justification (Equal Employment Opportunity Commission 1990).

Politics Feeds the Proliferation of Criminal Background Checks

Politicians of both parties have actively promoted new criminal background checks for employment, driven by sensational headlines and promising a false sense of security. Indeed, since the attacks of September 11, the number of industries and occupations requiring such checks keeps expanding. These new federal and state laws not only mandate criminal background checks, but they also expressly disqualify large numbers of workers from employment, often without regard to the age, seriousness, or relevance of the offense to the particular job.

To appreciate the bipartisan appeal for this issue, consider the latest law on criminal background checks passed by the 110th Democratic Congress. As part of the legislative debate to incorporate the recommendations of the 9–11 Commission, Senator Jim DeMint, a conservative Republican from South Carolina, moved to expand criminal background checks already required of the nation's port workers. Like most other laws targeting new industries for criminal background checks, the port worker legislation most impacts communities of color. Now more than ever before, the ports employ an especially diverse workforce, at least in terms of race. For example, in Oakland's port, African Americans comprise 40% of the workforce, compared to 37% for whites. Latinos represent another 22%, and fully 93% of the Oakland's port workers are men (Zabin et al. 1999).

Despite the 2002 federal law, which required background checks of more than one million port workers and disqualified many of those because of felony records dating back seven years (U.S. Congress 2002), Senator DeMint sought to eliminate the authority of the Transportation Security Administration (TSA) to determine the list of disqualifying offenses for port employment. In particular, he expanded and codified a list of disqualifying felony offenses aimed to screen out "terrorism" risks at the port, which broadly included anyone convicted of drug dealing and felony crimes of "dishonesty." In July 2007, the measure passed both the Senate and the House of Representatives by significant margins and became law (DeMint 2007).[3] As Senator DeMint proclaimed, "Serious felons are prime targets for those trying to smuggle a nuclear device or chemical weapon into our country, and we can't afford that risk. I appreciate the broad bipartisan support to strengthen our homeland security" (DeMint 2007:1).

In the rush to demonize anyone with a criminal record, the barrage of high-profile cases in the news also generates calls by lawmakers of both parties to require additional screening measures. Consider the 2007 case of James Mosqueda, the 51-year-old Bay Area truck driver who was hauling a gas tanker that exploded in the middle of the night near the San Francisco Bay Bridge (bringing down a major section of freeway that connects the congested highways leading to San Jose, Oakland, and San Francisco). Immediately after the incident, the state highway patrol reported that Mr. Mosqueda was traveling at an unsafe speed. Front-page news articles revealed that he had a criminal record for felony drug possession and possession of stolen property (Cabanatuan 2007). Despite his record, Mr. Mosqueda had successfully passed the TSA's background check because his offenses were more than seven years old. Nonetheless, just after the incident, U.S. Senator Barbara Boxer urged the use of tougher federal standards for drivers who haul hazardous materials (*ibid.*). Assemblyman Pedro Nava, the Democratic chair of the Transportation Committee, called for new state standards for drivers hauling hazardous material (Bulwa 2007; Cabanatuan 2007) while publicly proclaiming Mr. Mosqueda a "drug-using, gun toting, hit-and-run burglar" (Lum 2007).

When the dust finally settled, Mr. Mosqueda proved to be the victim of misleading and inaccurate attacks that undermined the merits of the debate to improve public safety and security in the trucking industry. Three months after the accident, state highway officials concluded that Mr. Mosqueda was not driving at an excessive speed. Rather, the cause of the accident proved to be the movement of the fluid in the tanker when he changed lanes, which experts agreed "is especially difficult for drivers to handle" (Chorneau and Yi 2007).[4] Mr. Mosqueda's flawless driving record and decade-long sobriety also came to light (Chorneau and Yi 2007). His felony convictions, all drug-related and committed during a three-year period more than 10 years earlier, turned out to have no bearing on the accident.

At the time of the incident, the only leading voices raising concerns came from conservative, not liberal, commentators. One op-ed writer for the *San Francisco Chronicle* wrote that if lawmakers throw "needless hurdles in ex-cons' rehabilitation, then every criminal sentence threatens to be a life sentence, and decades of playing it straight can count for nothing." She concluded, "But for once, let California have a disaster not followed by a stampede to pass laws that hurt the wrong people, because Sacramento cannot pass a law prohibiting steel from melting at 3,000 degrees" (Saunders 2007:B9). Another conservative pundit, writing for the *Sacramento Bee*, questioned Assemblyman Nava for attacking Mr. Mosqueda, concluding that "by all accounts, he paid his debt to society, reformed and became a very solid citizen—even offering to pay for his cab ride to the emergency room" (Walters 2007).

Interestingly, despite claiming to represent the interests of their constituents, elected officials appear disconnected from the public on this issue. According to a Zogby International poll conducted in February 2006, by almost a nine-to-one margin (87% to 11%), U.S. voters favored rehabilitative services for people in prison as opposed to a punishment-only system, and 78% favored legislation that would allocate federal funding to prisoner reentry (Krisberg and Marchionna 2006). Regarding criminal background checks more specifically, Americans have some serious concerns when the process applies broadly to workers who are not employed in safety-sensitive jobs and when the policies fail to protect privacy by, for example, relying on arrests, not just convictions (Bureau of Justice Statistics 2001). African Americans tend to be even more concerned than whites with abuses associated with criminal background checks (Bureau of Justice Statistics 2001).

What do we know about the true scope of federal and state laws denying employment to people with criminal records? Unfortunately, not nearly enough. At the federal level, no official inventory exists cataloging the occupations that require criminal background checks or the number of workers who were denied employment due to criminal records. We know that after the September 11 attacks, for the first time, the number of civil requests for rap sheets submitted to the FBI exceeded the number for criminal investigations. Nearly five million of the FBI's criminal record requests in 2004 were conducted specifically for employment and licensing purposes pursuant to federal laws authorizing background checks of the nation's truck drivers, port workers, nursing home workers, school employees, private security officers, and many other occupations.

Some of these federal laws extend beyond simply requiring criminal background checks. They also disqualify anyone with most kinds of felony records from employment. For example, 2.7 million truck drivers seeking permits to haul hazardous material (and necessary to work for any major trucking firm) must be screened by the FBI in accordance with the USA Patriot Act. As with port workers, if they have a felony record dating back seven years, they will be denied their "hazmat endorsement" in most circumstances, even with a stellar employment record and the strong backing of their employer. Conviction for drug sales, representing 20% of all state felony convictions, is the largest category of crimes resulting in disqualification (Bureau of Justice Statistics 2004).

Florida is the only state that has systematically cataloged its employment and licensing laws to evaluate their impact on job opportunities for people with criminal records. As authorized by an executive order issued by Governor Jeb Bush, every state agency was required to produce data to "determine the impact of the disqualifications on employment opportunities for ex-offenders in Florida" (State of Florida 2006:2). As a result, the Governor's Ex-Offender Task Force found that approximately one in 10 Floridians (1.7 million) has a felony or misdemeanor conviction on file with the state (nearly four times more have a record, including an arrest that did not lead to a disposition; Governor's Ex-Offender Task Force 2006). At least three million jobs, or nearly 40% of all jobs in Florida, require criminal background checks (Governor's Ex-Offender Task Force 2006). The task force has not yet provided a complete accounting of all those denied employment due to criminal records or other more detailed data on the age and seriousness of the offenses. However, according to data provided by selected agencies in California (conducting over 1.5 million criminal background checks a year for over 200 occupations), one in five applicants for licensing or certification under state laws "show" a criminal record (California State Assembly 2005).

Of special concern are laws imposing a *lifetime* barrier to employment based on a criminal record and other blanket disqualifications that fail to consider the specific circumstances of the individual, including work history, family ties, and success overcoming drug and alcohol dependence. As described above, employment policies imposing categorical exclusions that fail to judge the individual on the merits of his or her suitability for the job are most vulnerable to charges of unlawful race-based discrimination. Laws regulating unarmed private security officers—a growing entry-level occupation now employing more than one million workers—illustrate the problem of blanket and lifetime disqualifications. Of the 36 states requiring criminal background screening for unarmed private security officer positions, 24 have adopted a lifetime disqualification for anyone convicted of any felony (National Employment Law Project 2005). Only five states have adopted procedures to "waive" the disqualifying crime by taking into account evidence of rehabilitation or other mitigating circumstances.

Labor's Role in Holding the Line on Criminal Background Checks

Criminal background checks have expanded to nearly every trade and occupation heavily represented and actively organized by unions, including transportation, private security, health care, long-term care, and construction. Of special significance to unions, these requirements not only apply to new hires, they also threaten the jobs of incumbent workers who are often long-time members with solid, good-paying jobs. Despite significant institutional and political challenges, unions are playing a more active role advocating for more fair and effective policies on criminal background checks in response to these new realities.

To appreciate the major impact of criminal background checks on union industries, consider the laws enacted by Congress since September 11. Two months after the attacks on the World Trade Center and the Pentagon, Congress passed a law disqualifying anyone with a felony (and a number of misdemeanors) dating back at least 10 years from working in a secured area of an airport. The law provided no waiver procedure or other worker protections. About the same time, Congress passed the USA Patriot Act, requiring new background checks of the nation's truck drivers who haul hazardous material, a workforce represented by the International Brotherhood of Teamsters, with large employers including DHL and UPS. Next, in 2002, Congress enacted a maritime security law mandating similar criminal background checks on all the nation's port workers, who are heavily unionized by the longshore unions (the International Longshoremen's Association and the International Longshore and Warehouse Union).

The new federal laws are by no means limited to the unionized transportation workforce. They extend to entry-level workers, especially workers of color, in the service sector, where more unions are actively organizing. For example, in 2004, Congress authorized the private security industry to request a FBI background check, in addition to the background check now required by most states. A press release of the Service Employees International Union (SEIU) characterizes the union's national efforts to organize private security officers in major U.S. cities as "the largest of their kind since the Pullman Porters formed the Brotherhood of Sleeping Car Porters in 1925 to help create the black middle class" (Service Employees International Union 2007:1). Probably more than any other issue, criminal background checks play a pervasive role in limiting the employment opportunities of African Americans in the private security industry and thus their efforts to join the union. Expanded background checks also apply to most workers employed in long-term care facilities, another service industry where SEIU and other unions are actively organizing. Not unlike private security officers, these workers are largely people of color, and thus disproportionately likely to lose their jobs when routine criminal background checks are required and conducted.

Some unions have actively linked their effort to help promote the employment of people with criminal records with their organizing campaigns to build membership in urban communities of color. For example, in Los Angeles, the construction unions have actively recruited inner city youth, including those associated with gangs, in an effort to help rebuild the aging union membership and to regain their declining share of the market from non-union contractors (Quinones 2007). The unions have ramped up their community outreach with the help of pre-apprenticeship training programs. Although construction unions make clear they do not ask about criminal records specifically, an increasing number of larger contractors on projects involving schools, airports, and other government facilities require clearance based on an individual's criminal record. Citing the success of the outreach strategy in Los Angeles, some unions are reporting a shift in the diversity of their membership (Quinones 2007).

Still, the challenges for the unions to moderate the use of criminal background checks are significant, especially given a politically charged environment that remains hostile to unions and people with criminal records. Labor law also plays a countervailing role, as criminal background checks are not normally considered a mandatory subject of bargaining between the union and the employer. However, many unions whose members have been most directly targeted for new background checks have taken the lead in advocating for a more fair and effective background check process. Most notably, the International Brotherhood of Teamsters, the longshore worker unions, and the AFL-CIO Transportation Trades Department have consistently lobbied for protections for transportation workers impacted by the new federal background checks. These unions successfully advocated for a seven-year age limit on felony disqualifying offenses and a waiver procedure, both of which serve as model worker protections for federal and state legislation beyond the transportation sector. They did so despite considerable political and press attacks, as illustrated by a *Wall Street Journal* editorial accusing the unions of "muscling Congress" to protect port workers subject to the new background checks (*Wall Street Journal* 2006).

The Ways that Current Forces Directly Impact Employees and Employers

The policy developments and trends outlined above intersect to create enormous obstacles for job seekers with criminal records, despite the critical role employment plays in an individual's successful reentry and reintegration. They also exacerbate and reinforce employers' fears, making them unwilling or unable to hire individuals with criminal records despite their appropriateness for given jobs.

Employment Is Critical to Successful Reentry,
But the Options Are Increasingly Limited

Experts agree that there is a strong relationship between employment and decreases in crime and that helping former prisoners find and retain employment contributes to public safety (Maseelall et al. 2007). According to a preliminary study conducted by the U.S. Office of Probation and Pretrial Services, individuals released from federal prisons who were employed at the beginning and end of their parole supervision were seven times less likely to violate conditions of parole supervision than individuals who were unemployed (Johnson 2007). In New York state, 89% of individuals who violated their terms of parole supervision were unemployed at the time of the violation (New York State Department of Labor n.d.). According to a study in Illinois that followed 1,600 individuals recently released from state prison, only 8% of those who were employed for a year committed a new crime, compared to the state's 54% average recidivism rate (Lurigio 2005). Consistent with these findings, former prisoners themselves also identify employment as a key indicator of their ability to successfully reintegrate (La Vigne and Kachnowski 2005; Visher, Baer, and Naser 2006; Visher, La Vigne, and Farrel 2003; Visher, La Vigne, and Travis 2004).[5]

Moreover, the longer someone stays out of prison and keeps clear of the law, the less of a risk he or she poses to the community. A groundbreaking study found that those with a prior record who have not been arrested or convicted of a crime over a period of six or seven years are statistically no more likely than someone with no prior record to commit a crime (Kurlycheck, Brame, and Bushway 2006). Research further documents that job quality and stability are key to preventing recidivism (Travis 2005; Visher, Winterfield, and Coggeshall 2005). More specifically, jobs requiring more skills lead to better parole outcomes (Crutchfield and Pitchford 1997; Evans 1968). Sociologist Robert Sampson and criminologist John Laub argue that by strengthening social bonds, commitment to work reduces criminal activity (Sampson and Laub 1990). According to their longitudinal study, stable employment is an especially strong predictor of low levels of crime (Sampson and Laub 1993).

Yet people coming out of prison are hard pressed to find and obtain quality jobs (Piehl 2003; Western 2006). They often lack consistent work histories, educational backgrounds and hard skills demanded by the economy, and social networks to open employment opportunities. Moreover, for those coming home from prison, their needs for immediate work and frequent pay do not coincide with the training and other requirements needed to obtain a job with good long-term prospects. The impact of incarceration on labor market opportunities is severe. On an individual level, audit studies in Milwaukee and New York City found that a criminal record is associated with a 50% reduction in employment opportunities for whites and 64% for African Americans (Pager 2003).

Incarceration also depresses earnings by disrupting career paths among young men (Western, Kling, and Weiman 2001). Economist Jeffery Kling found that the effects of serving time in prison on earnings are quite large (around $500 per quarter) and that no major differences exist by length of time served between those serving violent or drug offenses (Kling 2002). Analyzing data from the National Longitudinal Survey of Youth, sociologist Bruce Western found that the average hourly wage for men involved in crime was much lower than men who never go to prison (Western 2006). Western also found that the wages of black men even before prison are less than those of white men after they have been to prison (Table 1). Testifying before a recent Congressional hearing evaluating the economic costs of incarceration in the United States, Western cautioned that "incarceration channels men into informal, secondary labor market jobs that offer little economic stability or upward mobility" (U.S. Congress 2007d). He concluded by noting that "these effects of incarceration on individual economic status are not new, but they are now playing out on a novel scale" (U.S. Congress 2007d).

Job seekers returning home from prison are less likely to be educated than other low-wage workers, further undermining their employment prospects. The Bureau of Justice Statistics reports that 41% of individuals in state and federal prisons and local jails had less than a high school education, compared to 18% of the general population age 18 and over (Harlow 2003). Moreover, the National Adult Literacy Survey of 2003 found that prisoners had lower average prose, document, and quantitative literacy levels than the general adult population (Greenberg et al. 2007).

TABLE 1
Average Wages by Race and Incarceration Status

Race	Hourly wages (2004 $)		
	Never incarcerated	Before incarceration	After incarceration
White	14.70	11.14	11.80
Hispanic	13.59	12.30	10.31
Black	12.34	10.25	9.25

Source: Western 2006:16.

The survey also estimated that a higher percentage of adult prisoners had been diagnosed with learning disabilities—17%—as compared to 6% of adults in households. An even larger disparity exists between the incarcerated population and the general population with regard to attaining any postsecondary education—12% and 48%, respectively (Greenberg et al. 2007).

In 2000, only half of state and federal prisoners were engaged in any kind of work activity, and those who were involved participated primarily in general maintenance jobs necessary to keep correctional facilities operating (Solomon et al. 2004). In 1997, just 32.2% of state prison inmates awaiting release had participated in vocational programs (Harlow 2003). Availability of and participation in postsecondary programs are even lower, at 13% for federal prisoners and 10% for state prisoners (Harlow 2003). Fifteen prison systems account for 89% of the 85,491 prisoners who participated in college courses during the 2003–04 academic year (Erisman and Contardo 2005), representing 5% of the total prison population. A major reason for this gap is the federal restriction on prisoners' being eligible to receive Pell educational grants.[6] When passed in 1994, the Violent Crime Control and Law Enforcement Act of 1994 reduced the availability of correctional education programs immediately, despite research demonstrating the strong correlation between the attainment of an education and a reduction in recidivism. By 1997, the American Correctional Association (1997) found that only 21 states offered formal postsecondary education programs in their prisons and enrolled less than 2% of the total prison population.

Demand Is Limited When Employers Discover a Criminal Record

Not surprisingly, studies show that employers prefer not to hire people with criminal records. A survey of more than 3,000 employers in four major urban areas (Atlanta, Boston, Detroit, and Los Angeles) found that only 40% of employers indicated they would consider hiring a formerly incarcerated individual to fill a job vacancy (Holzer, Raphael, and Stoll 2003). According to the study, a criminal record is evidence of untrustworthiness, and employers fear liability if they hire an applicant who later commits a crime on the job.

Employers increasingly use background check services as part of their screening processes. According to a survey conducted by the Society for Human Resource Management (2004), 80% of employers indicated they conduct background checks on potential employees, with medium- and large-sized businesses relying on this type of screening even more than smaller companies (85% and 86% respectively, compared to 69% for employers with fewer than 100 employees).

The unfettered use of criminal records is exacerbated by the lack of antidiscrimination laws protecting job applicants and employees with criminal records from employment discrimination. As discussed earlier, while the EEOC has determined that policies excluding individuals from employment on the basis of their arrest and conviction records may violate federal employment discrimination laws, few cases have been brought to test the weight or parameters of this policy guidance. In the most recent application of the EEOC guidelines, *El v. SEPTA* (2007), the U.S. Court of Appeals for the Third Circuit ruled against the plaintiff, an applicant for a paratransit driver position with a single 47-year-old murder conviction. The court concluded that Title VII requires criminal record policies to "accurately distinguish between applicants that pose an unacceptable level of risk and those that do not" (*El v. SEPTA* decision, p. 235). However, highlighting the need to update the EEOC's policies, the court also found that "it does not appear that the EEOC Guidelines are entitled to great deference."[7]

Moreover, few states have effective laws to govern how and under what circumstances an employer may consider an applicant's arrest or conviction record (Legal Action Center 2004) and few mitigate the stigma of a criminal record by permitting individuals to expunge or seal conviction records or obtain a certificate of rehabilitation (Legal Action Center 2004; Love 2007). In the small number of states where this relief may be available, the laws ordinarily require the passage of a period of time and apply only to first-time, nonviolent offenders.[8] These restrictions prevent those immediately returning home from prison from availing themselves of the relief expungement and sealing that laws might otherwise provide.

People with Criminal Records Tend to Obtain
Jobs in the Lowest Part of the Labor Market

Longitudinal surveys of individuals returning home from prison demonstrate that even when individuals with criminal records can find jobs, they are in the lowest part of the labor market. In a survey of 400 men returning home from prison in Illinois, of those working over a year after release, the average wage was $9.60 per hour (Kachnowski 2005). By way of comparison, this is only $2 higher than the Illinois minimum wage of $7.50 an hour and well below the Illinois median wage of $15.55 in 2006 or the Illinois male median wage of $17.70. Among prisoners returning home to Baltimore, the most common jobs include warehouse or factory work (29%), food service industry jobs (20%), and construction/demolition (11%; Visher et al. 2004). Similarly, among former prisoners returning to Cleveland, the most common jobs include construction and general labor (35%), factory work (17%), and food service (13%; Visher and Courtney 2007).

Reducing Barriers to Employment of People with Criminal Records and Promoting Good Jobs

While there are clearly many challenges to moving the millions of individuals coming out of the criminal justice system into the workforce, many opportunities exist to promote quality employment for these job seekers. These opportunities for reform build on the contributions of the reentry movement, including the advocacy efforts of formerly incarcerated people, to forge innovative policies that serve as models for federal, state, and local initiatives.[9] What follows are some of the most promising policies that can help shape a comprehensive reform agenda to regulate the expanding use of criminal background checks and create quality jobs.

1. *Inventory federal and state licensing laws:* In 2006, Governor Jeb Bush of Florida issued Executive Order 06-89, requiring an "inventory of all state laws and state agency practices that limit employment of people with criminal records." In addition, the directive requires collecting data to determine the impact on employment opportunities, while also generating state agency recommendations for reform, including "eliminated or modified ex-offender employment disqualifications." This is a critical first step for federal and state officials to document the impact of current occupational and licensing laws and develop appropriate standards to ensure a more fair and effective screening process while protecting public safety (U.S. Congress 2007b). The American Bar Association recommends that jurisdictions codify all collateral sanctions in a single chapter or section of the state's criminal code and inventory those related to employment and licensing in an effort to limit restrictions to those that are "substantially related to the particular employment" or that are "not designed to protect the public safety" (American Bar Association Commission on Effective Criminal Sanctions 2007).

2. *Adopt fair worker protections:* As required by the federal transportation security laws regulating port workers and hazmat drivers screened by the TSA for terrorism security risks (U.S. Congress 2002), all federal and state occupational and licensing laws should adopt standards that limit the age of disqualifying offenses and provide a "waiver" process. All workers with disqualifying offenses should be provided a meaningful opportunity to establish that they have been rehabilitated and do not pose a safety or security threat.

3. *Require disqualifying crimes be "directly related" to the job:* Consistent with the directives of the EEOC and the occupational licensing laws of half the states, all federal and state occupational and licensing laws should require that disqualifying crimes directly relate to the responsibilities of the job and that employers make individualized determinations about the appropriateness of hiring a job applicant with a criminal record (Love 2007). Of special concern, drug offenses should be closely scrutinized, given their disproportionate impact on people of color. In addition, broad categories of offenses, such as "dishonesty, fraud and misrepresentation," should be strongly disfavored.

4. *Limit criminal background checks until the final stages of the hiring process:* To ensure that applicants are evaluated on the merits of their qualifications and not unfairly discriminated against based on irrelevant criminal records, federal, state, and local officials should follow the lead of several major cities and counties (Boston, Chicago, Minneapolis, Oakland, Portland, St. Paul, San Diego, San Francisco, and the counties surrounding Oakland and Portland) in limiting consideration of criminal records until the final stages of the hiring process (National Employment Law Project 2008; *New York Times* 2006; *Star Tribune* 2007; Sulzberger 2007). Thus, except for especially safety-sensitive positions, such as law enforcement, job applicants for public employment (and for jobs with government contractors, as required in Boston) should not be asked about their criminal record as part of the initial job application.

5. *Enforce privacy and antidiscrimination protections regulating private employers and commercial screening firms:* The federal agencies in charge of enforcing the nation's privacy and antidiscrimination laws regulating criminal background checks (i.e., the EEOC and the Federal Trade Commission, respectively) should update their policies to reflect the vast reliance on criminal background checks and increase enforcement by targeting major employers and commercial screening firms that violate federal law (Nakashima 2007; U.S. Congress 2007c).

6. *Expand higher education, training and transitional jobs programs for people with criminal records:* Consistent with the research documenting that good jobs are required to reduce the record rates of recidivism, federal and state policy should build on model programs providing education, meaningful training, and transitional jobs to those in prison and returning to their communities. Access to postsecondary education programs is particularly critical to the long-term

success of people leaving prison (Batiuk et al. 2005; Saylor and Gaes 1996). So too is funding for job training in unionized construction now available in more communities (pending federal legislation would fund training or people with criminal records in green jobs; Reentry Policy Council 2004; U.S. Congress 2007a; Washington Corrections Center for Women n.d.). Finally, funding should be available for transitional jobs that provide support services for the hardest to employ (National Transitional Jobs Network 2007).

7. *Adopt "community benefit agreements" to promote employment of people with criminal records:* In addition to the city initiatives creating a more fair hiring process, local advocates and government officials have negotiated "community benefit agreements," with jobs created by taxpayer-subsidized projects like airports and convention centers. For example, an agreement negotiated between a major community group in Los Angeles and the LAX International Airport includes a "first source hiring" program for airport jobs (LAX Master Plan n.d.). The deal requires all airport employers, including most contractors, to make job postings available to the community oversight entity and to give preference in hiring to individuals from the community with criminal records and other "targeted" groups. Also, more jurisdictions should follow the lead of the city of Philadelphia and the states of California, Illinois, Iowa, Louisiana, Maryland, and Texas and offer tax credits to businesses that hire individuals with criminal records.

8. *Improve the accuracy and reliability of records:* Given their growing use, public and private sources of criminal records should be held accountable for keeping and disseminating accurate and reliable records. Federal law should be reformed to create a new system of FBI criminal background checks designed specifically for employment screening purposes. Of special significance, the FBI should be precluded from releasing rap sheets until they have been properly updated (as required by federal gun checks under the Brady Act), and workers should be automatically provided a copy of their records to help verify their accuracy (U.S. Congress, Emsellem Testimony 2007). Moreover, private consumer-reporting agencies need to comply with the accuracy and worker protection provisions established by the FCRA.

Conclusion

Nearly one in five of all adult Americans has a criminal record that will appear on a routine criminal background check for employment. Barring these individuals access to viable employment opportunities seriously compromises public safety and fails to provide them and their families the real chance to contribute to their communities and the economy.

A number of powerful forces have converged to create this new employment reality for many of the same communities already hardest hit by the limited availability of good jobs. Mass incarceration policies of the last four decades have left scores of individuals saddled with the stigma of a criminal record. A new industry of private screening firms has aggressively marketed criminal background checks to employers. Federal and state lawmakers have mandated that major industries employing people of color strictly limit the employment opportunities of people with criminal records. These largely unregulated forces often generate inaccurate and prejudicial criminal record information and compound the significant employment challenges facing workers with criminal records.

Building on the success of the many promising state and local initiatives that help hold the line in this new era of criminal background checks for employment, the opportunity exists to turn the tide and restore a sense of fairness and hope to those who have struggled to earn a second chance to transform their lives.

Endnotes

[1] According to the latest official state survey, 71 million people have criminal records on file with the states, including serious misdemeanors and felony arrests (Bureau of Justice Statistics 2006, Table 2). Because of overcounting, as a result of individuals who may have records in multiple states and other factors, to arrive at a conservative national estimate we reduce this figure by 30% (49.7 million). Thus, as a percentage of the U.S. population over the age of 18 (209 million according to the 2000 Census), an estimated 23.8% have criminal records on file with the states.

[2] 15 U.S.C. §§1681 et seq. Limits include requiring the employer to obtain the consent of the subject of the record before undertaking the check and providing an opportunity for the subject of the record to dispute the record's accuracy.

[3] The measure passed the U.S. House of Representatives by 354–66 and the Senate by 94–2.

[4] According to the chief of the California Highway Patrol, "He was maintaining a speed of 62 miles per hour, which is greater than the speed limit for commercial vehicles there of 55, but it is not excessive by any means at that time of the morning with no traffic on the roadway" (Chorneau and Yi 2007).

[5] The Maryland Pilot Study found that 97% of all participants agreed that finding a job upon release was important, and 90% agreed that employment was important in staying out of prison. The Illinois Prisoners' Reflections on Returning Home report demonstrated that 96% of all participants agreed that finding a job upon release was important, and 87% agreed that employment was important in staying out of prison (Visher, La Vigne, and Farrell 2003). In the Texas Prisoners' Reflections on Returning Home study, 93% of all participants agreed that finding a job upon release was important (La Vigne and Kachnowski 2005). The Ohio Prisoners' Reflections on Returning Home report found that 90% of all participants believed

that having a job was important in staying out of prison (Vishner, Baer, and Naser 2006).

[6] 20 U.S.C. § 1070(b)(8).

[7] *El v. SEPTA*, 479 F.3d 232 (3d Cir. 2007:25).

[8] For example, in Michigan, an individual convicted of no more than one offense can have a conviction record set aside five years after imposition or completion of the sentence, whichever is later. Certain exceptions apply, including traffic offenses, a range of sexual offenses, and serious offenses (Michigan Compiled Laws §780.621).

[9] Several important initiatives have focused much-needed attention on the challenges facing states and local communities in reintegrating the huge numbers of people leaving prison and jail each year in the United States. The Second Chance Act, a bipartisan piece of legislation pending in Congress, would reauthorize adult and juvenile offender demonstration projects, establish an interagency task force on federal programs and activities related to reentry, authorize research on offender reentry through the National Institute of Justice, and establish a resource center on a broad range of reentry issues. The Serious and Violent Offender Reentry Initiative (SVORI), now being evaluated, supported a range of jurisdictions tackling reentry through grants and technical assistance provided by the U.S. Department of Justice. The U.S. Department of Labor's Ready4Work Initiative currently funds several youth and adult demonstration projects aimed at improvimg reentry outcomes by providing mentorship and employment services to returning prisoners through community and faith-based organizations. Additionally, the Council of State Governments issued a Reentry Policy Council (2004) report, a set of blueprints for states to utilize to address prisoner reentry. The National Governors Association's Reentry Policy Academy has worked closely with seven states to address prisoner reentry through statewide interdisciplinary work teams. Similarly, the National Institute of Corrections' Transition from Prison to Community Initiative has provided technical assistance to several jurisdictions working through corrections to facilitate successful reentry.

References

American Bar Association Commission on Effective Criminal Sanctions. 2007. *Recommendation III Employment and Licensure of Persons with a Criminal Record*. <http://meetings.abanet.org/webupload/commupload/CR209800/newsletterpubs/Report.III.PDF.121306.pdf>. [September 6, 2007].

American Correctional Association. 1997. *Standards for Adult Correctional Institutions*, 1st ed. Lanham, MD: American Correctional Association.

Batiuk, Mary Ellen, Karen F. Lahm, Matthew McKeever, Norma Wilcox, and Pamela Wilcox. 2005. "Disentangling the Effects of Correctional Education: Are Current Policies Misguided? An Event History Analysis." *Criminal Justice*, Vol. 5, no. 1, pp. 55–74.

Bonczar, Thomas P. 2003. *Prevalence of Imprisonment in the U.S. Population, 1974–2001*. NCJ197976. Washington, DC: Department of Justice, Bureau of Justice Statistics.

———. 2007. *Prison Statistics*. Bureau of Justice Statistics, National Corrections Reporting Program. <http://www.ojp.usdoj.gov/bjs/prisons.htm#findings>. [October 17, 2007].

Bulwa, Demian. 2007. "Rush to Rebuild the Maze; Driver's History: Convictions for Drug Possession in the '90s, but a Clean Record in Recent Years." *San Francisco Chronicle,* May 1, p. A1.

Bush, George W. 2004. *State of the Union Address.* <http://www.whitehouse.gov/news/releases/2004/01/20040120-7.html>. [September 4, 2007].

Bureau of Justice Statistics. 2001. *Privacy, Technology and Criminal Justice Information: Public Attitudes Toward Uses of Criminal History Information.* NCJ 187663. Washington, DC: Department of Justice.

———. 2004. *Felony Sentences in State Courts, 2002.* NCJ 206916, Table 1. Washington, DC: Department of Justice.

———. 2006. *Survey of State Criminal History Systems, 2003.* NCJ 210297. Table 2. Washington, DC: Department of Justice.

Bureau of Justice Statistics and SEARCH. 2005. *National Focus Group on Identify Theft Victimization and Criminal Record Repository Operations.* <http://www.search.org/files/pdf/NatFocusGrpIDTheftVic.pdf>. [September 4, 2007].

Bushway, Shawn, Shauna Briggs, Mischelle Van Brakle, Faye Taxman, and Meredith Thanner. 2007. "Private Providers of Criminal History Records: Do You Get What You Pay For?" In Shawn Bushway, Michael A. Stoll, and David Weiman, eds. *Barriers to Reentry? Labor Markets for Released Prisoners in Post-Industrial America.* New York: Russell Sage Foundation, pp. 174–200.

Cabanatuan, Michael. 2007. "U.S. Says It'll Pay for the Maze Rebuild: Transportation Chief Tours Site, Makes First $2 Million Payment." *San Francisco Chronicle,* May 5, p. A1.

California State Assembly. 2005. Business and Professions Committee. Testimony of Maurice Emsellem. November 1.

Chorneau, Tom, and Yi, Matthew. 2007. "Update: The Maze Meltdown; Sloshing of Load Caused Crash, Early Finding by CHP Indicates." *San Francisco Chronicle,* July 14, p. B1.

Crutchfield, Robert D., and Susan R. Pitchford. 1997. "Work and Crime: The Effects of Labor Stratification." *Social Forces,* Vol. 76, no. 1, pp. 93–118.

DeMint, Senator Jim. 2007. *House Votes to Support DeMint Legislation Banning Serious Felons at U.S. Seaports.* Press release, July 17. <http://demint.senate.gov/public/index.cfm?Fuseaction=PressReleases.Detail&PressRelease_id=d535d843-1321-0e36-bafe-da0c4483bfce>. [September 4, 2007].

Department of Justice Office of the Attorney General. 2006. *The Attorney General's Report on Criminal Background Checks.* <http://www.usdoj.gov/olp/ag_bgchecks_report.pdf>. [September 5, 2007].

El v. SEPTA, 479 F.3d 232 (3d Cir. 2007).

Equal Employment Opportunity Commission. 1987. *Notice No. N-915, Policy Statement on the Issue of Conviction Records under Title VII of the Civil Rights Act of 1964.*

———. 1990. *Notice No. N-915-061, Policy Guidance on the Consideration of Arrest Records in Employment Decisions under Title VII of the Civil Rights Act of 1964.*

Evans, Robert Jr. 1968. "The Labor Market and Parole Success." *Journal of Human Resources,* Vol. 3, no. 2 (Spring), pp. 201–212.

Erisman, Wendy, and Jeanne Bayer Contardo. 2005. *Learning to Reduce Recidivism: A 50-State Analysis of Postsecondary Correctional Education Policy.* Washington, DC: Institute for Higher Education Policy. <http://www.ihep.org/Pubs/PDF/Recidivism.pdf>. [September 5, 2007].

Glaze, Lauren E., and Thomas P. Bonczar. 2007. *Probation and Parole in the United States, 2005*. NCJ 215091. Washington, DC: Department of Justice, Bureau of Justice Statistics.

Governor's Ex-Offender Task Force. 2006. *Creating Employment Opportunities for Ex-Offenders: Realizing the Idea of the Second Chance*. PowerPoint presentation, Slide 27. <http://www.djj.state.fl.us/AboutDJJ/Legislative_affairs/documents/TaskForceFinalReport.pdf>

Greenberg, Elizabeth, Eric Dunleavy, Mark Kutner, and Sheida White. 2007. *Literacy Behind Bars: Results from the 2003 National Assessment of Adult Literacy Prison Survey*. Washington, DC: United States Department of Education. <http://nces.ed.gov/pubs2007/2007473.pdf>. [September 5, 2007].

Harlow, Caroline Wolf. 2003. *Education and Correction Populations*. NCJ 195670. Washington, DC: Department of Justice, Bureau of Justice Statistics.

Harrison, Paige M., and Allen J. Beck. 2005. *Prisoners in 2004*. NCJ 210677. Washington, DC: Department of Justice, Bureau of Justice Statistics.

———. 2006. *Prisoners in 2005*. NCJ 215092. Washington, DC: Department of Justice, Bureau of Justice Statistics.

Holzer, Harry J., Steven Raphael, and Michael A. Stoll. 2003. *Employment Barriers Facing Ex-Prisoners*. Paper prepared for the Urban Institute Reentry Roundtable: Employment Dimensions of Reentry: Understanding the Nexus between Prisoner Reentry and Work (New York, NY, May 19–20).

JFA Institute. 2007. *Public Safety, Public Spending: Forecasting America's Prison Population, 2007–2011*. Washington, DC: Pew Charitable Trust, Public Safety Performance Project. <http://www.pewpublicsafety.org/pdfs/PCT%20Public%20Safety%20Public%20Spending.pdf>. [September 5, 2007].

Johnson, James, L. 2007. "Does Employment Help Reduce Recidivism for Federal Offenders?" *News and Views: A Biweekly Newsletter of the United States Probation and Pretrial Services System*, January 29.

Kachnowski, Vera. 2005. *Returning Home Illinois Policy Brief: Employment and Prisoner Reentry*. Washington, DC: Urban Institute. <http://www.urban.org/UploadedPDF/311215_employment.pdf>. [September 5, 2007].

Kling, Jeffery R. 2002. *The Effect of Prison Sentence Length on the Subsequent Employment and Earnings of Criminal Defendants*. Princeton, NJ: Woodrow Wilson School.

Krisberg, Berry, and Susan Marchionna. 2006. *Attitudes of US Voters toward Prisoner Rehabilitation and Reentry Policies*. National Council on Crime and Delinquency. <http://www.nccd-crc.org/nccd/pubs/2006april_focus_zogby.pdf>. [September 5, 2007].

Kurlycheck, Megan C., Roberta Brame, and Shawn D. Bushway. 2006. "Scarlet Letters and Recidivism: Does an Old Criminal Record Predict Future Criminal Behavior?" *Criminology and Public Policy*. Vol. 5, no. 3, pp. 483–504.

La Vigne, Nancy, and Vera Kachnowski. 2005. *Texas Prisoners' Reflections on Returning Home*. Washington, DC: Urban Institute. <http://www.urban.org/UploadedPDF/311247_texas_prisoners.pdf>. [September 5, 2007].

Langan, Patrick A., and David J. Levin. 2002. *Recidivism of Prisoners Released in 1994*. NCJ 193427. Washington, DC: Department of Justice, Bureau of Justice Statistics.

LAX Master Plan. n.d. "First Source Hiring Program for Airport Employers: Community Benefit Agreement. Exhibit C." <http://www.laxmasterplan.org/commBenefits/pdf/ExhC_CBA_LAXFirstSource_120804.pdf>. [September 6, 2007].

Legal Action Center. 1995. *Study of Rap Sheet Accuracy and Recommendations to Improve Criminal Justice Recordkeeping*. Unpublished report.
————. 2004. *After Prison: Roadblocks to Reentry*. <http://www.lac.org/lac/main.php?view=law&subaction=2>. [September 4, 2007].
Love, Margaret. 2007. *Relief from the Collateral Consequences of a Criminal Conviction: A State-by-State Resource Guide*. <http://www.sentencingproject.org/PublicationDetails.aspx?PublicationID=486>. [September 5, 2007].
Lum, Rebecca Rosa. 2007. "Truck Driver's History Raises Many Questions." *Contra Costa Times*. May 4.
Lurigio, Art. 2005. *Safer Foundation Recidivism Study*. Presentation at American Correctional Association, 135th Congress of Correction (Baltimore, August 6–11).
Maseelall, Aliya, Amanda Petteruti, Nastassia Walsh, and Jason Ziedenberg. 2007. *Employment, Wages and Public Safety*. Justice Policy Institute. <http://www.justicepolicy.org/images/upload/07_10_REP_EmploymentAndPublicSafety_AC.pdf>. [November 5, 2007].
McLean, Rachel L., and Michael D. Thompson. 2007. *Repaying Debts*. Council of State Governments Justice Center. <www.justicecenter.csg.org/files/RepayingDebts_Guide_final.pdf>. [November 5, 2007].
Nakashima, Ellen. 2007. "FTC Asked to Probe Background Checks on Rail Workers." *Washington Post,* July 12, p. D3.
National Employment Law Project. 2005. *The 'Smart on Crime' Agenda: Increase Public Safety by Reducing Legal Barriers to Employment of People with Criminal Records*. Presentation at Congressional Black Caucus Foundation 35th Annual Legislative Conference (Washington, DC, September 21–24).
————. 2008. *Major U.S. Cities Adopt New Hiring Policies Reducing Unfair Barriers to Employment of People with Criminal Records*. <http://www.nelp.org/nwp/second_chance_labor_project/citypolicies.cfm>. [September 6, 2007].
National Transitional Jobs Network. 2007. *Transitional Jobs Programs for Persons with Criminal Records*. <http://www.transitionaljobs.net/Resources/Downloads/Criminal_Records_new.pdf>. [September 6, 2007].
New York State Department of Labor. n.d. *Prime Objective: A Guide to Preparing the Job-Seeking Ex-Offender*. Albany, NY. <http://www.labor.state.ny.us/workforceindustrydata/PDFs/prime_objective.pdf>. [June 5, 2007].
New York Times. 2006. "Cities that Lead the Way." March 31, p. A18.
Office of Justice Programs. n.d. *Reentry*. Washington, DC: Department of Justice, Office of Justice Programs. <http://www.reentry.gov/>. [June 5, 2007].
Osborne, Jenny, and Amy Solomon. 2006. *Jail Reentry Roundtable Initiative: Meeting Summary*. Washington, DC: Urban Institute. <http://www.urban.org/UploadedPDF/411368_JRR_meeting_summary.pdf>. [June 5, 2007].
Pager, Devah. 2003. "The Mark of a Criminal Record." *American Journal of Sociology*, Vol. 108, no. 5, pp. 937–75.
Piehl, Ann. 2003. *Crime, Work, and Reentry*. Paper prepared for the Urban Institute Reentry Roundtable: Employment Dimensions of Reentry (New York, NY, May 19–20).
Quinones, Sam. 2007. "L.A. Gang Members Go Union." *Los Angeles Times*, May 21, p. A1.
Reentry Policy Council. 2004. *Charting the Safe and Successful Return of Prisoners to the Community*. <http://www.reentrypolicy.org/reentry/THE_REPORT.aspx>. [September 6, 2007].

Sabol, William J., Todd D. Minton, and Paige M. Harrison. 2007. *Prison and Jail Inmates at Midyear 2006.* NCJ 217675. Washington, DC: Department of Justice, Bureau of Justice Statistics.

Sampson, Robert J., and John H. Laub. 1990. "Crime and Deviance over the Life-course: The Salience of Adult Social Bonds." *American Sociological Review.* Vol. 55, no. 5, pp. 609–27.

Sampson, Robert J., and John H. Laub. 1993. *Crime in the Making: Pathways and Turning Points Through Life.* Cambridge, MA: Harvard University Press.

Saunders, Debra J. 2007. "Truck Driver with a Record." *San Francisco Chronicle*, May 2, p. B9.

Saylor, William G., and Gerald G. Gaes. 1996. *PREP: A Study of 'Rehabilitating Inmates Through Industrial Work Participation, and Vocational and Apprenticeship Training.* Washington, DC: Federal Bureau of Prisons.

SEARCH: The National Consortium for Justice Information and Statistics. 2005. *Report of the National Task Force on the Commercial Sale of Criminal Justice Record Information* <http://www.search.org/files/pdf/Report%20of%20NTFCBA.pdf>. [September 4, 2007].

Service Employees International Union. 2007. *Security Officers, African American Community Leaders, Mayor Villaraigosa Announce Major Breakthrough in Historic Effort to Create Good Jobs for Thousands of Black Workers.* Press release, May 20. <http://www.seiu.org/media/pressreleases.cfm?pr_id=1410>. [September 5, 2007].

Society for Human Resource Management. 2004. *SHRM Finds Employers Are Increasingly Conducting Background Checks to Ensure Workplace Safety.* Press release, January 20.

Solomon, Amy L., Kelly Dedel Johnson, Jeremy Travis, and Elizabeth C. McBride. 2004. *From Prison to Work: The Employment Dimensions of Reentry.* Washington, DC: Urban Institute. <http://www.urban.org/uploadedPDF/411097_From_Prison_to_Work.pdf>. [June 5, 2007].

Star Tribune. 2007. "Twin Cities Adopt Smart Job Stances: Effort is to Help Stop Revolving Prison Door." January 2, p. A3.

State of Florida. 2006. Office of the Governor, Executive Order Number 06–89.

Sulzberger, Arthur Gregg. 2007. "Job Form Changed to Drop Felony Question." *Oregonian*, October 31, p. D3.

Travis, Jeremy. 2005. *But They All Come Back: Facing the Challenges of Prisoner Reentry.* Washington, DC: Urban Institute Press.

U.S. Congress. 2002. House of Representatives. Committee on Transportation and Infrastructure. Maritime Transportation Security Act of 2002. 107th Congress, 1st session, November 25.

———. 2007a. House of Representatives. Committee on Education and Labor. Green Jobs Act of 2007. 110th Congress, 1st session, June 25.

———. 2007b. House of Representatives. Judiciary Committee, Subcommittee on Crime, Terrorism, and Homeland Security. Testimony of Maurice Emsellem. 110th Congress, 1st session, April 26.

———. 2007c. House of Representatives. Judiciary Committee, Subcommittee on Crime, Terrorism, and Homeland Security. Testimony of Sharon Dietrich. 110th Congress, 1st session, April 26.

———. 2007d. Joint Economic Committee. Testimony of Professor Bruce Western, 110th Congress, 1st session, October 4.

Visher, Christy, Demelza Baer, and Rebecca Naser. 2006. *Ohio Prisoners' Reflections on Returning Home*. Washington, DC: Urban Institute. <http://www.urban.org/UploadedPDF/311272_ohio_prisoners.pdf>. [September 5, 2007].

Visher, Christy, and Shannon M. E. Courtney. 2007. *One Year Out: Experiences of Prisoners Returning to Cleveland*. Washington, DC: The Urban Institute. <http://www.urban.org/UploadedPDF/311445_One_Year.pdf>. [September 5, 2007].

Visher, Christy, Vera Kachnowski, Nancy La Vigne, and Jeremy Travis. 2004. *Baltimore Prisoners' Experiences Returning Home*. Washington, DC: Urban Institute. <http://www.urban.org/UploadedPDF/310946_BaltimorePrisoners.pdf>. [September 5, 2007].

Visher, Christy, Nancy La Vigne, and Jill Farrel. 2003. *Illinois Prisoners' Reflections on Returning Home*. Washington, DC: Urban Institute. <http://urbaninstitute.org/UploadedPDF/310846_illinois_prisoners.pdf>. [September 5, 2007].

Visher, Christy, Nancy La Vigne, and Jeremy Travis. 2004. *Returning Home: Understanding the Challenges of Prisoner Reentry. Maryland Pilot Study: Findings from Baltimore*. Washington, DC: Urban Institute. <http://www.urban.org/UploadedPDF/410974_ReturningHome_MD.pdf>. [September 5, 2007].

Visher, Christy A., Laura Winterfield, and Mark B. Coggeshall. 2005. "Ex-Offender Employment Programs and Recidivism: A Meta-Analysis." *Journal of Experimental Criminology*, Vol. 1, no. 3, pp. 295–315.

Wall Street Journal. 2006. "Felons in the Dock." September 29, p. A16.

Walmsley, Roy. 2005. *World Prison Population List,* 6th ed. London: King's College London, International Centre for Prison Studies. <http://www.prisonstudies.org>. [September 5, 2007].

Walters, Dan. 2007. "Nava Milks Publicity from Crash." *Sacramento Bee*, May 4, p. A3.

Washington Corrections Center for Women. 2007. <http://www.doc.wa.gov/facilities/washingtoncc-women.asp>. [September 6, 2007].

Western, Bruce. 2006. *Punishment and Inequality in America*. New York: Russell Sage Foundation.

Western, Bruce, Jeffrey R. Kling, and David F. Weiman. 2001. "The Labor Market Consequences of Incarceration." *Crime and Delinquency,* Vol. 47, no. 3, pp. 410–27.

Zabin, Carol, Michael Reich, and Peter Hall. 1999. *Living Wages at the Port of Oakland*. Center for Labor Research and Education. <http://ist-socrates.berkeley.edu/~iir/livingwage/pdf/portoak.pdf>. [September 5, 2007].

CHAPTER 9

State and Local Policy Models Promoting Immigrant Worker Justice

AMY SUGIMORI
La Fuente

Immigrant workers—and particularly those who are undocumented—experience high rates of workplace abuse, including nonpayment or underpayment of wages and unsafe work conditions. While union representation makes a significant impact on all workers' wages and working conditions, many low-wage immigrant workers toil in workplaces and even entire industries, such as domestic work, that are not unionized. However, outside of the context of union organizing, growing numbers of immigrant workers across the country are organizing at the community level, through worker centers (Fine 2006) and with advocacy and service-provider allies to push for state and local policy changes that would address some of the particular challenges they face.

This chapter does not provide a comprehensive discussion of all state and local policies advanced by groups organizing immigrant workers. Rather, I look at three broad categories in which many of these policies can be gathered.

First, and significantly, many groups focus on improved mechanisms for enforcing workplace rights—in particular, wage and hour rights. Because immigration status and immigration law enforcement schemes have a significant impact on workers' ability to enforce labor and employment rights, this includes ensuring that undocumented immigrant workers have access to agencies and other means of enforcement.

Second, many groups focus on policies that create a climate in which immigrant workers are not too afraid or too unclear about their rights to speak up about workplace violations. A culture in which immigrants are treated as criminals creates obstacles to immigrant workers' ability to access agency assistance in enforcing rights and erodes their bargaining power in the workplace. Policies clarifying that municipalities and states are not participating in immigration enforcement can help bring workers out of the underground.

Finally, groups organizing workers often choose to adopt an industry-specific approach. Many immigrant workers are concentrated in industries that are structured in a way that has historically limited workplace rights, such as domestic work and day labor.

Why Focus on Immigrant Workers?

In order for labor and employment rights to have meaning, they need to be enforced, and there must be a baseline below which rights are not bargained or coerced away. This requires ensuring that the most vulnerable participants in the workforce are covered by labor and employment rights and have a means to enforce them.

In a March 2006 report by the Pew Hispanic Center, it was estimated that 7.2 million undocumented immigrants were employed in the U.S. in March 2005 (Passel 2006). Overall, foreign-born workers earn less than native-born workers. The Bureau of Labor Statistics reported that in 2006, the median weekly earnings of foreign-born full-time wage and salary workers was $532, compared with $698 earned by native-born workers (Bureau of Labor Statistics 2006a). Experience indicates that undocumented immigrants experience some of the most extreme violations of the right to be paid. While data on the prevalence of violations of wage and hour laws are not readily available, the high incidence of undocumented immigrants' earning wages near the minimum is an indirect indicator of the extent of violations. In 2004, the Urban Institute estimated that 6 million immigrants in the U.S. were working and that approximately two thirds of them made less than twice the minimum wage as compared with one third of all workers (Passel, Capps, and Fix 2004).

Another alarming trend is the increase in on-the-job deaths among immigrant workers. Fatalities among foreign-born workers have been increasing in a context in which the overall rate of workplace fatalities for all workers has actually been decreasing. The Bureau of Labor Statistics (2006b) found that from 1992 to 2006, foreign-born Latino workers experienced a 130% increase in the number of fatal injuries in the workplace. This upward trend occurred when fatal injuries among all workers in the United States decreased by 8% (Bureau of Labor Statistics 2006b).

A number of factors make immigrant workers vulnerable to exploitation, including lack of bargaining power, a legal framework in which undocumented workers are distinguished from other workers, and the informal nature of particular industries. In a report on worker protection and day laborers, the General Accounting Office (2002:11) stated that "immigrants to the United States, especially newer ones, are more willing to accept lower wages and substandard work that offers few benefits or protections, which makes them attractive to unscrupulous employers who may exploit them as a cheap source of labor."

Employers' relative power with respect to workers allows them, in some cases, to act in callous disregard for workers' safety and health. Human Rights Watch released a report in January 2005 that stated that "employers put workers at predictable risk of serious physical injury even though the means to avoid such injury are known and feasible. . . . These are not occasional lapses by employers paying insufficient attention to modern human resources management policies. These are systematic human rights violations embedded in meat and poultry industry employment" (Human Rights Watch 2005:2).

Immigration status plays a role in workers' ability to bargain for better wages and working conditions. UCLA researchers found that "respondents' legal status and lack of English skills had implications for their sense of vulnerability vis-à-vis the probability their employers would abuse them (e.g., put them at risk), and there would be nothing they could do about it because their employer would either fire them or turn them over to INS" (Brown, Domenzain, and Villoria-Siegert (2002:25). Similarly, researchers in North Carolina observed that "many immigrant workers believe that in a dangerous work situation, they have no choice but to perform the task, despite the risk" (North Carolina Occupational Safety and Health Project 2000:1). The GAO also connected the abuse of day laborers to fears about immigration law enforcement: "Being undocumented means that workers may not want to be found, so they will endure a higher level of abuse to remain undetected" (General Accounting Office 2002:11).

While federal and state legal workplace protections apply to all workers, regardless of immigration status,[1] in practice, immigrant workers face serious obstacles to realizing their rights in the workplace. Undocumented workers were legally distinguished from other workers through the 1986 passage of the Immigration Reform and Control Act (IRCA), which introduced penalties for knowing employment of undocumented immigrants (employer sanctions; Immigration Reform and Control Act 1986), as well as penalties for employees who provide false documents in order to obtain employment (Immigration Reform and Control Act 1986; 18 U.S.C. §1546 1970). Employers used this distinction to argue that undocumented immigrants did not have a legal right to work and thus were ineligible for protections and remedies under labor and employment laws.

Eventually, the question of IRCA's impact on rights under the federal labor law reached the U.S. Supreme Court. In a 2002 decision in *Hoffman*

Plastic Compounds v. *NLRB*, the court determined that an undocumented worker who was illegally fired for engaging in protected organizing activity was not eligible for the remedy of back pay—pay for the time he was not working due to the illegal firing—because of his immigration status. While the Supreme Court's ruling applied only to eligibility for back pay under the National Labor Relations Act, it has led to arguments by employers and their lawyers that undocumented workers should not be covered by the range of labor and employment laws and that they be ineligible for full remedies under those laws.

Moreover, immigrant workers face a range of barriers to enforcement of their legal rights in the workplace. Many immigrants fear accessing agencies such as federal and state departments of labor out of fear that this could lead to immigration proceedings. This perception can create serious problems for agencies that are primarily responsible for enforcing workplace protections. Workers are in the best position to identify violations of labor and employment rights. State labor department agents can best do their jobs with the cooperation of workers who can provide them with necessary information and report violations of labor and employment laws. Their jobs are much more difficult if they are identified as immigration agents. An extreme example of this reality took place July 2005 in North Carolina, when Immigration and Customs Enforcement agents posed as Occupational Safety and Health Administration agents in order to conduct a workplace raid. Following the raid, Allen McNeely, head of the North Carolina Labor Department's Occupational Safety and Health division, was strongly critical of that choice, saying that "the ruse eroded trust between the Labor Department and the workers it is trying to keep safe," and further, that "we are dealing with a population of workers who need to know about safety. . . . Now they're going to identify us as entrappers" (Associated Press 2005:B5).

It is within this context that community-based organizations, worker centers, day labor job centers, service providers, advocates, and unions have been pushing at the state and local levels for policies that would advance rights of immigrant workers.

Better Mechanisms for Enforcement of Workplace Rights

A primary focus of groups organizing or advocating on behalf of immigrant workers is the need to enforce existing workplace rights. Generally speaking, one of the problems most often raised by low-wage immigrant workers in non-unionized settings is wage theft—the failure of employers to pay for work performed. Many workers initially seek out worker centers for assistance recovering unpaid wages, and this can naturally lead to advocacy efforts to improve means of wage enforcement.

Workers' right to be paid is violated in a range of ways, including failure to pay overtime; improper deductions from paychecks, bringing actual wages received below the minimum wage; failure to pay for all hours worked; failure to pay workers who receive tips; daily or weekly pay rates that are not based on the hourly minimum wage; payment with bad checks; and improper classification of workers as independent contractors to avoid complying with workplace rights.

There are a number of policies that would help decrease the prevalence of wage and hour violations experienced by immigrant workers. First of all, more and better enforcement of the wage and hour laws by government agencies is needed. It is particularly important that agencies make it clear that they will enforce rights on behalf of all workers, because workers whose immigration status is in question have less means of privately enforcing workplace rights than other workers. Federally funded legal service programs are prohibited from providing legal assistance "for or on behalf of" most immigrant workers who are not lawful permanent residents (45 C.F.R. §1626.3 1983). Without the help of legal services, most low-wage immigrant workers are unable to hire an attorney to press their legal cases. Without strong enforcement by agencies, they are effectively prevented from enforcing their rights.

Need for Improved Agency Enforcement

Employers are particularly emboldened to cut corners on wage and hour laws when they are unlikely to face serious consequences for doing so. Absent strong enforcement of existing laws, the costs of violating wage and hour laws are actually lower—*even if any employer is caught*—than the costs of complying. This sends a perverse message to employers who might be inclined to cut corners. For example, workers are entitled to the full amount of wages, benefits, or wage supplements they are due. If the agency settles with employers who have violated the law for less than the full amount, employers can conclude is that there is no benefit to complying with the law.

A number of groups working at state and local levels have identified insufficient enforcement of existing wage and hour laws as a major problem. Part of this is attributable to declining resources for wage enforcement by federal and state agencies. The Brennan Center for Justice has reported that over the period from 1975 to 2004 "the number of Wage and Hour investigators declined by 14%" and "the number of compliance actions completed declined by 36%" (Bernhardt and McGrath 2005:2). In some cases, state laws provide wage and hour protections that are stronger than the federal law. However, the failure of state agencies to allocate sufficient resources to enforcement undermines legislative efforts to shore up the minimum wage. For example, the passage in 1997 of the Unpaid Wages Prohibition Act gave New York State one of the strongest wage enforcement laws in the country. In spite of this, studies indicate that New York's wage and hour laws are being sorely underenforced. In 2004, an investigation by *Newsday* revealed that enforcement of the minimum wage by the state Department of Labor has seriously declined since 1994 (Rau 2004). A 2007 report by CASA of Maryland documents that in spite of Maryland's strong wage and hour laws, rights have gone underenforced as budget and staffing of the Maryland Employment Standards Office declined from a high of more than 20 investigators to only 6 in 2007 (CASA of Maryland 2007). Similarly, though the California legislature enacted a garment worker antisweatshop law designed to crack down on pervasive violations in the industry, an advocacy report issued in 2005 found that the California Department of Labor Standards Enforcement failed to adequately enforce the law, recovering only a fraction of damages owed to workers (Sweatshop Watch 2005).

In order to draw attention to the need for improvements in agency enforcement, state and local groups have issued reports documenting the scope of the problem and calling for changes in agency practices. Community organizations and advocates in Colorado developed a Colorado Immigrant Worker Rights Taskforce in 2003 out of growing concern about workplace abuses faced by immigrant workers and particularly the phenomenon of wage theft: nonpayment of wages by employers. The task force made specific recommendations regarding how the Colorado Department of Labor could better enforce wage and hour laws on behalf of immigrant workers (Colorado Immigrant Worker Rights Taskforce 2005). In 2005, the Greater Boston Labor Council, AFL-CIO convened an ad hoc committee to look at the problem of wage and hour violations in Massachusetts and to advocate for better enforcement practices (Greater Boston Labor Council, AFL-CIO 2005). The Campaign to End Wage Theft, a New York coalition of community and advocacy organizations, identified the need for better agency enforcement and has provided a blueprint for wage enforcement best practices to the new New York State Commissioner of Labor who was appointed in 2007 (Campaign to End Wage Theft 2006). In January 2007· CASA of Maryland published a report highlighting the problem of wage theft and recommending ways that the state can address the problem (CASA of Maryland 2007).

"Post-Hoffman" Fixes: State Legislative or Agency Action

As discussed above, the U.S. Supreme Court's decision in *Hoffman Plastic Compounds v NLRB* raised questions about undocumented workers' rights and remedies. However, regardless of the federal

Hoffman decision, states have a right to exercise their police powers,[2] such as cracking down on worker abuse. This means that, in spite of federal immigration law, states can enact legislation specifically ensuring that all workers will be entitled to the same workplace rights and remedies.

Labor and immigrants' rights advocates in California pushed for such legislation immediately after the Supreme Court's decision in *Hoffman*. As a result, the California state legislature enacted a law clarifying that "all protections, rights, and remedies available under state law, except any reinstatement remedy prohibited by federal law, are available to all individuals regardless of immigration status who have applied for employment, or who are or who have been employed, in this state" (California Government Code §7285[a] 2002). This type of legislation is important because it sends a signal to employers that they will not be able to employ and abuse undocumented immigrants without having to pay the consequences of violating labor and employment laws. It also sends a signal to workers that they have rights and should seek means of enforcing them. Finally, it limits the unnecessary waste of time and resources to litigate questions of whether workers are covered by workplace laws and entitled to full remedies under them.

Short of enacting legislation, states can signal in other ways that workers are protected by labor and employment laws regardless of immigration status. This includes affirmative statements of policy by government agencies, opinions by state attorneys general directing agencies to protect all workers regardless of immigration status, and *amicus* briefings by state attorneys general urging state courts to apply labor and employment laws to all workers regardless of immigration status. Following the *Hoffman* decision and responding to communities' concerns about what it would mean with respect to New York State Department of Labor enforcement of wage and hour laws, the New York State Attorney General issued a formal opinion instructing the state Department of Labor to continue enforcing minimum wage and overtime laws regardless of workers' immigration status: "a backpay award to an undocumented worker for work that was not actually performed is fundamentally different from an award mandating payment of wages for work that the undocumented worker has already performed for the employer" (New York State Attorney General 2003:6). The California Department of Industrial Relations posted a statement on its website following *Hoffman* clarifying that it will "investigate retaliation complaints and file court actions to collect back pay owed to any worker who was the victim of retaliation for having complained about wages or workplace safety and health, without regard to the worker's immigration status"

(California Department of Industrial Relations 2002). The director of the Washington State Department of Labor and Industries issued a statement that undocumented immigrants continue to be entitled to remedies including wage replacement and medical expenses in workers compensation (Moore 2002).

Language Access

Limited English proficiency is another barrier immigrant workers face when they attempt to enforce their rights. If agencies that provide information about workplace rights or that enforce labor and employment laws do not provide information or communicate in languages workers can understand, workers are less likely to know about their rights and how to enforce them. One of the changes groups are seeking from state departments of labor to enhance their effectiveness is better access for workers who speak limited or no English. The current policies of some states provide a guideline for how agencies can provide better language access services.

Maryland has a language access law that requires all state agencies to provide services to individuals with limited English proficiency and all vital documents offered by state agencies to be translated into any language spoken by 3% of the overall population within a geographic service area. The law also requires all other state entities to regularly review their functions to determine the need to create further language access. (Maryland Senate 2002). Massachusetts unemployment compensation law provides that all notices and materials be available in English, Spanish, Chinese, Haitian Creole, Italian, Portuguese, Vietnamese, Laotian, Khmer, Russian, and any other language that is the primary language of at least 10,000 or .5% of all residents of the commonwealth (Massachusetts General Laws 1997).

On-the-job conditions are also adversely affected by linguistic communication barriers in the workplace itself. A possible factor identified as leading to the high rates of accidents and injuries among immigrant workers is difficulty in communication due to lack of a shared language between workers and management. In its report on day laborers, GAO suggested that limited English proficiency made workers less likely to be aware of workplace risks or to communicate risks to employers (General Accounting Office 2002:11). To address this problem, states can consider requiring employers to provide translators on the jobsite when a critical mass of workers do not speak the same language as supervisors. Both Nebraska and Iowa passed laws protecting non-English-speaking workers by requiring translators on the jobsite when over 10% of the employer's workforce speak the same non-English language (Nebraska Statute §48-2209 2003; Iowa Statute §91E.2 2006).

Eliminating Barriers Based on Social Security Number Requirements

State agency requirements of Social Security numbers (SSNs) create barriers to immigrants seeking access to services or enforcement of rights, as many immigrants are not eligible for SSNs (20 CFR §422.104. 2003). Moreover, the federal Privacy Act limits states' ability to condition benefits, rights, or privileges under law on disclosure of an SSN and requires state agencies that collect SSNs to inform individuals "whether that disclosure is mandatory or voluntary, by what statutory or other authority such number is solicited, and what uses will be made of it" (Privacy Act 1974 §552a [note]).

It is worthwhile for community groups to challenge state agency SSN requirements, either through policy advocacy or in the courts. In Florida, a provision of the workers compensation statute (Florida Statutes Section 440.192 1980) required injured workers to provide SSNs in order for their claim for workers compensation to be considered. This provision was ultimately struck down by the Florida Supreme Court as violating the Privacy Act (*Florida Division of Workers' Compensation* v. *Cagnoli* 2005). After organizing and advocacy by local community groups, a Rhode Island Department of Labor policy of improperly requiring workers seeking to enforce wage and hour rights to provide an SSN for their claims to be processed was discontinued (Pina 2006).

Routine practices and forms may create a perception that agencies are screening based on SSNs and deter workers from enforcing rights. Many state Department of Labor complaint forms include a space for an SSN. Workers may not be aware that a SSN is not required to file a complaint. The Department of Labor can make it clear that workers are not required to provide SSNs. This is good policy because it will maximize the effectiveness of the agency: The perception that SSNs are required to file a complaint deters immigrants from coming forward. Agencies do not need SSNs to assess a wage claim's validity or to enforce the wage and hour laws, and *even if* the DOL has a valid administrative convenience interest in requiring wage claimants to provide SSNs, these interests are outweighed by the primary interest in ensuring that all workers are paid the basic minimum wage and overtime pay.

Private Rights of Action and Limiting Risk of Retaliation

While serious enforcement by state agencies would be needed to ensure broad compliance with workplace laws, legislation ensuring that private entities have the power to enforce laws and seek civil penalties helps to fill gaps in the absence of agency enforcement. An example of such legislation at the state level is the California Labor Code Private Attorneys General Act of 2004, which allows private individuals to sue for civil fines or penalties for violations of certain California laws. Previously, this power was left to state agencies. Similarly, when groups advocating on behalf of day laborers pushed for increased protections under Illinois law, one of the elements adopted in the Illinois Day Labor Law was a provision that any party could seek penalties (Illinois Public Act 094-0511 2006). This means that private entities can ensure that the costs of violating the law are higher than the costs of compliance, even absent strong agency enforcement.

As I have discussed, immigrant workers, particularly those whose status is in question, are especially vulnerable to retaliation when speaking up about their rights. One way to minimize the risk of retaliation is to allow third parties, such as community-based organizations, worker centers, and unions, to bring complaints for violations of workplace rights on workers' behalf. In 2003, community groups and advocates pushed for San Francisco to adopt the highest minimum wage in the country (San Francisco Administrative Code §12R 2003). The city ordinance also authorizes third parties and entities such as community groups and unions to file complaints for violations of the minimum wage (San Francisco Administrative Code §12R 2003). This is useful when individual workers are discouraged from making complaints due to possible employer retaliation.

Firewall Between State and Local Agencies and Federal Enforcement of Immigration Law

As has been discussed, better and increased enforcement of workplace protections, such as wage and hour laws, can have a positive effect on reducing worker abuse. Experience has shown that enforcement of federal immigration law by state and local agencies does not have such a positive effect. In fact, fear of immigration enforcement keeps workers silent about workplace abuses as they increasingly perceive all agencies as potential immigration enforcers. This problem has been articulated by the head of the federal Occupational Safety and Health Agency (OSHA): "in responding to immigrant worker deaths, the agency (OSHA) encounters a difficult situation because sometimes workers are afraid to speak out about unsafe or unhealthful conditions for fear of being deported" (California Working Immigrant Safety and Health [WISH] Coalition 2002:13). As the general attitude increasingly favors prosecution and deportation of undocumented immigrants, undocumented workers are increasingly likely to be wary of approaching any agencies—even those whose mission is to assist victims of crime or abuse.

Overcoming Challenges to Labor Standards Enforcement in an Increasingly Hostile Environment

If labor standards are to be maintained across the board, it is essential that they be enforced on behalf of all workers, including those who do not have work authorization. This becomes increasingly difficult in a political climate that is often hostile to undocumented immigrants. While a number of states and localities continue to adopt sensible policies that further the rights of all workers, regardless of immigration status, increased attention has been focused on initiatives specifically targeting and penalizing immigrants and those who interact with them.

This has a number of effects on workers' rights. For one thing, it diverts attention and resources from proactive initiatives that advance workers' rights. For another, it creates a climate of fear in which many workers are pushed further into the underground. Moreover, it creates divisions among working people and undermines the solidarity needed to counter the general erosion of workers' rights. Finally, it emboldens and galvanizes anti-immigrant forces and those who would use anti-immigrant rhetoric for political advancement to vigorously oppose any initiatives that are seen to represent official recognition of undocumented immigrants. For these reasons, it is essential that those advocating for worker rights confront state and local anti-immigrant initiatives and work to promote a climate conducive to defending worker rights across the board.

When the perception exists that state and local agencies are participating in immigration enforcement, it becomes much harder to encourage immigrant workers to come forward and report workplace abuses. Because of this, for years cities and towns have adopted policies specifically stating that they will not assist in enforcement of federal immigration law. In the 1980s, San Francisco, among others, declared itself a "sanctuary city" (San Francisco Administrative Code §12H.1 1989). The legal context in which localities can refuse to cooperate with immigration enforcement was somewhat restricted in 1996 and 1997, but such policies are still permissible (*The City of New York and Rudolph Giuliani v. The United States and Janet Reno* 1997; *The City of New York and Rudolph Giuliani v. The United States and Janet Reno* 1999). In 2003, unions and community groups around the country organized the Immigrant Workers Freedom Ride. Caravans of immigrant workers and organizers traveled across the country from California to New York to highlight the need for comprehensive immigration reform and protection of labor and civil rights of immigrant workers. The political momentum generated by the Freedom Ride provided the context in which a number of local laws were enacted preventing local enforcement of immigration law.

The current New York City Executive Order 41, which was adopted as the Freedom Ride reached New York, provides an example of the type of policy permitted under federal law. Rather than being immigration specific, it is a broader privacy protection policy that protects information relating to a range of private matters, including receipt of public assistance, immigration status, status as a victim of sexual assault or domestic violence, status as a crime witness, and income tax records. The order prohibits city workers from asking individuals about private matters unless it is necessary to provide service or they are required by law to do so. In addition, the order provides that law enforcement officers, such as police and corrections officers, can make inquiries only when they are investigating "illegal activity" *other than* simply possible immigration status violations. The policy also stipulates that city workers may not share any "confidential" information they have about individuals unless they are required by law or have written authorization from the individual to do so. In addition, law enforcement officers can share immigration status information only when investigating "illegal activity" other than simply possible immigration status violations.

Shortly after the New York order was signed and made public, the Philadelphia city solicitor issued a memorandum clarifying Philadelphia's policy regarding confidential information. The memorandum went on to outline a confidentiality policy similar in language and structure to the one in New York City. The Philadelphia policy also requires that written authorization by an individual for city workers to share "confidential" information must be provided "in a language that [the individual] understands." It also specifies valid forms of photo identification when a city worker is required to establish the identity of a person seeking city services: a state-issued driver's license or non-driver's license, a photo consular identification issued by the nation of a foreign national, or a valid passport. Finally, the Philadelphia policy lists examples of city services that should be made readily available to all city residents regardless of personal or private attributes. It also includes examples of benefits programs that may require that a person be a "qualified" immigrant in order to access services. These additions are significant because they increase the likelihood that immigrants will know when they may properly be asked about their immigration status. The additions also provide guidance to city workers about types of identification they can request and that immigrants are likely to have.

In addition to the growing number of cities and towns with such policies, two states have adopted measures limiting the state's role in immigration enforcement. Maine's policy was adopted through an executive order of the governor, "An Order Concerning Access to State Services By All Entitled Maine Residents" (Maine Executive Order 2004), and Oregon's policy was enacted into law (Oregon Revised Statutes 2001).

While towns continue to consider the benefits of such policies, they also come under attack, particularly as attention has increasingly been focused on initiatives targeting immigrants. The passage of HR 4437, the Sensenbrenner-King immigration bill, in the federal House of Representatives in December 2005 signaled an approach of treating undocumented immigrants and those who interact with them as criminals. Following the bill's passage, an increasing number of states and localities considered, and in some cases passed, legislation that criminalized or penalized undocumented immigrants and required a broader range of actors—from local agencies to employers, landlords, and others—to engage in immigration enforcement. Members of Congress have also introduced bills seeking to deny funding to localities that have policies of noncooperation with immigration enforcement (Koppelman 2007).

In 2006, Colorado, Georgia, and Louisiana passed legislation requiring employers and local government to play a larger role in immigration enforcement (Colorado House Bill 06-1343 2006; Colorado Senate Bill 06-090 2006; Georgia Security and Immigration Compliance Act 2006; Louisiana Senate Bill 753 2006). In 2007, Oklahoma passed an extremely broad law regulating treatment of immigrants in the state (Oklahoma Illegal Immigration Taxpayer and Citizen Protection Act 2007). At the local level, Hazelton, Pennsylvania, drew national attention when it passed extremely broad legislation targeting immigrants (Hazelton Illegal Immigration Relief Act 2006). Other towns, including Riverside, New Jersey, adopted similar ordinances.

This movement at state and local levels has diverted energy and resources from attempts to find proactive solutions addressing the problems of employer abuses. Moreover, the reality is that anti-immigrant initiatives have resulted in costs but no benefits for the states and localities that have adopted them. In addition to being unconstitutional, state and local laws targeting immigrants have proven to be an expensive exercise in bad policy. Local laws targeting immigrants have been determined unconstitutional, and localities have been obliged to spend resources defending the laws in court. The Hazelton law, for example, was ultimately struck down in federal court (*Lozano et al.* v. *City of Hazelton* 2007). A number of other local initiatives have also been called into question by federal courts around the country (*Garrett* v. *City of*

Escondido 2006; *Reynolds* v. *City of Valley Park, MO* 2006; *Stewart* v. *Cherokee Country* 2007; *Vasquez* v. *City of Farmer's Branch* 2007). A year after passing a series of laws targeting immigrants, Colorado found it had spent millions of dollars implementing the laws but had seen no benefits (Couch 2007). Riverside, New Jersey, actually voted to rescind its law after realizing that it was unworkable, had led to unnecessary divisiveness and discrimination, and had a negative impact on local business (Puerto Rican Legal Defense and Education Fund 2007).

Though political effect has outweighed sensible policy choices in a number of recent examples, hopefully this will not completely prevent states and localities from adopting sensible policies that further civil and labor rights. Fortunately, as anti-immigrant initiatives capture public attention, the list of localities adopting policies of noncooperation with immigration enforcement continues to grow. In 2007, the city of Detroit, Michigan, adopted an ordinance that prohibits profiling on the basis of a number of statuses, including immigration status (Detroit City Code, *Bias-Based Policing and Solicitation of Immigration Status* 2007). Those who are concerned about maintaining a climate in which labor, civil, and human rights can be upheld will have to stand up to the rhetoric and political posturing that push elected officials to adopt useless and costly anti-immigrant initiatives.

At the same time, this rhetoric has galvanized and politicized opposition to initiatives that are seen as proimmigrant. The recent history of driver's license policy in New York State provides an instructive example. Over the past several years, a statewide coalition of labor, community, religious, and advocacy groups had drawn attention to the need to reverse an internal policy of the Department of Motor Vehicles that conditioned access to driver's licenses on proof of immigration status. That policy put an expiration date on the livelihood of tens of thousands of New Yorkers who would be unable to renew their licenses. It also threatened to push people into the shadows as they became unable to identify themselves, cooperate with law enforcement, and participate in daily life.

In September 2007, Governor Spitzer announced that New York would roll back the immigration status requirement to access driver's licenses and adopt antifraud measures to ensure the security and validity of New York's licenses. While there was broad support for this policy from a range of labor, community, and other groups as well as national security experts and elected officials, it was met with loud opposition nonetheless (Schlesinger and Traub 2007). Anti-immigrant groups that equated immigrants with terrorists led the outcry, which was then picked up by elected officials criticizing the governor (New York Immigration Coalition 2007). Voices of support and of immigrant communities were drowned out by extremist rhetoric and anti-immigrant sound bites, and the governor's favorability rating was reported to have plummeted (Bindrim 2007). In this context, the governor retreated twice. He first proposed a modified plan that made concessions on a number of key principles supported by immigrant worker advocates; then he dropped the plan altogether (Schlesinger and Traub 2007). Ultimately, New York was left without a solution to the problem of hundreds of thousands of New Yorkers who are unable to obtain driver's licenses and auto insurance, sending the unfortunate message that it is politically risky to support policies that are seen to benefit undocumented immigrants.

Industry-Specific Approaches

In some cases, the best way to lift the floor of wages and working conditions is to address the realities and structure of entire industries. Certain sectors that are characterized by low wages and poor working conditions are also ones in which many immigrant workers are employed. While workers in those sectors face a range of abuses associated with their immigration status, the particular structures of the industries also leave workers vulnerable to abuse. In many cases, an industry-specific approach is an essential component of what is needed to address widespread exploitation of workers. In some cases, as I will discuss below, this is because of the legal framework governing the industry or the short-term or contingent nature of the work. Moreover, certain employer strategies of chiseling wages and benefits predominate in particular industries. Finally, worker organizing and building power are essential to raising standards—as has been demonstrated by labor unions. A number of worker centers have adopted industry-specific strategies to worker organizing—focusing, for example, on the restaurant, taxi, garment, domestic work, and day labor industries. This chapter looks at two of these industries, domestic work and day labor.

Domestic Workers[3]

The domestic work industry is dominated by women of color and immigrant women in particular (Domestic Workers United and DataCenter 2006). The isolated nature of their work puts them at a disadvantage in negotiating with their employers for better work conditions. Moreover, they face pervasive violations of the rights they do have under the law.

Domestic workers, such as those who care for children or perform housecleaning, have historically been systematically excluded from workplace protections under federal law. The National Labor Relations Act, which protects workers' rights to organize and bargain collectively, specifically excludes domestic workers from definition of "employee" (NLRA 1935), thus excluding them from the act's protections. Until 1974 all domestic workers were completely excluded from coverage under the Fair Labor Standards Act (FLSA; Fair Labor Standards Act 1938; Fair Labor Standards Amendments 1974), which provides for minimum wage and overtime. The FLSA still excludes from coverage those domestic workers who are considered "casual" employees, such as babysitters and "companions" for the sick or elderly. Furthermore, domestic workers who live in the employer's home, unlike most other employees in the U.S., are not entitled to overtime under FLSA. The regulations associated with the Occupational Safety and Health Act, which regulates health and safety conditions in the workplace, explicitly exclude domestic workers from the act's protections "as a matter of policy" (29 CFR 1975.6 1972). Title VII bars employment discrimination on the basis of "race, color, religion, sex, or national origin" but applies only to employers with 15 or more employees, thus for practical purposes excluding domestic workers (Civil Rights Act 1964). They are similarly excluded from the Family Medical Leave Act (FMLA), which protects workers' right to take up to 12 weeks unpaid leave due to illness, birth, adoption or foster placement of a child, or need to care for an ailing spouse, child, or parent, because the FMLA protects only those employed by employers with at least 50 employees (Family Medical Leave Act 1993).

Exclusion from state protections. Domestic workers have been excluded from protections under state laws as well as under federal laws. Just two of many examples can be found in the California and New York overtime provisions. California provides for an overtime exemption for workers who are "personal attendants," meaning their work consists of caring for children, seniors, or patients (California Wage Order 15-2001 2001§1[B]). Only domestic workers who spend 20% or more time cleaning or performing housework are eligible for overtime under California law.[4] Under New York regulation, domestic workers who live in an employer's home are only entitled to overtime at a rate of 1.5 times the minimum wage, as contrasted with the normal overtime rate of 1.5 times the regular rate of pay, and then only after 44 hours of work in a week, as contrasted to the normal overtime threshold of 40 hours of work in a week (12 NYCRR §142-2.2 2004). As under federal law, domestic workers are excluded for practical purposes from New York state employment discrimination protections, which apply only to employers with more than four employees (New York Executive Law §292[5] 2007). Finally, domestic workers are not even guaranteed coverage under workers compensation. For example, under New York State law, those who work more than 40 hours per week for the same employer are covered, but only if the employer has chosen to secure workers compensation insurance (New York Workers Compensation Law §2[4] 2007).

In addition to being denied basic workplace protections, many domestic workers are unlikely to have any of the additional benefits that might be voluntarily provided by employers, such as paid sick leave, paid vacation leave, severance pay, days off from work, paid holidays, and advance notice of termination. Moreover, many domestic workers are unaware of the rights they have or how to enforce them. Because of this, a number of groups across the country have been organizing domestic workers, pushing for recognition of a standard employment contract and for legal change to address the historical injustices they face (Domestic Workers United and DataCenter 2006).

Employer noncompliance with existing protections. A study of domestic workers in New York conducted by Domestic Workers United and DataCenter (2006) reported that "forty-one percent (41%) of the workers earn low wages. An additional 26% make wages below the poverty line or below minimum wage. Half of workers work overtime—often more than 50–60 hours a week. Sixty-seven percent (67%) don't receive overtime pay for overtime hours worked." A study conducted by students at George Washington University of domestic workers in Maryland determined that 75% did not receive the overtime pay due to them and that approximately 50% did not receive the state minimum wage (CASA of Maryland 2007). In California, a survey conducted by the Coalition for Domestic Worker Rights together with the Data Center determined that 11% of domestic workers in the San Francisco Bay area earned less than the state minimum wage (National Employment Law Project 2006). The survey also determined that 22% of domestic workers were paid less than agreed upon with their employer, and 16% were not paid for their work at all or paid with a bad check.

Domestic worker bills. Some progress has been made at the local level. Legislation passed in New York City and Nassau County, New York, regulates agencies that place domestic workers in jobs. Agencies must provide a written description of employee rights and employer obligations to both employees and potential employers (Nassau County Administrative Code §21-9.10.02 2006; New York City Administrative Code §20-771 2003). When the agency arranges for a worker to apply for a position, it must provide a written job description (Nassau County Administrative Code §21-9.10.03 2006; New York City Administrative Code §20-772 2003).

However, this is only a start. Comprehensive legislation at the federal or state level would be needed to right the wrongs that have developed in an industry that has gone largely unregulated throughout history. Organizers and advocates have chosen to focus on passing legislation at the state level. In 2006, the California Coalition for Household Worker Rights presented legislation, AB 2536 (Montañez), that proposed equality in overtime protections for personal attendants and liquidated damages for all domestic workers. The legislation passed but was vetoed by Governor Schwartzenegger (Schwarzenneger 2006).

In 2007, as a result of advocacy by Domestic Workers United, legislation has been reintroduced in the New York State legislature that would provide a broad "Domestic Worker Bill of Rights." The bills are A00628A in the Assembly and S 5235 in the Senate. This legislation would phase in a living wage for domestic workers and, in addition to the means of enforcing their rights, would provide for overtime pay for hours worked over 40 a week; one day off per week; family medical leave; paid vacation, holidays, and sick days; and severance pay and advance notice of termination.

Day Labor

The most comprehensive national study on day labor reports that "on any given day, approximately 117,600 workers are either looking for day-labor jobs or employed as a day laborer" (Valenzuela et al. 2006:i) The study also reports that day laborers are widely subjected to wage theft, on-the-job injuries, and harassment. Wage and hour problems confronting day laborers take many forms, including complete nonpayment and late payment of wages, payment of less than the agreed-upon rate, and payment by checks with insufficient funds. Furthermore, as a report issued by the U.S. General Accounting Office notes, there are certain lawful practices under the FLSA, such as permissible wage deductions for items such as meals and transportation, that can adversely impact day laborers, bringing their take-home pay well below the minimum wage (General Accounting Office 2002). Day labor employers often delay payments of promised wages until the completion of a job. Upon completion, day laborers are commonly left with less than they were promised or a void check.

Chicago groups, including the Union Latina and the San Lucas Worker Center, pushed Illinois to enact a strengthened Day Labor Services Act (Blagojevich 2005). This follows on the successful campaign to get the city of Chicago to enact a citywide day labor ordinance. Like the majority of other state-level laws regulating day labor, the Illinois and Chicago laws largely serve to regulate labor intermediaries—"day and temporary labor service providers" and third-party employers who contract with those intermediaries for labor

(National Employment Law Project 2005a). While the regulation of labor intermediaries is a good idea, it is only one piece of what is needed to address the conditions faced by most day laborers. According to the national day labor report, the vast majority of day laborers seek work at informal sites in front of businesses and on busy streets (Valenzuela et al. 2006). Thus, most of them contract directly with worksite employers and do not interact with labor intermediaries, who may be easier to regulate.

While day laborers would benefit from enhanced legal protections and regulation of direct worksite employers (National Employment Law Project 2005b), the most pressing problem is the lack of means for them to enforce the wage and hour rights they already have under state and federal laws. Similarly, the occupational health and safety problems faced by day laborers are not simply due to lack of legal protection. Many day laborers fall within the jurisdiction of the federal Occupational Safety and Health Administration (OSHA). Limited investigative resources, the fleeting nature of day labor employment, and the complaint-driven nature of OSHA enforcement result in a virtual absence of health and safety enforcement for day laborers. In theory the complaints process that drives enforcement of the Occupational Safety and Health Act makes it possible for any employee to report a health or safety violation. However, many researchers and agencies dealing with day laborers agree that day laborers underreport their concerns about workplace safety and health because they believe no corrective action will be taken, and they are willing to risk their safety as long as they are paid (General Accounting Office 2002). This is particularly troubling because "few if any, day laborers receive personal protective equipment or safety training" (p. 15). So in practice, fear of retaliation, the short-term nature of day labor, and limited enforcement resources have severely restricted OSHA monitoring of day labor worksites. OSHA's focus on larger projects and employers results in a lack of oversight of smaller employers more likely to employ day laborers.

Day labor community job centers. In order to address the workplace abuses faced by day laborers, a number of groups around the country have turned to organizing and developing day labor centers. Abel Valenzuela of UCLA and Nik Theodore of the University of Illinois studied 61 groups that specifically organize day labor centers around the country (Theodore, Valenzuela Jr, and Meléndez 2008). Day labor centers bring order to the often-chaotic competition of work in public rights of way or parking lots. They also raise the wage floor and serve many of the same roles as other worker centers.

Both the National Day Labor Study (Valenzuela et al. 2006) and the GAO report identify day labor community job centers as an effective and immediate means to address the labor violations faced by day laborers. In its report, the GAO concluded that an effective way for agencies to improve their enforcement efforts is to develop relationships with agencies that serve day laborers—such as day labor community job centers. In fact, GAO worked with a number of groups that work with or run such centers to gather the information for its report (General Accounting Office 2002).

In addition to helping government agencies improve their enforcement activities, day labor community job centers engage in a range of activities to address violations themselves. As described in the GAO report, centers provide day laborers with rights education. Many provide booklets to help workers record information about jobs performed and hours worked. They help workers negotiate with employers for wages owed. When employers refuse to pay, they engage in direct action, such as picketing, to pressure employers to pay; they assist workers in filing claims with government agencies; sometimes they refer workers to private attorneys or to the State Attorney General's office (General Accounting Office 2002). Moreover, the National Day Labor Study describes the broader mediating role played by centers: They monitor employer practices, they help organize and normalize the hiring process, they provide opportunities for workers to develop skills and find better jobs, and they help to mediate community tensions and involve other community stakeholders in addressing the challenges faced by day laborers (Valenzuela et al. 2006).

Public officials and police around the country have spoken in support of day labor job centers (National Employment Law Project 2005c), and a growing number of towns and cities have decided to provide funds and support for them. For example, Montgomery County council member Tom Perez said the following in a January 2005 news release:

> This center renews our commitment to include everyone in Montgomery County's economic development. The successful partnership between business, government and CASA of Maryland has shown that matching employers and employees in a safe and organized environment benefits families, small businesses, and the community. The rising tide of Wheaton redevelopment must lift all boats to succeed (Montgomery County, Maryland 2005).

Conclusion

Ultimately, broad approaches that build power for all workers and minimize the differences that are exploited to underpay and abuse workers would have the biggest impact on eliminating sweatshop conditions.

Such broad approaches include meaningful, comprehensive immigration reform that maintains workers' rights, and increased rates of unionization of all workers, immigrant and nonimmigrant alike. However, organizing at a community level around local and state policies aimed at addressing immediate problems identified by immigrant workers can help to build power among immigrant workers and develop a climate in which it is harder for employers to use workers' differences to divide and exploit. As increasing numbers of workers find themselves on the outside—not members of unions, and uncertain of whether they will ever be able to adjust their immigration status—it is particularly important to identify policies to ensure that those workers are not forever doomed to operate in an abusive underground as well.

The intensity of anti-immigrant rhetoric following the failure of attempts to pass comprehensive federal immigration reform legislation has led to a political climate that threatens to push already vulnerable immigrant workers further underground. Policies that pit workers against each other based on immigration status undermine worker organizing and lower standards for everyone. Thus the task for those concerned with advancing civil and labor rights is twofold: Ensure that labor rights, including the right to be paid and the right to organize, are upheld for everyone, and counter the latest wave of anti-immigrant scapegoating that divides workers into a two-tiered workforce and diverts attention away from addressing real problems.

Endnotes

[1] See, for example, the following: U.S. Department of Labor Wage and Hour Division, Fact Sheet #48, *Application of U.S. Labor Laws to Immigrant Workers: Effect of Hoffman Plastics Decision on Laws Enforced by the Wage and Hour Division* at http://www.dol.gov/esa/regs/compliance/whd/whdfs48.htm [September 30, 2007] (stating that it will fully and vigorously enforce the Occupational Safety and Health Act [OSHA]) the FLSA, the Migrant and Seasonal Worker Protection Act [AWPA], and the Mine Safety and Health Act without regard to whether an employee is documented or undocumented); New York State Attorney General Formal Opinion No. 2003-F3, 2003 N.Y. AG LEXIS 20 at 12 (stating that "a backpay award to an undocumented worker for work that was not actually performed is fundamentally different from an award mandating payment of wages for work that the undocumented worker has already performed for the employer"); EEOC press release, *EEOC Reaffirms Commitment to Protecting Undocumented Workers from Discrimination* (June 28, 2002; "Hoffman Plastics . . . does not affect the government's ability to root out discrimination against undocumented workers" and has "directed its field offices that claims for all forms of relief, other than reinstatement and post-termination backpay for periods after discharge or failure to hire, should be processed in accord with existing standards, without regard to an individual's immigration status"); *Balbuena v. IDR Realty LLC,* 2006 N.Y. LEXIS 200; 2006 NY Slip Op 1248 (N.Y. Feb 21, 2006; holding undocumented workers are not precluded from recovering lost earnings in tort).

[2] *New York State Conf. of Blue Cross & Blue Shield Plans* v. *Travelers Ins. Co.*, 514 U.S. 645, 654 (1995); see *Rice* v. *Santa Fe Elevator Corp.*, 331 U.S. 218, 230 (1947; "[W]e start with the assumption that the historic police powers of the States were not to be superseded by the Federal Act unless that was the clear and manifest purpose of Congress"). See also *Locke* v. *United States*, 529 U.S 89, 108 (2000); *Jones* v. *Rath Packing Co.*, 430 U.S. 519, 525 (1977; "assumption" is triggered where "field which Congress is said to have pre-empted has been traditionally occupied by the States"); *California* v. *ARC America Corp.*, 109 S.Ct. 1661 (1989).

[3] See Domestic Workers United and DataCenter, *Home Is Where The Work Is: Inside New York's Domestic Work Industry* (July 2006) at 10 (reporting that "[n]inety-five percent of the domestic workers who responded to the survey are people of color and 93% are women. Three-fourths of workers [76%] are not U.S. citizens"); Peggie R. Smith, *Regulating Paid Household Work: Class, Gender, Race, and Agendas of Reform*, 48 AM. U.L. REV. 851, 923 (April 1999, observing that domestic workers are "disproportionately women of color," and "likely to be undocumented workers").

[4] See *Opinion Letter from California Labor Commissioner Donna M. Dell to Barbara Biglieri* (Dell 2005), dated November 23, 2005, Re: Interpretation of IWC Wage Order 15: Definition of "personal attendant," note 3 (stating that "[t]he DLSE has historically adopted a standard that 'does not exceed 20 percent of total weekly hours worked' [as used in the Federal regulations regarding companionship services, 29 CFR 552.6] in determining what is 'significant.' Accordingly, 20% or less of total weekly hours worked will not be deemed to be significant"; available at http://www.dir.ca.gov/dlse/opinions/2005-11-23.pdf [September 30, 2007]).

References

18 U.S.C. §1546. 1970. *Fraud and Misuse of Visas, Permits, and Other Documents.*

20 CFR §422.104, as amended. 2003. *Who Can Be Assigned a Social Security Number.*

29 CFR 1975.6. 1972. *Policy as to Domestic Household Employment Activities in Private Residences.*

29 U.S.C. §201, et seq. As amended 1974. *Fair Labor Standards.*

45 C.F.R. §§1626 et seq. 1983. *Alien Status and Eligibility.*

Associated Press. 2005. "State Labor Officials Complain about Immigrant Arrests." *News & Observer,* July 8.

Bernhardt, Annette, and Siobhan McGrath. 2005. *Trends in Wage and Hour Enforcement by the U.S. Department of Labor, 1975–2004.* <http://www.brennancenter. org/programs/downloads/trendswageshours.pdf>. [September 30, 2007].

Bindrim, Kira. 2007. "New Yorkers Bash Spitzer License Plan: Poll." *Crains*, November 13. <http://www.crainsnewyork.com/apps/pbcs.dll/article?AID=/ 20071113/FREE/71113010/1097>. [November 25, 2007].

Blagojevich, Rod. 2005. *Governor Blagojevich Announces New Labor Laws that Ensure Fair Wages and Better Conditions for Thousands of Workers.* Press release. <http://www.illinois.gov/PressReleases/ShowPressRelease.cfm? SubjectID=3&RecNum=4556-02-925>. [September 30, 2007].

Brown, Marianne P., Alejandra Domenzain, and Nelliana Villoria-Siegert. 2002. *Voices from the Margins: Immigrant Workers' Perceptions of Health and Safety in the Workplace.* <http://www.losh.ucla.edu/publications/voicesreport.pdf>. [October 14, 2007].

Bureau of Labor Statistics. 2006a. *Foreign-Born Workers: Labor Force Characteristics in 2006*. <http://www.bls.gov/news.release/forbrn.nr0.htm>. [November 18, 2007].

————. 2006b. *Census of Fatal Occupational Injuries Charts, 1992–2006*. <http://www.bls.gov/iif/oshcfoi1.htm#2006>. [December 2, 2007].

California v. ARC America Corp. 1989. 109 S.Ct. 166.

California Department of Industrial Relations. 2002. *Undocumented Worker Rights*. <http://www.dir.ca.gov/QAundoc.html>. [May 20, 2008].

California Government Code. 2002. Cal. Govt. Code §7285.

California Wage Order. 2001. California Wage Order 15-2001 1(B).

California Working Immigrant Safety and Health (WISH) Coalition. 2002. *Improving Health and Safety Conditions for California's Immigrant Workers: Report and Recommendations of the California Working Immigrant Safety and Health (WISH) Coalition*. <http://socrates.berkeley.edu/~lohp/graphics/pdf/wishrept.pdf>. [November 18, 2007].

Campaign to End Wage Theft. 2006. *Protecting New York's Workers: How The State Department of Labor Can Improve Wage and Hour Enforcement*. <http://brennancenter.org/dynamic/subpages/download_file_47027.pdf>. [November 18, 2007].

CASA of Maryland. 2007. *Wage Theft: How Maryland Fails to Protect the Rights of Low-Wage Workers*. January. <http://www.casademaryland.org/docs-pdfs/wagetheft.pdf>. [November 18, 2007].

The City of New York and Rudolph Giuliani v. The United States and Janet Reno. 1997. 971 F. Supp. 789.

The City of New York and Rudolph Giuliani v. The United States and Janet Reno. 1999. 179 F.3d 29.

Civil Rights Act. 1964. Title VII. 42 U.S.C.A. §2000e.

Colorado House Bill 06-1343. 2006. <http://www.leg.state.co.us/clics2006a/csl.nsf/fsbillcont3/D44C4D655410B398872570CB005DB438?Open&file=090_enr.pdf>. [November 18, 2007].

Colorado Immigrant Worker Rights Taskforce. 2005. Letter to Colorado state representatives Rosemary Marshall and Mike Cerbo and state senator Jennifer Veiga. On file with author.

Colorado Senate Bill 06-090. 2006. <http://www.leg.state.co.us/Clics2006A/csl.nsf/fsbillcont3/B80D87B97639B67187257118006CCD41?Open&file=1343_enr.pdf>. [November 18, 2007].

Couch, Mark P. 2007. "Pricey Immigration Law, State Agencies, $2 million cost and No Savings." *Denver Post*, January 25, p. B6.

Dell, Donna M. 2005. Opinion letter from California Labor Commissioner Donna M. Dell to Barbara Biglieri, Re: Interpretation of IWC Wage Order 15: Definition of "personal attendant." November 23. <http://www.dir.state.ca.us/dlse/opinions/2005-11-23.pdf>. [November 18, 2007].

Domestic Workers United and DataCenter. 2006. *Home Is Where the Work Is: Inside New York's Domestic Work Industry*. <http://www.domesticworkersunited.org/media/files/6/homeiswheretheworkis.pdf>. [November 18, 2007].

Equal Employment Opportunity Commission. 2002. *EEOC Reaffirms Commitment to Protecting Undocumented Workers from Discrimination*. Press release. <http://www.eeoc.gov/press/6-28-02.html>. [November 18, 2007].

Fair Labor Standards Act (FLSA). 1938. Ch. 676, 52 Stat. 106029 U.S.C. §213(a)(15); 29 U.S.C. §213(b)(21), as amended, 29 U.S.C. §201, et seq.

Family Medical Leave Act (FMLA). 1993. 29 U.S.C. sec. 2601 61.60. 29 U.S.C.A. §2611 (2)(B)(ii).

Fine, Janice. 2006. *Worker Centers: Organizing Communities at the Edge of the Dream.* Ithaca, NY: Cornell University Press.

Florida Division of Workers' Compensation v. *Cagnoli.* 2005. No. SC05-220.

Florida Statutes §440.192. 1980.

Garrett v. *City of Escondido.* 2006. No. 06 CV 2434 JAH (S.D. CA December 15, 2006).

General Accounting Office. 2002. *Worker Protection: Labor's Efforts to Enforce Protections for Day Laborers Could Benefit from Better Data and Guidance.* GAO-02-925. <http://www.gao.gov/new.items/d02925.pdf>. [November 18, 2007].

Georgia Security and Immigration Compliance Act. 2006. <http://www.legis. state.ga.us/legis/2005_06/fulltext/sb529.htm>. [November 18, 2007].

Greater Boston Labor Council, AFL-CIO. 2005. Report on file with author.

Hazelton Illegal Immigration Relief Act. 2006. Ordinance 2006-18. <http://www. hazletoncity.org/090806/2006-18%20_Illegal%20Alien%20Immigration%20Relief% 20Act.pdf>. [November 18, 2007].

Hoffman Plastic Compounds v. *NLRB.* 2002. 535 U.S. 137.

Human Rights Watch. 2005. *Blood, Sweat, and Fear: Workers' Rights in U.S. Meat and Poultry Plants.* <http://www.hrw.org/reports/2005/usa0105/>. [November 18, 2007].

Illinois Public Act 094-0511. 2006. <http://www.ilga.gov/legislation/publicacts/94/ 094-0511.htm>. [November 18, 2007].

Immigration Reform and Control Act. 1986. 8 U.S.C. §1324a.

Iowa Statute. 2006. I.C.A. §91E.2.

Jones v. *Rath Packing Co.* 1977. 430 U.S. 519, 525.

Koppelman, Alex. 2007. "Congress to New York (and Chicago and L.A.): Drop Dead." *Salon*, October 4. <http://www.salon.com/news/feature/2007/10/04/ sanctuary/index.html>. [November 25, 2007].

Locke v. *United States.* 2000. 529 U.S 89, 108.

Louisiana Senate Bill. 2006. Louisiana Senate Bill 753.

Lozano, et al. v. *City of Hazelton.* 2007. No. 3:06cv1586 (M.D. Pa. July 26, 2007).

Maine Executive Order. 2004. *An Order Concerning Access to State Services By All Entitled Maine Residents.* <http://www.maine.gov/tools/whatsnew/index.php? topic=Gov+News&id=2172&v=Article-2006>. [September 30, 2007].

Maryland Senate Bill 265. 2002. <http://mlis.state.md.us/2002rs/bills/sb/sb0265e.rtf>. [September 30, 2007].

Massachusetts General Laws. 1997. Mass. Gen. Laws Ch. 151A §62A.

Montgomery County, Maryland. 2005. *Duncan Announces New Wheaton Day Laborer Site 2005.* Press release. <http://www.montgomerycountymd.gov/ apps/News/press/PR_details.asp?PrID=1269>. [May 20, 2008].

Moore, Gary. 2002. Statement by Gary Moore Director of the Department of Labor and Industries. <http://www.nelp.org/iwp/reform/state/appendixwadol.cfm>. [July 29, 2008].

Nassau County [New York] Administrative Code. 2006. Nassau Cty Admin. Code §21-9.10.02.

———. Nassau Cty Admin. Code §21-9.10.03.

National Employment Law Project. 2005a. *A Comparison of Day Labor Statutes as of September 2005.* <http://www.nelp.org/docUploads/State%20DL%20chart% 20090605%5F100505%5F133648%2Epdf.> [October 14, 2007].

————. 2005b. *Drafting Day Labor Legislation: A Guide for Organizers and Advocates*. <http://www.nelp.org/docUploads/Guide%20to%20Drafting%20Day%20Labor% 20Legislation%20030804%2Epdf>. [October 14, 2007].

————. 2005c. *Quotes from Public Official in Support of Day Labor Centers*. <http://www.nelp.org/docUploads/quotes%20from%20local%20officials%20on% 20day%20labor%20centers%2Epdf>. [September 30, 2007].

————. 2006. Rights Begin at Home: Defending Domestic Workers? Rights in California, p. 9. <http://nelp.org/docUploads/california%20guide%20oct%206% 202006.pdf>. [July 29, 2008].

National Labor Relations Act (NLRA). 1935. 49 Stat. 449, as amended, 29 U.S.C §§ 151–69.

Nebraska Statute. 2003. NE ST §48-2209.

New York State Attorney General. 2003. New York Attorney General Formal Opinion No. 2003-F3. <http://www.oag.state.ny.us/lawyers/opinions/2003/formal/2003_ f3.html>. [September 30, 2007].

New York City Administrative Code. 2003. NYC Admin. Code §20-771.

————. 2003. NYC Admin. Code §20-772.

New York City Codes, Rules and Regulations. 2003. 12 NYCRR §142-2.2.

New York Executive Law. 2007. NY Exec. L. §292(5).

New York Immigration Coalition. 2007. *"F.A.I.R. Hearings": An Analysis of the Intimate Connections Between "Experts" Testifying Against the New State DMV Policy and the Anti-Immigrant, Nativist Group F.A.I.R.* <http://www.thenyic.org/ templates/documentFinder.asp?did=774>. [November 25, 2007].

New York Workers Compensation Law. 2007. NY Work Comp Law §2(4).

New York State Conf. of Blue Cross & Blue Shield Plans v. *Travelers Ins. Co.* 1995. 514 U.S. 645, 654.

North Carolina Occupational Safety and Health Project. 2000. *Immigrant Workers at Risk: A Qualitative Study of Hazards Faced by Latino Immigrant Construction Workers in the Triangle Area of North Carolina.* <http://www.coshnetwork.org/ cpwrstudy.pdf>. [November 18, 2007].

Oklahoma Illegal Immigration Taxpayer and Citizen Protection Act of 2007. 2007. <http://www.sos.state.ok.us/documents/Legislation/51st/2007/1R/HB/1804.pdf>. [November 18, 2007].

Oregon Revised Statutes. 2001. OR. Rev. St. 181.850.1.

Passel, Jeffrey S. 2006. *The Size and Characteristics of the Unauthorized Migrant Population in the U.S.* <http://pewhispanic.org/files/reports/61.pdf>. [October 14, 2007].

Passel, Jeffrey S., Randy Capps, and Michael Fix. 2004. *Undocumented Immigrants: Facts and Figures.* <http://www.urban.org/UploadedPDF/1000587_undoc_ immigrants_facts.pdf>. [October 14, 2007].

Pina, Tatiana. 2006. "Group Aims to Protect Workers." *Providence Journal,* October 27. <http://www.projo.com/news/content/nowork27_10-27-06_ KI2IRG7.33976c2.html>. [November 18, 2007].

Puerto Rican Legal Defense and Education Fund. 2007. *Riverside Rescinds Local Anti-Immigration Ordinance.* Press release. <http://prldef.org/Press/Press %20Releases/Riverside/Riverside%20Rescinds%20Local%20anti-immigration %20ordinance.pdf>. [November 18, 2007].

Privacy Act. 1974. 5 USC §552a (Note).

Rau, Jordan. 2004. "NY Labor Law Enforcement: A Fight for Fair Pay, State Labor Agency's Reinforcement of Rules Requiring Proper Wage for Workers Has Waned During Pataki's Tenure." *New York Newsday,* April 11, p. A6.

Reynolds v. *City of Valley Park, MO.* 2006. No. 06-CC-3802 (St. Louis County Cir Ct., September 27, 2006).

Rice v. *Santa Fe Elevator Corp.* 1947. 331 U.S. 218, 230.

San Francisco Administrative Code. 2003. San Francisco Admin. Code §12R.

———. 1989. San Francisco Admin. Code §12H.1 Ord. 375–89.

Schlesinger, Andrea Battista, and Amy Traub. 2007. "Immigrant Drivers License Plan Unravels." *The Nation,* November 14. <http://www.thenation.com/doc/20071126/schlessinger_traub>. [November 25, 2007].

Schwarzenegger, Arnold. 2006. *Governor Schwarzenegger's Veto Messages.* <http://gov.ca.gov/pdf/press/ab_2536_veto.pdf>. [September 30, 2007].

Smith, Peggie R. 1999. *Regulating Paid Household Work: Class, Gender, Race, and Agendas of Reform.* 48 Am. U. L. Rev. 851, 923.

Stewart v. *Cherokee County, GA.* 2007. No. 07 CV 0015 (N.D. GA, January 4, 2007).

Sweatshop Watch. 2005. *Reinforcing the Seams: Guaranteeing the Promise of California's Landmark Anti-Sweatshop Law.* <http://sweatshopwatch.org/media/pdf/AB633Report_ExeSum.pdf?PHPSESSID=3361df65f656b31ddb6d463e94f2e693>. [November 18, 2007].

Theodore, Nik, Abel Valenzuela, Jr., and Edwin Meléndez. 2008. *Day Labor Worker Centers: New Approaches to Protecting Labor Standards in the Informal Economy.* Chicago: Center for Urban Economic Development, University of Illinois at Chicago.

Valenzuela Jr., Abel, Nik Theodore, Edwin Meléndez, and Ana Luz Gonzalez. 2006. *On the Corner: Day Labor in the United States.* <http://www.sscnet.ucla.edu/issr/csup/uploaded_files/Natl_DayLabor-On_the_Corner1.pdf>. [November 18, 2007].

Vasquez v. *City of Farmer's Branch.* 2007. No. 3-deCV2376-R (N.D. TX January 11, 2007).

Chapter 10

Fighting and Winning in the Outsourced Economy: Justice for Janitors at the University of Miami

Stephen Lerner
Service Employees International Union

Jill Hurst
Service Employees International Union

Glenn Adler
AFL-CIO

On February 12, 2006, *The New York Times* (2006) Sunday magazine ran a story about the luxurious 9,000-square-foot official residence occupied by University of Miami (UM) president Donna Shalala in Coral Gables, Florida.

Headlined "An Academic Retreat," the article was filled with details about Shalala's Lexus SUV, her dining table for 24, the four beds for her dog, Sweetie, and her 29-foot motorboat that "is for sale" because she just doesn't use it enough.

Most readers probably chalked it up as another "lifestyles of the rich and famous" story, made somewhat more interesting because of Shalala's status as a former Secretary of Health and Human Services during Bill Clinton's White House years. But for 400 low-wage workers who held unenviable jobs as janitors, landscapers, and cleaners on Shalala's UM campus, the story became a galvanizing moment in their campaign to win better wages, benefits, and union rights.

For nearly a year, the workers had been struggling to pressure their employer, the national cleaning company UNICCO, and UM, which contracted with UNICCO for cleaning services, to raise standards for campus janitors. The janitors, the majority of whom were Cuban American, were earning as little as $6.40 an hour, with no health benefits. Many of them had held their jobs for 15 to 20 years. As workers in a right-to-work Southern state under Republican control, their quest seemed unlikely to succeed.

Yet it did. Just a little over six months after the article about Shalala appeared in the *Times*, the Miami janitors ratified a four-year union contract that will increase wages by as much as 51% over what they were earning when they began their campaign, that guarantees secure, affordable health benefits, and that increases their paid vacation time. "We were told it could not be done in Florida. But our need was great," said UM janitor Clara Vargas. Joining with Vargas to announce and celebrate the contract victory, Rob Schuler, president of Service Employees International Union (SEIU) Local 11, with whom the UM janitors united, noted, "Florida needs jobs that lift workers out of poverty, not drive them deeper into it" (Service Employees International Union 2006c).

The UM workers' victory poses a double mystery: How were janitors—among the most marginalized workers in the global economy—able to organize, fight, and defeat two powerful adversaries, and how were they able to succeed in a Southern right-to-work "red" state with apparently few natural allies? It is not among these workers—and certainly not in Miami—that one would expect union organizing to thrive.

In many respects, factors specific to Miami contributed to the victory. The incredible gap between Miami's rich and poor, for instance, made it easier to dramatize and make visible the janitors' poverty. More important, Miami workers and students were willing to dramatize the crisis through increasing actions: rallies, marches, an Unfair Labor Practice (ULP) strike by the workers, and a widely publicized hunger strike that both students and workers joined. As time wore on, and as the resolve of workers did not wear out, support from the Miami community grew. More and more high-level politicians got involved, the Cuban American state legislators in Tallahassee began to take notice (because the strike was thoroughly covered in the Cuban American press), and even the mayor of Miami came to talk to the hunger strikers. And for Shalala and other university leaders, there was the sobering thought of a graduation day that stood to be overshadowed by thousands of people demonstrating in support of the janitors.

But the victory also must be understood as part of an unfolding strategy developed by SEIU's "Justice for Janitors" (J4J) campaign to rebuild its membership. Janitors, the historic base of SEIU, had seen their union devastated by outsourcing and deunionization in the 1970s and 1980s. Many in the labor movement believed that they could not fight back against these trends and that low-wage workers were not organizable. Indeed, even in SEIU many argued that we should give up organizing and representing janitors outside our remaining union bastions in New York, Chicago, and San Francisco. But as it became apparent that these changes were permanent and spreading throughout the economy, that no occupational category or city was immune to their effects, we were able to win space to experiment with new approaches and develop a strategy that responds effectively to the challenge of organizing among low-wage workers. This new strategy required that we focus our campaigns on the top of the money chain where money and power are concentrated, rather than only on the direct employer.

This strategy of focusing on the corporation ultimately purchasing the service, rather than on a subcontracting firm, has been successful, and as a result there are more unionized janitors in absolute numbers today than ever before. With the union's janitorial foundation once again secured by 2000, J4J set its sights on extending from northern cities into their suburbs, and from the North into the South. J4J's reach enabled the UM fight to be nationalized, attracting powerful allies while engaging constituencies that mattered to the university and the company. And as the UM campaign benefited from J4J's strength, in turn the UM victory contributed to a cascade of new organizing as UNICCO agreed to go union in other cities where it operates.

Even though the UM janitors were the very picture of workers marginalized and exploited by the global economy, their story is a model for how, in the outsourced economy, workers can develop their own weapons for countering employers' race to the bottom. Moreover, these same strategies and tactics have been extended occupationally to new groups of unorganized workers, including subcontracted security guards, who are organizing through SEIU's "Stand for Security" campaign. These campaigns offer important lessons of how workers, their unions, and community allies can challenge the reorganization of the economy, rebuild their unions, and turn low-wage jobs into middle-class jobs as part of a broader campaign to win economic and social justice.

Finally, the victory points to new challenges and opportunities posed by the global economy, which is transforming the property services world in front of our eyes into a truly global industry. Symbolic of this ineluctable trend, an Australian company recently bought out UNICCO. Workers will have to keep pace with these changes and develop true global unions capable of countering the power of global companies. Otherwise we will repeat the mistakes of the 1970s, when unions were caught flat-footed by corporate restructuring and the devastation it brought.

The Rise, Fall, and Rebirth of the Janitors' Union

In the 1970s and 1980s it was among the seemingly weakest, most vulnerable, and most invisible workers that corporations started to experiment, testing what they could get away with and searching for new ways to cut costs and increase their profits and power. There was no press release announcing that "work will be part-timed, health insurance and pensions eliminated, and jobs outsourced." The wealthiest corporations in the U.S. didn't say, "Wouldn't it be great if we could outsource millions of cleaning and security jobs, cut wages, and then say we aren't responsible for the poverty we have created because we don't directly employ these workers any longer!" Instead, they quietly poked, prodded, pushed, and tested new ways to work people harder for less, and as they succeeded—relentlessly, and with increasing speed—spread these new practices farther and wider in the economy.

Practices once thought outrageous and on the margins, like unilaterally declaring that janitors are "independent contractors," and thus no longer covered by unemployment or workers compensation, have become the norm for workers and occupations once thought insulated from these kinds of abuses. What started at the bottom of the economic ladder has metastasized upward and throughout the economy, and with globalization it has been exported.

Unionization

Cleaners in major urban centers such as New York, Chicago, and San Francisco successfully organized, often through strikes, during the labor upsurge in the 1920s, 1930s, and 1940s. Janitors and other workers (doormen, elevator operators) employed directly by local real estate owners bargained citywide master contracts, providing in one agreement the same wages and benefits for tens of thousands of people employed by hundreds of different employers.[1] As late as the 1970s, the majority of janitors employed in the commercial office sector in the larger northern cities were full-time workers protected by union contracts that provided health insurance, pension benefits, vacation time, and decent wages. Janitors' working conditions mirrored the standards of other unionized urban workers; far from being a poverty-level job, janitorial work provided entry into the middle class for poor workers and their families.

Deunionization

Starting in the 1960s and 1970s, and then with increasing momentum into the 1980s, five major changes came close to destroying the janitors' union and drove wages and benefits below poverty levels.

- *Consolidation of real estate ownership:* National and international companies bought and consolidated office building ownerships and then drove for "efficiencies" to cut costs and increase profits.

- *Outsourcing/contracting out:* Instead of employing janitors directly, building owners increasingly hired cleaning contractors, and they forced contractors to compete over who could cut costs the most in order to win contracts. This same phenomenon played out for building security workers, as owners hired private contractors rather than directly employing security guards.

- *Reclassification of workers:* Building owners often changed workers' classifications, though not their functions, such as when they redefined janitors as independent contractors who were ineligible to join unions. A lesser known technique was applied to security workers. In New York, for example, building owners redefined workers who performed multiple tasks, such as door opening, concierge, and reception, as performing security functions. This shift gave the employer the right to pull these workers out of the union under an obscure provision in the labor law (section 9[b][3] of the National Labor Relations Act) that allows security officers to choose a mixed union that represents guards and nonguards as their representative only if the employer voluntarily agrees.

- *Immigration:* The work force very quickly shifted to immigrants, many of whom were undocumented and susceptible to employer abuses.

- *National and international consolidation of cleaning contracts:* Cleaning contractors morphed from "mom and pop" enterprises to national and international companies employing hundreds of thousands of workers, increasing their size, power, and geographic spread.

Starting first with small contractors in the non-union suburbs of major cities and then spreading to smaller, weaker union markets and ultimately to New York City, Chicago, and San Francisco, cleaning contractors, at the behest of the real estate industry, demanded and won huge economic concessions. Again and again the union was caught off guard as the concessions won in one market were exported to places of former union strength. Work was part-timed, wages were cut, benefits were eliminated. Building owners successfully forced unionized janitors to compete with new non-union cleaning contractors (which were often non-union "double-breasted" companies owned by the same union contractors) to see who would work for the least. If the union didn't agree to concessions, the union contractor was fired and replaced by a non-union company.

More than 100,000 union jobs were lost as citywide master collective bargaining agreements were destroyed. SEIU seriously considered giving up organizing and representing janitors outside of New York City, Chicago, and San Francisco, the three cities where the union represented commercial cleaners, security workers, residential apartment and condominium doormen, porters, elevator operators, and other workers. In these three cities, SEIU's historic strength combined with higher labor movement–wide union density and political strength created conditions that allowed it to continue to negotiate collective bargaining agreements directly with the association of building owners and thus sidestep some of the worst pitfalls of outsourced work. Where the union negotiated directly with building owners, it was able to preserve full-time work, benefits, and citywide master agreements, even if subcontractors did most of the work.

In the 20 other cities with high union density in the Northeast, Midwest, and West, SEIU was far weaker and wages and benefits were lower prior to the employer attack. In these cities the union was either destroyed or became so weak that the wave to cut wages, eliminate benefits, and make work part-time totally swamped the market and union. The growing consensus within the union was that it was impossible to win in an industry that was now dominated by part-time, undocumented workers employed by giant cleaning contractors who in turn worked for the wealthiest corporations in the country, intent on driving costs to the lowest possible level.

In city after city, outsourcing and deunionization spread from commercial cleaning to security, to universities and to the public sector. And instead of having a coherent analysis and plan to address the changes in the industry, SEIU fell into two traps. The first was a tendency to view immigrant workers as the enemy; rather than embracing and organizing immigrants, many in SEIU blamed them for the growth of non-union low-wage contractors. The second was believing the battle should be fought—as it always had been—with the cleaning contractors who were the direct employers, rather than with the building owners who controlled the money.

SEIU's failure to develop a plan that could confront the reorganization of industry and the economy fed the argument that it was impossible to win in the new environment. This same process played out through the entire economy, as what was once seen as a problem for a small number of immigrant janitors has increasingly become the model driving business more generally. At every level, public and private corporations have adopted the tactic of hiding behind outsourced companies as justification for squeezing out "inefficiencies" like health insurance while eliminating the most basic benefits and job security.

In 1986, SEIU launched its first Justice for Janitors campaigns in Denver and Washington, DC. For this first campaign we deliberately went to local unions willing to try something new. The Denver union in particular was an "amalgamated local" (with membership across the sectors in which SEIU organized) and didn't carry the historical baggage of the old ways of organizing among janitors. On its own initiative it had been experimenting with new approaches and was eager to begin organizing among the city's janitors. The local welcomed the campaign and provided the space to demonstrate that it was possible to win. Together we put many people and a lot of time into a fight that was relatively small, but where no one was telling us what would or would not work. Nobody thought we could succeed, but when we won big, it opened the door.

Through marches, building community coalitions, and civil disobedience SEIU successfully organized 1,200 janitors in Denver alone and demonstrated that it was possible to win with undocumented, contracted-out, part-time workers. The Denver victory led to SEIU's officially adopting a "rebuilding program" that launched Justice for Janitors nationally. And in learning to win in these cities, the union organized and welcomed undocumented workers and directly confronted the building owners and the people who financed them.

Reunionization

To reunionize an industry that had adopted many of the characteristics of so-called "unorganizable contingent work" required an analysis and strategy focused not on the bottom where contractors dwell, but on the top of the money chain where money and power are concentrated. We began to untangle the complicated relationships between janitors' direct—or legal—employer (the contractors) and their secondary—or *de facto*—employer (the building owners), who set the terms on which contractors do business. This meant concentrating on the building owners who dominate the industry by examining their financial, regulatory, political, and operational situations and the key relationships, especially with investors. It meant focusing on the pension funds and banks that finance the building owners' operations, identifying various ways to affect these corporations and the people who control them. By refusing to accept the idea that building owners had shed their economic and moral responsibility by hiring subcontractors, the union was able to reassert—in the context of the new outsourced economy—its traditional role of dealing directly with those who have power to raise wages and benefits.

The J4J leaders learned how to integrate economic strategies with powerful public campaigns built around alliances with community, religious, and political leaders. Janitors who clean fancy buildings for the richest corporations can win support and sympathy from many who are not normally pro-union because immigrant workers so vividly capture the moral contradictions of poverty amid plenty.

In addition to challenging the industry through economic and moral pressure, J4J also retooled the strike and the organizing of non-union workers. Union and non-union workers involved in organizing campaigns learned how to use offensive strikes as a critical ingredient in both organizing and bargaining. Rather than striking to stop buildings from being cleaned—a near impossible task given the relatively unskilled work force—the strike was transformed into an opportunity for hundreds and thousands of workers to be freed from their regular jobs to become full-time activists. By organizing, campaigning, demonstrating, and disrupting day-to-day business operations—often through mass civil disobedience—workers could create a crisis for the business elite that helped pave the way for citywide settlements.

In deploying these approaches, SEIU learned the hard way that it could not make gains by organizing building by building; even if a contractor allowed its workers to unionize, it did so at its own peril, as it would likely be undercut when the contract to clean these buildings next went out to bid. So we scaled upward, reckoning that the resources needed to wage a fight in a single building could be more efficiently deployed in winning a contractor's entire portfolio across a city, and by doing this with multiple contractors in a citywide campaign, we could take the entire commercial office cleaning industry. Crucial to this was developing the "trigger": After a contractor agreed to go union, SEIU would not raise wages until a majority of its competitors also went union, ensuring no contractor was put at a competitive disadvantage.

And the union learned that the janitors had hidden power: Their critical, though invisible, position in the finance, insurance, and real estate industries meant they could not be off-shored. Powerful constituencies rallied to the demand for justice in their communities for janitors who earned poverty wages while cleaning the offices of multi-billion dollar companies.

The campaign not only recovered membership SEIU lost during the 1980s, it organized an additional 100,000 janitors, first by consolidating and increasing membership in the cities where the union has traditionally been strong. From this base, the union has been able to follow its union contractors as they consolidated and expanded into new markets to ensure that they go union even in traditionally non-union regions (See Table 1 for a list of major citywide campaigns).

TABLE 1
Citywide Justice for Janitors Campaigns

City	Year campaign began	Date of first master contract	Number of workers
Denver, CO	1986	1987	1,200
Washington, DC	1987	1997	5,000
Los Angeles, CA	1988	1995	8,000
San Jose–Oakland, CA	1991	1996	2,500
Sacramento, CA	1996	1999	1,500
Fairfield County, CT	1999	2000	3,000
Orange County, CA	2000	2000	2,000
Northern New Jersey	2001	2001	6,000
Baltimore, MD	2001	2001	1,700
Houston, TX	2005	2006	5,300
Miami, FL	2005	2006	400
Cincinnati, OH	2006	2007	1,200
Columbus, OH	2006	2007	1,200
Indianapolis, IN	2006	2008	1,500

Since 2000 the focus has been on following building owners from downtown commercial centers into the surrounding suburbs, and then organizing in new cities where they also operate. This strategy was in part facilitated by the master agreements SEIU won in its core cities, which include language permitting workers to honor picket lines against their employer, even if the violations occurred elsewhere. Thus bargaining in union strongholds was put in service of union growth elsewhere as workers who already enjoy the benefits of a union take risks to organize the unorganized. In 2006 this and other strategies yielded the biggest victory yet: recognition and winning a strike and first contract for 5,300 janitors in Houston.

The battle at UM is a critical case for understanding unions' ability to respond to the challenges of the outsourced economy. Can strategies and tactics that work in the North and areas where unions still have some strength succeed in traditionally non-union areas like the South?

University of Miami: "Yes We Cane"

The battle in Miami pitted 400 immigrant Cuban and Haitian janitors against the University of Miami, its president, Donna Shalala, and UNICCO, a cleaning contractor with $1 billion in revenue and 20,000 employees. UM subcontracted its cleaning and maintenance work to UNICCO, and despite multiple efforts by students and faculty to win a living wage for the janitorial workers over several years, the university had refused to raise wages and benefits. UNICCO was unionized

elsewhere, especially in the Northeast, but it had long resisted unionization in the South and other areas. Even in markets where it was unionized, UNICCO had led employer opposition to shifting from part-time
to full-time work, leading to a 2002 citywide janitor strike in Boston.

Despite appeals from workers, students, and community and religious leaders, the university adopted a position far different from that of
other major universities, such as Harvard. Instead of embracing a living
wage policy or encouraging UNICCO to resolve the matter, the university claimed it was "neutral" and not party to the dispute. Despite the
fact that the university employed and paid UNICCO to clean and maintain the campus, it hid behind the contractor, claiming no responsibility
for the conditions of janitors, including the ones who personally cleaned
Donna Shalala's house.

There was no doubt, as we had learned with building owners in
other janitor struggles, that the university controlled UNICCO's
behavior and ability to settle. This created the moral issue of a program of economic apartheid at UM, in which the institution's direct
employees enjoy traditional benefits, while contracted-out workers—
overwhelmingly people of color and immigrants—live in poverty. The
university's attempt to obscure its own control over the janitors' economic conditions set the stage to test, in a new battlefield, whether
strategies and tactics that worked in Los Angeles and Chicago could
work in Florida.

Strategies and Tactics: The Workers Lead the Way

The successful effort to improve conditions for janitors and maintenance workers at the university began with the building of an organized group of workers who supported unionization. Simultaneously,
students, faculty, and religious leaders were organized to support that
effort. Previous failed efforts had left a small core of faculty who felt
change was needed but had little hope that they could win, due to the
opposition of the university and UNICCO and the weakness of labor
in Florida.

As in most organizing efforts, a base of supporters was needed to
lead the effort. But this effort differed from previous attempts in several
ways. First, this time workers were directly engaged in large numbers.
Second, SEIU's success in other cities and at other universities provided
a roadmap, with technical knowledge and hope. Finally, the effort was
not restricted to the campus; the entire union was engaged in assisting—
janitors in other cities, including UNICCO employees; top leadership;
pension and investor liaisons; political organizers; communications staff;
and, of course, organizers.

Multiple tactics were used to dramatize the moral issues and to create a crisis that forced action. Previous attempts at improving the conditions of workers had used education and moral suasion to try to create pressure for change. These efforts, while laudable, allowed those responsible to delay action until whatever pressure had been created drifted away. Fundamentally, what led to the success of this campaign was the willingness of both workers and students to take increasingly militant action to sharpen and dramatize the crisis.

Initially there was informational leafleting, followed by rallies to demonstrate widespread support, followed by an unfair labor practices (ULP) strike. Throughout this effort, workers did not just walk on picket lines. As J4J has done in northern cities, the strikers functioned not only as a mobile demonstration, but also as organizers and spokespeople. Educational forums were held in several university departments. Dormitories agreed to hold forums where both UNICCO and the workers presented their stories. Indeed, at one forum, UNICCO was forced to concede that the university set its wage rates and that UNICCO would provide whatever conditions the university requested. These efforts kept the faces and stories of workers in front of the students, the faculty, the community, and the press.

SEIU also began distributing to other building owners and their investors the facts about the situation at UM. Since the university was ultimately responsible, SEIU also began talking about Donna Shalala's decision to allow these workers to earn minimum wage with no health benefits, a message conveyed to constituencies she might care about.

Minority Strike and Civil Disobedience

From the beginning, an overwhelming majority of the 400 janitors supported the drive to join SEIU Local 11 for union representation. But when the time came to go out on a ULP strike, a majority did *not* support walking off the job. But those who did support the strike were militantly in favor of it, and they made a crucial decision to respect the desires of the workers who did choose to go back to work. Rather than condemning those workers, they instead encouraged them to function as a kind of "inside" committee that would continue to sign up workers to support the union. Meanwhile, the strikers became full-time organizers in their communities and their churches, traveling around the country building support for the campaign.

The workers led the community and students in increasingly dramatic actions. Every time the university adjusted to one strategy or set of activities, a new set began. In short, there was no magic bullet, just ever-escalating actions operating at multiple expanding levels, first in Miami and then throughout the country, creating the reality that the janitors and their union were in this for the long haul.

Making Poverty Visible: Donna's World . . . and Zoila's

But back to the fallout from the *Times* article about Shalala.

The UM president's remarks in an otherwise innocuous article helped transform the campaign from a local dispute to a national battle about low wages, the lack of affordable health care, and the growing gap between rich and poor. The campaign became a metaphor for poverty in the face of plenty, with UM claiming it could not afford to pay janitors better wages.

Publicizing the moral issues and putting a face and reality to the conditions for janitors has been a central tactic in every J4J campaign. In the UM fight, many actions were used to tell the story and to create newsworthy events. In the online political blogosphere, where the campaign put a lot of effort into magnifying its message in a medium not often used by unions, reaction was swift, whether it was in such cheeky blogs as "Wonkette" or the labor-oriented "Working Lives" written by Jonathan Tasini. But one of the most empowering follow-up articles was in the mainstream *Miami Herald*. One of the campus janitors, Zoila Garcia, agreed to be interviewed by *Herald* columnist Ana Menendez. The resulting column contrasted Shalala's lavish lifestyle with the daily struggles of a UM janitor (*Miami Herald* 2006). Garcia, at 51, had worked as a university janitor for many years, and she was earning just $6.70 an hour, without health insurance. Menendez asked Garcia to answer some of the same questions that had been posed to Shalala: What is your "perfect day," your "favorite vacation spot," and the "possession that best defines you?"

The contrasting answers were dramatic. Shalala's perfect day begins with getting a $10 million donation for the campus and ends with three sets of tennis; for Garcia, the perfect day is "Friday, when I get my check and know that I'll be OK for a few days." Shalala's favorite vacation is a trip to the Kingdom of Bhutan; Garcia would like to take her grandchildren to the Miami amusement park Parrot Jungle, but she can't afford it. Shalala drives a Lexus hybrid SUV; Garcia drives a 1995 Ford Aerostar, and "when it rains outside, it rains inside." Shalala had chosen a drawing by Susan Kapilow as the possession most defining her; Garcia chose "my smile. I always have a smile for everyone."

Another stunning contrast: While Shalala said her current reading is about health care, because she is teaching a class, Garcia needs a $4,000 operation to take care of a blood clot that has formed on the back of her calf, but she has to put it off because she can't afford it.

Who could read that and not be outraged? From this point forward, the janitors' campaign began to pick up more and more news coverage, community support, and attention from politicians. The marginalized, exploited "invisible" workers were rapidly becoming visible.

Escalation: Workers and Students United

One of the key leaders of the J4J campaign was Maritza Paz, who was in many ways representative of UNICCO's 400-person janitorial, cleaning, and landscaping work force. Paz had been working as a UNICCO janitor at UM for more than a decade, managing to raise two kids on poverty wages. Like the other UM janitors, she had to scramble to pay for medicine, doctors' visits, food, and rent. Paz was very familiar with having to simply do without. During the campaign, she was able to stand up for the first time, tell her story, be heard, and fight for a better life.

Even though UNICCO and the university were showing no signs that they would talk with the striking janitors, much less reach a deal with them, the janitors were determined to stay on strike until they won. And the fact that they were picking up support from students, faculty members, the community, and religious and political leaders gave them a true sense of empowerment.

Feliciano Hernandez, for instance, was one of six pro-union workers who were suspended from their jobs by UNICCO, ostensibly for refusing to haul an 80-pound floor stripper up several flights of stairs without the proper equipment. Instead of bowing to this pressure from the company, the six filed new ULP charges against UNICCO. By this time the National Labor Relations Board had already issued a complaint against UNICCO for violating the rights of UM janitors to form a union.

"From here, I see only strength, commitment, and courage," said Hernandez. "We are no longer invisible. Before, our voice was a whisper. Now when we say we will stand up for our rights, our voice is loud and strong enough to be heard" (Service Employees International Union 2006a).

When it comes to the student body, the University of Miami is decidedly not an activist campus. But a minority of the students did support the janitors' campaign, and a core group was very active in their support. Once the ULP strike began, the level of student support grew. A group known as STAND (Students Toward a New Democracy), dedicated to creating a culture of activism at UM, sponsored a march and rally in support of the janitors. The march, which began in a campus courtyard and proceeded past Shalala's office, attracted a swell of support from students, faculty, workers, and community leaders. As STAND spokespersons Liza Alwes and Jacob Coker-Dukowitz noted in their press materials, UM was cited by the *Chronicle of Higher Education* in 2001 as being the second-worst in the nation out of 195 colleges for what it paid janitors (*Chronicle of Higher Education* 2001). Playing off the name of the school's football team, the Miami Hurricanes, STAND said the goal of the march was to point out to university officials that "Poverty Is Not a Cane Value." The march was a display of progressive activism that Miami had not seen in years. It served to give janitors and their supporters a sense that victory was a distinct possibility.

As the ULP strike dragged on, with workers committed to sticking it out and with UNICCO and the university unwilling to establish a process chosen by the workers to form a union and to resolve outstanding civil rights violations, it was the janitors' student supporters who came up with the idea of a hunger strike. It was a tactic that had been used successfully in support of workers at other campuses, and as the UM students discussed the idea with the janitors, the workers decided that they, too, should participate. It was also clear at that point that a more dramatic action was needed to increase the sense of crisis.

So on April 5, 2006, a group of eight janitors and six students began a fast for justice. They set up an outdoor venue for their fast that they dubbed "Freedom City." Located outside the university entrance, Freedom City quickly became a 24-hour-a-day tent city with daily prayer services and rallies. Students, faculty, and other supporters slept out overnight with the hunger strikers. Cuban democracy activist Ramon Saul Sanchez was one of the community supporters helping to kick off the fast. He pledged to work within the Cuban American community to continue broadening support for their goals. "Civil rights are universal and no company has the right to violate them. Immigrants have made an incredibly positive contribution to our society and their rights should be respected here in Miami, just as in any other part of the country," Sanchez said (Service Employees International Union 2006b).

The fast upped the ante considerably. It was a bold way to dramatize the seriousness of the janitors' campaign and of the workers' and students' commitment. For the entire 17 days of the hunger strike, the press—and, increasingly, community and religious leaders—were drawn to Freedom City. There were solidarity visits from politicians, community activists, religious leaders, and international labor leaders. Midway through the hunger strike, an urgent update was sent out to inform supporters that Feliciano Hernandez, one of the campaign leaders taking part in the fast, had to be rushed to the hospital. He eventually was released, in good spirits, and the hunger strike continued. The campaign's website, *yeswecane.org*, also began posting daily video podcasts from the hunger strikers, helping generate thousands of e-mail letters of support from around the world. All of this was yet another signal to the university and UNICCO that the campaign was gaining momentum and broader support.

Nationalizing the Campaign

As all of this activity was happening in and around the campus, the janitors were pushing forward on several other fronts. Union members honored picket lines that spread from Florida to cities throughout the Northeast where UNICCO is predominantly unionized with SEIU. This was the case in Boston, one of UNICCO's largest markets. Campus workers at Harvard University, the company's largest account, began talking about honoring picket lines. This came at a time when Harvard was searching for a new president, and one of those on the list of potential candidates was Shalala. Since the Harvard presidency is a matter of great concern to the local community, the Cambridge City Council sent a representative to Miami to investigate the janitors' situation at UM. The council eventually passed a resolution that stated its opposition to Shalala's becoming Harvard president because of the controversy it would bring. The use of both fronts—pressuring UNICCO and publicizing Shalala's lack of action—turned Boston into a central focus of a fight fifteen hundred miles away.

In the meantime, the hunger strike dragged on, and two more workers were pulled off the fast because of health problems. Despite being asked to come off the hunger strike by both the union and religious leaders, workers refused, chanting in Spanish from their wheelchairs during a march, "union or death" (la unión o muerte). The workers eventually were persuaded to stop the fast when SEIU president Andy Stern and SEIU executive vice president Eliseo Medina met with them in Miami and agreed to personally take over the fast for the workers. Medina, a widely respected labor leader who had started as a farm worker and became a leader with Cesar Chavez in the United Farm Workers, stayed on a water-only fast for 11 days; he ate again only when victory was announced.

As some large real estate investors began questioning the wisdom of using a company like UNICCO who could not resolve such bitter labor disputes in buildings in which they invested, it became clear that key cleaning accounts around the country were ready to fire UNICCO and hire contractors that were not the focus of a national dispute. With graduation day on the horizon, UM realized that it very well could become a day marked not by celebration, but by thousands of angry demonstrators demanding justice for the campus janitors.

When this juncture finally was reached—the point where all parties wanted the issue settled—victory finally came. The university mandated that contractors on campus provide their employees with higher wages and health insurance. By May 1, the UNICCO janitors won the right to form a union by the method of their choosing. They chose a majority sign-up process, which was completed several weeks later. They then negotiated a four-year contract with UNICCO that provided annual raises, guaranteed affordable health insurance, three additional vacation days, and three new holidays (Christmas Eve, New Year's Eve, and the day after Thanksgiving).

As janitor Clara Vargas, a bargaining team member, said, "Today, we have hope for a more secure future, a chance to make our lives and the lives of our children better" (Service Employees International Union 2006c).

All in all, it seemed like the perfect day; not the one expected by the university, but the one envisioned by 400 workers who proved they could be a force for justice, even in an outsourced economy.

Building on the Past, Preparing for the Future: A Cascade of Organizing

The victory at UM provides many lessons and gives us much to celebrate. But what is less known is that as part of the settlement UNICCO agreed to a process that would allow thousands of their workers elsewhere in the United States and Canada to win a union. The campaign in Florida was won in part because the union used its strength in unionized cities to pressure UNICCO, and in winning Florida the union again used its strength to win a union for thousands of other UNICCO employees in other non-union cities. In this way, Miami was an open-ended achievement, not merely an end in itself, continuing a process of cascading victories, building ostensibly local disputes into a broader national advance.

As SEIU has made these gains in the U.S. property services industry, the industry continues to mutate under the pressure of globalization, offering both new perils and new opportunities. By 2000, the largest owners and contractors were becoming global companies operating in dozens of countries. An increasingly small group of global property owners, global contractors, and global pension funds has come to dominate the property services world. Tellingly, an Australian company recently purchased UNICCO, the focus of the University of Miami strike.

In their wake these companies are spreading worldwide the practices they perfected in the United States. These trends were visible in a recent meeting in London of janitors who were organizing with the Transport and General Workers' Union (T&G) at the huge Canary Wharf complex.[2] The workers—immigrants from East Asia, Africa, and

Latin America—spoke a host of languages, but they recounted the same daily struggle to survive on poverty wages in one of the most expensive cities on earth. They described the impact of their employer's relentless drive for efficiency and cost-cutting: more area to clean with fewer workers, long hours, and the absence of a voice at work.

We could have had the same meeting in Miami, Los Angeles, or Boston, in Johannesburg or Jakarta. There is a common thread in London. The contractor is global: a Danish company called ISS. The key building owner is global: the New York–based bank Morgan Stanley. The pension money that makes it all work is drawn from around the world and managed globally. Even the workers are global. The only thing that is local is the union.

If we remain a local entity in a global world, we will find ourselves—for all our gains—reduced to one small part of a global company's worldwide operations, with little or no countervailing power.

This future is not inevitable. We were meeting the Canary Wharf janitors as part of an effort to organize globally in the property services sector. We were working with T&G, which was enthusiastic about organizing janitors in London, and ISS was a key piece of the campaign. At first ISS raised wages to try to avoid the union, but then the company recognized T&G and (at the time of writing) is negotiating not just for Canary Wharf, but citywide in London.

Another example: SEIU has a history of mutual solidarity with Australia's Liquor, Hospitality, and Miscellaneous Workers Union (LHMU). When LHMU wanted to counter the race to the bottom in their country's burgeoning property services industry, SEIU collaborated with them and with New Zealand's Service and Food Workers Union (SFWU) as they launched the "Clean Start" campaign, a multicity, industrywide effort to organize janitors in both countries. As in London, the employers' response was to make marginal improvements to stave off the union, but they are now negotiating agreements, and the unions' membership is up.

Extending the Model from Cleaning to Security

Nowhere are the trends of consolidation and globalization—and the prospects for global union activity—clearer than in the security industry.

In the past, security officers, like janitors, were direct employees of the building owners, companies, and other institutions they were hired to protect. However, unlike janitors, who worked under the terms of SEIU's master contracts in big northern cities, security officers had little experience of strong unionism. Under the Congress of Industrial Organizations (CIO), the United Auto Workers and United Steelworkers signed up guards when they organized entire factories. The officers' willingness to stand with their striking brothers and sisters prompted a reaction under the Taft-Hartley revisions specifically barring the National Labor Relations Board from certifying a bargaining unit if the union—or a federation to which it affiliates—has nonguard members (National Labor Relations Act 1935; see Section 9[b][3]). A number of independent unions sprang up in the gap, none with significant membership or the power to win against large employers. The changes placed security officers outside the mainstream of the labor movement and denied them the power that strong national unions could provide.

As with janitors, security officers were the targets of building owners' massive outsourcing from the 1980s. They too experienced the race to the bottom, becoming the direct employees of private security companies engaged in cutthroat competition to secure contracts. In addition to the low wages, poor or missing benefits, and insecurity that are the familiar consequences for workers of this competition, officers' daily exposure to physical risks was heightened by poor training and shoddy equipment provided by cost-cutting companies.

These conditions gave rise to distinctive grievances among officers, who often invited SEIU to organize by pointing out the huge gap in wages and benefits between themselves and the unionized janitors at their worksite—sometimes as they were escorting our organizers out of the building! Their position did not improve in the deluge of security spending after 9/11, little of which trickled down to the guards. Instead the pressure intensified on officers struggling to provide a professional service while caught between the public's rising demands for security and their employers' cost-cutting.

In 2000 we began investigating whether we could adapt our J4J model to organize contract security officers. We began researching the largest companies in the U.S.: their structure, leadership, clients, investors, and expansion plans. We found that their structural position was similar to that of the cleaning companies we organized and that the real power was at the top, with the building owners and other corporate clients who set the terms of the contract competition. Moreover, we learned that notwithstanding the NLRB's 9(b)(3) rule, there was no prohibition on security companies' reaching private agreements to recognize SEIU.

In 2002 SEIU launched the "Stand for Security" campaign, with the goal of organizing security officers citywide in the 10 largest cities in the U.S. We began discussions with the five largest companies and a number of other regionally based companies toward an agreement on a partnership to improve labor standards in the industry.

In support of this goal, SEIU's primarily immigrant janitor locals committed themselves to using their financial resources as well as their industrial and political power to organize African American and other workers marginalized by the new economy. Contrasting the wages and benefits of unionized cleaners with those of non-union security officers has been the most powerful evidence that unionizing the service sector can turn low-wage jobs into middle-class jobs. In Los Angeles, the campaign calculated that if security officers had the same wages and benefits as janitors, it would add $50 million to the city's poorest neighborhoods.

But in the course of the campaign, the U.S. industry underwent unprecedented globalization and consolidation: A Swedish company, Securitas, bought two large U.S. firms and overnight became the largest security company in the country. In 2002 Wackenhut, the number two U.S. company, was bought by the Denmark-based Group 4 Falck, which in turn merged in 2004 with the United Kingdom–based Securicor to form Group 4 Securicor (G4S), with headquarters in London. Securitas and Group 4 Securicor between them employ more than 160,000 security officers in the U.S. and nearly three quarter of a million workers worldwide. To remain competitive, security companies that operate primarily in the United States have also consolidated. Once the dust settled on this corporate reshuffling, the top five companies employed some 215,000 workers in an industry that used to be dominated by mom-and-pop firms.

We understood that as companies globalized, we could not win better standards for guards through a national campaign alone. Our bargaining power had declined as we became just one market—albeit a large one— in the new parent companies' worldwide operations.

Our first global effort focused on Securitas. Owing in large measure to the solidarity of the Swedish Transport Workers' union, the company signed an agreement in March 2003 allowing workers to organize city-wide in multiple cities when a majority of workers sign cards for the union. Securitas had earlier acquired Pinkerton's, and the agreement took union this once-notorious strike-breaking company!

Following on that success, we focused the Wackenhut effort on collaboration with the Danish unions, who had high density in Group 4 Falck in Copenhagen, where employees enjoyed representation on its board of directors. After fruitless discussions with the company, in October 2003 we launched in Geneva a global campaign against Group 4 Falck at a meeting of the property services sector of the global union federation Union Network International (UNI).

We soon learned that support from the home country unions was not sufficient if a company refuses to bargain. Indeed, in the course of the campaign the Group 4 Falck–Securicor merger moved the center of power to the United Kingdom, sidestepping whatever influence the Danish unions could have brought to bear.

In response, we decided to locate our power not in the relationships between the parent company and its home unions, but in collaboration with unions outside Europe that were engaged in similar fights with the company and that had aspirations to organize security officers in their countries. We learned that unions in Indonesia, Kenya, South Africa, India, Uruguay, and other countries were already pursuing their own separate fights with demands similar to those we have raised in the U.S. The Indonesian union, ASPEK, had already embarked on a major strike against the company for refusing to bargain over the Group 4 Falck–Securicor merger's effect on the workers' terms and conditions. We reckoned that coordinated and joint efforts would have a much more robust effect on Group 4 Securicor than were our individual and separate fights.

From mid-2005 we have worked to build a true global campaign focusing on Group 4 Securicor for a global labor rights agreement in which the company would respect the rights of its employees everywhere to join a union of their choice. Such an agreement would be the basis for the allied unions to establish a strong base in the security sector, from which they could then launch active organizing efforts to raise standards throughout the industry. This focus strengthened the strategic importance of UNI as a coordinating center for the national unions engaged in the campaign.

In November 2006, UNI convened a meeting of trade unionists from 19 countries to begin a global campaign. Participants came from Asia, Africa, Europe, and North and South America; they agreed to hold a follow-up meeting and to send a fact-finding delegation to Africa in April 2007. UNI organized a meeting in Johannesburg of unions representing guards in eight African countries, as well as representatives of European and American unions, nongovernmental organizations (NGOs), and human rights organizations. Following the meeting, delegates took fact-finding trips to Malawi and Mozambique, where they met with union officers, G4S employees, and government officials; the company declined to meet the delegations.

UNI, along with the British union UNITE and the NGO War on Want, issued a report, *Who Protects the Guards: The Facts Behind G4S in Southern Africa*, on the eve of G4S's 2007 annual general meeting in London (Union Network International and Alliance for Justice at Group 4 Securicor 2007).

The report spelled out the racist and exploitive practices of G4S in Africa, and it set the stage for ongoing work with a British parliamentary group and for UNI work with unions in Africa. Meanwhile, the campaign has compelled G4S to clean up some of its worst practices in Africa. For example, G4S has signed a nationwide collective agreement in Uganda—

where it was the only major nonunion security contractor—for about 400 guards and a recognition agreement in Malawi for 13,000 guards.

And, as a result of the campaign, security workers in Indonesia represented by ASPEK were able to declare victory in July 2006 after a 15-month-long strike and an outpouring of community and international support pressured the multinational firm to respect human rights. The dispute stemmed from the international merger between Group 4 Falck and Securicor. On April 25, 2005, about 500 security guards engaged in a legal strike to demand clarity from the company over whether they would remain permanent employees with the same rights following the merger. The workers maintained that if they were being transferred to a new company they were due severance pay under Indonesian law. Rather than pay severance or guarantee the workers that their terms of employment would remain the same, the company fired 238 striking workers in the capital city, Jakarta, and an additional 24 in Surabaya. The firings were followed by a campaign of harassment and intimidation using outdated Indonesian laws that criminalize behaviors allowed in most democracies.

In the settlement, Securicor Indonesia agreed to pay severance plus 11 months of back pay to the fired workers in Jakarta. Criminal charges brought against the ASPEK president and several union members were dropped. Each worker received twice the PMTK, or legally guaranteed minimum severance, plus 11 months of back pay.

Meanwhile, the Wackenhut campaign in the U.S. continues. Overall, the Stand for Security campaign has made enormous progress, as Wackenhut's major competitors have all agreed to work with SEIU to improve standards in the industry. Security officers in Boston, Washington, Minneapolis, Chicago, Seattle, San Francisco, Oakland, and Los Angeles have won recognition from these companies and (at the time of writing) are negotiating or have negotiated first-ever citywide master security contracts. Dozens of local, regional, and national security contractors have signed similar "majority sign-up agreements."

Stand for Security and the successful efforts to organize janitors in London, New Zealand, and Australia demonstrate that the lessons learned in the J4J campaign can be extended, not only geographically to southern U.S. cities, but to other countries and to new groups of contract workers, such as security officers.

Going Global

All this takes us to the biggest issue. Just as workers cannot win in one city anymore, they cannot win in one country alone. The numbers of workers organized in the janitorial and security industry are relatively small in relation to the size of U.S. and world economies. But they demonstrate that not only can we win, but this may be our greatest opportunity to win in the biggest possible way.

In the face of years of decline, it may sound preposterous to argue that we believe we are now entering a moment of incredible opportunity for workers and their unions. But there are times when a mixture of events not of our making unleashes social forces and contradictions that create the possibility—not the guarantee—of creating a movement that lets us accomplish things we had never imagined possible. We are now in such a time.

How do we challenge corporate power through a campaign to organize workers into trade unions strong enough to raise wages and to unite communities into organizations powerful enough to win decent housing, schools, and medical care? How do we build on the critical experience gained by janitors and security officers, who have learned that they are far stronger working together than they would have been had they focused efforts on one building, one company, or one group of workers? How do we anticipate where the economy is going, instead of ending up on the defensive as it morphs and changes?

Organize Globally

Most trade unions still focus their resources and activity in one country. Despite a hundred years' rhetoric about the need for workers to unite beyond borders, most global work is symbolic solidarity action and not part of a part of a broader strategy. The economy is interrelated and global, and so must our organizing.[3]

Corporations, Not Countries

A campaign to change the world needs to focus on the corporations that increasingly dominate the global economy. To raise wages and living standards, we must force the largest corporations in the world to negotiate a new social compact that addresses human rights and labor rights in enforceable agreements that could lift tens of millions out of poverty. This campaign needs to be grounded in the worksites of the corporations that drive the economy and in the cities where they are located and from which they get much of their capital.

Union, community, religious, and political leaders need to lead a campaign calling on the 300 largest pension funds in the world to adopt responsible capital investment policies covering their 6.9 trillion euros (US$9 trillion) in capital. Responsible contractor policies require that the contractors servicing their investments maintain certain minimum standards for their workers. These policies ensure quality services by requiring fair and humane treatment of workers.

Global Workers, Global Unions, Global Cities

We must create truly global unions, spread across six continents, whose mission and focus is on the new global economy. But they do not need to be in every country or major city to have the breadth and reach to tackle the largest global corporations. The challenge of building global unions isn't to ask how we can be everywhere in the world, but instead to ask what is the minimum number of countries and cities we need to be in to exercise the maximum power to force corporations to adopt a new social compact? This means organizing janitors, security, hotel, airport, and other service workers in some of the 50 or so global cities that are central to the operations of these corporations.[4] The goal is to improve immediate conditions and to build a union that organizes not only where workers labor but also in the neighborhoods and communities where they live.

A Moral and Economic Message

It is not enough to organize workers and their workplaces. The campaign needs a powerful message about the immorality of workers' living in poverty amid incredible wealth. Religious, community, and political leaders need to embrace and help lead the campaign, because it highlights the moral issues of poverty, points a finger at the corporations responsible for it, and offers solutions good for workers and the community as a whole.

There are signs that elements of this campaign are becoming politically fashionable. Public opinion polls suggest significant concern about the rising inequality between rich and poor. In a national *Los Angeles Times*/Bloomberg poll released in December 2006 (*Bloomberg News* 2006), nearly three quarters of respondents said they consider the income gap in America to be a serious problem.

To organize successfully at the worksite and in communities, immigrants and migrant workers need to be brought out of the shadows of second-class status in the countries where they work. This campaign needs to take the lead in each country, and globally, to defend the rights of immigrant and migrant workers. It must promote laws that give immigrant and migrant workers full legal rights so they can organize, unite with native-born workers, and help lead this fight.

Disrupting—and Galvanizing—the Global City

It would be naïve to imagine that traditional union activity, moral persuasion, and responsible investment policies are enough to change corporate behavior or the world. These are starting points: small steps that allow workers and their allies to win victories, solidify organization, and increase the capacity to challenge corporate power. As activity and tension increase, the global business elite will go back and forth between making minor concessions to placate workers and attacking workers at the workplace, in the media, and in political circles. But in the end, we only get real change by executing both pieces of a two-pronged strategy: galvanizing workers, community leaders, and the public in a city around the need to lift up our communities, and creating a crisis that threatens the existing order.

Conclusion

This moment is so exciting and ripe with opportunity. In the last century, industrial workers learned how increasingly coordinated industrial action could cripple national economies, topple governments, and win more just and humane societies. This strategy worked for more than 50 years. But production has been redesigned and shifted across the globe, dispersing the power of workers and their unions. The rapid convergence of global corporations and workers in 50 global cities—where corporations are concentrating, not dispersing—has created new conditions and contradictions. These allow us to imagine how organized service workers can capture the imagination of people in their communities who are disturbed by poverty and income inequality, while simultaneously learning how to disrupt the "engine rooms" in cities across the globe. In so doing we can start to tip the balance of economic power in the world.

Global capital can operate smoothly in these cities because business leaders from around the world can fly in and out of their airports, stay in their hotels, and travel their streets to offices, banks, finance houses, and stock exchanges. Global cities, and the corporations that have centered the economic life of the world in them, cannot operate without the global workers who literally feed, protect, and serve the planet's richest and most powerful corporations and people. By learning how to disrupt these airports, offices, and hotels, service workers can exert their newly found and previously unimagined power, not for a day, but for weeks and months in an escalating campaign demanding decent wages and living conditions for workers and a stronger, more prosperous future for entire communities and cities.

It is astonishing that these are the workers whom the labor movement had written off as "unorganizable" a few short years ago. The Justice for Janitors and Stand for Security campaigns have demonstrated that it is not only desirable but possible for low-wage workers to fight back and win, even against corporations on the cutting edge of global outsourcing. In using their power, these workers can take the lead in creating a new world where the incredible technological progress, wealth, and economic advances of the global economy lift up the poor, empower the powerless, and inspire all of us to fight for justice.

Endnotes

[1] For a discussion of this largely unknown history of SEIU's organizing among janitors and an assessment of J4J strategy, see Milkman (2006).

[2] T&G recently merged with Amicus to form a new union, UNITE.

[3] For a more detailed discussion of the argument in favor of developing global unions, see Lerner (2006).

[4] See Sassen (2006) on the concentration of service sector jobs in global cities.

References

Bloomberg News. 2006. "Americans See Rich–Poor Gap Worsening." December 14.

Chronicle of Higher Education. 2001. "How Much Should Colleges Pay Their Janitors?" August 3.

Lerner, Stephen. 2006. "Global Unions: A Solution to Labor's Worldwide Decline." *New Labor Forum*, Vol. 16, no. 1 (Winter), pp. 23–37.

Miami Herald. 2006. "While Shalala Lives in Luxury, Janitors Struggle." March 1.

Milkman, Ruth. 2006. *L.A. Story: Immigrant Workers and the Future of the U.S. Labor Movement*. New York: Russell Sage Foundation.

National Labor Relations Act. (1935).

New York Times. 2006. "An Academic Retreat." February 12.

Sassen, Saskia. 2006. *Cities in a World Economy*. Thousand Oaks, CA: Pine Forge Press.

Service Employees International Union. 2006a. *Janitors Vote Overwhelmingly to Authorize Strike at University of Miami Over Unfair Labor Practices Committed by Janitorial Services Giant UNICCO*. Press release, February 25. <http://www.only2press.com/desk/200602/1140904800-21273.htm>.

———. 2006b. *Janitor and Student Hunger Strike Begins at UM*. Press release, April 5. <http://dfa.meetup.com/173/messages/boards/view/viewthread?thread=1790686&listpage=120>.

———. 2006c. *First Contract Provides Hope For Better Life; Lifts Hundreds of Janitors at UM Out of Poverty*. Press release, August 23. <http://www.seiu.org/media/pressreleases.cfm?pr_id=1333>.

Union Network International and Alliance for Justice at Group 4 Securicor. 2007. *Who Protects the Guards: The Facts Behind G4S in Southern Africa*. <http://www.focusong4s.org>.

CHAPTER 11

New Directions for the Living Wage Movement

PAUL K. SONN
National Employment Law Project

STEPHANIE LUCE
University of Massachusetts–Amherst

In the first few decades after World War II, U.S. public policy distributed the benefits of growth broadly by establishing a strong national wage floor that employers and unions then improved upon through collective bargaining. But both components of this system began to collapse beginning in the 1970s. In the years since, real wages have been stagnant or eroding for the majority of U.S. workers (Mishel, Bernstein, and Allegretto 2006). Congress allowed the federal minimum wage to erode substantially in real terms. At the same time, our labor law and collective bargaining system became increasingly ineffective at protecting workers' ability to organize (Compa 2004). This transformation of our labor policy has limited the ability of workers in the new service industries to unionize, contributing to a sharp decline in private sector union density as service jobs have replaced the base of unionized manufacturing jobs that sustained our nation's middle class during the decades of postwar prosperity.

These changes led policy makers and advocates for working families to begin exploring new options beyond collective bargaining and federal policy for seeking better wages. Beginning in the 1990s, new coalitions led by grassroots groups, the labor and faith communities, and immigrant worker centers emerged across the country focused on using the legislative arena, especially at the local level, to seek better wages through the enactment of new wage laws. This "living wage" movement had surprising success, with more than 130 cities and counties passing living wage ordinances in just over 10 years. However, the impact of these early laws has been limited in many ways. In most cities, they cover only a small percentage of the workforce since they extend just to employers who receive contracts or subsidies from the local government. Moreover, in many cities, enforcement of these living wage laws has been weak.

In more recent years, however, the living wage movement has expanded in new directions. First, grassroots groups have worked to raise the wage floor more broadly, winning substantial increases in the minimum wage in many states and ultimately helping to pass the first federal minimum wage increase in 10 years. Second, they have continued to broaden local living wage laws as tools for promoting good jobs above the minimum wage floor. Third, they have launched new initiatives to improve enforcement of wage protections, especially for immigrant workers. Fourth, they have begun to engage more broadly with the economic development process in an effort to ensure that growth delivers living wage jobs and other benefits that communities need. Finally, they have begun to build international links, helping activists in other countries launch living wage campaigns.

This chapter reviews these new directions in the living wage movement, both in the United States and globally.

Living Wage Laws

The first modern "living wage" law was enacted in Baltimore, Maryland, in 1994. Community organizers there decided to push for higher wage standards at the local level after concluding that it would not be realistic to win substantial increases in the state or federal minimum wage at that time. At the local level, by contrast, they found that elected leaders were more responsive to community needs and concerned about the growth of working poverty.

That first living wage law enacted by the Baltimore city council—which has since become known as a "traditional" living wage law—set a higher minimum wage for employers doing business with the city government. The law focused on employers who contracted with the city because in most states, city regulatory authority is broadest over such employers.

In the years that followed, campaigns for similar laws emerged in cities and counties across the country. Many wage advocates saw local action as a place where policy change could be achieved using the "people power" of grassroots organizing rather than the greater financial resources and lobbying strategies that are required at the state or federal level.

After more than a decade of living wage campaigns, activists had achieved considerable success, with more than 130 laws enacted in cities and counties around the country. The campaigns had been successful in building new grassroots coalitions and educating the public about the growth of working poverty. And the resulting higher wages were making a significant difference in the lives of the workers covered by the new wage laws.

At the same time, though, there were many limitations to the approach. First, most of these early living wage laws do not cover many workers, since they reach only employers that do business with local governments. In small cities, the number of workers covered could be fewer than 100. While in larger cities like New York the number covered could be as high as 60,000, even that figure reflects just a small portion of the city's low-wage workforce.

Second, many of the early living wage laws have not been effectively implemented. Lack of commitment by officials in some cities resulted in poor enforcement. In others, the laws allowed city officials to grant waivers to many employers, effectively circumventing the new wage protections. These enforcement problems echo the broader challenges in enforcing all wage standards: Widespread noncompliance with minimum wage and overtime laws is an increasing problem in many low-wage industries (Bernhardt, McGrath, and DeFilippis 2007).

Finally, the local focus of the first wave of living wage campaigns was also a limitation. By working at the municipal level, where lawmakers are often more responsive to community needs, labor and community groups were able to sidestep the obstacles to reform at the state and federal levels, including the lobbying clout of low-wage employers. But activists recognized that the impact of wage laws confined to a single locality was, of course, limited. In response, they began to explore ways to build on the success of the early living wage movement to address wages more broadly and to develop ties with workers in other cities, states, and countries.

State and Federal Minimum Wage Increases

In an effort to improve wages more broadly for low-income workers, the living wage movement set its sights on campaigns to raise the minimum wage at the state and, ultimately, federal level. Using the organizing capacity that it had built through local campaigns and drawing on demonstrated public support for stronger wage protections, living wage activists over the past five years have begun the process of restoring the U.S. minimum wage to a more robust level.

This focus emerged gradually on a state-by-state basis. It gained momentum as the value of the federal minimum wage—which the Republican Congress and the Bush administration froze at $5.15 an hour for 10 years—continued to fall. In 1999, just 10 states and the District of

Columbia had minimum wages higher than the federal level (Fiscal Policy Institute 2006). By early 2007, 33 states representing more than 70% of the U.S. population had raised their minimum wages—some more than 50% higher than the then-federal minimum wage of $5.15.

Most of these campaigns for statewide minimum wage increases have been focused on state legislatures. Grassroots groups joining with allies from the labor movement and the faith community have successfully organized to persuade their lawmakers to increase wages in states across the country.

Another important tool for minimum wage activists has been the ballot initiative. While polls show strong public support for raising the minimum wage in just about all 50 states, a significant number of legislatures have still refused to act. In states where they are authorized, ballot initiatives give wage activists a way to go directly to the voters, who can approve wage increases that have been blocked by their state legislatures.

After successful campaigns for minimum wage ballot initiatives in the 1990s in Oregon, Washington, and California, this approach gained momentum in 2004 when activists organized successful ballot initiatives in Florida and Nevada to raise the minimum wage and—equally important—to provide for annual cost-of-living increases in future years to prevent the minimum wage from eroding again. The Florida and Nevada initiatives were approved by overwhelming margins, and they helped engage low-income voters in the political process, as they appeared on the same ballot as the 2004 presidential election.

Building on those successes, activists began to organize ballot initiative campaigns in eight more states in 2006. Just the threat of a possible ballot initiative campaign enabled wage activists to win minimum wage increases in Michigan and Arkansas. When organizers began to gather signatures for minimum wage initiatives—which had the potential to bring low-income voters to the polls in a year of hotly contested elections—the conservative legislatures in those states reversed their longstanding opposition to the minimum wage and approved substantial wage hikes in order to get the issue off the ballot.

In six more states—Arizona, Colorado, Missouri, Montana, Nevada, and Ohio—minimum wage initiatives were approved to appear on the November 2006 ballot. Lobbyists for low-wage industries poured millions of dollars into campaigns attempting to persuade voters to reject the initiatives. But although supporters had virtually no television or radio advertising of their own, the measures passed easily in every state. Even in states like Montana and Missouri, where the races for the U.S. Senate were excruciatingly close, voters approved the minimum wage hikes by 76% and 74% margins. Polling showed that support was solid among virtually all demographic groups, including middle- and upper-income voters, and among both Democrats and Republicans.

The campaigns also showed that minimum wage increases do not need to be combined with other concessions in order to be politically feasible. This stands in contrast to Congress's recent practice of attaching unrelated business tax cuts to each of the last several federal minimum wage hikes.

Ballot initiatives have been especially important in helping living wage activists win key reforms that have proven elusive in the legislatures. One reform is the adoption of annual cost-of-living increases for minimum wage laws so that they do not erode again in the future. Nine of the 10 states that have adopted this important reform to date did so through initiatives. And activists have been able to use initiatives to get many states to close outmoded loopholes that deny millions of deserving workers, such as home health aides, seasonal farmworkers, and tipped workers, full protection of the minimum wage.

In the wake of the ballot initiative victories, however, in several states lobbyists for low-wage employers began pushing to roll back, in whole or in part, the voter-approved increases. In Ohio, for example, just weeks after the election, low-wage employers launched a rollback campaign under the guise of "implementing" the new wage hike. In Montana, the attack came from the restaurant industry, focusing on rolling back the minimum wage for tipped food service workers—one of the state's largest low-wage sectors. In Missouri, the restaurant industry simply refused to pay their waiters and waitresses the increased wage, arguing that the new minimum wage did not apply to tipped workers (Sonn 2007).

In both Montana and Missouri, minimum wage supporters were able to block these efforts through organizing and advocacy. In Ohio, however, they were unable to prevent the conservative legislature from rushing through an implementation law that purported to reverse many of the new protections contained in the minimum wage initiative. But incoming Governor Ted Strickland—a minimum wage supporter—was able to work with advocates to minimize the impact of the rollback legislation. For example, the Strickland administration determined that a careful reading of the rollback law indicated that it did not strip minimum wage protections from home health aides and migrant farmworkers as industry representatives had claimed.

One lesson of these rollback fights is that if minimum wage supporters organize and expose these attacks for what they are—attempts to cut pay for working families—the broader public is with them, and lawmakers pushing the rollbacks may back down. But the campaigns require real organizing, together with help analyzing the true impact of the roll-back proposals, which are often presented as "technical" rule changes.

The 2006 state ballot initiatives and the living wage movement's years of organizing around the needs of the working poor encouraged the Democrats to make the minimum wage a central plank of the platform on which their congressional candidates ran that year. When those elections carried them back to power, Congress was able to push through the first federal minimum wage increase in 10 years by attaching it to an Iraq war spending bill. But while long overdue, this increase—to $7.25 by 2009—is just a first step toward restoring the minimum wage to a meaningful level.

Already, living wage activists have joined with Senator Edward Kennedy to chart the next phase of this campaign, with planned legislation that would finally restore the federal minimum wage, in real terms, to its level during the postwar decades of prosperity, and then increase it each year based on the cost of living. But as the living wage movement works to build support in Congress to pass this key reform package in the years ahead, all indications are that states will continue to lead the way in demonstrating the depth of national support for restoring a robust minimum wage.

New Directions: Expanded Living Wage Laws

While restoring the minimum wage at the state and federal levels has been a major focus of living wage activists in recent years, it is just one of several new directions. Another focus has been exploring new ways to expand the coverage of municipal living wage laws in order to raise pay more broadly.

Initiatives to expand the coverage of living wage laws have taken several forms. One approach has been to enact broader wage laws that raise the minimum wage for all or most employers in a city. These measures, called "citywide minimum wage laws," have been pursued chiefly in cities with high costs of living where the state minimum wage is too low to adequately support low-wage workers. The first cities to enact such laws were Santa Fe and San Francisco, which as of 2008 had city minimum wages of $9.50 and $9.36, respectively. The number of cities exploring this approach has been limited, in part because cities' legal authority to adopt broad wage laws varies from state to state.

Another emerging approach has been using living wage laws to promote good jobs in key low-wage industries that are expanding in communities. For example, in 2006, living wage activists and labor allies in Emeryville and Los Angeles, California, successfully enacted the nation's first two industry-targeted living wage laws for hotel jobs. Low-wage hotel employers immediately brought lawsuits challenging these new measures. A federal district court rejected a legal challenge to the Emeryville law in 2006. However, one of the major hotels affected by the measure has continued to resist paying the living wage, forcing the city to bring a lawsuit seeking compliance. The Los Angeles law was initially blocked by a state court judge, citing alleged procedural defects with the way in which it was enacted. But that ruling was reversed on appeal in late 2007 and the law is now expected to go into effect.

In Chicago, grassroots groups have been campaigning for the first living wage law for retail jobs—one of the largest low-wage industries. The proposal was a response to the rapid expansion of "big box" retailers in the city as the industry discovered Chicago's underserved urban market. While city residents welcomed the expanded retail services, they objected to the low wages and limited benefits that the new stores paid. Pointing to the fact that some retailers, such as Costco, were already paying a $10 living wage and providing health benefits to their workers in Chicago, activists proposed a living wage law to require that all large retailers in the city do the same.

The proposed living wage was overwhelmingly popular with residents and consistently polled at above 70% (with even higher support among African Americans and Latinos). The Chicago city council approved it 35-to-14 in July 2006. However, Mayor Richard Daley used his first veto in 17 years in office to block the bill, and the city council fell just short of the two-thirds majority needed to override the veto.

More recently, the District of Columbia has enacted a new wage law for the city's security guard industry, a fast-growing sector where low pay and poor training were fueling high staff turnover, jeopardizing public safety. Adopted with the support of both the security industry and unions, this new ordinance extends the federal Service Contract Act's prevailing wage and benefits standards to all security guards employed in office buildings in the city. When it took effect in 2008, the measure boosted pay for thousands of guards to $11.51 per hour and guaranteed them at least $3.16 per hour in benefits or supplemental pay.

Yet another new direction that living wage expansion is taking focuses on asking developers seeking taxpayer-funded subsidies to ensure that workers at the development will receive living wages. For years, it was only in a few cities that living wage laws covered businesses receiving municipal economic development subsidies (Elmore 2003). Recently, however, living wage activists have begun to extend wage standards more broadly to include businesses receiving such taxpayer-funded assistance. For example, activists in New York City won new laws at both the city and state levels extending living wage standards to the city's chief tax incentive program for new housing construction, the 421-a program. As a result, all new apartment buildings whose developers elect to receive this tax benefit must pay their janitors and security guards living wages. Activists are now working to extend similar standards to economic development subsidies awarded by industrial development agencies across the state.

Finally, activists and policy makers are increasingly translating living wage standards to the state level by requiring all businesses receiving state contracts to pay a living wage. Several states have for many years mandated prevailing wages and benefits for service employees such as janitors, security guards, and cafeteria workers employed by businesses that supply services to state agencies. In recent years, living wage activists have broadened such laws to reach more state subsidized workers. For example, Connecticut's Service Worker Act adopted in 2000 requires prevailing wages and benefits for businesses receiving state service contracts and those operating cafeterias under franchise agreements at state agencies, state university campuses, state-owned airports, and state highway rest areas. In 2007, Maryland became the first state to adopt an actual living wage for state contractors. Recognizing differences in the state's economy, the law establishes one living wage rate for urban and suburban areas, and a lower one for rural counties.

Enforcing Minimum Wage and Living Wage Laws

Another increasingly important focus of living wage and minimum wage organizing is better enforcement of wage protections. In recent decades, wage and hour violations have become endemic in scores of low-wage industries (Bernhardt, McGrath, and DeFilippis 2007). While immigrant workers, both documented and undocumented, are especially vulnerable to such abuses, these widespread practices affect low-wage employees of all backgrounds in all regions of the country. In response, living wage activists are joining with immigrant worker organizers to fight for better enforcement of these basic protections.

These campaigns have taken different forms depending on whether their focus has been on enforcing living wage laws or minimum wage laws. We have discussed elsewhere the challenges of implementing "traditional" living wage laws, which extend to businesses receiving city contracts or subsidies (Luce 2004). As outlined in that book-length analysis, local activists have worked to enforce living wage laws using a combination of inside channels (such as implementation advisory boards) and outside channels (such as filing grievances and lawsuits, holding rallies, and getting media attention).

To date, several of the largest-scale violations of local living wage laws have involved the industrial laundry giant Cintas. In three cities, workers have brought lawsuits charging the laundry company with accepting city contracts and then reneging on its obligation to pay the applicable living wage. Workers at laundry facilities in Hayward and Los Angeles, California, and Madison, Wisconsin, sued the company for violating living wage laws. In Madison, after the lawsuit was filed, city officials shifted the laundry services contract to another firm. In Hayward, the lawsuit was approved as a class action, and the company was ordered to pay 219 workers at two facilities over $1 million in back wages and penalties (Russell 2005). In Los Angeles, the case is still pending after the courts ruled that it may go forward as a class action.

In other cities, living wage enforcement campaigns have focused on workers at municipal stadiums where employers have not complied with living wage laws. In Miami, organizers and advocates helped publicize the plight of 188 janitors who have not been paid the living wage to which they are entitled under the city's law for cleaning city-owned property, including the Orange Bowl (Chavez 2007). After the workers filed an enforcement suit with the assistance of legal services lawyers, the janitorial services contractor agreed to settle and repaid the workers nearly $100,000 in back wages. Similarly, organizers are fighting the failure of the Baltimore Orioles and the Camden Yards baseball park to pay Baltimore's mandated living wage to the more than 100 building service workers at the stadium (Zirin 2007).

Beyond living wage enforcement, the past five years have seen growing grassroots activism focused on improving enforcement of the minimum wage and other basic workplace protections. Worker centers and immigrant rights organizations are leading this movement to publicize the pervasive wage-related violations in dozens of major industries—practices such as forcing employees to work off the clock, paying less than the minimum wage, making illegal deductions from hourly wages, failing to pay overtime, and failing to pay on time. The workers who are most vulnerable to these abuses include immigrants, especially the undocumented, ex-offenders, and those transitioning off of public assistance. However, employers' growing use of these illegal practices affects workers of all backgrounds in all regions of the country. Increasingly, the grassroots community and labor activists of the living wage movement are joining these wage enforcement campaigns, recognizing that widespread wage and hour violations undermine job standards for all low-wage workers.

Immigrant worker groups and advocates are developing a variety of initiatives to address this growing problem. For example, in some states,

immigrant workers and allies are working to overhaul the wage enforcement systems of their state departments of labor (Gordon 1999). Staffing
levels for wage enforcement personnel have remained flat for decades—
despite rapid growth in the low-wage workforce during that period
(Bernhardt and McGrath 2005). Moreover, few departments of labor
have modernized their enforcement systems to respond to changes in
low-wage industries and labor markets. The lack of an effective response
to wage violations has helped fuel the growth of such practices in many
industries (Bernhardt, McGrath, and DeFilippis 2007).

To tackle this problem in New York, immigrant worker centers,
legal service lawyers, and advocates came together to develop a plan
for overhauling the state's wage enforcement system. The New York
State Department of Labor has welcomed the working group as a part-
ner, and together they are identifying and testing a range of model
reforms for making the system more effective, especially in problem
industries (Campaign to End Wage Theft 2006). Their aim is to
develop reform models that can serve as a blueprint for eventual mod-
ernization of the U.S. Department of Labor's wage enforcement system after 2008.

A similar campaign is under way in Maryland. Led again by immigrant worker centers, it is grappling with the enforcement challenges
presented in a state where previously the state department of labor
enforcement program consisted of just seven staff and a $300,000
budget. Having documented widespread wage violations occurring in
occupations and industries such as nursing homes, garment production, restaurants, domestic work, and day labor, the coalition is
advocating for increased funding and staffing and for other reforms
such as having the agency issue regular reports and work more closely
with the state attorney general, prosecutors, and community groups
(Bruillard 2007).

In some states, activists are also exploring local-level strategies for
improving wage enforcement. These include local wage theft laws aimed
at increasing the penalties for employers who don't pay workers their
wages. In most places, failure to pay a worker is considered just a civil
offense. But in cities like Phoenix, Denver, and Kansas City, activists
have helped enact new laws classifying nonpayment of wages as a type of
theft under the municipal code (González 2006; Valenty 2006). Although
workers previously had the ability to file complaints with the state
department of labor against employers who didn't pay wages owed, that
process is slow and cumbersome. By creating the threat of criminal
charges, local wage theft laws can speed up the process of charging
employers and getting wages paid (Verga 2004).

In other states, advocates are pursuing a similar strategy by creatively using existing "theft of services" laws to enforce workers' right to be paid. These laws, which have been on the books for years in many places, have typically been used to prosecute business customers who fail to pay for services. By persuading local prosecutors to apply them to employers who fail to pay wages owed, immigrant worker activists have created the threat of criminal charges, which helps secure faster repayment by employers.

In another approach, advocates for immigrant restaurant workers in New York are urging the city council to use its licensing authority to respond to the problem of wage violations in the restaurant industry, one of the largest low-wage sectors. Their proposed "responsible licensing" policy would require the city to examine a restaurant's record of wage violations in the same way that it now considers food safety violations when determining whether its operating license should be renewed.

Unions representing workers in low-wage industries have also been increasingly active in helping enforce state and local minimum wage and living wage legislation. Unions representing industrial laundry workers have helped non-union laundry workers recover unpaid wages, as in the lawsuits against Cintas discussed above. Similarly, unions representing building service and home care workers play a leading role nationally in helping low-wage workers enforce their rights under state and local wage laws. In just one example, in 2004 a union representing building service workers filed a complaint with Connecticut officials on behalf of janitors at the University of Connecticut, Bradley Airport, and the state Department of Transportation who were not being paid their mandated wage under the state's Service Worker Act discussed above. As a result, 350 janitorial employees won approximately $1.7 million in back wages. According to John Magnesi of the Connecticut Department of Labor's Wage and Workplace Standards Division, "This was a huge recovery and significantly advanced these workers toward something approaching truly 'livable wages' "(Magnesi 2007).

These snapshots of the growing number of wage enforcement initiatives highlight both the increasing importance of the issue and the challenges that these campaigns pose for low-wage workers and advocates. Overhauling wage enforcement by city or state authorities can be a complex, multiyear project. It often requires coalitions to grapple with technical questions such as expanding enforcement budgets and overhauling bureaucratic systems. And campaigns to enforce living wage laws have not generated broad support because the laws' narrow coverage means that they affect fairly few workers. Still, as recognition of the problem of wage violations grows, enforcement campaigns are likely to become an increasingly important focus for living wage and immigrant worker activists nationally.

Community Benefits Agreements and Accountable Development Campaigns

At the same time that they are working to raise the minimum wage, living wage activists are beginning to explore ways to promote the creation of more good jobs for low-income families above that basic wage floor. A key focus is the municipal economic development process—the set of policies that cities and counties use to stimulate and shape new job and business growth in their communities. As they engage with the development process, activists are seeking new approaches for ensuring that economic development delivers good jobs and the other benefits that low-income communities need.

One promising strategy is the use of community benefits agreements (CBAs), agreements that community coalitions negotiate with developers to establish a baseline set of standards and commitments that the developer will honor on a new development project. The idea is that when a new development project is planned for a community—whether it is a new shopping center, a housing development, or a sports arena—the developer should negotiate with local stakeholders to ensure that the development responds to community needs for good jobs, affordable housing, and livable communities. As Julian Gross, a leading advisor of community groups in CBA campaigns, explains, "[CBAs] allow community groups to have a voice in shaping a project, to press for community benefits that are tailored to their particular needs, and to enforce developers' promises" (Gross, LeRoy, and Janis-Aparicio 2005). CBAs typically require that some or all of the resulting jobs be paid a living wage and that local residents receive priority for them. They may also include requirements that the development adhere to certain environmental standards, be built with union labor, or include childcare facilities and public park space.

CBAs allow community-labor coalitions broad latitude in negotiating with developers. Since CBA agreements are private contracts between community groups and the developer, they may include requirements that cities cannot as easily address through legislation—for example, that the developer agree to neutrality in any union organizing campaign. Among the incentives for developers to negotiate CBAs is that they demonstrate community support for the project, a factor that can be important as a developer seeks zoning approvals, permits, or subsidies from city officials or competes with other bidders for the right to develop city-controlled land.

It has been community-labor activists in Los Angeles who have pioneered the CBA approach. Beginning with the Staples Center development project in 2001, they have negotiated over a half-dozen such agreements around local development projects. Illustrative was the CBA that they negotiated in 2004 for the expansion of Los Angeles International Airport (LAX). It provided for job training for 500 local residents each year and a local hiring preference for the new jobs created at the airport—jobs that already pay a living wage as a result of the Los Angeles living wage law. The agreement also included funding for public health programs and noise abatement and air pollution reduction measures to address the impact of the expansion on surrounding communities.

CBAs have quickly become a key tool for grassroots groups by allowing local communities to have a voice in new development to ensure that they share in its benefits. In recent years, CBAs have been negotiated in Denver, New Haven, San Diego, Minneapolis, and Milwaukee (LeRoy and Purinton 2005).

One of the challenges involved with CBA campaigns is that they can require specialized expertise on legal and technical issues, such as city planning and zoning, economic development funding, and real estate development. The strategy may also be most effective in cities with strong and growing economies where developers are competing with one another to build. And the fact that CBAs must be negotiated one project at a time means that the approach is resource intensive.

For this reason, leaders of the accountable development movement are exploring ways to "scale up" the CBA approach. Their goal is to reorient city economic development policy more broadly to make creating permanent, living wage jobs, affordable housing, and livable communities its chief focus. In Los Angeles, for example, community-labor activists have organized to appoint reformers to the board of the city's economic development agency. With this new leadership, the agency is shifting its priorities to make community benefits a major priority for its entire economic development program.

Following Los Angeles's lead, a new campaign in New York City is working to broaden the city's approach to economic development. Using the opening provided by the upcoming 2009 city elections, activists are building a coalition focused on reforming the city's economic development systems—everything from the planning process and business subsidies to land use and the housing code—to promote a more equitable and livable city. Their platform includes strategies for preserving affordable housing and neighborhood businesses, upgrading the city's rapidly growing low-wage industries, improving mass transit in underserved neighborhoods, and creating good jobs in new green industries.

This new movement for accountable development is clearly still in its early stages. It is likely to be a growing focus of grassroots groups in the coming years as local residents and city agencies test and develop new strategies for leveraging economic development to deliver the jobs and benefits that communities need.

Going International

In addition to the new directions for living wage and minimum wage campaigns in the U.S., there is increasing interest in this strategy internationally. The American living wage movement arose as a response to eroding wage standards, weaker labor and employment law enforcement, and a labor law system that became increasingly ineffective at protecting workers' ability to organize. Over the past 20 years, this U.S. model of labor market deregulation has begun to take root in a range of other nations. These include developed countries of North America and Europe that have traditionally had stronger labor market standards than the U.S. as well as developing countries that are experiencing external pressure to keep labor market standards low.

In response, labor supporters in some of these countries have begun looking to the U.S. living wage movement for organizing and policy strategies for rebuilding wage standards. In the United Kingdom this movement began in 2001, when a community-labor coalition came together to begin pushing for living wages for service workers in London, a city with one of the world's highest costs of living. In 2004, they won an agreement from Mayor Ken Livingstone guaranteeing a living wage for employees of the Greater London Authority and some public contractors. In the years since, they have extended these living wage agreements to British universities such as the London School of Economics and Queen Mary College, to the agency in charge of the 2012 London Olympics (London 2012 2007), and to large banks such as Barclays and Citigroup (Wills 2007). Additional campaigns are under way, including a citywide initiative for living wages for immigrant workers launched in 2006 by a network of community organizations.

Living wage campaigns are also under way in Canada. Canada does not currently have a national minimum wage; instead wages are set by each province. Labor and community groups are working to raise provincial minimum wages. Their new initiative, "Make the Minimum Wage a Living Wage," calls for the provinces to raise their minimum wages to $10 Canadian an hour (Howlett 2005). They are also proposing that the federal government reestablish a national minimum wage of $10 an hour and that it be automatically increased each year to keep pace with the cost of living. In addition, some of these Canadian wage activists are now working with organizers in Mexico to explore the concept of a "continental living wage campaign"—connecting minimum wage efforts in Canada, the U.S., and Mexico (Albo 2007).

Outside of Europe and North America, unions in India have been exploring the idea of coordinated wage standards for garment workers across Asia. With support from U.S.-based labor advocates, they have developed a proposal for an Asian garment worker wage floor. They estimate that about six out of every 10 garments produced in the world come from a few Asian countries, including China, India, and Bangladesh. If workers in the Asian countries could establish similar wage standards, they could begin to eliminate the whipsawing competition among the three nations that has helped keep wages low. This strategy does not necessarily require that the wage rates be identical in each country. It would be sufficient that they be within a reasonable range of one another, perhaps set using similar formulas that are established through coordinated campaigns. The strategy is not to seek a legislative increase in the minimum wage, which would be politically infeasible in these countries, but rather to organize campaigns targeting leading firms in each nation that appear able to pay wages higher than the national minimum. The hope is that establishing a higher standard at a group of leading companies in each country would raise pay levels throughout the industry and bring more marginal firms at least up to the minimum wage, which many currently violate (Tewari 2006).

Labor and community activists have also pursued living wage campaigns in a range of other countries and regions around the world, including Japan, Hong Kong, Australia, New Zealand, and South Africa. These initiatives have taken different forms, similar to the range of U.S. campaigns. In Japan, for example, unions have been working to pass a "Fair Public Contract Law," which would mandate a living wage and employment retention for workers employed under competitively bid government contracts. In Hong Kong, activists have been fighting to establish a more adequate minimum to protect the region's 300,000 to 400,000 workers who currently earn poverty level wages (Cheng 2006; Smith 2006). After a campaign calling on the government to enact an adequate minimum made little progress, activists and legislators have shifted to a legal strategy, arguing that Hong Kong's constitution requires that the government set a minimum wage for workers whose wages fall below the poverty line.

Finally, as in the U.S., ensuring enforcement of basic wage standards is a key problem that is gaining attention, in both the developed and developing world. While many workers would like to see an increase in the minimum wage, they are first concerned about ensuring regular payment of wages currently promised. Studies from across the globe document cases of workers who are promised wages that they never receive. It is impossible to get accurate data on the number of workers worldwide affected by nonpayment of wages or the amount of money owed, although researchers have attempted to estimate the numbers in various countries. For example, an International Labour Organization (ILO) analysis of China estimates that approximately 14 million workers were owed wage arrears of about $4 billion (U.S.) as of 2000 (Greenfield and Pringle 2002/3). Another ILO report outlines how nonpayment of wages—a violation of ILO Convention 95—is a significant problem in the Russian Federation, where 7.3 million workers were owed approximately $1 billion (U.S.) as of 2005 (International Labour Organization 2006). Protests demanding the payment of wage arrears are common activities by labor unions and NGOs in a number of countries. As in the U.S., there is a pressing need across the globe for developing new approaches for monitoring compliance, increasing enforcement resources, and mobilizing workers and NGOs to press employers and state agencies to address the issue.

Conclusion

When the Democrats swept to power in Congress in the November 2006 national elections, a strengthened minimum wage was a center-piece of the platform on which they ran. Where the minimum wage was on the ballot that year, bipartisan majorities of voters decisively endorsed increases. And after congressional Democrats delivered the first federal minimum wage increase in 10 years, they are preparing to introduce legislation calling for yet another round of minimum wage increases to continue restoring the wage floor to its historical level.

This broad base of support for a restored minimum wage marks a significant evolution from the 1990s, when action to increase the minimum wage generated muted enthusiasm from Congress and came with over $20 billion in business tax cuts. We believe that it has been the work of the living wage movement over the past decade that accounts for much of this shift. Beginning 13 years ago with labor and community organizers in Baltimore, Maryland, this movement has changed the politics around wage policy in the United States through organizing, advocacy, and education. By placing the concerns of the working poor back on the national agenda, living wage activists have made restoring the minimum wage one of our top policy priorities.

As this movement has grown in its organizing capacity and policy vision, living wage activists are successfully promoting new approaches for raising the minimum wage, for improving enforcement of wage protections, especially for immigrant workers, and for making economic development programs a vehicle for creating good jobs above the minimum wage floor. And activists are exporting this policy and organizing model to both developed and developing nations, where campaigns for strengthened wage standards are beginning to take root. In this fashion, the living wage movement is beginning to generate a more comprehensive public policy agenda responding to the growing problems of low-wage work and widening inequality in our economy.

References

Albo, Greg. 2007. "Income Inequalities, Living Wages, and Union Organizing." *MRZine*. March 15. <http://www.monthlyreview.org/mrzine/albo150307.html>. [April 1, 2007].

Bernhardt, Annette, and Siobhán McGrath. 2005. *Trends in Wage and Hour Enforcement by the U.S. Department of Labor, 1975–2004*. New York: Brennan Center for Justice.

Bernhardt, Annette, Siobhán McGrath, and James DeFilippis. 2007. *Unregulated Work in the Global City: Employment and Labor Law Violations in New York City*. New York: Brennan Center for Justice.

Bruillard, Karin. 2007. "Groups Demand State's Help in Fight Against Wage Abuses." *Washington Post*, January 9, p. B05.

Campaign to End Wage Theft. 2006. *Protecting New York's Workers: How the State Department of Labor Can Improve Wage-and-Hour Enforcement*. New York: Brennan Center for Justice.

Chavez, Juan Carlos. 2007. "Empleados de Limpieza Exigent Salario Digno." *El Nuevo Herald,* March 28, p. 1.

Cheng, Jonathan. 2006. "Minimum Wage Fight in Courts." *The Standard*. December 5. <http://www.thestandard.com.hk/news_detail.asp?pp_cat=11&art_id=33381&sid=11189666&con_type=1&d_str=20061205&sear_year=2006>. [April 1, 2007].

Compa, Lance. 2004. *Unfair Advantage: Workers' Freedom of Association in the United States Under International Human Rights Standards*. Ithaca, NY: Cornell University Press.

Elmore, Andrew. 2003. *Living Wage Laws and Communities: Smarter Economic Development, Lower Than Expected Costs*. New York: Brennan Center for Justice.

Fiscal Policy Institute. 2006. *States with Minimum Wages Above the Federal Level Have Had Faster Small Business and Retail Job Growth*. <http://www.fiscalpolicy.org/FPISmallBusinessMinWage.pdf>. [August 23, 2007].

González, Daniel. 2006. "Phoenix Treats Cheating Laborers as a Criminal Act." *The Arizona Republic*. February 11. <http://www.azcentral.com/arizonarepublic/news/articles/0211wagetheft0211.html>. [March 21, 2007].

Gordon, Jennifer. 1999. *Campaign for the Unpaid Wages Prohibition Act: Latino Immigrants Change New York Wage Law*. Carnegie Working Paper No. 4, August. Washington, DC: Carnegie Endowment for International Peace.

Greenfield, Gerard, and Tim Pringle. 2002/3. "The Challenge of Wage Arrears in China." *Labour Education,* Vol. 128, no. 30, p. 8. Geneva: International Labour Organization.

Gross, Julian, Greg LeRoy, and Madeline Janis-Aparicio. 2005. *Community Benefits Agreements: Making Development Projects Accountable.* Washington, DC: Good Jobs First.

Howlett, Dennis. 2005. "The Call for a Living Wage: Cross Canada Campaigns." *Canadian Dimension,* May/June. <http://canadiandimension.com/articles/2005/05/01/27/>. [April 1, 2007].

International Labour Organization. 2006. *Comments by the Committee of Experts on the Application of Conventions and Recommendations. 77th Session.* <http://webfusion.ilo.org/public/db/standards/normes/appl/appl-displayAllComments.cfm?hdroff=1&ctry=0640&conv=C095&Lang=EN>. [April 2, 2007].

LeRoy, Greg, and Anna Purinton. 2005. *Community Benefits Agreements: Ensuring That Urban Redevelopment Benefits Everyone.* Neighborhood Funders Group. <http://www.nfg.org/publications/community_benefits_agreements.pdf>. [November 2, 2007].

London 2012. 2007. *Olympic Delivery Authority and London Citizens Agree to Work Together on London Living Wage.* Press release. February 15. <http://www.london2012.com/news/media-releases/2007-02/olympic-delivery-authority-and-london-citizens-agree-to-.php>. [August 21, 2007].

Luce, Stephanie. 2004. *Fighting for a Living Wage.* Ithaca, NY: Cornell University Press.

Magnesi, John. 2007. E-mail to Stephanie Luce, January 11.

Mishel, Lawrence, Jared Bernstein, and Sylvia Allegretto. 2006. *The State of Working America 2006/2007.* Ithaca, NY: ILR Press.

Russell, Jesse. 2005. "Landmark Living Wage Case Forces Cintas to Pay over $1 Million." *Workers Independent News.* <http://www.laborradio.org/node/1604>. [March 22, 2007].

Smith, Patrick L. 2006. "Reining in Freewheeling Hong Kong; City Known for Laissez Faire Considers More Regulations." *The International Herald Tribune,* August 16, p. 3.

Sonn, Paul K. 2007. "The Fight for the Minimum Wage." *The American Prospect.* June 4.

Tewari, Meenu. 2006. *Targeting Global Supply Chains: Innovations in Labor Organizing in the Indian Garment Industries.* Paper prepared for the Conference on Multinationals and Labor Rights, September 22–24, Chapel Hill, University of North Carolina.

Valenty, Richard. 2006. "Council to Talk Wage Theft." *Colorado Daily.* January 15. <http://www.saveourstate.org/forums/lofiversion/index.php/t7205.html>. [March 21, 2007].

Verga, Rita. 2004. *An Activist's Toolkit: Using Criminal "Theft of Services" Laws to Enforce Workers' Rights to Be Paid.* New York: National Employment Law Project.

Wills, Jane. 2007. "Low Pay, No Way: When a Campaign in Support of Contract Cleaners at Canary Wharf Shamed Barclays Bank into Announcing a Living Wage for All Its London Workers, It Marked an Effective New Alliance between Trade Unions and the Wider Community." *Red Pepper.* Aug.–Sept. <http://www.redpepper.org.uk/article414.html>. [March 21, 2007].

Zirin, Dave. 2007. "Cleaning Up After the Orioles." *The Nation.* September 4.

CHAPTER 12

Mighty Monolith or Fractured Federation? Business Opposition and the Enactment of Workplace Legislation

DAVID WEIL
Boston University

Under H.R. 800, the misnamed "Employee Free Choice Act," union organizers could force businesses to accept "card-check" agreements. This tactic means that union organizers would approach employees one on one to publicly sign a card indicating union support, a method rife with the possibility of intimidation. Indeed, you would lose your voice in the process, and you could even be fined for offering improved benefits or working conditions to your employees—under H.R. 800, that's viewed as a threat to your employees' "free choice."[1]

The American Hotel and Lodging Association opposes H.R. 800 and S. 1041 [the Employee Free Choice Act] in the strongest possible terms, and urges Congress to reject this brazen assault on workers. . . . It would be unconscionable for Congress to eliminate the right of their constituents to vote in private ballot elections in their workplaces when those Members enjoy that right in their workplace—the halls of Congress.[2]

In 2007, Congress considered the Employee Free Choice Act (EFCA), legislation that would revise the National Labor Relations Act (NLRA) by allowing card-check recognition of unions, first contract arbitration, and increased penalties for unfair labor practices. The legislation—and in particular the card-check proposal—engendered the vehement opposition of business organizations, as illustrated by the opening quotations from the National Federation of Independent Businesses (NFIB) and the American Hotel and Lodging Association. But they were not alone: Virtually the entire spectrum of the business community, from the Business Roundtable (representing Fortune 500 companies) to small business representatives like NFIB and the Chamber of Commerce, worked together in opposition to the legislation.

Legislation affecting the workplace has been a lightning rod for business opposition since Congress began to address employment conditions at the turn of the last century. Every attempt to alter the NLRA in the past 35 years has been met with a near unanimous and virulent response from the business community and the failure to achieve reforms of that law. It is therefore easy to conclude that business opposition is a reflexive response to any effort by Congress or the White House to dabble in workplace affairs and that the business community acts as a monolithic impediment to progressive legislation.

Legislative solutions to redress conditions in the sectors and workplaces representing "gloves-off" employment practices must be crafted in this political context. Many of the problems described in this volume arise from changes in the forces governing the workplace over the last 30 years: the increasingly global basis of competition in many industries, transformations in technology and work organization, deregulation of product and labor markets, and the entry of millions of new immigrants into low- and high-skilled labor markets. These changes make workers in many sectors more vulnerable to the inevitable churning of the labor market. The decline of union density, decreasing resources for enforcement of existing policies, and the growing use of subcontracted employment have only intensified the risks facing workers. A number of the prior chapters have discussed means to redress this vulnerability, in part through passage of new public policies.

An overview of business positions on a variety of workplace policies would provide little reason for optimism regarding the prospects for legislation to address these problems. Table 1 summarizes the position of five business associations on a variety of federal policies that have been proposed in since the late 1970s. The table indicates that in virtually all of the cases, the formal business position was one of opposition.

Yet significant federal workplace legislation has been passed over the past quarter century, often in bursts of sustained legislative activity. In 1940, the U.S. Department of Labor administered 18 regulatory programs; by 1960 it administered 40; in 1975, 134; by 1994, 189; and now it oversees close to 200 statutes related to the workplace (see Weil 2007 for a discussion of this "installed base" of legislation).

How has legislation made it past seemingly uniform business opposition? Does business really act as a monolithic barrier to legislation? If not, in what cases has it been divided, and how did those divisions affect

TABLE 1
Recent Workplace Legislation and the Initial Position of Major Business Groups

	Business association[a]					
Workplace policy	BRT	NAM	C of C	NFIB	NRF	Major business supporters
Labor Law Reform (1977)	Oppose	Oppose	Oppose	Oppose	Oppose	None
High Risk Occupational Disease Notification and Prevention Act (1988)	Oppose	Oppose	Oppose	Oppose	Oppose	Chemical Manufacturers Association; American Electronics Association
WARN (1989)	Oppose	Oppose	Oppose	Oppose	Oppose	None
Civil Rights Act (1991)	Support	Oppose	Oppose	Oppose	Oppose	AT&T; other BRT members
Family and Medical Leave Act (1993)	Oppose	Oppose	Oppose	Oppose	Oppose	None
Comprehensive Occupational Safety and Health Reform Act (1994)	Oppose	Oppose	Oppose	Oppose	Oppose	None
Workplace Fairness Act (1993)	Oppose	Oppose	Oppose	Oppose	Oppose	None
Employee Free Choice Act (2007)	Oppose	Oppose	Oppose	Oppose	Oppose	None

[a] BRT: Business Roundtable; NAM: National Association of Manufacturers; C of C: Chamber of Commerce; NFIB: National Federation of Independent Businesses; NRF: National Retail Federation.

political outcomes? What other factors created the political conditions to enact legislation in recent decades, such as the Workers Adjustment Retraining and Notification Act (WARN) or the Family and Medical Leave Act (FMLA)? Are there lessons from these successful cases—as well as from the failures—that could inform future legislative initiatives? How might some of these problems be dealt with through means in a political environment where business can successfully block new progressive legislation?

This chapter examines the role of business opposition in affecting the passage of workplace policies. I argue that, rather than acting as a monolithic and unified barrier to all legislation, in many cases schisms have emerged within the business community that created a political space for policies to move forward. Although one seldom finds overt support for workplace legislation among business groups, segments of the business community have had reason to move from a position of strict opposition to one of negotiation. In these cases, and in the presence of a broad coalition of legislative advocates, Congress has been able to pass legislation.

The chapter begins with a broad framing of the factors surrounding political economy of regulatory policy generally and workplace policy in particular. I then review the history of three workplace policies in detail to illustrate the impact of business, labor, and other groups on legislative outcomes: the WARN Act of 1988, the FMLA of 1993, and finally a suite of attempts to reform the NLRA. The history of these and other recent workplace policies reveals several common features regarding when business stands as a monolith against any new policies versus where fractures emerge that bring key players to the negotiating table, thereby allowing enactment of new policies. I conclude the chapter with a discussion of the implications of this analysis for prospective workplace legislation.

The Political Economy of Workplace Regulation

Workplace policies are not established in a vacuum. Like any form of regulation, those policies entail changing behavior toward, and therefore imposing costs on, a targeted group of organizations in order to benefit a different set of individuals. This inevitably creates stakes for both the targets and beneficiaries of the regulation to become politically engaged. A rich political science and economics literature addresses this political economy of regulation (e.g., Becker 1983; Olson 1971; Stigler 1971; Wilson 1980).

Regulatory policies almost always impose concentrated costs on the regulated in order to achieve a larger public purpose. The parties that bear the cost of regulation have high incentives to become involved in the legislative process. On the other hand, since the benefits of regulation are often diffused across a large number of individuals, their individual stakes in becoming involved are comparatively small. What is more, they face a free-rider problem, where the benefits of letting someone else shoulder the task of engaging in the political fight undermine collective participation in the political process (Olson 1971). As a general matter, then, those who bear the costs of regulation enjoy a substantial political advantage over those who benefit from the regulation. As noted by James Q. Wilson (1980:370): "Since the incentive to organize is strong for opponents of the policy but weak for the beneficiaries, and since the political system provides many points at which opposition can be registered, it may seem astonishing that regulation of this sort is ever passed."

Workplace policies are classic examples of the dilemma described by Wilson and others. Federal workplace policies affect employers in one of three ways: requiring them to follow a set of baseline practices regarding the employment relationship (e.g., paying the minimum wage); establishing a procedure for them to set workplace policies in conjunction with labor unions (the basis of the Railway Labor Act and the National Labor Relations Act); or creating procedural rules for employers to work within when setting broad areas of human resource policy (as, for example, under various antidiscrimination laws). All three pathways affect important business decisions and therefore raise costs to employers. It is not hard, in this sense, to understand the unanimity of business viewpoints on workplace policies shown in Table 1.

Although a large numbers of workers may directly benefit from some policies (e.g., low-wage workers in many industries from minimum wage laws), most workers may not perceive the benefits from a given workplace policy or believe them to be very significant. Workers therefore face the same collective action problem as in any regulatory situation. Historically, labor unions have helped to redress this problem, by serving as the political voice of those directly represented by unions as well as of unorganized workers (Freeman and Medoff 1983). Yet as union density has declined, the ability to play this role in the political process has been diminished.

The political economy of regulation would seem to make passage of any workplace legislation unlikely. What accounts for the successful cases of legislative enactment? Do these cases amount to political victories through the creation of least-common-denominator laws or regulations? Or do they represent true instances of legislators overcoming the entrenched interests of the politically powerful?

The Political Economy of Workplace Policies: Three Cases

Protecting Workers from Plant Closings, or Companies from Plant-Closing Legislation?

Concerned over the economic impacts of intensifying global competition in the manufacturing sector and facing political fallout from a growing number of high-profile plant closings and mass layoffs, Congress debated a variety of proposals in the late 1970s and early 1980s. Policy options ranged from restricting employer rights to close major facilities to creating industry-based policies to improve competitiveness and major modifications of the unemployment insurance system (see, for example, Magaziner and Reich 1982 and Bluestone and Harrison 1983 for discussion of this range of policy options).

Congress ultimately selected a more modest approach to the problem: requiring companies to provide advanced notice to affected workers and communities in the event of a plant closing or large-scale layoff. The aim of imposing such a requirement was to improve post-layoff and plant-closing outcomes for displaced workers as well as to provide communities facing significant economic impacts with time to find alternative solutions or make adjustments for the impending closings. The original bill, introduced by Ohio's Democratic Senator Howard Metzenbaum in 1985, required companies to provide workers and the surrounding community 90 days' advance notice prior to a shutdown or layoff affecting 50 or more workers.

From the beginning, the bill was vigorously opposed by a coalition of business groups. Business lobbying, coupled with Reagan administration opposition, left the bill in committee for the remainder of the congressional session. Business and conservative critics of advance notice argued that it would lead customers, suppliers, and capital markets to overreact, making already weakened companies less able to recover and expand. If advance notice was to be required, they argued, it should be provided a relatively short time prior to plant closing. It should also exempt wide classes of employers whose decisions to reduce employment reflected the normal ebb and flow of production rather than more profound, long-term reductions in employment (see Ehrenberg and Jakubson 1990, pp. 39–46).

Continued increases in plant closings in manufacturing led Metzenbaum and Congressman William Ford (Democrat, Michigan) to reintroduce the bill in 1987, this time increasing the amount of time for advanced notice for very-large-scale closures. To improve the likelihood of passage, the legislation was incorporated into a larger international trade bill that had the support of centrist Democrats as well as Republicans. The increasing likelihood of passage led to rifts within the business coalition, particularly between large and small employers potentially affected by a plant-closing law.

As a result, although many business associations maintained a public position opposing the plant-closing notification bill, their representatives began to negotiate over specific provisions. The number of days required for notice fell from 90 days in the original bill to only 60 days. Similarly, although virtually all workers at covered employers—hourly, salaried, and managerial—were entitled to notice, the extent of employer coverage became the topic of debate. In the end, private and not-for-profit employers were exempted from notification requirements if they had fewer than 100 workers (and employees were excluded from that count if they had worked for less than six months in the past year or worked fewer than 20 hours per week on average). That meant that the vast majority of small businesses were not required to provide advance notice of layoffs or closings.

The definition of plant closing and mass layoff also left many potential company decisions involving large employment cuts outside of the law's disclosure requirement. A covered employer was required to provide advance notice if an impending shutdown would lead to a loss of 50 or more workers in a 30-day period. Mass layoff was defined narrowly as reducing employment at any site of 500 or more workers or laying off 50 to 499 workers if that number represented at least a third of the workforce. In addition, covered employers were not required to provide advance notice for a variety of "unforeseeable" business reasons, for natural disasters, or where it could be shown that even the 60-day disclosure would cause irreparable harm to the business's viability.

Enforcement powers were also the object of negotiations, resulting in a stripped-down apparatus for implementing the law. Unlike most federal labor policies, the advance notice requirement did not vest a particular division of the U.S. Department of Labor with authority to investigate or enforce the law. Enforcement was provided instead through lawsuits lodged by workers, their representatives (if present), and/or local governments in federal courts. An employer found in violation of the disclosure requirement could be required to pay the affected workers back pay and benefits for the period when notice was not provided (up to 60 days) and potentially pay modest civil penalties of up to $500 for each day of violation.

With these amendments in place, Congress passed the bill as part of a larger piece of trade legislation. When President Reagan vetoed the entire trade bill, Metzenbaum reintroduced the plant-closing bill as a self-standing piece of legislation, called the Worker Adjustment and Retraining Notification Act (WARN).[3] WARN was passed by Congress, and this time it became law, but without the signature of the president.

The divergence between big and small business interests ultimately created the political space to pass WARN. Nonetheless, the resulting compromise produced a law that covers a relatively small percentage of plant closings and large-scale layoffs given the large percentage of the workforce employed in workplaces with fewer than 100 workers and the fact that the vast majority of employment reductions (even in large workplaces) do not fall within the narrow definitions of employment loss described in the regulation (Ehrenburg and Jakobson 1990; General Accounting Office 2003). A series of investigative reports in 2007 documented major plant closings where a combination of the broad exemptions to the law and noncompliance denied workers of advanced notice even in the face of large-scale layoffs (Drew and Eder 2007; Eder and Drew 2007).

Family and Medical Leave: High-Road Benchmark or Pyrrhic Victory?

The passage of the Family and Medical Leave Act of 1993 is often cited as one of the first major legislative accomplishments of the Clinton administration. In fact, the legislation represented the end of a decade-long fight to create family leave policies.

The growing participation of women in the labor force and the changing structure of the typical American household created a pressing need for public policies addressing working families. During the 1980s, when the effort to pass a family leave policy gained momentum, the proportion of households with two income earners went from 52% in 1980 to 63% in 1988. At the same time, the number of single-parent households rose by 23% from 1980 to 1988 (Hyland 1990). The prevalence of two-income and single-parent households and the entry of women into new occupations and industries placed new pressures on the workplace and on households attempting to strike a work–family balance (Hochschild and Machung 1989; Kanter 1989). Providing employees with leave occasioned by the birth or sickness of their children represented one of the challenges posed by these labor market changes.[4]

The first parental family medical leave bill was introduced in Congress by Howard Berman and Patricia Schroeder in 1984.[5] The bill—like all of those to follow—did not require that employers pay for time off for workers, but simply allowed for 18 weeks of unpaid leave with a guarantee of reinstatement arising from a birth, adoption, or serious illness of a child (Marks 1997). This contrasted with many European countries that already required employers to provide paid medical leave.

Given the large and growing number of women in the workforce, the "family-friendly" nature of the policy, and an emerging popular discourse on work–family balance, the legislation appeared likely to garner bipartisan support. Early co-sponsors included conservative Republicans like Henry Hyde of Illinois and Christopher Smith of New Jersey (Marks 1997). Supporters of the bill included not only the AFL-CIO and labor unions but a range of women's groups (e.g., the National Organization of Women [NOW] and the Women's Legal Defense Fund [WLDF]), social service organizations, religious organizations, health professional associations, and other policy advocates, including the American Association of Retired Persons (Elison 1997).

Yet early in the legislative process, support for the bill began to polarize, particularly as business groups became involved. The greatest opposition came from small-business organizations led by the Chamber of Commerce and the National Federation of Independent Businesses (NFIB) as well as other industry-based organizations representing predominately smaller businesses. A poll by NFIB in 1986 found that 83% of its membership opposed a parental medical leave bill (Elison 1997). A concerted campaign by the small-business community to stop the legislation entirely was initiated in 1986, fueled in particular by concerns over the disruption that a mandated leave bill would have.

A significant percentage of larger-scale businesses in the U.S. already provided medical leave for their workers (Kanter 1989). A Bureau of Labor Statistics survey in 1989 found that 36% of employees in medium and large firms in the private sector already provided maternity leave and 19% provided paternity leave. Similar to FMLA, the vast majority of policies allowed for unpaid leave only. Among those private employers offering unpaid leave, the average duration for maternity leave was about 19 weeks versus 18 weeks for paternity leave (Meisenheimer 1989).[6] Yet business groups representing larger businesses objected to a government-mandated leave requirement on the grounds that it would lock them into those arrangements or in some cases require them to be more generous (Martin 2000). Groups like the Business Roundtable and the National Association of Manufacturers therefore supported the public position taken by the more vehemently opposed small-business lobby.

The intensity of small-business opposition (and reserved opposition from larger business organizations) made it difficult for the legislation to move out of the House subcommittee in charge of markup. With support largely polarized around party affiliation, negotiations in markup focused on raising the minimum size for small-business exemptions, increasing the length of time employees would need to be eligible for medical leave, and reducing the amount of mandatory time prescribed by the law.

However, when Democrats regained control of the House in 1986, the bill made it out of committee and began to move forward, while a companion bill was introduced in the Senate. The bills in both chambers continued to be the target of intensive lobbying by the small-business community, joined increasingly by representatives of big business as it became clear that some legislation would be reported out. In the ensuing negotiations, small business pressed for raising the exemption threshold. As a result, the bill exempted firms with fewer than 50 workers in the first three years after passage and fewer than 35 workers after that.

By the time the bill emerged on the House floor, however, businesses with fewer than 50 workers were uniformly exempted from coverage. An analysis by WLDF concluded that this had the effect of exempting about 50% of the private sector workforce. The period of coverage had also been reduced to a total of 12 weeks. The Senate ratified the House bill with no modifications, but it was subsequently vetoed by President George H.W. Bush in 1990.With the election of Bill Clinton in 1992, the coalition behind FMLA reintroduced it in the following congressional session with the major features of the legislation from prior negotiations largely in place. After the bill made it through Congress, President Clinton signed FMLA into law in 1993 (Monroe, Garand, and Teeters 1995).

In the end, the broad coalition of FMLA proponents successfully moved the policy to enactment over the course of a decade of political machinations. This reflected the breadth of the coalition supporting the legislation that included not only the labor movement, but NOW, WLDF, the American Civil Liberties Union, and AARP.[7] But it also reflected subtle schisms in the business community. While the small-business community perceived the legislation as fundamentally against its interests, the willingness of other segments of business to accept a policy that in some sense codified its existing practices created the political space for eventual passage.

Several studies of FMLA subsequent to passage have found that it led to an expansion of parental leave coverage among firms both covered *and* not covered by the act. A Bureau of Labor Statistics Employee Benefits Survey found that among medium and large firms (100 employees or more), the proportion of full-time employees with maternity leave coverage increased from 37% in 1991 (shortly before passage) to 84% in 1995. Among small firms (where a substantial percent were exempted from the act) coverage went from 18% in 1992 to 47% in 1994.[8] There is also evidence that the take-up rate for leave (that is, the percentage of workers entitled to leave who actually use it) also increased significantly following passage of FMLA (Waldfogel 1999). This implies that once the political logjam blocking parental leave was finally broken, FMLA had impacts beyond those workers who already received coverage.

Workplace Representation Policy as the Political Third Rail

"Labor law in America is hard to change. This may be the understatement of the century." (Kochan 2007:101)

This chapter opened with quotations reflecting the virulent opposition of the business community to the Employee Free Choice Act (EFCA), labor reform legislation that failed to be approved by a

Democratic-controlled Congress in 2007. Yet EFCA was only the latest of a long line of defeats. Every legislative effort to reform federal labor laws has met defeat for more than 30 years. Public policies relating to worker representation seem to represent the third rail of political engagement.

In 1974, after painstaking negotiations among building trades unions, contractor associations, and key construction users, Secretary of Labor John T. Dunlop brokered a deal that would have altered features of labor relations in the construction sector to allow for "common situs" picketing on construction sites (common situs picketing occurs when a union pickets a construction site where multiple contractors are present, resulting in economic pressures being placed on contractor[s] not directly involved in the dispute, resulting under current law in an illegal secondary boycott). Last-minute concerns about the political backlash from the wider business community and other conservative supporters led President Gerald Ford to veto the very bill his own labor secretary had painstakingly crafted.[9]

Three years later, a modest set of reforms to the NLRA failed to become law even though it was supported by President Jimmy Carter and a Democratic-controlled Congress. Despite such a favorable political climate, the policy was defeated by means of a Republican filibuster, and through the concerted pressure of the business community. Robert Thompson of the U.S. Chamber of Commerce noted at the time, "Business is more unified in the outright defeat of this bill than in any other labor issue I've observed over the past 25 years" (Freeman and Medoff 1983:203).[10]

The Workplace Fairness Act of 1993 sought to overturn the longstanding Supreme Court doctrine established in *NLRB v. Mackay Radio & Telegraph Company* (304 U.S. 333, 1938), which provides employers the right to hire permanent replacements for strikers.[11] A series of long, high-profile strikes in the 1980s and early 1990s (e.g., Greyhound and Caterpillar) demonstrated the limited utility of the strike as a tool of union leverage, in part given the Mackay doctrine. Proponents of striker-replacement legislation therefore argued it would rebalance power at the bargaining table that had shifted toward management, particularly given the decline in union density beginning in the mid-1950s and deepening in the 1970s and 1980s.[12]

Opponents of the act—cutting across both the union and non-union segments of the business community—characterized the ability to hire permanent replacement workers as a fundamental tool of collective bargaining, allowing business to survive the effects of strikes. Rather than rebalancing the collective bargaining environment, businesses argued, the legislation would give labor unions decisive leverage, leading to widescale work disruptions, losses in productivity, and dire macroeconomic impacts (Estreicher 1994; Singh and Jain 2001). Striker-replacement measures had been introduced unsuccessfully in the House in 1991 and Senate in 1992. The legislation was reintroduced by Senator Howard Metzenbaum and Congressman William Clay at what seemed to be another propitious political window of opportunity: during the brief period of time when Democrats controlled both the Congress and the White House in 1993. Indeed, Bill Clinton had pledged support for the bill as a presidential candidate and its reintroduction in the 103rd Congress as the "Cesar Chavez Workplace Fairness Act."

Yet the same broad business coalition that had fought the Labor Law Reform Act of 1977 reassembled once again and, despite the presence of Democrat majorities, successfully prevented the bill from making it out of Congress.[13] With Republicans retaking control of Congress in 1994, the bill never again moved forward, although it was reintroduced in the 104th through 106th congresses.

The near unanimity of business opposition to these initiatives is striking. In the cases of WARN and FMLA, segments of the business community moved from a position of complete opposition to negotiation over provisions of the legislation. In contrast, efforts to expand the extent of collective bargaining or the relative balance of labor–management power in it have repeatedly galvanized the business community. As a result, legislative efforts in this arena led not to political compromise, but to the failure to achieve enactment in any form.[14]

The inability to pass legislation relating to collective bargaining is thus a situation reflecting the "monolithic face" of business community opposition. But it also represents the difficulty the labor movement faces in gaining passage of legislation where it lacks broad coalition partners who have a strong and direct vested interest in the legislation. As Freeman and Medoff (1983) pointed out 25 years ago, the labor movement has been far more successful in the political arena in championing "social movement" legislation that in large part affected workers far beyond their existing membership than legislation specifically directed toward more direct interest in workplace representation. The continued erosion of union density only further contributes to the difficulty of passing policies focused specifically on workplace representation.

What Determines Passage of Workplace Policies?

What accounts for the passage of some workplace policies (WARN, FMLA) and not others (the suite of policies relating to collective bargaining)? Many proximate factors affect why some pieces of legislation eventually make it through the political labyrinth into law and others do not. For example, public crises often play an important role in at least temporarily breaking through Wilson's political economy of concentrated costs and diffuse benefits. The scandals at Enron and Worldcom in 2001, for example, started the legislative cycle that ultimately led to passage of the Sarbanes-Oxley financial reporting laws of 2003.[15]

Nonetheless, in the cases I have described, two critical dimensions help explain why proponents of workplace policies overcame the demanding constraints posed by the political economy of regulation. First, divergences in the prospective benefits and costs of proposed regulation created schisms within the "monolithic" business community that provided the political space necessary for legislators to craft a workplace policy. Second, the breadth as well as strength of the coalition supporting regulations played an important role in keeping Congress and the White House engaged.[16] Table 2 provides a summary of these two dimensions as well as several other factors related to the enactment of the policies discussed above as well as other relevant cases.

Divergent Interests: When Small Business and Big Business Diverge

Although regulatory costs are concentrated on a relatively small number of players, they often are not shared equally across regulated entities. The divergence in costs of workplace policies across the business community represents a first critical determinant of policy enactment. Business in general may share a common interest in keeping as much discretion as possible over employment policies. But competitive, political, and social factors may convince some businesses that they have more to lose from proposed legislation than others in the business community.

Firms facing greater competitive pressure, producing products or services that allow for less specialization or niche marketing, and/or having a larger proportion of costs associated with labor will have a greater incentive to oppose new workplace policies. Other firms may have a lesser stake in opposing policies if they have already adopted a set of human resource practices largely in keeping with them. Often, the intensity of opposition to a workplace policy varies with the size of the business enterprise.

Virtually all of the major business groups initially opposed the proposed workplace policies listed in Table 2. Reflexive opposition arises from the regulatory calculus described by Wilson (1980), Becker (1983), and others: the costs of these interventions are concentrated on the business community. Broad-based business opposition accounts in part for the moderate nature of initial policy proposals: A rash of plant closings

TABLE 2
Political and Institutional Factors Regarding Selected Federal Workplace Policies

Workplace policy	Small-business opposition?	Large-business opposition?	Broad political coalition partners beyond labor movement?	Related state-level policies prior to federal legislation?	Crisis or major public event related to the legislation?	Legislative outcome
Davis-Bacon Prevailing Wage (1931)	Yes, but not well organized	No	Yes	Yes	Yes[d]	Passed
Fair Labor Standards Act (1938)	Yes, but not well organized	Mixed[a]	Yes	Yes	No	Passed
Labor Law Reform (1977)	Strong	Strong	No	No[b]	No	Failed
Hazard Communication Standard (1983)	Strong	Mixed[c]	Yes	Yes	No	Passed
WARN (1988)	Strong	Moderate	No	Yes	Yes[e]	Passed with significant exemptions
Family and Medical Leave Act (1993)	Strong	Moderate	Yes	Yes	No	Passed with significant exemptions
Workplace Fairness Act (1993)	Strong	Strong	No	No[b]	No	Failed
Employee Free Choice Act (2007)	Strong	Strong	No	No[b]	No	Failed

[a] Law supported by manufacturers based primarily in northern states; opposed by manufacturers in southern states and those operating in both areas.
[b] Federal preemption does not allow state-level policies related to NLRA. Several state-level attempts to restrict the use of permanent striker replacement, for example, were ruled unconstitutional (LeRoy 1993).
[c] Standard opposed by business groups that would be required to provide significant levels of disclosure (e.g., Chemical Manufacturers Association); Supported by downstream chemical users who saw benefit in disclosure (see Fagotto and Fung 2003; Fung, Graham, and Weil 2007).
[d] Depth of the Depression; federal construction projects were the linchpin of recovery efforts.
[e] Many major plant closings in manufacturing sector in late 1980s.

across the manufacturing sector elicits a requirement for advanced notification; the need to address work–family pressures leads to a requirement to provide unpaid time off of work. Even where the potential costs of proposals may be inconsequential for particular business subgroups—e.g., increases in minimum wage levels on the employment costs of large employers represented by the Business Roundtable—the stake they have in future alliances involving more consequential legislation may lead them to sign on to opposing initiatives (or at least to sit on their hands).

Yet in the case of WARN and FMLA, a realignment occurred as the legislation proceeded. Small business remained for the most part implacably opposed to the policy. However, other segments of the business community began to negotiate about the legislation itself rather than simply trying to thwart its passage.[17] Thus, in the case of WARN, the length of time required for advanced notice, the extent of coverage, the structure of enforcement under the act, and the procedures for notification became active areas of political negotiation. For FMLA, larger businesses at a certain point moved from opposition to negotiating for amendments in the legislation that moved it to more closely conforming with existing leave policies already prevalent among a subset of major companies.

Underlying motivations. The divergence in business community interests arises in part from the underlying motivations driving different segments of the business community. The strong and consistent opposition toward workplace regulation from the small-business community reflects both practical and ideological concerns. From a practical perspective, small businesses tend to have a higher proportion of their costs related to labor, employ a higher proportion of low-wage workers, and generally operate in more competitive product markets. Taken together, these factors mean that workplace regulations directly impact their costs and profitability. Ideologically, many of the positions that small-business lobbies like NFIB stake out—often explicitly in their testimony against proposed legislation—are based on the premise that attempts to regulate one aspect of the workplace inevitably lead to wider and more onerous regulation. This ideological orientation—accompanied by a political ethos that venerates small businesses—promoted a highly antagonistic response to virtually all major workplace regulation introduced over the last 30 years.

Big business's reflexive initial opposition to most workplace legislation is sometimes viewed as puzzling, particularly in cases like increasing the minimum wage, since it is argued that they already comply with such policies. For example, there is abundant evidence that workers in larger companies receive higher earnings are more likely to receive various types of benefits and generally work under better conditions than comparable workers in small companies (e.g., Brown, Hamilton, and Medoff 1990; Harrison 1997). Why not, then, "level the playing field" by requiring smaller competitors to treat their workforce commensurately?

This view misses several factors underlying the strategic position of the big business community. First, large-scale enterprises share a common and wider political agenda with the small-business community in terms of tax, economic, and general regulatory policies. Because of that broad common interest, the risks from breaking ranks with the coalition are significant, producing incentives to join the wider business coalition initially.

Second, one must question the premise that many of the firms in business associations like the Business Roundtable (Fortune 500 corporations) in fact compete directly with the typical firms in the Chamber of Commerce or the National Federation of Independent Business. Although there are cases where this may be true, the memberships of these organizations tend to compete in distinct industries and markets and therefore do not directly benefit from a more level playing field. What is more, where there is overlap, such as among National Association of Manufacturers and Chamber of Commerce members, smaller businesses often play a role as a secondary set of suppliers to large firms. Given that role, larger businesses have political interests allied with small firms in preventing further regulation that would have the secondary effect of raising their costs or increasing their incentive to seek offshore alternatives.

Nonetheless, the cases I have outlined (and other examples noted in Table 2) suggest that big-business associations have shifted their strategy from pure opposition to a negotiating stance in the course of some legislative battles. For example, during the years between the initial proposal of FMLA in 1984 and its passage in 1993, big-business representatives seemed to have decided to negotiate for a more delimited medical leave policy rather than simply attempting to block that legislation. The reasons for doing so arise from two sources.

The impact of state-level legislation. One factor driving the big-business community to diverge from small-business interests can be traced to passage of state-level legislation during the course of legislative efforts. The costs of complying with varied requirements state by state can quickly dwarf the costs of a common federal standard. Many of the cases in Table 2—FMLA, Right-to-Know, and WARN as well as the recent passage of an increase in the federal minimum wage—arose in the wake of passage of similar, often more stringent, statutes at the state level and the specter of pending legislation in other states (e.g., Wisensale and Allison 1989). Big businesses, operating in multiple markets, face these costs (and the consequent incentives to bargain) far more than their small-business counterparts, creating incentives to negotiate.[18]

Federal preemption under the NLRA has a reverse effect on business incentives to negotiate. Because the NLRA anchors labor law firmly—virtually exclusively—at the federal level, states cannot pass separate legislation affecting activities either protected or prohibited by the act (e.g., Freeman 2006; Sachs 2007). So preemption removes the threat of states' passing more stringent representation laws, increasing the "mighty monolith" face of business in this area of policy.

Who controls the branches. Party control of the White House and Congress plays an additional role in creating divergences in the political strategy taken by different segments of the business community (see generally Vanden Bergh and Holburn 2007). The two polar cases— Democratic control of the White House and Congress versus Republican control of both branches—not surprisingly are associated with profoundly different strategies. In cases where Republicans controlled both branches of government, the strategy for small and big business has been to oppose and block workplace policy initiatives. Given the variety of legislative initiatives of common interest under such a favorable political context, the incentives for big-business groups to join with small-business allies leave little room for negotiating over policies.

On the other hand, where both branches are controlled by Democrats, as during the first two years of the Clinton presidency, representatives of big business face greater incentives to move from opposition to negotiation. Although they join their small-business allies in initially opposing proposed legislation, the incentive to engage in some negotiation in order to shape policies is significant.[19] Moving to a negotiating stance under FMLA, for example, allowed the big-business lobby to push for a policy that codified many of the practices already being followed by those businesses (e.g., in setting the terms and eligibility for leave) rather than risk facing more stringent regulations that would force them to substantially alter their internal policies.

In the two intermediary cases of divided government, the small-business lobby locked into a "no-negotiation" strategy, either by standing behind a blocking strategy from the White House to Democratic congressional initiatives (e.g., during the Reagan and George H.W. Bush eras) or lining up behind congressional efforts to block initiatives or introduce legislation that seeks to roll back workplace policies (e.g., the latter six years of the Clinton administration, when Republicans controlled Congress). Big-business stances, on the other hand, reflected a more strategic approach to shifting from blocking to negotiating based on the strength of political support for the bill from Congress, the White House, and proponents.

Divergence in business interests helps explain why small-business exemptions are often a central aspect of negotiations. The political compromise that led to passage of WARN and FMLA included exempting a significant percent of the small-business community from coverage. Similar exemptions exist under other federal workplace policies, including the Civil Rights Act of 1964, the Americans with Disabilities Act, and the Age Discrimination in Employment Act. Given the greater incentive for small business to resist legislation and for big business to enter negotiations, small-business exemptions become a way for negotiators to find common ground with the segment of the business community that is least resistant to the proposed legislation.

In contrast to the cases described, business interests are indeed monolithic when it comes to expanding the scope of representation or the bargaining leverage of labor unions. Even among companies with union representation, the incentive to oppose expansion of collective bargaining is high given the continuing erosion of union density in the private sector and subsequently the increasing perceived benefit of operating union-free in markets where fewer competitors are covered by union contracts. This means large non-union, and union employers share a common front with the largely non-union medium- and small-business communities in opposing *any* revision to current policies. In fact, given the role of labor unions as the center of larger coalitions that press for other workplace policies (see below), policies that might expand the labor movement have further spillover effects that are deleterious to common business interests.

The Breadth of Coalitions Supporting Legislation

A second dimension affecting the enactment of workplace policies concerns the political strength of organizations representing their beneficiaries. As I have noted, organized labor has long provided a partial solution to Wilson's and Olson's diffused benefit/collective action problem by providing legislative voice for workers they represent in collective bargaining and increasingly for segments of the workforce they do not. The support and influence of the labor movement has been a necessary condition for passage of virtually all major pieces of workplace legislation over the last 50 years.

With the growing diversity of the labor force, the increase in dual-income and single-parent families, and the resulting impact of household structure on family–work balance, many recent workplace policies have engaged groups beyond the labor movement. Antidiscrimination policies, for example, have engaged political coalition partners from the NAACP, the Urban League, NOW, and groups representing the disabled. The breadth of the resulting coalitions, including but extending beyond the perimeter of the labor movement, plays an important role in explaining the cases of successful legislation reviewed earlier. Coalition breadth is of particular importance given the long-term decline in union density. The FMLA case illustrates the importance of broad coalition partners to policy enactment. Almost a decade passed from the time that parental leave policies were first proposed to when they were finally signed into law in 1993. Although the nature of business opposition changed over that time, it was the persistence of the broad coalition favoring legislation that kept it alive through five Congresses and three presidencies. WARN similarly required repeated legislative rounds before passage. The breadth of coalition partners provided supporters access to resources as well as a broadened span of legislative supporters beyond long-standing labor allies (Martin 2000). In addition, it was more difficult for opponents of the bill to paint a policy like FMLA as "special interest" legislation given its array of supporters, including such influential groups as AARP. Other policies, like the American with Disabilities Act and various pieces of antidiscrimination legislation, benefited similarly from broad-based coalitions.

The repeated failure of workplace representation legislation again provides the flip side to this argument. Although a coalition of groups supported and provided support for workplace representation legislation, the labor movement represented its principal proponent. Thus, even though the Labor Law Reform Act of 1977 and EFCA sought to bring representation to workers not currently covered by collective bargaining, the legislation could be painted by opponents as being advocated in the narrow self-interest of "big labor."

Political Economy Lessons for Future Workplace Legislation

[T]he most common and durable source of factions has been the various and unequal distribution of property. . . . A landed interest, a manufacturing interest, a mercantile interest, a moneyed interest, with many lesser interests, grow up of necessity in civilized nations, and divide them into different classes. . . . The regulation of these various and interfering interests forms the principal task of modern legislation, and involves the spirit of party and faction in the necessary and ordinary operations of the government." (James Madison in Hamilton, Jay, and Madison 1941:56)

"I am shocked—*shocked*-to find that gambling is going on in here!" (Captain Louis Renault, prefect of police, in the film *Casablanca*)

Powerful parties have sought to influence public policies since the inception of republics, as Madison's quote from the Federalist Papers attests. But should we be any more surprised about this than Louis Renault was about the presence of gambling shortly before collecting his night's winnings at the roulette table?

The recurring role of business in blocking or shaping workplace policies should come not as shocking or even novel, but as nothing more than the participation of "a manufacturing interest" in seeking to shape the "ordinary operations of the government." Each age undoubtedly imagines itself to be suffering through the era of greatest corruption of the political process. Madison reminds us that powerful interests have sought and will always seek to win at the roulette wheel.

Yet in a time of weakened institutions representing workers, understanding how business influence has played out in a variety of legislative battles, and in particular the impact of diverging interests within that community, is critical to contemplating passage of future workplace policies. Persuasive arguments and the presence of strong coalitions of labor unions will not on their own be sufficient to enact workplace legislation, as most recently demonstrated with EFCA. A successful legislative policy must include a clear mapping of where business coalitions may differ in their underlying opposition.

This volume has focused on industries and employers where workers face the full brunt of the contemporary labor market's downside risks: low pay, minimal benefits, little job security, limited opportunity for voice. Legislative initiatives to redress these risks will face the same broad-based business opposition as the workplace policies I have discussed. The party controlling the White House and Congress plays an important impact on those stances, but even Democratic control of the White House and Congress in no way ensures political success (as vividly illustrated by the first two years of the Clinton administration). Several political implications should be highlighted.

The Importance of Enforcement

Given the political economy of workplace policy, an agenda to address "gloves-off" employment practices must not rely solely on legislative solutions. The more than 200 federal regulations overseen by the U.S. Department of Labor represent an installed base of workplace regulations that offer many basic protections for workers. The authority to set strategies and procedures for enforcement and administration of this installed base rests with the federal executive branch. Providing resources for policies requires congressional authorization subject to the political dynamics discussed earlier. However, budget authorization is time-delimited by the annual appropriation cycle and tends not to draw the level of political heat created by new legislation. Focusing on enforcement and implementation of existing policies thus affords opportunities for a new administration to address workplace problems immediately. Using scarce political resources to create innovative tools and approaches for enforcing the installed base can produce more significant results in a shorter amount of time than a wish list of new legislation.

Between 1975 and 2004, the number of Department of Labor investigators devoted to wage and hour enforcement declined by 14%. Over the same period, the number of workers in the labor force increased by 71% and the number of workplaces by 112% (Bernhardt and McGrath 2005). Decline in the investigative staff of other workplace agencies has been similarly accompanied by tremendous growth in the workforce covered by those agencies. Redressing the huge imbalance between enforcement resources and the number of covered workplaces represents an essential foundation for an enforcement policy.

Effective enforcement also requires targeting workplaces where employers are most likely to be violating the law, particularly where workers are least likely to be able to protect themselves. Rather than playing a workplace-by-workplace "cat and mouse" game of inspection, agencies should seek to influence key actors in industry supply chains, networks of contractors, and other key players in industry settings that can in turn influence the incentives for others in those networks to comply (see Weil 2005 and Weil and Mallo 2007 for an example of such an approach). Policy should draw on a range of carrots and sticks that lead to long-term changes in compliance behaviors at the firm level and industry level.

Finally, a responsive regulatory strategy must engage the workforce by encouraging the exercise of rights granted under existing statutes. Most federal workplace policies require that workers or their representatives act as the frontline of enforcement and implementation. Reducing the fear of retaliation by ensuring whistleblower protections, creating a more "user-friendly" complaint process, and reaching out to groups that assist in exercising rights can improve the protections afforded by the installed base of workplace regulations for the vulnerable workforce.

A new administration could undertake such an enforcement agenda without major changes in federal legislation. Significant advances in workplace conditions could thus be accomplished starting on day one of a new administration (see Weil 2007 for extensive discussion of this issue).

Selecting Politically Viable Workplace Policies

A legislative strategy to address repercussions of "gloves-off" practices must focus on salient issues where the formidable political obstacles described in this chapter can be surmounted. One recent example is the passage of an increase in the federal minimum wage in 2007 after a battle of almost a decade. Along with the change in political control of Congress, passage was spurred on by the adoption of higher, state-level minimum wage policies in more than 30 states by July 2007. Several prospective workplace problems offer similar political opportunities. One example discussed elsewhere in this volume is the use of subcontracting and other forms of balkanized employment relationships that give rise to low pay, poor working conditions, and pervasive violations of labor standards. An important area for legislative initiatives in this regard is curbing the use of worker misclassification as a means to escape regulatory and tax policies. Passage of federal legislation is promising, since many states have recently introduced legislation regarding misclassification and related problems while others have increased enforcement of existing statutes. This movement at the state level alters the political calculus of multistate businesses in regard to federal legislation. The interest of state and local governments (seeking lost tax revenue), along with community, immigrant, and worker rights groups, creates the basis for a broader coalition to support such initiatives, further increasing its chance of becoming law.[20] Changing employer liability for subcontracting represents a related area of opportunity.

Family–work issues present another major area that appears politically tractable. Expanded family leave policies have been the target of state-level initiatives in the last five years. Family-friendly policies that build on the foundations created by FMLA also offer the opportunity to build broader alliances and greater incentives to bring segments of the business community to the table (see, for example, Kochan 2005).

The Prospects for Representation Reform

The foregoing analysis paints a pessimistic picture concerning the possibility of passing significant labor law reform, even with a Democrat in the White House. Estreicher (1994:602), in discussing the failure to pass the Workplace Fairness Act during the brief period of time in the 1990s when Democrats controlled both Congress and the White House, notes that future efforts to "reform . . . the rules regarding strikes should not be viewed in isolation but as part of a comprehensive reexamination of federal labor law aimed at making the system work better in an era of competitive product markets." Kochan (2007) similarly has clearly laid out the need to base discussions of labor law reform in a larger context of improving both representation and productivity in U.S. workplaces.

The legislative experience reviewed in this essay implies that the prospects for such reform are dim given the unanimity of business interest in opposing labor law reform and the absence of state-level political pressure because of federal preemption in this policy area. Expanding opportunities for workplace voice in low-wage workplaces, then, requires labor to engage a very broad and enthusiastic coalition in support of such changes. Rather than seeking to convince other groups of their interests in a revived labor movement per se, this requires creating a vision of workplace representation around a broader focal point that intersects with core objectives of other constituencies.[21]

Alternatively, it requires other means of workplace representation that offer workers voice mechanisms, for example, through increasing the use of health and safety committees or expanding requirements for representation under alternative dispute resolution systems. New avenues for voice could form the basis for a broader political coalition and create the political incentives to bring segments of the business community to the legislative bargaining table.

Conclusion

The political challenges to addressing the problems facing a significant percentage of low-wage workers are formidable, but they are not insurmountable. Past success at passing progressive workplace policies provides both reason for hope and guidance on how new initiatives should be crafted and navigated through demanding legislative processes. Rather than decrying the obstacles created by entrenched interests against such policies, attention would be better spent in coming to understand the recurring fissures in the business coalition and gaining the widest possible support among groups with significant stakes in improving workplace conditions.

Endnotes

[1] Statement of the National Federation of Independent Businesses. <http://cawiz.com/nfib/issues/alert/?alertid=9617401>. [July 6, 2007].

[2] Statement of the American Hotel and Lodging Association. <http://www.ahla.com/public_view_brief.asp?mstr=60>. [July 6, 2007].

[3] Worker Adjustment and Retraining Notification Act, PubL 100–379, Aug. 4, 1988, 102 Stat 890 (codified at 29 USC §§2101–2109 [2000]). The Department of Labor published final regulations on the law in 20 CFR 639 (2006).

[4] This account draws from Marks (1997), Elison (1997), and Martin (2000).

[5] Elison (1997) reports that the initial legislation was drafted by representatives from the Women's Legal Defense Fund and several academics from Georgetown University.

[6] A segment of the business community was already affected by the state-level family medical leave polices in Maine, Minnesota, Oregon, Rhode Island, Wisconsin, and Vermont. Larger firms operating in multiple states therefore had some incentive to support a consistent federal policy.

[7] AARP support was secured by broadening the scope of leave to include care for elderly parents and grandparents.

[8] Data from a series of Bureau of Labor Statistics survey reported in Waldfogel 1999. Similar increases in the incidence of paternity leave were found over this time period.

[9] Dunlop resigned as Secretary of Labor shortly thereafter, feeling that his credibility to the parties had been undermined by Ford's actions. See Kaufman (2002) for Dunlop's account of the events surrounding the "Common Situs Picketing" bill.

[10] The concerted national effort to defeat the bill included the National Association of Manufacturers, the U.S. Chamber of Commerce, and the Business Roundtable (which had initially agreed not to oppose the bill). It was complemented by an aggressive grassroots campaign against the bill by the small-business community (see Freeman and Medoff 1983, pp. 202–4).

[11] The issue in the Mackay case was in fact narrower, involving the refusal of the Mackay Radio and Telegraph Company following the end of a strike to reinstate five of the most vocal union members (although all other striking workers were allowed to return to their jobs, which had been filled by replacements during the strike). In the end, the court supported the view of the NLRB that the employer had discriminated against the five employees. However, in the larger decision, the court noted that it was not "an unfair practice to replace striking employees with others in an effort to carry on the business." The court went on to note that although the NLRA supported the right to strike, an employer "is not bound to discharge those hired to fill the places left by strikers, upon the election of the latter to resume their employment, in order to create places for them" (NLRB v. Mackay Radio 1938:346–7).

[12] A number of books and articles on related topics also became part of the active policy discussion regarding the need to reform labor laws, including Weiler (1990), Craver (1993), Gould (1993), and Weiler and Mundlak (1993).

[13] There were 53 votes in favor of the bill in the Senate. Because 60 votes were needed to close floor debate and end a filibuster against the bill, the Republicans were able to kill the bill in the Senate. (See "Senate Vote to End Filibuster on Striker Replacement Fails," Bureau of National Affairs, *Daily Labor Reporter*, No. 155, August 13, 1993, p. A–2.)

[14] Recent efforts to reform workplace legislation to favor business interests have also proven unsuccessful. In 1997, a business-backed effort to relax section 8(a)(2) of the NLRA to allow a wide range of employee participation activities (the Teamwork for Employees and Managers, or TEAM, Act) also ended in failure, demonstrating the ability of labor unions and their political allies to resist changes in the other direction. But in contrast to the growing influence of business on Capitol Hill, labor's influence has waned.

[15] Legislative initiatives regarding the workplace have only occasionally been preceded by major crises. A series of devastating mining accidents precipitated the congressional activity that led to the Mine Safety and Health Act of 1969 and the Occupational Safety and Health Act of 1970 (Ashford 1976). To a lesser extent, the rash of major plant closings in the steel, auto, and other manufacturing sectors in the 1980s focused public attention on "deindustrialization," which led eventually to the WARN Act.

[16] This section builds on a framework developed with my colleagues Archon Fung and Mary Graham as part of our study of transparency policy. See Fung, Graham, and Weil (2007), chapter 5, for a complete discussion.

[17] One of the foundations of modern workplace policy, the Davis-Bacon Act of 1931, began with broad support from the business community. The Davis-Bacon Act requires payment of prevailing wages for construction work undertaken for the federal government. It was enacted in the depths of the Depression as the economy struggled with the twin problems of unemployment and wage/price deflation. Craypo (1997) notes that Davis-Bacon's passage arose from a broad coalition of support, not only from building trades unions and the American Federation of Labor, but also from major segments of the construction industry. Prominent business associations like the General Contractors Association, representing large-scale contractors who were most likely to bid major federal jobs, supported the notion of prevailing wage laws (although it disagreed with labor on how those wages would be set). Other business associations also supported attaching prevailing wage legislation to major public works initiatives. Failure to do so, it was thought, would "put the government in the politically embarrassing position of seeming to undermine jobs and wages at a time when it was trying to revive industry and earnings through public projects" (Craypo 1977: 223). This support built on a more general desire by the business community to expand public construction work as an important element of an economic recovery strategy (Bernstein 1970). The segments of the construction sector with the most to lose from prevailing wage legislation—contractors using the large number of itinerant, unemployed workers—lacked effective political representation. And the major end user affected by the law—the Hoover administration—favored the bill as part of its economic revitalization program.

[18] This is not an atypical political dynamic. The political logjam preventing passage of a number of transparency policies (for example, nutritional labeling) broke as companies began to be covered by state-level disclosure laws. See Fung, Graham, and Weil (2007), chapter 5, for a discussion of these cases.

[19] Big-business associations entered immediately into a negotiating stance in only two of the workplace policies in Table 1. In both cases, the response from the wider business community and key members of the Republican Party has been harsh. When the Business Roundtable (BRT) decided to work with civil rights group in fashioning the Civil Rights Act of 1991, they were bitterly criticized by the other major business lobbies and the George H.W. Bush administration (see Gould 1993, chapter 8). John Sununu, the White House chief of staff, commented publicly to a representative of the National Stone Association (an opponent of the bill), "Maybe you could get a stone manufacturer to create a little tombstone with 'BRT' on it. Not as direct as a horse's head, I guess" (Holmes 1991:A10). Similarly, the decision by the American Electronics Association and Chemical Manufacturers Association to help draft the Occupational Disease Notification Act of 1987 led prominent Senate Republicans

like Orrin Hatch to rebuke those associations from the Senate floor on behalf of individual association members (Jacobs 1999, chapter 8).

[20] A first step in this direction is the Independent Contractor Proper Classification Act of 2007, introduced by Senators Obama, Durbin, Kennedy, and Murray. The bill would close tax loopholes created by the "Safe Harbor" provision of federal tax law as well as increase enforcement of misclassification of independent contractors.

[21] For example, using workplace committees to address safety and health has been an area of recurring interest among business groups, labor unions, and health and safety advocates since the early 1990s. Although there remain significant debates about the form those committees should take and their permissibility under section 8(a)(2) of the NLRA, the strategy potentially represents an area for fashioning innovative policies and new directions in labor policy. It might also offer the best path for improving the prospects for employee voice in many private workplaces through legislative mechanisms.

References

Ashford, Nicholas. 1976. *Crisis in the Workplace: Occupational Disease and Injury.* Cambridge, MA: MIT Press.

Becker, Gary. 1983. "A Theory of Competition Among Pressure Groups for Political Influence." *Quarterly Journal of Economics*, Vol. 98, no. 3, pp. 371–400.

Bernhardt Annette, and Siobhan McGrath. 2005. "Trends in Wage and Hour Enforcement by the U.S. Department of Labor, 1975–2004." New York: Brennan Center for Justice, New York University Law School.

Bernstein, Irving. 1970. *The Turbulent Years: A History of the American Worker, 1933–1941.* Boston: Houghton Mifflin.

Bluestone, Barry, and Bennett Harrison. 1983. *The Deindustrialization of America: Plant Closings, Community Abandonment, and the Dismantling of Private Industry.* New York: Basic Books.

Brown, Charles, James Hamilton, and James Medoff. 1990. *Employers Large and Small.* Cambridge, MA: Harvard University Press.

Craver, Charles B. 1993. *Can Unions Survive? The Rejuvenation of the American Labor Movement.* New York: New York University Press.

Craypo, Charles. 1997. "Alternative Perspectives on the Purpose and Effects of Labor Standards Legislation." In Bruce Kaufman, ed., *Government Regulation of the Employment Relationship.* Madison, WI: Industrial Relations Research Association, pp. 221–51.

Drew, James, and Steve Eder. 2007. "Without Warning: Flaws, Loopholes Deny Employees Protection Mandated by WARN Act." *Toledo Blade*, July 15.

Eder, Steve, and James Drew. 2007. "Compromises Diluted Bill's Original Intent." *Toledo Blade*, July 15.

Ehrenberg, Robert, and Gary Jakubson. 1990. "Why Warn? Plant Closing Legislation." *Regulation*, Vol. 13, no. 2, pp. 39–46.

Elison, Sonja Klueck. 1997. "Policy Innovation in a Cold Climate: The Family and Medical Leave Act of 1993." *Journal of Family Issues*, Vol. 18, no. 1, pp. 30–54.

Estreicher, Samuel. 1994. "Collective Bargaining or 'Collective Begging'? Reflections on Anti-strikebreaker Legislation." *Michigan Law Review*, Vol. 93, no. 3, pp. 577–608.

Fagotto, Elena, and Archon Fung. 2003. "Improving Workplace Hazard Communication." *Issues in Science and Technology*, Winter, pp. 63-68.

Freeman, Richard, and James Medoff. 1983. *What Do Unions Do?* New York: Basic Books.

Freeman, Richard. 2006. "Will Labor Fare Better Under State Labor Relations Law?" *Proceedings of the 58th Annual Meeting of the Labor and Employment Relations Association* (Boston, January 6–8), Champaign, IL: Labor and Employment Relations Association, pp. 125–32.

Fung, Archon, Mary Graham, and David Weil. 2007. *Full Disclosure: The Perils and Promise of Transparency.* New York: Cambridge University Press.

General Accounting Office. 2003. *The Worker Adjustment and Training Notification Act: Revising the Act and Educational Materials Could Clarify Employer Responsibilities and Employee Rights.* Washington, DC: General Accounting Office.

Gould, William B. IV. 1993. *Agenda for Reform: The Future of Employment Relationships and the Law.* Cambridge, MA: MIT Press.

Hamilton, Alexander, John Jay, and James Madison. 1941. *The Federalist.* New York: Modern Library.

Harrison, Bennett. 1997. *Lean and Mean: Why Large Corporations Will Continue to Dominate the Global Economy.* New York: Guilford Press.

Hochschild, Arlie, and Anne Machung. 1989. *The Second Shift: Working Parents and the Revolution at Home.* New York: Viking Penguin.

Holmes, Steven. 1991. "Talks on New Rights Bill Divide Large and Small Companies." *New York Times*, April 19, pp. A10–11.

Hyland, Stephanie. 1990. "Helping Employees with Family Care." *Monthly Labor Review*, September, pp. 22–6.

Jacobs, David. 1999. *Business Lobbies and the Power Structure in America.* Westport, CT: Quorum Books.

Kanter, Rosabeth Moss. 1989. *When Giants Learn to Dance: Mastering the Challenge of Strategy, Management, and Careers in the 1990s.* New York: Simon and Schuster.

Kaufman, Bruce. 2002. "Reflections on Six Decades of Industrial Relations: An Interview with John Dunlop." *Industrial and Labor Relations Review*, Vol. 55, no. 2, pp. 324–45.

Kochan, Thomas. 2005. *Restoring the American Dream: A Working Family Agenda for America.* Cambridge, MA: MIT Press.

———. 2007. "Updating American Labor Law: Taking Advantage of a Window of Opportunity." *Comparative Labor Law and Policy Journal*, Vol. 28, no. 2, pp. 101–23.

LeRoy, Michael. 1993. "The Mackay Radio Doctrine of Permanent Striker Replacements and the Minnesota Picket Line Peace Act: Questions of Preemption." *Minnesota Law Review*, Vol. 77, pp. 843–69.

Magaziner, Ira, and Robert Reich. 1982. *Minding America's Business: The Decline and Rise of the American Economy.* New York: Harcourt, Brace, Jovanovich.

Marks, Michelle Rose. 1997. "Party Politics and Family Policy: The Case of the Family and Medical Leave Act." *Journal of Family Issues*, Vol. 18, no. 1, pp. 55–70.

Martin, Cathie Jo. 2000. *Stuck in Neutral: Business and the Politics of Human Capital Investment Policy.* Princeton, NJ: Princeton University Press.

Meisenheimer, Joseph. 1989. "Employer Provisions for Parental Leave." *Monthly Labor Review*, October, pp. 20–5.

Monroe, Pamela, James Garand, and Holly Teeters. 1995. "Family Leave Legislation in the U.S. House: Voting on the Family and Medical Leave Act of 1990." *Family Relations*, Vol. 44, no. 1, pp. 46–55.

NLRB v. Mackay Radio & Telegraph Company (304 U.S. 333, 1938).

Olson, Mancur. 1971. *The Logic of Collective Action: Public Goods and the Theory of Groups.* Cambridge, MA: Harvard University Press.

Sachs, Benjamin. 2007. "Labor Law Renewal." *Harvard Law and Policy Review,* Vol. 1, no. 2, pp. 375–400.

Singh, Parbudyal, and Harish Jain. 2001. "Striker Replacements in the United States, Canada, and Mexico: A Review of the Law and Empirical Research." *Industrial Relations,* Vol. 40, no. 1, pp. 22–53.

Stigler, George. 1971. "The Theory of Economic Regulation." *Bell Journal of Economics and Management Science,* Vol. 2, no. 1, pp. 3–21.

Vanden Bergh, Richard, and Guy L.F. Holburn. 2007. "Targeting Corporate Political Strategy: Theory and Evidence from the U.S. Accounting Industry," *Business and Politics,* Vol. 9, no. 2. <http://www.bepress.com/bap/vol9/iss2/art1>. [September 10, 2007].

Waldfogel, Jane. 1999. "The Impact of the Family and Medical Leave Act." *Journal of Policy Analysis and Management,* Vol. 18, no. 2, pp. 281–302.

Weil, David. 2005. "Public Enforcement/Private Monitoring: Evaluating a New Approach to Regulating the Minimum Wage." *Industrial and Labor Relations Review,* Vol. 52, no. 2, pp. 238–57.

———. 2007. "Crafting a Progressive Workplace Regulatory Policy: Why Enforcement Matters." *Comparative Labor Law and Policy Journal,* Vol. 28, no. 2, pp. 101–30.

Weil, David, and Carlos Mallo. 2007. "Regulating Labour Standards via Supply Chains: Combining Public/Private Interventions to Improve Workplace Compliance." *British Journal of Industrial Relations,* Vol. 45, no. 4, pp. 805–82.

Weiler, Paul. 1990. *Governing the Workplace.* Cambridge, MA: Harvard University Press.

Weiler, Paul, and Guy Munlak. 1993. "New Directions for the Law of the Workplace." *Yale Law Journal,* Vol. 102, no. 8, pp. 1907–25.

Wilson, James Q. 1980. "The Politics of Regulation." In James Q. Wilson, ed., *The Politics of Regulation.* New York: Basic Books, pp. 75–121.

Wisensale, Steven, and Michael Allison. 1989. "Family Leave Legislation: State and Federal Initiatives." *Family Relations,* Vol. 38, no. 2, pp. 182–9.

ABOUT THE CONTRIBUTORS

Glenn Adler is deputy director at the Center for Strategic Research in the AFL-CIO's Organizing Department. He was previously research coordinator in SEIU's Stand for Security campaign to organize contract security officers. Prior to joining SEIU in 2001, Adler was involved for many years with the South African labor movement. For 10 years, he taught labor studies and sociology at the University of the Witwatersrand in Johannesburg and was senior researcher at the National Labour and Economic Development Institute, the research arm of the Congress of South African Trade Unions.

Annette Bernhardt is policy co-director at the National Employment Law Project. She coordinates NELP's policy analysis and research support for campaigns around living wage jobs, immigrant worker rights, and accountable development. A leading scholar of low-wage work, Bernhardt has helped develop and analyze innovative policy responses to the changing nature of work in the United States. She has published widely in journals including the *American Journal of Sociology*, the *American Sociological Review*, and the *Journal of Labor Economics*. Her most recent book is the co-edited *Low-Wage America: How Employers Are Reshaping Opportunity in the Workplace*, published by the Russell Sage Foundation.

Heather Boushey is currently a congressional staffer. Her research areas are the U.S. labor market, social policy, and work and family issues. Her work ranges from examinations of current trends in the U.S. labor market and how families balance work and childcare needs to how young people have fared in today's economy. Boushey has testified before Congress and authored numerous reports and commentaries on issues affecting working families. She co-authored *The State of Working America 2002–3* and *Hardships in America: The Real Story of Working Families*. Previously, she was at the Center for Economic and Policy Research.

Laura Dresser is the associate director of the Center on Wisconsin Strategy at the University of Wisconsin, Madison, a research and policy center supporting high-road economic development. She has worked with labor, education, community, and business partners to improve job access and career advancement for workers in Wisconsin. An expert on workforce development and low-wage jobs, Dresser has published research on service sector jobs, unions and workforce development, and black women's economic opportunities. She has served as a consultant/technical advisor to the AFL-CIO, the State of Wisconsin Department of Workforce Development, and local employment and training projects.

Maurice Emsellem is policy co-director of the National Employment Law Project, a research and advocacy organization that partners with local communities to deliver on the nation's promise of economic opportunity. Ensellem has worked on collaborations that have successfully modernized state unemployment insurance programs, created employment protections for workfare workers, and reduced unfair barriers to employment of people with criminal records in state laws and in city hiring practices. He was a Soros Justice Senior Fellow in 2004 and a Stanford Public Interest Law Mentor in 2003.

Sarah Gammage is a social affairs officer with the Economic Commission for Latin America and the Caribbean in Mexico and an affiliate at the Center for Women and Work at Rutgers University. She has worked for a number of development organizations, including the United Nations Development Programme, the International Center for Research on Women, the Global Policy Network, and the International Institute for Environment and Development. Gammage has written about gender and trade, poverty, migration, and economic development for journals including *World Development, Development and Change, Human Organization, Ambio*, and *Latin American Perspectives*.

Ana Luz Gonzalez is a Ph.D. student in the Department of Urban Planning at the University of California, Los Angeles. She was the project coordinator for the National Day Labor Survey. Her research interests focus on poverty, labor markets, and economic development. Currently she is working on a study that will document the prevalence of workplace violations among low-wage workers in Los Angeles, Chicago, and New York.

Mark H. Greenberg directs the Poverty and Prosperity Program at the Center for American Progress in Washington, DC. He previously was the executive director of the center's Task Force on Poverty, which issued *From Poverty to Prosperity: A National Strategy for Cutting Poverty in Half*. Greenberg is also a senior fellow at the Center for Law and Social Policy, where he was previously the director of policy, and is engaged in developing the Georgetown University Center on Poverty, Inequality, and Public Policy.

Jill Hurst is the director of strategic organizing at SEIU. She has worked for SEIU for 10 years: She served as secretary treasurer of the Boston SEIU Property Services Local, was a leader in the national Justice for Janitors campaign, and was the Connecticut State Council director. Hurst directed the University of Miami comprehensive campaign around the country. Prior to joining SEIU, she worked for the Connecticut Federation of Teachers.

Stephen Lerner is assistant to the president for SEIU's North American and International Strategic Initiatives and Campaigns. At SEIU, Stephen has launched and led efforts by janitors, security officers, and other property services workers to lift themselves out of poverty in the Justice for Janitors and Stand for Security campaigns. Lerner has been an organizer for a number of different unions. He started organizing with the United Farm Workers of America on the grape and lettuce boycott. He also organized garment workers in North Carolina, South Carolina, and other southern states. Lerner also serves on SEIU's executive board.

Elizabeth Lower-Basch is a senior policy analyst at the Center for Law and Social Policy and a member of the workforce team. Her areas of focus include welfare policy, job quality, and supports for low-income working families. From 1996 to 2006, Lower-Basch worked for the Office of the Assistant Secretary for Planning and Evaluation at the U.S. Department of Health and Human Services.

Stephanie Luce is an associate professor at the Labor Center at the University of Massachusetts–Amherst and distinguished lecturer at the Joseph S. Murphy Center for Worker Education, City University of New York. Her research focuses on low-wage labor markets, in particular the impact of living wage campaigns on workers and communities. She is the author of *Fighting for a Living Wage*, published by Cornell University Press.

Edwin Meléndez is professor of management and urban policy at Milano, The New School for Management and Urban Policy in New York City. He has conducted considerable research in the areas of Latino studies, economic development, labor markets, and poverty. In addition to numerous scientific papers and other publications, Meléndez is the co-editor of the recently published *Latinos in a Changing Society* (Praeger, 2007) and the author or editor of 10 books, including *Communities and Workforce Development, Working on Jobs: The Center for Employment Training*, and *Hispanics in the Labor Force*.

Ruth Milkman is professor of sociology and director of the Institute for Research on Labor and Employment at the University of California,

Los Angeles. Her research and writing has ranged over a variety of issues surrounding work and labor organization in the U.S. Her most recent book is *L.A. Story: Immigrant Workers and the Future of the U.S. Labor Movement* (Russell Sage Foundation, 2006).

Debbie A. Mukamal joined John Jay College of Criminal Justice in 2005 to develop and direct its Prisoner Reentry Institute. She previously served as a staff attorney at the Legal Action Center, where she founded and directed the National H.I.R.E. Network, a clearinghouse for information related to the employment of people with criminal records. In addition, Mukamal co-authored *After Prison: Roadblocks to Reentry—A Report on State Legal Barriers Facing People with Criminal Records.*

Paul K. Sonn is co-legal director of the National Employment Law Project (NELP). With a staff of lawyers and social scientists, NELP works with government leaders and grassroots coalitions to respond to the key problems of the U.S. labor market in the 21st century. Sonn founded and co-directed the Economic Justice Project at New York University's Brennan Center for Justice, which merged with NELP in 2007. His work has been profiled in the *New York Times Magazine*, the *Nation*, and the *New York Law Journal*.

Amy Sugimori is the executive director of La Fuente, a not-for-profit organization that hosts projects, including the New York Civic Participation Project and the Long Island Civic Participation Project, that develop community–labor partnerships to engage in organizing and leadership development to promote civic participation in immigrant communities. Prior to joining La Fuente, Sugimori was an attorney with the National Employment Law Project, where she provided support to labor and community groups organizing and participating in policy advocacy around the country to advance the rights of low-wage immigrant workers.

Nik Theodore is director of the Center for Urban Economic Development and associate professor in the urban planning and policy program of the University of Illinois at Chicago. His current research examines economic restructuring and dynamics of labor market change.

Chris Tilly, director of the Institute for Research on Labor and Employment and professor of urban planning at the University of California, Los Angeles, specializes in labor, income distribution, and local economic development. His research focuses on aspects of low-wage work (including race and gender inequality) in the U.S. and Mexico and on grassroots movements for social change in the U.S. and Latin America. Tilly's books include *Stories Employers Tell: Race, Skill,* *and Hiring in America* and *Work Under Capitalism*. He served on the editorial collective of *Dollars and Sense* magazine from 1986 to 2006 and is a member of the editorial board of the Rose series of sociological monographs.

Abel Valenzuela Jr. is professor of urban planning and Chicano studies and director of the Center for the Study of Urban Poverty at the University of California, Los Angeles. Valenzuela has published numerous articles on day labor, other immigrant workers, immigrant settlement, and urban poverty.

David Weil is professor of economics and Everett W. Lord Distinguished Scholar at Boston University School of Management and co-director of the Transparency Policy Project at the Kennedy School of Government, Harvard University. His research includes workplace regulatory policy, industrial and labor relations, and labor union strategy. He is the author of numerous articles and three books, most recently *Full Disclosure: The Perils and Promise of Transparency*. Weil serves as an advisor to the U.S. Department of Labor, OSHA, and other government agencies as well as a mediator and advisor to labor unions and labor–management groups in the U.S., Canada, United Kingdom, and Australia.

Noah D. Zatz is acting professor of law at the University of California, Los Angeles. His research focuses on the legal regulation of work and inequality. Specific interests include how the law identifies "work" and "workers," especially as those concepts are shaped by gender, race, and distinctions between the market economy and other social institutions. His recent scholarship explores these issues through analyzing welfare law's enforcement of work requirements and employment law's application to prison labor. Before beginning his academic career, Zatz practiced as an attorney at the National Employment Law Project in New York City.